The Raja's Magic Clothes

JOANNE PUNZO WAGHORNE

The Raja's Magic Clothes

Re-Visioning Kingship and Divinity in England's India

THE PENNSYLVANIA STATE UNIVERSITY PRESS
UNIVERSITY PARK, PENNSYLVANIA

Library of Congress Cataloging-in-Publication Data

Waghorne, Joanne Punzo.
    The raja's magic clothes: re-visioning kingship and divinity in England's India /
Joanne Punzo Waghorne.
        p.   cm. — (Hermeneutics, studies in the history of religions)
    Includes bibliographical references and index.
    ISBN 0-271-01066-5 (alk. paper)
    1. Pudukkottai (Princely State)—Kings and rulers—Religious
aspects.   2. India—Kings and rulers—Religious aspects—Case
studies.   3. Pudukkottai (Princely State)—Politics and government.
4. India—Politics and government—19th century.   I. Title.
II. Series.
BL1215.K56W35   1994
294.5′3′095482—dc20   93–20133
                                                              CIP

Published by The Pennsylvania State University Press,
Suite C, Barbara Building, University Park, PA 16802-1003

Unless otherwise noted,
all of the photographs in this book are by Dick Waghorne.

As always, in memory of my father
Henry R. Punzo

Contents

List of Illustrations

The captions on the paintings and photographs reproduced in this book are designed to be read as a running essay within the larger text. In general, the sequence of the plates reflects chronological changes in Pudukkottai and all plates, including the color plates, are therefore numbered consecutively. The numbers with asterisks (*) indicate color plates, which are in the color section of the book.

Preface

The spent and sightless eyes of James Frazer stare out from one of the last photographs taken of the grand old man of sacral kingship. Those eyes should serve as a warning that Sir James secretly doomed any would-be successors to his study of kings to endlessly write and rewrite, edit and enlarge, as he had done. I have learned that no matter how small the royal domain or how seemingly remote the royal lord, the project explodes beyond its small borders into issues that open the eyes and then blind the mind to easy words and simple discourse. My fellow wearied travelers on India's royal roads know what I mean when I say that in spite of its ten-year gestation and its present length, this book remains a work in progress.

But why should a book about the royal rituals in a 1,200-square-mile domain in a hinterland of South India take on such length? S. Radhakrishna Aiyar, in his five-hundred-page *General History of the Pudukkottai State*, begins answering the same imagined jibes: "Some might say 'Show us the Pudukkottai State for which we have here a history of this size.' And others might curtly remark 'More area or less bulk.' " The beleaguered Radhakrishna then answers with long lists of the cultural contents of the tiny state with its overlays of "hundreds of dolmens or 'sepulchral urns,' " fifteen rock-cut temples, the ruins of several Jain and Buddhist temples and monasteries, and 1,000 inscriptions (1916, vii–viii). Later he adds the important connections of the rajas here to the Muslim nawab of the Carnatic and then to the rise of British power in South India.

This tiny slice of South India has seen it all. And I wonder what slice of royal India that survived into the twentieth century has not. While temples can retain some cultural (if not economic) independence protected by rules of purity and by the reluctance of all but a few zealot foreign lords to invade such sanctuaries, royal courts cannot. Rajas are bound to history and to their overlords. They must amalgamate, imitate, and consolidate the contemporary paraphernalia of power. A. M. Hocart, who also wrote and rewrote his own works on kingship, argued that it is in the nature of kings to draw all things to themselves, to incorporate, to absorb divinity and humanity, to hold diverse powers. I find both Radhakrishna's long listing of the aggregate cultures in Pudukkottai, and Hocart's category of "king" as conglomerate by his very "nature," true to my own experience in Pudukkottai. The scholar who cuts into the royal body in this tiny kingdom finds the world spilling out.

To imply that the world exists in any microcosm, however, is dangerous in today's intellectual environment. We live in an era of the search for indigenous categories and for the "native point of view." We warn one another—quite rightly—to eschew universal categories that turn out to be nothing more than disguised ethnocentrism of the dominant culture. The grandiose schemes of a James G. Frazer or an F. Max Müller or even a more cautious A. M. Hocart defining "King" and "God" and "Science" and "Magic" seem now to be false searches for fabricated "essences" that exist nowhere but in the head of the scholar. And yet I begin to talk of kings and invoke the dangerous Sir James and speak of the world inside my Pudukkottai oyster! A serious critic might well warn me to avoid any "essentializing" strategy in such a book. That charge will be leveled at many a book during the next decade. Thus, I run the risk here of being accused of remaining a true daughter of the much-maligned Sir James Frazer—a charge that I in part accept. A full argument in defense of the comparative project would require a serious apologia, but it requires no apology. In this book I remain very critical of much of the nineteenth-century search for easy universals, but not of the possibility of humans to meet, to borrow, to somehow "know" each other, and to create anew.

Put simply, I reserve the right to essentialize, because this era between 1850 and 1947 was by its very nature an age of the confluence of cultures, of *lived* comparison, of the need to create a common vocabulary in which such words as "divinity," "religious," and "authority" began to take on a common use if not a common meaning. The most important discovery I made in researching and writing this book was this overlay of the modern imperial, "global" culture. I tried desperately for several years to extract the *real* India, the *real* Hindu voices from the texts. This project failed precisely because I had "bracketed" the most interesting area in this whole question of sacred kingship: the messy places where "British" and "Indian" had already coalesced in concrete people and places. In fact, if I were to rewrite the book in the next five years, I would emphasize not only the British and "Hindu" pieces of this little kingdom but the Muslim as well. That was the reality in Pudukkottai in the late nineteenth century. And I contend that, in spite of the years of searching for indigenous categories and real Hindu voices, confluence—a native essentializing between "cultures"—remains an important part of modern India and the contemporary world.

This same confluence of cultures that marked the late nineteenth century is happening now more than ever. New consciousness of ethnicity and nationalism exists in the same India as the modern media, blue jeans, and Bajaj scooters. Supporters of "fundamentalist" attempts to build a temple at the Babri Masjid in Ayodhya can be spotted in newspaper photos wearing blue jeans under their long saffron shirts. There is no need to forge artificial comparisons, as Max Müller or Frazer did—putting together Frankenstein worlds out of decaying pieces of fragmented culture parts. The world presents to scholars—as it did in the late nineteenth century—composite cultural organisms with strong tendencies toward fragmentation but equal centripetal strength. We must be aware of both forces, giving consideration to the very particular voices of peoples with their own special nuances, but we cannot pretend that at the same time many of the same voices also speak out to the world. They translate the world into their life, and they are translated into the daily life of others far away and yet never so very far.

Yet with all my defense of "comparison," this book remains in many respects "deconstructive." I refuse to see the two enterprises as incompatible. The book is a study in the countervoice of both orthodox India and conventional political and religious discourse in Britain. The point—that the conglomerate culture, the global culture, lived in Pudukkottai and shared in the empire must be read between the lines of official discourse, in the corners of official photographs and commissioned paintings, in the folds of folktales, and in the subtext of orthodox scripture—may be an odd one. In later chapters I develop the importance of the king and his court as outsiders, as sinners, and as "naked" forest-dwellers. However, rather than seeing these aspects of kingship as tangential to the king's dharmic role, I see the "illusion," the *māyā,* of the ornate king as built into the system. The king's body is not stable, but very bound to time. There are points at which he must divest himself of power and authority, must become "naked" in order to be divine.

Here my use of such terms as "God" and "Goddess" can be genuinely misunderstood. I capitalize the terms because these are not secondary or lesser to the Judeo-Christian God. They do, however, function differently in space and time. Neither the Gods' nor the king's divine bodies are stable in their visible form as icons of flesh, metal, or stone. In the book's conclusion, in fact, I ask for a reappraisal of our usual equation of "God" with eternity and stability. Thus, a sensitivity to theo-logy, and open discussion of the ways in which deity and time are related, can make sense of the issues.

No historian of religion with my early orientalist training in Sanskrit could possibly be unaware that issues of deity and time and matter and spirit have been discussed many times over in Indian philosophy. The problem is that I became disturbed at hearing the constant pounding of the hammer of those same texts that emphasized the immaterial nature of the universe in India. That hammer was forged in Max Müller's workshop as much as in India, and the Hindu (and British) voices that have thereby been forced into silence are the very ones I try to give a voice in this book. I have not rounded up the usual orthodox Hindu theologians and philosophers, because the Hindu system in Pudukkottai was ignored as much by the Hindu pandits as by the British scholars, for the many reasons I outline in Chapters 6, 7, and 8. There is an important set of Hindu texts, the Agamas, which do speak of the icon and of the embodiment of Gods. Fortunately, the patient work of a few scholars in India and the United States on the Agamas is paying off. When these texts are given the same critical attention as the much-translated Vedas, there will be a new Hindu theological voice to consider in the study of South Indian kingship. But at this point Hindu voices that were consciously ignored by mainstream scholarship—the voices of the royal women, of the old courtiers, are added here along with their articulate faces. Thus, I try to retain the counterdiscourse and in that sense remain deconstructive while refusing to eschew what I dare not call universalisms but could name "macro-discourse."

I have not yet mentioned one crucial point. I am a historian of religions. Our business is precisely to talk about what I call "theo-logy"—the nature of divinity, of matter and spirit, of human and divine relationships. As fully trained specialists, we do this with caution, with care, with a deep concern for facts and for history, but as scholars of religions we also must dare to discuss broad issues within the concrete world of our study. To exorcise statements on materialism or divinity or kingship from this book would be to rid the book of the very elements that make it an essay in hermeneutics.

This book, like the little kingdom it presents, was made in many places and with the experiences of many people. I did research and wrote in London, in Pudukkottai and Madras, and at home in a Victorian house in Boston and my present house, which was constructed by Carolina Quakers when the East India Company first began to erect its grand empire. I cannot possibly mention all the many passing conversations, little hints from bystanders, discussions, and the very complex conversations that provided the ideas for the book. In Pudukkottai, I do remember in particular the very old members of the palace establishment who often strained their memories for details and searched their own boxes of memorabilia to share pictures and documents with me. I think of the palace Head Harikar Sri K. Subramanian, Dasi Saraswati of Tirugokarnam, Agama Sastriar Sri M. Bala-subramanian Sastri, the great musician Vinaividwan Tirugokarnam Ramachandra Aiyar, and the descendant of the royal bodyguards, K. Sathiamurti Rao. I think of many Pudukkottaians who sat and reminisced with me recalling a song or a sight or sending over a poem or reading from an old manuscript: N. Sadasivam, Ganesa Sharma, K. A. Pan-chapagesa Dikshitar, P. R. Minakshi Sundaram Pillai, Tiru A. R. Seshia Sastri, T. N. Olaganathan, Sai Matha Brinda Devi, Rajkumari Meena Vijaya Raghunatha Tondaiman. I also remember the gracious subcollector of Pudukkottai, Sheela Balakrishna I.C.S., who made the many hours in the Darbar office comfortable and productive. I also remember the expert help of K. Mahalingam, who translated many of the complex inam grants for me; the indefeasible knowledge of P. M. Sastri; and the energetic Major P. R. Sastri, Indian Army Ret., for introducing me to so many people in Pudukkottai. The Tirugokarnam temple Devasthanam kindly permitted my photographer-husband to extensively photograph the temple. But when I think of Pudukkottai I most remember Rani Rema Devi with great respect and affection, as well as my friend K. Lakshminarayanan, then director of the Government Museum of Pudukkottai and now curator of the Government Museum of Udagamandalam, a consummate scholar and a committed public servant. Both made this book possible.

In Madras I much appreciate the good help of the directors and the staff of that city's libraries and archives. I am especially grateful to M. K. Raman, then of the U. V. Swaminatha Iyer Library; T. Shankaran of the Tamil Isai Sangam; M. Arunachalam of the Tamil and Sanskrit and Other Languages Research Institute, Egmore; and the late R. Aiyaswamy, for sharing his private folklore collection with me. All who work in Madras have long known T. N. Jayavelu, antiquarian book dealer par excellence. The director and staff of the Oriental Manuscripts Library at the University of Madras were very helpful in providing copyists and recommending an excellent translator, K. Venkataraman, retired Tamil pandit. As always, I relied on the help and good offices of the Department of Politics and Public Administration of the University of Madras, especially Dr. C. N. Perumal and Dr. Chandra Y. Mudaliar. But above and beyond academic work, I had the constant support of my friend Mythili Raman and her family.

London remains a hospitable city for scholars. Its libraries have generously extended all of their services to me: The British Library and the (then) India Office Library, especially the Department of Prints and Drawings; the Library of the School of Oriental and African Studies. The Duke Humphrey's Library at Oxford kindly allowed me to see the Max Müller papers.

The research for this book was made possible by grants from the U.S. Office of Education (Fulbright Faculty Research Abroad) and the Social Science Research Council. My husband and I were able to complete much of the photography for this book while in India in 1986–87 researching Hindu temples under a fellowship from The American Institute of Indian Studies. I was able to revise the manuscript as a fellow at the Institute for the Arts and Humanities, University of North Carolina, Chapel Hill. My university has also extended help with grants to prepare the final manuscript, and the Department of Religious Studies made three excellent research assistants available to me. Jeff Ruff and Jay Ford aided with preparing the final copy, and Neal Keye created the index. All are graduate students in the department. But as important as these grants was the timely help of Robert L. De Gregorio of Cambridge Trust Company, whose financial advice in 1986 allowed me to take a year to work full-time on the first draft of this manuscript.

I save mention of my husband, Dick Waghorne, for last. He has accompanied me on all of my research in India as photographer and Old India Hand who can buy a rail ticket in fifteen minutes and negotiate his way through a crowd carrying thirty pounds of equipment in one hand while eating an onion uttapam with the other. Unless otherwise noted, all the photographs in this book are his. His keen eye has vitalized this book as his constant support has enlivened my life for the last twenty-four years.

"Wag End"
Eli Whitney, North Carolina

Treatment of Key Terms in a Conglomerate Language

The languages of formal correspondence and official documents in Pudukkottai stabilized as English and Tamil in the twentieth century, but this particular "Tamil" and "English" at times only reflected the use of either *script*. Pudukkottai passed through a succession of official languages, beginning with Telugu, then Marathi, Persian, Sanskrit, English, and Tamil, that remained part of its working vocabulary. These languages originated with the dominant overlord or various Brahman communities imported into Pudukkottai from time to time to provide ritual and clerical services. By the late nineteenth century, the "English" language that dominated the official documents was truly an Anglo-Indian bureaucratese, with many of the same words that Henry Yule and A. C. Burnell formalized into a delightful "Glossary of Colloquial Anglo-Indian Words" entitled *Hobson-Jobson* ([1903] 1984). The Government of Madras recognized the developing conglomerate language and appended its own thousand-page glossary to the *Manual of the Administration of the Madras Presidency* (1893).

Rather than do violence to this perfectly understood bureaucratic language, I have not tried to re-create the "original" language by adding many complex diacritical marks. I purposely avoided a text filled with words that are treated as foreign terminology, because that would imply that the material in the book should be understood as foreign—something that needs "translation"—when, in fact, such terms formed a common language for those who worked and wrote under the umbrella of the British Raj. No member of the Indian Civil Service—Indian or British—would have considered writing *darbār* when Durbar or Darbar would be better understood. I have modernized this practice only in that I do not capitalize these terms when they are used as common words. The Victorian practice of capitalizing many nouns simply looks odd today. The following types of words, then, are treated as common English words. Many have already passed into American English and appear even in the *American Heritage Dictionary:* durbar, dewan, Moghul, nawab, raja, rani, zamindar, viceroy. The glossary that follows provides the original language sources for many important terms. The glossary is not exhaustive—producing such a glossary for southern India would be a project in itself—but readers with philological and linguistic interests can see exactly how conglomerate the language became.

xxiv   Treatment of Key Terms

I do not capitalize the titles of British administrative officers or nobility, as would have been the case in imperial records, unless those titles are part of a proper name. Thus I use, for example, dewan-regent, political agent, the raja of Pudukkottai, the nawab of the Arcot, the queen. An exception to this rule is the names of the officials at the raja's court, which are capitalized in order to distinguish them from the common terms used to denote servants or services rendered for the public. In the palace, even common butchers or cooks had the status of officers of the state and until 1888 were paid in special rent-free gifts of land from the raja. Thus I follow the common practice in Pudukkottai for English documents and write Sirkele, Harikar, Jamedar, Purohita. The Huzur Establishment is the entire palace staff, and the Dignitary Establishment is just the inner circle of emblem-bearers. Both are capitalized because they were considered official government offices, as are the sets of records generated by administrative offices: Darbar Files, Huzur Records, Palace Records.

The bureaucratic language used throughout the empire, and especially the more specialized language of records within South India, however, was never codified and left considerable room for regional and individual variations. I have adopted many of the spellings used by the clerks in Pudukkottai's records offices, which betray the tendency, when in doubt, to "Tamilize" spellings no matter what the original source language. These regionalisms will be apparent to anyone who reads Tamil. The most common of the Tamilizations is the insertion of vowels after consonants in contravention of Sanskrit or Persian forms, and the addition of familiar Tamil prefixes and suffixes to non-Tamil root words instead of affixing the source language's own forms. In spite of this, the clerks' spellings would have been recognizable throughout southern India and in most cases throughout the Indian empire.

Alongside the conglomerate bureaucratic Anglo-Indian, a common theological language also developed from "Grantha"—Sanskrit words borrowed by the Tamil pandits and Tamilized by eliminating the aspirated "s" and by adding an "m" to Sanskrit words ending in "a" and writing all this either in Tamil or in Roman script. Sometimes Tamil words are joined to Sanskrit to form linguistically odd but perfectly understood terms—for example, *kumpa*(Tamil)+*abhiṣēka*(Sanskrit)=*kumpapisēkam,* but then written (usually by Tamil Brahmans who were the clerks) as "Kumbabhishekam" in English records. The difficulties of dealing with this hybrid Tamil-Sanskrit have yet to be resolved. The problems of transliterating it into English are great. Again, I follow the practice of the Indian clerks in the records offices of Pudukkottai and use their common Anglo-Indian theological vocabulary. I also follow their practice of capitalizing these Tamil-Sanskrit words to distinguish them from either pure Sanskrit or pure Tamil. Thus I write Prasadam, Tirtham, Pattabhishekam, Dassara.

For Indian proper nouns, I follow the most common spelling used in late English language records. S. Radhakrishna Aiyar's *General History of the Pudukkottai State* has been my guide for most spellings: Pudukkottai, Tanjore, Trichinopoly, Raja Ramachandra Tondaiman, Raja Martanda Bhairava Tondaiman, Dewan A. Sashia Sastri (I have not used the older Sashiah or the honorific Sastriar), Sadasiva Brahmendra, Tirugokarnam temple, Dakshinamurti temple, Brihadambal. Where Radhakrishna Aiyar provides no guidance, I follow the most common spelling of the terms used by the clerks in the various record offices in Pudukkottai.

When a word was considered foreign even to the writers of Indo-English, or when I quote from a Tamil or Sanskrit text, I follow the current practice in the social sciences and transliterate and italicize the word with clear diacritical marks the first time it is used, and thereafter only when necessary for clarity. When I use such words repeatedly, I treat them as common terms and write inam, devadasi, darsan, etc. The transliteration follows the *Tamil Lexicon* published by the University of Madras (1936).

Glossary of Common Anglicized Terms

This glossary contains common anglicized terms from the hybrid administrative and ceremonial language of the nineteenth century. It provides the source language(s) for each term, for readers interested in the linguistic construction of this ostensible language once openly called Anglo-Indian. When possible, the literal translation of the term precedes the definition of the term as it functioned in South India. I indicate when the term had a special use in Pudukkottai.

The original classical source language is given in parentheses with both literal and contextual meanings following. A/ = Arabic, S/ = Sanskrit, T/ = Tamil, Te/ = Telugu, P/ = Persian, H/ = Hindustani (now Urdu or Hindi, but at the time the unified lingua franca of northern India). When the word was commonly used in two languages or derived from a combination of two languages, both are given. A word marked A-P/, for example, would be an Arabic-Persian word.

Abhishekam (S/ *abhiṣēka*). A "sprinkling," anointing with holy water and other substances to consecrate a divine image, temple, or person.

Adappakkaran (T/ *aṭaippa+k+kāraṉ*). The man who holds the "betel bag." A royal servant in charge of the ritual distribution of betel nut at all formal court ceremonials.

Agama (S/ *āgama*). Tradition. Medieval Sanskrit texts central to temple worship. Many were composed in southern India.

Ahambadiyan (T/ *akampaṭi+yaṉ*). An "insider." A caste in southern India connected to service inside a palace or temple.

Aranmani (T/ *araṇ+maṉai*). A fort-house. Palace.

Bahadur (H/ *bahādur*). Brave man. A title of distinction granted by the Moghul court in Delhi and then adopted by the East India Company to honor service.

Baragiri (P/ *bārgīr*). A cavalry man who does not own his own horse but serves a higher authority. A palace servant connected with the royal guard.

Biruthus (T/ *pirutu,* S/ *viruda*). Crying

out, proclaiming. A royal banner or emblem.

Bogi (T/ *pōki*).   Palanquin bearer.

Bokkusham (**from S/** *bhoga*).   Things of enjoyment; treasures. The treasury in a palace.

Bokkushakkar (*Bokkusham*+ T/ *kāran*).   Treasurer.

Brihadambal (S/ *bṛhat*+ T/ *ampāḷ*).   The Great Mother. The name of the tutelary Goddess of Pudukkottai.

Brihannayaki (S/ *bṛhat*+ T/ *nāyaki*).   The Great Protectress. Another name for Brihadambal.

Carnatic (T/ *kār+nāṭu*).   The black country. A Tamil designation adapted by the East India Company to indicate the area of India from Madras to Madurai. Later indicated all of South India.

Cervaikar (T/ *cērvai+k+kāran*).   Service to a sacred person. The Tamil title used for members of noble families who were considered kin to the raja and who provided troops in war. Also spelled Servaikar. Used interchangeably with Sardar.

Chamaram (S/ *camara*).   A yak. A fan made from a yak's tail, a premier sign of royalty. The term was normally interchangeable with the Hindustani term, Chowrie, but in Pudukkottai the Chamaram came to mean a fan of swan and peacock feathers while the Chowrie was the yak-tail fan.

Chobdar (P/ *chūb-dār*).   Mace or staff bearers, but also the staffs. The staffs, usually made of silver, were a sign of authority. In Pudukkottai the silver staffs were called "rods" in English; the term above was used especially for the two gold staffs pre-

sented by the East India Company and always carried next to the raja.

Chola (T/ *cōḻam*).   An ancient Tamil kingdom. The powerful dynasty that dominated much of southern India culturally, if not politically, from the capital in Tanjore in the tenth to thirteenth centuries C.E. A style of art and architecture associated with the period.

Chowrie (H/ *chaunrī*, from S/ *camara*).   A fan made of a yak's tail. A major emblem of royalty. *See also* Chamaram.

Dakshinamurti (S/ *dakṣiṇa+mūrti*).   The south-facing image; also implies the more orthodox "right-handed" as opposed to "left-handed" rites in certain ritual practices. The form of Shiva as the preceptor of the Gods embraced by the Tondaimans as their dynastic deity.

Daffedar (P/ *dafʿa-dār*).   Head peon. In Pudukkottai, the head of the palace guards, the Dalayets, who also served as palace menials.

Dalayet (H/ *ḍhalāyat*).   Armed attendant. In Pudukkottai, a member of the menial royal bodyguard, not associated with the state militia, who served essentially as peons in the palace.

Dampathi (S/ *dam+pati*).   Master of the house. A personal gift to servants from the master, but especially the gift from the raja to Brahmans often in the form of clothing.

Darbar (P/ *darbār*).   An audience hall. In Pudukkottai this particular English spelling of the Persian term came to mean the official power of the state, the government, as distinguished from "durbar." *See also* durbar.

Dassara (S/ *daśaharā*. Possibly from *daśaha*, a ceremony lasting ten days.) The ten-day-long celebration, especially important for South Indian Hindu kings, honoring the Goddess in her forms as the deity of war, wealth, and learning. In northern India the same festival celebrates the victory of Lord Rama over the demon-king Ravana. Celebrated in October–November according to the lunar calendar. *See also* Navaratri.

devadasi (S/ *deva+dāsī*). The female servants of God. Dedicated from childhood to temple service, these women wrote and performed dance dramas, danced, and executed certain ritual services inside the sanctum of the temple for the pleasure of the presiding deity. They also served the Hindu king.

dewan (P-A/ *dīwān*). The book of accounts; later the keeper of accounts; finally, the one who sat on the seat next to the king. The chief administrative officer, the prime minister, in the royal states of India. The term came into English as "divan," an elegant sofa.

Durga (S/ *durga*). The Goddess of victory and war, especially important to Hindu kings.

Dunka (H/ *dankā*). A pair of kettledrums carried on a horse or, as in the case of Pudukkottai, on an elephant. An important emblem of royalty.

durbar (P/ *darbār*). An audience hall. The ceremony in which the raja sat in state with all of his court to hear petitions and make official pronouncements. The practice became an important ceremonial both for Hindu rajas and for high British officials. *See also* Darbar.

Faisal Registry (P/ *fayṣal*). A judicial judgment or decree. In Pudukkottai, a collection of judgments contained in bound volumes. The term was used especially of the records determining ownership of and taxes on former inam lands in the 1880s.

Gadi (H/ *gaddī*). Seat, throne. The royal throne.

Gajalakshmi (S/ *gaja+lakṣmī*). A form of Lakshmi, the Goddess of wealth and well-being, seated on a lotus surrounded by elephants bathing her with water from their trunks. The form is especially auspicious and is used to signify overflowing royal wealth.

Gandabherunda (T/ *kaṇṭa+pēraṇṭam*). An enormous legendary two-headed bird able to hold an elephant in its claws. An important emblem of royal power in Pudukkottai.

Grantha (S/ *granthi*). Knotted together. The name given to a hybrid form of Sanskrit written in Tamil script and used primarily by temple priests for texts utilized in rituals.

Guruswami (S/ *guru+svāmin*). The master teacher. The chief spiritual adviser to a Hindu king. In Pudukkottai, the superior of the staff of priests who served in the palace. *See also* Rajaguru.

Harikar (T/ *arikkāraṉ*). A messenger. The Brahmans used as messengers during war because of the religious prohibition against killing them. In Pudukkottai, the Brahman chief of staff in the palace who directed all ceremonies and acted as the raja's official emissary in carrying royal gifts and invitations.

Huzur (A/ *ḥuẓūr*). Literally, "the presence." A term of great respect used to address an exalted person. In Pudukkottai, the term came to indicate the palace as the seat of authority.

inam (A/ *inʿām*). A benefice. Especially a gift of rent-free land from a king to reward military service, to recognize special talent, to compensate for service in the palace, or to recognize close kinship.

Jagir (P/ *jāgīr*). A large hereditary estate granted by a monarch along with the rights to collect taxes. In Pudukkottai, only the raja's close kin and a collateral royal line held such estates.

Jagirar (P/ *jāgīr-dār*, T/ *jakir+ār*). The holder of a Jagir.

Jamedar (P/ *jamʿ-dār*). Leader of an army unit. In Pudukkottai, the head of the palace guards. The term was also used as a rank in the British Indian army.

Jyothisa (S/ *jyotiṣa*). An astrologer. In Pudukkottai, the court official who set the yearly religious calendar for all palace and state rituals.

Kalasa (S/ *kalaśa*). Water pot. The sacred vessel used for ceremonial ablutions and for the anointing rituals in the consecration of a king or divine icon. *See also* Abhishekam and Kumbam.

Kallar (T/ *kaḷḷan*). "Thief," but here in the honorific form the name of a caste once associated with banditry in southern India; later a dominant landholding group in southern Ta-

milnadu. The caste of the rajas of Pudukkottai.

Kamadhenu (S/ *kāma+dhenu*). The giver of all desires. The mythical cow that grants all wishes especially associated with the Goddess as mother.

Kaval (T/ *kāval*). Watchman. A guard in the palace usually assigned to watch certain areas.

Kodaikkar (T/ *koṭai+k+kāran*). Umbrella bearer. A servant who carried the royal umbrella behind an Indian monarch when he processed in state. The umbrella is a primary emblem of royalty.

Kothal (P/ *kūtal*). A plumed horse led before a dignitary in procession as a sign of honor. Now seen only in circus parades.

Koyil (T/ *kōyil*). Palace or temple. Dwelling place of a divinity. Usually applied to temples or churches but not to mosques. *See also* Mandir.

Kudumiamalai (T/ *kuṭumiyan+malai*). A town twelve miles west of Pudukkottai city that contains and now gives its name to a very old rock-cut temple, properly called the Sikhanatha temple. The temple was the site of the earliest coronation ceremonies for the rajas of Pudukkottai.

Kumbabhishekam (T/ *kumpa+* S/ *abhiṣēka*). Anointing with water from a holy vessel. The ritual of consecration for the deities within the sanctum of a temple.

Kumbam (T/ *kumpa*). Water pot, especially the vessel holding the holy water used for rituals of consecration. The Tamil equivalent of the Sanskrit term "Kalasa."

Kurumbas (T/ *kurumpar*). A caste of hunters and shepherds. An aboriginal tribe that legends assert first conquered and ruled southern India.

Kurava (T/ *kurava*). A caste of itinerant fowlers, snake charmers, and fortune tellers. The Gypsy of southern India.

Lakshmi (S/ *lakṣmī*). The Goddess of good fortune, wealth, and well-being. Especially associated with the largest of Hindu rajas.

Madikaval (T/ *māṭi+kāval*). Watchman in the upper story of the palace, which in Pudukkottai was the ladies' quarters.

Mahakumbabhishekam (S/ *mahā+* T/ *kumpa+* S/ *abhiṣēka*). The rite of consecration for a newly built or newly refurbished temple. Holy water is poured from the holy water pot onto the top of the spires covering the sanctums of the temple.

Mahal (A-P/ *maḥall*). A residence or apartment within a palace complex, especially the ladies' quarters within a royal palace.

Mandapam (T/ *maṇṭapam*). A permanent or temporary pavilion within a temple or palace complex used for such rituals as a marriage or to prepare the deity or king before processions.

Mandir (T/ *mantiram*, S/ *mandira*). House, palace, or temple. Usually a neutral term for any sacred building or hall. Can be applied to a mosque or a temple but not usually to a church. *See also* Koyil.

Maravar (T/ *maravār*). A caste of hunters, but this honorific form refers to a dominant landowning community. The caste of the rajas of Ramnad.

Nadhaswaram (S/ *nādasvara,* also T/ *nāka+curam*). A large musical instrument, like a clarinet, with a bellowing tone used in rituals and processions.

Nagarakhana (P/ *naqqāra-khāna*). The kettledrum house. A porch or archway where the royal drums were sounded at intervals throughout the day. In Pudukkottai a band that played Persian, "nawabi" (*see* nawab), music throughout the night.

Navaratri (S/ *nava+rātri*). The nine nights. The annual nine-day festival to honor the Goddess in her many forms. A tenth day was celebrated by kings in southern India to mark the Goddess's ultimate victory over demons. *See also* Dassara.

nawab (A-P/ *nawwāb*). A deputy. In the bureaucracy of the Moghul empire in India, a governor appointed by the court in Delhi. Later a title of respect for both British and Muslim gentlemen. When written as Nabab or Nabob, a European merchant living in rich Oriental style in India or at home on profits from the East India trade. In Pudukkottai and elsewhere, used as an adjective, "nawabi," to mean anything related to the former Moghul empire or to Moghul-Persian culture.

Nizam (A/ *niẕām*). Regulator. The hereditary title of the Muslim rulers of Hyderabad state who once controlled a territory reaching far into present Tamilnadu state.

Ondiyiruppu (T/ *oṇṭiyiruppu*). Sitting

the term for the holy water used in the ritual bathing of deities and the king. *See also* Abhishekam.

Tirugokarnam (T/ *tiru+kō+karanam*). Literally "lord of the cow's ear." The town next to Pudukkottai city that contained the state temple. Usually called the Tirugokarnam temple, it is more properly the Gokarnesvara temple. The name refers to the important legend about the founding of the temple.

Valaiyan (T/ *valaiyan*). "Net-man." Primitive hunters in the forests of southern India. In Pudukkottai, the caste of hunters who served the raja as foresters and purveyors of game.

Vastram (S/ *vastra*). Clothes, vestments. Used for clothing the raja gave as a gift of honor to members of his court to mark their weddings and other family rituals, to honor Brahmans, or to recognize poets and scholars.

Vedaikari (T/ *vettai+k+kāran*). Huntsman. The palace officer in charge of supplying the raja with meat and other products of the forest. Head of the Valaiyans.

Vellalar (T/ *vellālār*). A dominant landowning caste in southern India associated with the rich wetlands. In South Indian hierarchy, the highest non-Brahman caste.

Viralimalai (T/ *virāli+malai*). A hill in Pudukkottai accommodating a famous ancient temple to the God Murugan, who was patronized by the rajas. The temple usually takes its name from the hill, but it is more properly called the Sri Subrahmanya temple at Viralimalai.

yali (T/ *yāli*). Lion. A legendary animal combining the features of an elephant and a lion. A paramount emblem of royal power.

zamindar (P/ *zamīn-dār*). Landholder. A quasi-independent ruler of a vast estate who paid taxes directly to the paramount authority with judicial powers and the right to levy taxes within his estate. Zamindars in southern India continued to use the title "raja," but they were not readily recognized as rajas by the British. Often spelled zemindar.

zamindary (P/ *zamīn-dār*). The estate of a zamindar. The British adopted the system from the Moghuls and created it as one step in power below a Native State. The differences between the two were often subtle, but in the case of Pudukkottai, a Native State, and nearby Ramnad, a zamindary, the crucial distinction was tribute to the overlord. Pudukkottai paid no taxes to the British. Also spelled zamindari.

Toward a Recovery of Religious Things: *An Introduction*

Many years ago there lived an Emperor, who cared so enormously for new clothes that he spent all his money upon them, that he might be very fine. He did not care about his soldiers, nor about the theatre, and only liked to drive out and show his new clothes. He had a coat for every hour of the day; and just as they say of a king, "He is in council," one always said of him, "The Emperor is in the wardrobe."

—Hans Christian Andersen

The king is dead, or to say it as it was said in the little kingdom of Pudukkottai in India, *kālañcenratu*—his time lapsed. Raja Ramachandra Tondaiman, who died in 1886, remains embodied in a series of portraits and in pages of old records kept in archives in London, New Delhi, and his old capital city. His once-dashing successor, His Highness Sir Martanda Bhairava Tondaiman, G.C.I.E., died in Paris in 1928 but leaves his vitality in a portrait with his British knightly robes elegantly draped over his silk brocade frock coat. He had been to England to see the queen. Old court officials still keep a reproduction of this portrait printed as a keepsake at the time of his death (Plate 1). The present Raja Rajagopala Tondaiman safeguards many of these mementos of his erstwhile kingdom in his palace in nearby Trichinopoly. Like all such "Native States," Pudukkottai was amalgamated into the Indian union in 1948. Now *Putukkōṭṭai kālañcenratu.*

Gone too are the British civil officers of "the Raj," as the British government of India came to be called. Ironically their portraits now rest alongside those of rajas whose lavish spending

Plate 1.   A memento distributed at the death of His Highness Martanda Bhairava Tondaiman in 1928. The caption reads in very anglicized Tamil: "His Highness Sri Brihadambadas Raja Sir Martanda Bhairava Tondaiman, G.C.I.E. Born 26-11-1875. Died 28-5-1928." The cameoed portrait is a popular painting of the raja rendered by Venkatarayalu Raju in 1914. (A gift of the palace Head Harikar Sri K. Subramanian.)

was so often the occasion for their stern reprimands. In His Highness's palace in Trichino-poly, the face of the British tutor from Cambridge who carefully trained the young Martanda Tondaiman so long ago is fixed forever in a hunting scene. He sits among the tusks of elephants with his guns and tents, looking much like a raja in his own domain (Plate 2). Portraits of British governors who sat under the royal canopy with the raja "in durbar" (in a formal audience with the full court) (Plate 3) are now hung next to the very men whom they doubted were fit to rule. The great dewan Sir A. Sashia Sastri, appointed by the British to bring order to Raja Ramachandra's domain, has left his face and corpulent figure seated appropriately between British officers and the raja in durbar (Plate 4, color section). The spirit of the queen-empress whom they all served has been distributed all over India into the many bronze and stone statues in front of the old offices and universities built in her name. Sometimes a garland can still be seen draped over the bronze shoulders of one such Victoria who sits in front of the University of Madras, her eyes glancing toward the Bay of Bengal.

As living memory fades, time has turned the rajas and the rulers of the imperial past into the very bric-a-brac that has become a popular cliché for anything Victorian. There was something about the heyday of the British Empire that left a myriad of mementos. Our Victorian attics, those public museums and private palaces throughout London and the former Indian empire, are stuffed with grand ornaments, crowns and turbans, and paintings of people bedecked in the same. This intense interest in decoration and in a world of public

Plate 2. Neither the subject nor the artist is identified in this painting, which hangs in His Highness's palace in Trichinopoly, but several photos of Mr. F. F. Crossley in the royal family's photo albums make the identification certain. Crossley, who tutored the young Raja Martanda for seven years, encouraged the raja's hunting and apparently accompanied him throughout India on such adventures, ostensibly to increase the young king's knowledge of India. This painting may date from 1893, when the raja went on an elephant hunt in nearby Travancore State. Crossley, on the far right, a graduate of Cambridge University, shed his bookish vocation here and basked in royal glory as he confidently struck the pose of a big-game hunter. The young man seated on the far left may be Raja Martanda.

display was shared by Britain's queen, India's many rajas, and even aspiring middle-class families in Britain and the empire whose carefully preserved parlors and elegant front porches were created for the public eye like the court of any prince. In the middle-class homes, the first photo albums, often hand painted by the ladies of the house, brought the opportunity to share in this world of the gilded image. But the centerpiece for this world of display was always the Raj in India embodied in public statues and popular etchings of Victoria on her throne (Plate 5), sometimes surrounded by India's many bejeweled rajas, all paying obeisance to this queen-empress.

So I begin by making a suggestion: Indians who attended "princes" like the raja of Pudukkottai, the British who served in these "Native States," and perhaps even the British public, who eagerly made the Raj and its exotic princes part of the decor of their homes, came to share a common culture. This is not a radical thesis for a modern cultural historian. There have been excellent works on the revival of royal rituals in Britain, and detailed studies on the construction of a "ritual idiom" for the Raj in India (see Lant 1979; Hobs-

Plate 3.   In this detail of a larger painting, Raja Ramachandra Tondaiman shares his throne with the visiting governor of Madras, Sir Grant Duff, in the last year of the raja's life. The paint on the cloth canvas is now badly cracked after a century of summer heat, but Sir Grant can still be seen sitting with complete aplomb as an honored guest, but also as the representative of the "Paramount Power." The painting, now in the keeping of the Government Museum in Pudukkottai, is signed by Ravi Varma and dated months after the raja's death. Although the faces are executed with fine detail, the painting overall lacks Ravi Varma's usual grace. This piece was probably created from memory or from a photograph by one of Varma's students and completed by the artist to commemorate the last glorious moment of the now-deceased king. Raja Ramachandra had patronized the well-known artist throughout his life, commissioning several major works.

bawm and Ranger 1983). Pudukkottai has been the subject of a fine study that details, among other aspects of kingship, the importance of the rajas' gifts of *pirutus,* honors, which often took the form of the right to wear certain ornate clothing and other ritual garb (Dirks 1987). In all these studies, the decorative elements, the items of fancy dress or elegant decor, are understood within the political and social contexts of the day. These "symbols" or "ritual idioms" were means to legitimize rule, to express both social solidarity and social segmentation. They were valued "texts" that if properly read have much to say about the complex configuration of the state in both India and Britain.

Plate 5. A group of Parsi gentlemen look up curiously at a newly installed marble image of Queen Victoria in this Bombay park sometime in the 1870s, after Victoria became the Empress of India. The ornate statue portrays a young Victoria and may have been modeled on Sir George Hayter's famous painting of the queen now in the National Portrait Gallery (see Bayly 1990, 331). Apparently unable to accept the then matronly Victoria, both Hayter and this sculptor re-created her seated upon the throne, young and vigorous on her coronation day—not as she was when she assumed the Indian imperial title. (Photo by T. W. Scadden. Courtesy of the Oriental and India Office Collections, The British Library.)

In this book, however, I take a more radical tack. As a historian of religions, my foray into the domain of history has other purposes than to reveal the nature of cultural transitions or to explore the changing nature of the state or of society. The domain of symbols and of ritual has long been the special province of the comparative study of religions. When "symbols" appear in ritual texts, we are accorded the right to discuss their theological significance along with their social or political import.

The reader should be warned, then, that this study is neither a history of Pudukkottai or the empire, nor a history of ideas. This is a work of "ethno-theology," the study of the nature of divinity within the historical moment. The particular moment in question was what I will term "iconic." I use "iconic" not in the later sense of Peirce's philosophy but more literally, for in this world of surface display, photos, paintings, books, and even persons were concretized into icons, into valued *things*.

This is not to say that many in the British empire willingly admitted to participating in such a system. And I do not want to suggest that this was not also a period deeply involved with principles and purposes, an era that worked hard to bring all hidden motivations, religious or secular, into consciousness. These same times of grand royal ritual also developed science as we know it, and intense belief in rationalism, and the very modern disciplines that study ritual and religion. In spite of this, or perhaps because of it, I argue that in the often unspoken and many times denied—but lived—world of display, the Victorian period left us with what it has most to contribute to our modern understanding about religion: its intense involvement with the ornamental and the decorative, with highly prized *things*. Moreover, this intense involvement with valued things was not simply another convenient form of communication in an age when a vast empire made a shared vocabulary of words much less effective than a shared stock of ritual images. I would argue instead that this was a new age of "idolatry." A multitude of new icons, holy persons, and sacred things were available to the British openly in places like Pudukkottai and in camouflage as "political" pageant at home.

The court rituals of a little kingdom like Pudukkottai, or even the controversies over Victoria's own royal ceremonials, might now be only of passing interest to the modern study of religion if it were not for one important fact. The founders of the comparative study of religion as well as of modern anthropology lived in this same imperial world of royal display. The push and pull between a desire to share in a renewed chance for ritual splendor that an empire made possible, and an old allegiance to a rationalism free of frivolity, vexed scholars as much as civil servants and queens.

Friedrich Max Müller, the period's most influential scholar of India, and James George Frazer, the young man whose name would become synonymous with the study of sacral kings, both lived in tension with the empire. During his early career, Max Müller was supported by funds from the East India Company and the later British Government of India. He served as an examiner for candidates for the Indian Civil Service. His papers contain numerous invitations to Buckingham Palace. At the end of his life, Queen Victoria named Müller to her Privy Council. Yet he, more than any other scholar, was responsible for creating a great counterimage of India as the model of a truly spiritual, nonmaterialistic culture. His work helped to make the ornamented lords, like the raja of Pudukkottai, insensible to several generations of scholars and to reformist Indians alike. Yet ironically, just after his death, a number of his fellow scholars openly criticized his pride in worldly success and the vanity of his stylish clothes (Chaudhuri 1974, 372).

James Frazer, too, deplored the modern materialistic culture of his day. His famous tome, *The Golden Bough*, opined the tragic mistakes of a ritual world that was built upon a fantasy, the fantasy that human beings could control matter. Although his own life was simple, his books were ornate. If photos reveal much about the man, then Sir James wore his knighthood with considerable pride.[1] The scholars, the very agency of modern theory about ritual, were thoroughly a part of the Victorian world that made ritual with one hand and wrote it off with another. They delighted in knightly robes and silk cummerbunds, but spoke of the foolishness of magic and the glorification of infinite spirit.

Only a Victorian scholar, however, would have the bold sense of grandeur to argue this case with the entire empire as a subject. In our age of much smaller aspirations, the theater here can be more modest, but the script need be no less complex. The small princely state of Pudukkottai is enough to stage the argument as long as the reader keeps in mind that in the backdrop to every scene must be painted the empire. There was an astonishing circulation of

---

1. See photographs entitled "Sir James and Lady Frazer, annual dinner of the Royal Literary Fund, London, 1930" (Ackerman 1987, plates 9 and 10).

ideas, as well as things, throughout India and from India to Britain, even in a place as small as this fifty-square-mile kingdom in the dry lands of South India. This will become clear in the pages that follow. Furthermore, I claim the right to insinuate such scholars as F. Max Müller and James Frazer into this tiny set, precisely because their ideas and their books helped to veil the religiousness, the very sacredness, that operated here among the fly whisks, fans, and fancy plumage of the rajas' courts. They were the real phantoms of this small but still grand opera.

Ironically, Pudukkottai became one of those places where the British could permit themselves real access to such sacral things, precisely because the British civil service officers classified court rituals as "political ceremonials" and the scholars did nothing to change that designation. Yet in places like Pudukkottai, divinity had the most to do with material things, particularly with one certain thing: the body of the king. If we replay the drama of the British participation here and then rerun the story a second time with the spotlight on this royal court in its own South Indian scenery, then a fuller range of *theo-logies* can be revealed.

The reader, then, can expect a book in two parts. The first to explore and deconstruct an encounter of the Raj with its rajas, looking at this tiny kingdom in South India with a wide-angle lens, and the second to return to Pudukkottai with an eye focused close up and with a mind intent on reconstructing its rajas in their fullest ceremonial context. The opening set will be the small princely state of Pudukkottai and its own central scene, the durbars—the ritual occasions in which the raja and his entire court would assemble in full state dress to give what in Britain would be called an audience, a hearing, but what in Pudukkottai was considered a *darśan* (also *darśana*), a seeing, a gift of a splendid sight.

The durbar and other rituals of display were part of the courtly life of most Indian princes, and the British quickly adopted these "ceremonials," as they called them, and participated in the durbars of their feudatory princes. In such places as Pudukkottai and in the capitals of the three Presidencies that comprised British India and in the imperial capital, the British created their own durbars. In the great Delhi Durbar of 1877, which honored the assumption of the title of Empress of India by Queen Victoria, the British proved that they could at times excel in this ritual medium, a fact that made some British at home uncomfortable (Cohn 1983b, 206). In Pudukkottai they succeeded in yoking the British lion to the Indian elephant and pulling off a very good show indeed. Here the Hindu and the British Christian, as well as the British rationalist, played together for a time with royal *things* and, as we shall see, made and unmade Gods.

The reader must be warned that the world I am constructing/reconstructing existed only for some of the people, some of the time. This was equally a time of antiroyalism in Britain and of the bitter Irish struggle for Home Rule. In most of India, the rule of queens or princes must have seemed remote because British India was a bureaucratic state. Only in the third of India under "native rule" did this royal world survive. Many of the British civil servants who experienced, even reveled, in these Native States did so with a divided conscience and a divided mind. Many were Scotsmen, Presbyterian Calvinists unsure of both ritual and royalty; others were good bureaucrats committed to a rational system of government, who considered ceremonials a sad necessity in this oriental world.

Yet some of these same staid servants of the empire also betrayed an overly keen interest in the very ceremonials they found so irksome. Some officials—such as Sir Charles Tupper and William Lee-Warner—spent years sorting out the proper ceremonial relationships between the queen-empress's regal status and that of the Indian princes. Tupper confidently declared these princes to be ruling "chiefs," but not kings, noting Pudukkottai as a prime example of a state whose dewan had to be reprimanded after daring to call his raja a "royal" person. Tupper, quoting Sir Henry Maine from a memo dated 1864, reminds his reader, "There may be found in India every shade and variety of sovereignty, but there is only one independent Sovereign, the British Government" (Tupper 1895, 19–20).

Others in the empire, including Victoria herself, were never comfortable with all this bulky garb of the empire. There was a running battle between the queen and those who organized her now-famous Golden Jubilee over Her Majesty's attire. The queen refused to appear in full state dress and absolutely would not use the gold state coach. The grand queen-empress thus refused to appear in the way she was so often portrayed in India, seated in state with crown and scepter. Instead, she wore a bonnet and insisted on riding in an open carriage to a simple service in Westminster Abbey. The queen was not enamored of ritual and was decidedly "low church." As Jeffrey Lant put it, "Not only did she like her religion simple, she liked it short and sweet. When it was otherwise, the Defender of Faith was given to fidgeting" (1979, 162). How very disappointing it must have been to the Charles Tuppers of the empire to see the likes of a raja of Pudukkottai who ruled an area measured in square miles more capable of a grand show than this dowdy queen on whose empire even the sun never set. But when the queen would not oblige by putting on her crown, the print-makers, the engravers, the painters, and the sculptors would supply the proper dress. The empress of India always wore her crown, even when Victoria, queen of Great Britain, wore a bonnet as she drove alone in her old landau.

While the queen fidgeted in her crown, while a Scotsman governor uncomfortably shared in native rituals, while Max Müller was dismissed by fellow scholars for the vanity of his dress, the raja of Pudukkottai sat on his throne. Neither a privy councillor nor considered a royal personage of the empire, Raja Ramachandra Tondaiman sat with his silks, his jeweled turban, and his bejeweled courtiers "in durbar."

The durbar was the ultimate ritual of display. The raja sat under his brocade canopy surrounded by a group of "servants" called the Dignitary Establishment, each of whom held one of his royal emblems, which included fly whisks, maces, and silver rods. On the left side of the raja's canopy sat his immediate family, usually brothers and uncles and the Sardars—military officials who were understood as kinsmen. On the right were the court administrative officials, the dewan (chief minister), and various judicial and tax officials. All were splendidly attired in court dress that carefully displayed their rank and their status in the realm. The durbar ritual itself was this very display followed by presentation of a coin to the raja by the raja's kinsmen and of a lemon by his officers. At the close of the ceremony the raja distributed "attar and pan," the traditional parting gift to guests of rose water perfume from an ornate decanter and sweetened betel nut, both offered on a tray. The same kind of display occurred more publicly outside the durbar hall when the raja rode in procession with the Dignitary Establishment surrounding him and all of his courtiers ahead. In earlier days, the Tondaimans rode in state around the borders of their capital city every night. In Raja

Ramachandra's time, the raja rode in procession during certain festivals associated with the state temple and later to mark special imperial holidays.

When asked today to explain this display of the raja, old members of the court agree: The raja was displayed in order to allow his subjects to "take *darśan*"—a term usually used in connection with the ornamented images of deities displayed in the sanctum of a temple. The God embodied in the bronze or stone image within the temple is believed to grant devotees this power-laden vision, a revelation of divine presence. Similarly, the sight, the darsan, of the rajas had this same divine power. So powerful was this vision of the raja that a person experiencing exceptionally good luck was asked, "Have you seen the raja's face today?" During interviews in Pudukkottai the last living devadasi, who had served as a dancer for rituals in the palace, and the old Agama Sastri, who had been the chief priest in charge of properly performing all state ritual, openly declared that the raja was "God" (here both Sanskrit, *devatā*, and Tamil, *cāmi*)—much to the surprise of a very modern member of the Pudukkottai royal family!

In spite of such open statements about the raja's position as a "God," the meaning of the divine status of the Indian king has been much debated and often misunderstood, as scholars have tried to apply Western theology to a place like Pudukkottai (Gajendragadkar 1962, 421; Gonda 1969, 134; Dumont [1966] 1970, 72). Many scholars even as late as the 1970s assumed that divine powers belonged to only the Brahman priesthood as the mirror of the Gods on earth. For example, political scientist Charles Drekmeier felt justified in insisting that when Brahmanic texts used divine terminology to describe the king, the language had to be understood as metaphor:

> The word deva is often translated by Western scholars as "god." Deva is used, however, to connote moral superiority rather than omnipotent divinity in the Judeo-Christian sense. It meant resplendent or awe-inspiring and was applied to that which possessed more than ordinary power. When the king is described in the ancient scriptures as devata, his importance to the community is extolled, and we are not justified in reading more into the term. (Drekmeier 1962, 251)

But Ramachandra Tondaiman seated "in durbar" is neither an omnipotent nor an omnipresent God, nor is his divinity simply an aggrandized mask of status or power. At the center of the durbar sat a "god," but not "in the Judeo-Christian sense." Raja Ramachandra Tondaiman in durbar, like the many objects that surround him, must also be understood as an icon. This special nature of this living icon is at the heart of the entire culture of display. The pages that follow verify that we are justified in reading much more than metaphor into the terms *devatā* and *cāmi*.

Given the continued downplaying of the sacredness of the Hindu king, is it any wonder that the early British civil servants never ventured officially to disclose this religious aspect of the durbar? Although it was undisclosed, they did not fail to notice the fact. The British official in the field may not have chosen intellectually to justify the raja, but their descriptions of what was clearly some form of divine kingship fill the pages of that once-popular literary genre "memoirs-of-my-years-in-Injha." One such late memoir records with wonder how "one Hindu ruler, highly cultured and well known in London drawing-rooms, poses as a semi-divinity in his own State" (Barton 1934, 61). E. M. Forster described quite elegantly in *The Hill of Devi* how the raja, whom he served as private secretary, functioned at the very least as a priest, if not a God, in the ceremonies of his realm ([1953], 102–20). But in the official records of the Raj the durbars are strictly classified as "political" and are called simply "ceremonials." No official record I reviewed gave even the slightest hint that the British "Resident," the official representative of the Government of India to the rajas, or any member of the Political Department that oversaw the Native States, openly revealed the religious nature of this ceremony. Even the Indians that prepared the official administrative manuals in English for states like Pudukkottai tended to follow the British classification and wrote that the raja's household and all the "servants" that formed his court existed to enhance his "dignity."

The British saw the splendor of the durbar and imitated its form in their own ceremonials, but they did not ask how it all worked. And scholars of the realm, who should have been able to say much about such sacral kingship, never directed their attention to these Native States. Max Müller was not interested in such modern creations. Frazer, who wrote the most extensive discussion of the sacral king ever attempted, let his pen roam the ancient world from Japan to Rome to seek examples, but somehow passed over the capitals of the Raj, where British governors were sitting down under silk canopies with rajas they saw as men but whose people saw them in some important sense as embodied divinity.

This is not to say that everyone in South India or even everyone in Pudukkottai acknowledged Raja Ramachandra and his successors as a "god" or even as a king. Antiroyal feelings were not foreign to India. There is a strong tradition that suspected the divine power of kings and even tried to write sacral kingship out of orthodoxy. In modern times, there were those in Pudukkottai who supported the developing movement of the 1920s to free "the millions of people in the Indian States suffering under the autocratic rule of their Princes" (Chudgar 1929, v), and a more recent history of the freedom struggle in the princely states records the work of the All-Indian States' Peoples' Conference (Handa 1968), which was active in Pudukkottai. But for many of the people much of the time, if Raja Ramachandra did not take this ornamented throne someone else would have occupied it in the same posture that he so conspicuously assumed.

The very culture of ornamentation in Pudukkottai was not fragmented by either an Age of Reason or a previous age of theology whose arguments against the real presence of divinity in ritual had triumphed. That divinity could take concrete form in a king or a saint, or even a seeming madman, is not a serious question here. To put it another way, there is no commandment against "idolatry." And here is the rub. A "chief" of one of the smallest Native States in India can openly display his divinity to those who cared to look, while Her Majesty and a whole retinue of those participating in the ceremonials of an empire stand embarrassed in their own lordly array.

I have heard it said that the Tondaiman family were not really kings because this family were upstarts. The most sarcastic statement came from a well-known collector of folktales about royal families who wrote to tell me he did not collect material from Pudukkottai because these kings were really just "made by the British." And this indeed is the supreme irony. Many of the Tondaimans' honors—their titles, their rights to land, even their right to carry certain gold sticks—were conferred by the East India Company and later by Her Majesty's Government of India. Collection of such honors made a warrior lord into a king and, more important, into a divine personage. Those who saw nothing of splendor in the Tondaimans saw them as mere puppets of the British. But for those who acknowledged the Tondaimans as rajas, the British honors were simply a part of the accoutrements that added to their lord's regal status and thus to his divinity. In spite of British attempts to classify all these rituals as "ceremonials" and the rajas as "chiefs," at some level, they participated in this act of king-making and, ironically, God-making. And if the Pudukkottai raja was considered divine, what could be said of his liege lady? Who was Victoria?

In this empire where a Calvinist sat on a throne with lavish princes, actions belied words. Images belied events when Victoria's jubilee bonnet in Britain became a crown in India. Articulated principles inherited from the Enlightenment are at odds with the culture of a new royal age where the British must make kings (and Gods) as part of their great Raj. This is the problem in restructuring the memory of even this tiny kingdom in the imperial galaxy. There have been several decades of discussion about the "Westernization" of India, but near silence on the "Easternization" of Britain. The assumption is that the only influence India had was through the few Hindu reformers and preachers who filled the language of intellectuals in Britain with words like "karma" and "dharma" and filled their heads with images of India as the last haven for the nonmaterialistic people of the world.

As Ronald Inden now asks in his provocative reevaluation of the Euro-American "imagining" of India, "European discourses appear to separate their Self from the Indian Other—the essence of Western thought is practical reason, that of India, dreamy imagination. . . . But is this so?" (1990, 3). The answer is indeed no. But the real conjunction of "West" with "East" may well have occurred in a place like Pudukkottai without words, silently, so that normal discursive language failed to announce the event and so that, ironically, all participants actually remained free to act and move together in a space that slipped beyond and between the hard pen of imperial discourse.

Historians of religions have too long looked only at words. Religion can exist as much inside a durbar hall as in a temple. Clues to the presence of a religious culture can be as much embedded in a decorated elephant as in an ancient myth. The official printed schedule of ceremonials to be observed for a visiting governor reveals another side to kingship that orthodox Brahman texts from the eighth century cannot disclose. The word of bureaucratic documents, the paraphernalia of the court, the style of dress, the colors of a painting—all these "things" must be added to the words of theological and mythic discourse we have learned to read so well.

Not all forms of religious history can be reduced to science with hypothesis, data, and conclusion. Historians of religions, like lawyers, journalists, or novelists, must convince their public to accept a certain configuration of events, a particular evaluation of characters, a certain reading of material evidence as "true." That reconstruction changes as time passes. This book is not structured around a central "thesis" on the topic of sacral kingship that I intend to "prove" by marshaling all possible evidence. Rather, I am asking readers to begin by looking at a curious phenomenon: a common interest in both India and Britain in king/

queen/rajas. Moreover, instead of supposing that India forced Britain to take its rajas seriously because of its own ritual instincts, let us allow for the possibility that Britain was equally if not more involved with creating a new royal age. Moreover, and more important, scholars were not aloof from the enterprise of empire. They must be added to the script, not dropped from it. Intellectually, they represent what Ronald Inden has called the "loyal opposition" (1990, 66), but their own work and even their own careers were englobed by the world of ornamentation.

The central problem then becomes why this world of ritual splendor was so readily embraced in praxis by the British but not in open theory. Why the doubts, the near subterfuge, the embarrassment? And India shares in the same embarrassed loving of its own ornamented lord and its lavish rituals. This is not a case of a materialistic West subverting an ascetic East into a foolhardy attempt to emulate the splendor of an empire, nor is it a pageant-plagued, vain, and effeminate East seducing a staid soldier of Christ. The rajas of Pudukkottai, no less than the nearby British civil servants, shared in a culture that gloried in ritual splendor but also felt a nakedness underneath this garish garb. This story does have a central mystery: What is this drawing toward royal splendor and, at the same time, how can we explain away the equal repulsion? Frazer suggested a dark side to kingship, but after rewriting his story three times in thirty years, he never fully told his anxious audience what that darkness might have been.

Setting the Scene

This study depends primarily on an analysis of images, not of concepts. The argument is created not through a progression of ideas but in a chronological progression of portraits and photographs, a play of images. The point is to convince the reader that ornamentation—particularly in the crucial image of the ornamented raja seated in state (or, as more commonly put, "in durbar")—defines a serious form of religiousness in this tiny state. This seeming oriental ostentation both absorbed British styles into its own forms and in many subtle ways allowed the British to experience their own intense fascination with the same kind of sacredness.

This book reverses the assumption of the British that it was Indians who could not bring their own history and culture to consciousness. Here we see the British as willing and sometimes eager participants in a system that they at first denied, then understood pragmatically, and ultimately rejected. Comparative studies of the royal court in India and in Britain had to wait until the late 1920s, and then were largely ignored by the public and by scholars (for example, Buckler 1985 and Hocart 1970).

The progression of images dates from 1858 to 1928, from the moment the British woke up to the importance of "ceremonials," to the time when their political, religious, and social interests in this ornamented world waned. Ironically, only in the very last period of the Tondaiman rule of the Pudukkottai state do the British sufficiently disappear from the picture to leave room to reconstruct a memory of what this ornate sacral kingship might be without their presence. But by then India was moving toward independence with a program that abjured the irrationality and wastefulness of the "pageant princes." The British never dissolved the Native States, and in fact insisted that their old treaties with the princes be honored in the new republic. This became one of the issues that delayed negotiation for independence. It took the new Government of India to dissolve the states one year after independence, much to the surprise and great anger of many of the rajas. The British could never and perhaps would never have annexed all of this princely world into their dominion. There were ties that bound the British to the rajas that went well beyond the good rationality that was supposed to rule the rest of India. But again, it is the complexities of this shared world of ornamentation, not the world of commerce, that our old attic of images can begin to reveal.

The best introduction to this kind of argument is to stop and take a close look at an early set of Victorian images of Raja Ramachandra Tondaiman in durbar, all of which were produced between 1858 and 1886. The first is a photographic portrait dating from 1858 produced for the East India Company. The second is a painting of the same scene by an Indian artist in a traditional style. The third is a painting by a well-known British artist that probably dates from the 1860s. The last canvas, dated 1886, bears the name of an Indian artist whose mastery of European technique made him famous in his time.

The reader-viewer must realize at the beginning of this excursion into the Victorian trove of images that the paintings that serve as the text for much of the discussion here and in the ensuing chapters were commissioned by the rajas of Pudukkottai and have remained with the Tondaimans. To this day, they bedeck the walls of His Highness's palace in Trichinopoly; of the "Residency," the grand house built for the use of British officials and visiting dignitaries, and now the home of the family of the raja's brother; and of the nearby Government Museum, once the private palace of a most engaging rani of Pudukkottai. The condition of the paintings reflects their survival as living artifacts. They appear here, as they do in Pudukkottai—on the walls and in the life of this family. The photographs seen here and in later chapters, preserved in albums in India, also wear the stains and the insect bites of daily life. The British photographs have had a less rigorous life on the guarded shelves of the old India Office Library, now the Oriental and India Office Collection of the British Library.

"Photographic Views of Poodoocottah"

His Excellency Ramachandra Tondaiman sits under a gold brocade canopy surrounded by his court. The camera has stilled this ceremonial durbar (Plate 6), leaving an image of royal ritual in one of the smaller kingdoms in British dominated India. The image appears very oriental, a photo from a land still under ancient native rule. The bejeweled raja and his courtiers in traditional Moghul court dress still silently nod to the tutelary overlordship of the Muslim king of Delhi. But this photograph was taken in 1858, a watershed year. The

Plate 6. Raja Ramachandra Tondaiman seated with his court in durbar. The photo, taken in 1858 by Captain Linnaeus Tripe, is part of a series of photographic folios documenting the southern provinces of the East India Trading Company. A sample of Captain Tripe's extensive photography was displayed in a 1984 exhibit organized by the Victoria and Albert Museum, "The Golden Age of British Photography, 1839–1900." The catalog of the exhibit mentions that Tripe, infantryman turned photographer, traveled to Pudukkottai in 1856 and again in 1858 (Haworth-Booth 1984, 105). "Photographic Views of Poodoocottah" was produced for the library of the Secretary of State for India. Each page of the still-beautiful folio is embossed with Tripe's own seal: "LT" forming a cameo in a floral frame. (Courtesy of the Oriental and India Office Collections, The British Library.)

British ruled as administrators from Calcutta but continued until now to let that pensioned "pageant prince," the Moghul emperor in old Delhi, provide the ceremonial cloth for the British Raj. The British had tolerated, or had planned merely to tolerate, all such pageantry as a necessity in this land of endless ritual. The Moghul emperor, and even this little king, were all part of the same image of the "effeminate life of Asiatic pageant royalty" that caused the resigned smile so often pictured on the faces of the British civil servants in India (Clunes 1833, 38; see also Thompson 1943, 279). But this was the year of the great Indian Mutiny. The British nearly lost their domain to rebels whose first political act was to march to Delhi and seat their pageant prince back on the Peacock Throne. The British did not laugh at their finely bejeweled and feathered friends after that. Pageant apparently held power. This photograph of odd oriental splendor was now more serious business.

Look carefully for a moment at this image of Ramachandra Tondaiman seated with his full court. The eye behind the lens was not an Indian, but Linnaeus Tripe, an East India Company officer turned photographer. Captain Tripe was commissioned by the company to photograph people and places of antiquarian, historical, or ethnographic interest in the southern dominions (Haworth-Booth 1984, 105). Ramachandra Tondaiman in durbar was part of a series of photographs of oriental exotica created for British eyes. Here, then, are Ramachandra's court ministers seated in European chairs. The raja, having moved during the long exposure, presents a shadowy face at the edge of the depth of field. His Dignitary Establishment, those turbaned figures holding vague objects in hand, form a blurred back-drop out of the focus of the lens. The geometric center of the image is the raja, but the real objects that dominate the photograph are the European crystal chandelier and two crystal wall sconces ironically illuminating the multiple pillars so reminiscent of a Hindu temple.

This photo clearly pleased the raja but was really meant to be enjoyed in the libraries of London, where the album still resides in the Oriental and India Office Collection of the British Library. The camera of Linnaeus Tripe makes the raja look both exotic and familiar. The viewer meets His Excellency literally through European glass in the light of the grand chandelier. This Victorian glass chandelier and the prominent chair in the foreground seem to mediate between the raja and the viewer like radical new artwork safely framed in familiar gold gilt.

A Very Large Indian Miniature

The raja commissioned painters, both Indian and British, to portray the same durbar scene. The work of a traditional Indian artist, Govindasamy Maistry, presents some interesting contrasts (Plate 7). The painting measures 64″ × 36″ but adopts the style of miniature painting. Many of the same persons and objects in the photographic scene are present, but arranged in a very different order. Missing are the European chairs; the ministers are packed into the edges of the portrait. The Dignitary Establishment, all clearly in focus, surround the raja, whose body now swells to a disproportionate size. He sits at the geometric and the

Plate 7.   This painting entitled "Ramachandra Tondaiman in Darbar," by Govindasamy Maistry, has no date but is probably from the same period as Tripe's photograph (Plate 6). This painting was photographed and cataloged in *The Pudukotah Portraits* by Percy MacQueen in 1926 (16) and remains in the Government Museum at Pudukkottai. Here His Excellency wears flowing Moghul court robes rather than a brocade coat and pants, which betrays concessions to English style in Tripe's photograph. But the glass chandelier still hangs above and is even mirrored below the painting.

actual center of vision. On the top of the painting is again that chandelier, diminished in size and sharing the foreground with a set of objects miniaturized to present a uniform band across the bottom of the painting (Plate 8, color section), a decorative style familiar on friezes of Hindu temples. But here tiny jeweled elephants and ornately decorated horses with grooms share the stage with crystal candlesticks, glass-cased clocks atop Victorian tables, and repeated miniatures of the same grand chandelier.

The European furnishings are truly decontextualized. The chandelier is valued as an object of pure grandeur. The clock, the couch, and the table (Plate 9) serve no purpose in the frieze other than "decorative." Yet the importance of these valued things is not diminished. As reflected in their size, they are given a position equal to the jeweled elephants and the Kothal Horse, the decorated horse used for processions. The Kothal Horse and the Jeweled Elephant (Plate 10) were the two primary signs of kingship in Pudukkottai. Clearly the British "decorations" have joined these other powerful signs of an enhanced royal status. The Indian painter has read the chandelier now as part of the raja's own domain.

Plate 9.   In this detail of Maistry's painting, Raja Ramachandra shows a good sense of what constituted basic elegance for his new overlords. No British house of any status would be without a fine table, an ornate clock, and a proper couch. Of course, the raja's couch is a throne, and his clock a new sign of royal authority perhaps over time itself. It is interesting that the Persian term *divan* became "dewan," meaning both the seat of administration and the chief administrator in India, but in Britain became the most elegant word for the parlor couch, "divan."

Lewis's Romantic Flourish

After a lifetime of world travel as an artist, F. C. Lewis spent much of his later years painting commissions for many of India's ruling princes. A catalog from a 1982 exhibit at the Victoria and Albert Museum, *India Observed: India as Viewed by British Artists,* describes Lewis as obtaining "generous patronage from Indian rulers who at that time were equipping their palaces with European paintings and furniture. He specialized in large durbar scenes, which included portraits not only of the rulers and their courtiers but also of the British Residency staffs" (Archer and Lightbrown 1982, 133–34). The catalog places Lewis in Pudukkottai between 1851 and 1854 but he was clearly in possession of Tripe's photographs

Plate 10.   Here Maistry's care with painting the Kothal Horse and the Jeweled Elephant, along with their groom and the mahout, respectively, reflects the importance of these emblems in the realm.

when he created his durbar scene for Raja Ramachandra. The number, dress, pose, and position of the courtiers and the Dignitary Establishment is too similar to be a coincidence. Lewis more likely painted this portrait from the photograph rather than strictly from life, later in the 1860s when he toured India for a second time.

A portrait photographer's images, no matter how interpretive, are bound to persons and places more strictly than a painter's. Lewis kept the outlines of Tripe's photographic image, but he added key elements and subtracted others (Plate 11). Gone is the grand chandelier that so dominated both Tripe's photograph and Maistry's "Miniature." Gone too are the ornate pillars of the raja's durbar hall, which are replaced by generic arches that Lewis used in paintings of other such durbar scenes. The colors are subdued. The vibrancy that Lewis subtracted from things was added to the human face. The uniformed Dignitary Establishment standing behind the courtiers wear the bold expression of honest English yeomen. Their ceremonial rods become real weapons in their hands as they stand ready to defend their lord (Plate 12). The courtiers now are poised at the edge of their chairs, ready for some quick decision (Plate 13). Lewis embellishes the face of this raja whose family had not seen battle for sixty years, and provides him with the curled moustache and testy expression of a

Plate 11.   Frederick Christian Lewis, 1813–1875, toured the royal courts of South India and Rajasthan, including Pudukkottai in 1851–1855 (Archer and Lightbrown 1882, 133). The brass plate on the painting now kept in His Highness's palace in Trichinopoly sets the date at 1853. Lewis also painted striking individual portraits of the raja and his brother (MacQueen 1926, 3, 19, 20). Lewis reportedly returned to India in 1863–1866, traveling in nearby Travancore but not in Pudukkottai. Tripe's photograph of the durbar scene is dated 1858, but he was in Pudukkottai earlier, in 1856. The overall similarity of the two durbar scenes, however, is striking. Photographs of the actual durbar room in the last chapter of this book show that Lewis's arches simply mute the already blurred details in Tripe's work. The pillars in the durbar room are quite ornate. Lewis may have painted the royal portraits in 1853, but his durbar scene may well have been painted later from Tripe's vision, not from life.

bold warrior lord (Plate 14, color section). Lewis provides his Indian characters with very European expressions. Their features are certainly Indian, but not their demeanor, which evokes King Arthur and the Knights of the Round Table rather than the indolent pageant princes a British viewer a half century earlier might have expected. It is interesting to note that Tennyson had just published his popular *Idylls of the King* in 1859. The more ornate second edition of 1862 was dedicated to the memory of Prince Albert, whose tragic death put the queen and the empire into mourning. Tennyson's poetry created verbal images of splendor, of grandly dressed maidens and shining knights, that might have seemed to come

Plate 12.   The faces of the Dignitary Establishment (out of focus) in Tripe's photograph give Lewis leeway for a most telling flight of fancy. With eyes that gleam even in the back row with sharp white paint against very black pupils, these household officials become bold warriors, a technique in sharp contrast to Lewis's otherwise soft palette.

to life in this lavish Indian court rather than in England, where a joyless queen would continue to prefer black for the rest of her reign. By muting the Indianness of the place and by creating familiar faces, Lewis left viewers with room to fill in their own location for this scene of royal splendor.

Here are two civilizations, each learning to incorporate the other into its own image of grandeur, but both have much in common. There is the common need for such splendor, and yet there is the common loss of real sovereignity for both this Indian house and the British royal house. Raja Ramachandra was now under the watchful eye of the British political agent, and Victoria commanded little but her own privy purse. Jeffrey Lant (1979) labels the pageants of the Windsor "insubstantial," and Nicholas Dirks (1987, 356) terms the ceremonial emblems of the Tondaimans "fetishized things." Just as court life in Britain was once the center of real political power, so too the display of the highly decorated person of the raja was a central feature in the royal ritual in Pudukkottai.

Plate 13. Lewis paints the raja's immediate family sitting on the edge of their seats as if events might demand an act worthy of noble heritage.

The durbar itself, in the early eighteenth century, was at the same time both a ritualized public display of the grandeur of the raja and a place to conduct official business. For any court officer to speak "in full and open Durbar" was to take an official stand (Board of Control's Collection, 245/5541, letter from W. Blackburne dated October 21, 1807). Thus the durbar both sanctified and legitimized public actions. When the raja was seated "in durbar" surrounded by his court, his very presence became sacred. The awe surrounding the raja did not diminish, but his power to move armies, to tax, and to give and take away land gradually ceased.

When the political power of kingship declined, all that was left was the ritual state. This was as true in Buckingham Palace as it was in Pudukkottai. Walter Bagehot in *The English Constitution* (1867) had actually made this point and openly recommended the aggrandizement of royal ritual in England. In Pudukkottai the first act of a new claimant to royal power was to hold a durbar. If a substantial number of important people attended and paid him honor, he reigned. If not, he and all of his armies remained a band of mercenaries. As history would have it, the ritual of the king seated in state was the first act and the last remnant of kingship. Ramachandra Tondaiman, no less than Victoria, shared her fate and her power as a thing of pageant rule. The commonality of this tale of two cities is apparent in the next painting of Ramachandra Tondaiman in durbar.

Plate 17.   Not only has the British governor shared the raja's throne, but British and Indians sit beside each other with remarkably similar clothing. British and Indian courtiers wear the same style of coat, with sashes indicating their rank. Only the headdress and the lower garments differentiate the two, as if their commonality at the torso must be sandwiched between their difference at the head and the foot.

At 10:45 A.M. His Excellency the Governor and party will drive for Durbar escorted by Troopers by the Pududvayal Tope Road, and when the old battery is passed a salute of 21 guns will be fired.

His Excellency and party will enter the palace by the Western Gate, and on arrival at the Palace Square they will be received by the Commandant and the Dewan Peishkar at the carriage door and conducted to the foot of the staircase.

His Excellency and party will be received at the foot of the staircase by the Assistant Dewan, the band playing.

At the top of the staircase, His Excellency and party will be received by His Highness the Rajah and the Dewan-Regent and conducted to the Canopy where the State Sofa is placed.

His Excellency and His Highness will take their seats on the Sofa.

After His Excellency and party have taken their seats, the Dewan-Regent and members of the Rajah's family and all Durbarees will assume their usual seats in two rows.

A little nautch [performance by the palace dancers and musicians] will then take place, heralds proclaiming the ancient titles of the Rajah.

The nautch over (10 or 15 minutes), His Highness will rise to present garlands, sandal, attar and *pan supari* [prepared betel nut] to His Excellency the Governor and party. The sandal and *pan supari* will simply be touched and the garlands worn.

This over, all will resume their seats for a minute or two and then rise on His Highness and His Excellency rising, when the Durbar will break up.

His Excellency the Governor and party and His Highness the Rajah and the Durbarees will then if convenient sit for a photo. (Residency Records, R2/21, 1884–95, "Ceremonials")

Sastri's account leaves little to suspect that anything of sacred significance will happen here. Only the photo will preserve the scene.

In contrast to the stodgy words of Dewan Sastri, Ravi Varma painted a holy scene. The raja and His Excellency, Sir Mountstuart Elphinstone Grant Duff, G.C.I.E. (see Plate 3), present a delightful contrast. Devoid of frivolous finery, the governor wears no insignia of his rank save that grave expression of indisputable authority. Raja Ramachandra, in the jeweled turban of state, shines in gold braid. The British officers do not share their chief's simplicity; they sport their share of gilded finery. But the raja and the governor are not really so disparate. In place of his former Moghul court dress, Ramachandra Tondaiman now wears a suit that could have been made by the governor's own tailor. In the foreground of the painting is neither chandelier nor jeweled elephant. Instead, incense—usually reserved for images of deities—burns in a large elaborate stand in front of this scene. Varma's vivid painting seems to hint that by coming under the raja's sacred canopy the British had joined the world of the Gods.

Alone, these four images of Raja Ramachandra in durbar do not tell the whole story, but they may well be the best synopsis of a complex tale. Moreover, these images are self-fulfilling statements. The paintings and photograph depict a glittering raja in court, but they also are clearly meant to confirm what they display. This is the primary image the raja wanted to project, and the British were willing, it seems, to buy into this same scene.

The origins of the durbar as a political and cultural ceremony are not as important as the fact of its common acceptance. It would be foolish to claim that because the British willingly entered the picture they had fully joined in all the cultural and religious nuances this image had in Pudukkottai. Likewise, because the raja's durbar hall was lighted by a European chandelier does not mean that European purposes highlighted his intentions for rule as he sat in state. But nonetheless, when two cultures share the same space at the same time using the same valued things, something is happening there, even if no one quite acknowledges what it is. Certainly after 1858, when Ramachandra sat in durbar, there was always some thing of Britain there. Whatever occurs under that sacred canopy is meant to be seen in London as much as in Pudukkottai. Once those British things and British people entered so deeply into his realm under the sacred canopy that covered the throne, they could no longer be called purely British again.

Just as British civil servants found themselves inside the sacred canopy of India rajas as part of that ornamental world, the scholarly world of Oxford and Cambridge was about to erase such a picture from consideration as part of the "real" India. The search for the real India was the ironic attempt of British and continental scholars to once again define a pure Indian tradition from the hybrid culture of the new modern India. This "real" India was then to be used as a model for reforming the Raj into a system that was supposedly more palatable to Indian cultural sensitivities. A new era of the "Orientalists" changed much of the course of scholarship on India and changed the way many in the Indian Civil Service defined their purpose in India: to salvage and restore the golden days of Indian culture, to do for Indians what they had failed to do for themselves.

Thus began the odd bifurcation of practice from theory that was to mark much of scholarship that affected the empire. The British began to reject in theory the very world that they had created in fact. Friedrich Max Müller and James George Frazer are part of the memory of Pudukkottai precisely because their style of scholarship made the raja so difficult to see for so long. These scholars differed in their material and their methods. Frazer was not primarily interested in India, and Max Müller never discussed kingship. But Frazer produced a picture of kingship, and Müller an image of India, that bypassed the modern world. If Britain had real material links to the many pieces of the empire, those bonds were in the hoary past. The modern situation was presented as a radical dichotomy of cultures whose commonality could be found only in a shared tribal dark past revealed by exotic texts and remnants of strange ritual behavior. Müller was especially fond of citing these ancient bonds and then ending his many lectures with grand suggestions of some future day when this British Lion and the Indian Lamb would sit together in peace. The point here is that Britain and India were already sitting together. The confluence of culture was there, but it was written out of existence because it was left out of the books that were to influence the coming century.

To return to the initial thesis of this study, the ornamental world of the rajas of Pudukkottai was part of a larger culture of ornamentation. The Victorian period, with its growing visual technologies, such as photography, may well have allowed greater opportunities for presentation of visual images than anytime previously. And the visual image itself gave to ritual a form of concreteness that such courtly ceremonials rarely had in the past. In medieval South India, kings built temples as monuments to their wealth. Occasionally their faces were carved in stone sculpture as donors with hands folded at the entrance to the temple. Friezes on the temple walls depict royal armies and scenes from court life. But only the late Moghul miniature painting began a tradition of painting the portrait of the rajas outside of the temple context. Following the Moghul Empire, the British painter and photographer made it possible to record the durbar in all its richness. Yet at the same time, the rising new discipline of the comparative study of religion turned "Hinduism" into words and into books, and turned interest from ceremonials to a fascination with India's own great "books." But all this occurred in the context of the larger culture of display that ironically turned the very books of comparative religion into ornamental things.

The complexity of the heyday of the empire demands that we learn how to "read" the image of Raja Ramachandra and how to "see" the new study of comparative religion in the context of this culture of display. But it is also important to remember that in Britain this period of flirtation with the ornamental never culminated in a legitimate marriage of "East" and "West." The culture of display in this ultimately Protestant country was always at best an open secret. But in India the case was quite the opposite. Raja Ramachandra ultimately must been seen as part of a *religious* system in which the ornamentation and the public display of Gods and of the king is as central to theology as it is to ritual. This theology may not have a textual base, but it is sanctioned by a long ritual and poetic tradition.

Thus, what is officially classified as political ceremony in British records must be reclassified as religious ritual in Pudukkottai. To move between British ceremony and Hindu ritual is to see the same forms but to recognize that ceremonials in India were never really decontextualized for modern Indians as they were for the British, who had no other real referent for their experiences in India except the long-lost days of knights and kings that had only lately been re-created in the imagination of the modern Victorians. Only James Frazer seemed close to consciously connecting the British experience of the empire to "religion," but the connections he drew were not with the bright and shining world of perfect princes, but rather with a dark, melancholy world of crime, death, and the hapless wait for a promised rebirth. Frazer subtly reminded Britain that it had a serious religious link to sacral kingship, but that it also went with a sad tale of an itinerant preacher put to death as a would-be king. The associaton of sacral kingship with lavish splendor was only one side of the story. There was a darker side of royal nakedness, loss, and failure, that was an open secret in Pudukkottai but a "forgotten" mystery in England.

The recent popularity of the films of James Ivory and the television film series "The Jewel in the Crown" recalls the importance to a new generation of British and American audiences of the unspoken attempts at mutual clarification that marked the encounters of the British in India. Ivory's films often center on the royal court and invoke once again the glittering and seductive image of the Hindu raja in his court. In fact, much of the new British "Indomania," the "Show-Business Epidemic" that even merits headlines in *Parade* magazine, plays endless reruns of British Civil Servant Meets Hindu Prince. The shadowy faces of the raja of Pudukkottai and of others like him seem still to sit on the edge of the depth of field of Western consciousness—just enough in focus to catch the eye, but still too tantalizingly unclear to ever consign to a "scientific" objectivity and then by degrees to esoteric studies.

His Excellency Ramachandra Tondaiman sits in durbar as a "god." The nature of his divine body will never be revealed to "objective" eyes, because such eyes will too quickly pull off the king's magic clothes to reveal some "truth," some lesson in polity, some certain fact of the real India underneath. But the raja of Pudukkottai exists now in the surface of those images still available for another darsan by Western eyes. This raja never was a phenomenon for India alone. He was a king experienced deeply by the Hindu and fretfully by the British, but experienced nonetheless. His importance still lives in the nexus where Britain met India in the precarious splendor of an imperial age.

Part One

An Encounter of Near and Far

Philosophy as we have received it from the Greeks and perpetuated it in the West will be unequal to this concrete universal as long as no serious encounter and no mutual clarifications have brought these civilizations into the field of our experience and at the same time removed its limitations. This encounter and this mutual clarification have not yet already taken place. They have taken place for some men and for some groups and they have been the great concern of their lives.

—Paul Riceour

Plate 18.   The edifice of the Royal Pavilion, Brighton, was completed in 1826 by the king's architect, John Nash. The Indian facade was one of the last layers and was the brainchild of the king, who personally decided that "the Pavilion should assume an Eastern character, and the Hindoo style of Architecture was adopted in the expectation that the turban domes and lofty pinnacles might from their glittering and pictur- esque effect, attract and fix the attention of the Spectator" (Dinkel 1979, 36). Within twenty years of the king's death, the pavilion at Brighton was sold and eventually allowed to fall into ruin. When Britain finally reenchanted the Raj, such Anglo-Indian extravaganzas would be built not in England but at the very site of the Moghul empire in "New" Delhi.

own middle-class values without both critique and the usual pangs of nostalgia for the grand majesty of heroic days past. By 1877, Victoria, a shining empress of India, would be actual- ized not on English soil but on the other side of the world.

In his *Victorian Frame of Mind,* Walter Houghton describes the Victorians as keenly aware of their age as "transitional," but he points out that "the past which they had outgrown was not the Romantic period and not even the eighteenth century. It was the Middle Ages" (1957, 1). Houghton presents the final loss of a medieval past with its "rule of the king" and supposedly fixed social structure as the central definition of "feudal." France had its upheaval of the old order while England's royalty slowly lost power to a changing economic structure (1). Houghton argues that the ambivalences of the age stem from a gnawing sense of individual helplessness in the jaws of a growing mechanization that caused a "compensation" in the realm of imagination. Here kings and knights still reigned. The phenomenon of hero-worship was, for fifty years, "a major factor in English culture" (310). Hero-worship was virtually synonymous with the land of King Arthur and company, who sailed back from Avalon to live in the poems of Tennyson and the essays of Carlyle.

In Houghton's analysis, this longing for a new heroic age never went beyond the pages of fiction or the shining imaginations of the essayists. England dreamed of heroes and yet trudged on as a nation of shopkeepers. The empire, although touted by intellectuals as a stage for heroic effort, was yet another matter of business—a "divorce of theory from practice"—for the average English businessman. What Houghton fails to consider is that a colony such as India was more than a business proposition to England. As long as there was an Indian empire, a stage existed on which to play out a feudal dream in a very real world. In that distant land, there were six hundred real princes who took up their places and knew how to play their roles well. Lewis's 1860s portrait of Raja Ramachandra in durbar easily made this native court in India into a living world of knightly splendor. But the move from a world of literature, a world of pure imagination, into the concrete ritual world of royal India posed some serious problems for the British.

As early as 1755, well before Victoria and Tennyson, officers of the East India Trading Company began to move into the Indian ceremonial world in both the royal palaces and the temples. In a diary from 1772 to 1774, George Patterson described the British governor in Madras going for an official visit to the palace of the nawab of the Carnatic, "in State, with all the Country Musick and other ensigns of his dignity before him" (Diary of George Patterson, 8:158–59). The Company frequently sent troops and bands to march in the processions that accompanied festivals at the temples in their newly acquired domains. By the 1840s the issue of British participation in such "idolatry" reached the floor of Parliament. Direct connection to temple rituals was soon severed, but by an interesting sleight of the hand, participation in the rituals of the Indian royal courts was never categorized as religious and thus never became a matter of open debate. As the British pulled out of direct participation in openly religious rituals, however, they began to insinuate themselves into the existing royal rituals in the Native States. Removed from the temple, the royal courts may have been a safe place for construction of a new ritual world—free from religious overtones and thus theological controversy. The problem with Britain then, and with its historians even now, is to admit that this longing for a medieval past, for ceremonial, for pomp, for ritual splendor, was at its roots tangled with religious problems and was no more free of the problems of "idolatry" than was the earlier participation in the temple festivals. In short, as soon as the British adopted Indian ceremonials, willingly or not, they entered into some very complex theological problems. The task here is to illustrate how, even in the little state of Pudukkottai, issues of finance, of management, of "good" government can also be read as a conflict over the nature of authority—*divine* authority.

The British Empire was from the start a ceremonial empire. The officers of the East India Company quickly adopted the rituals and pageant that traditionally accompanied power in India. But as soon as such ensigns of power were adopted, the British began to tell themselves out loud that such ceremony was necessary only to satisfy the emotional hunger for pageant among their ritualistic subjects. This voiced rationale for maintenance of ceremony began as early as 1804, when a British officer defended maintaining all ceremonial respects toward the pensioned raja of Tanjore so that other allies may not "be taught to fly from a connection which involves as a necessary consequence not only the loss of sovereign power but the decay of that decent reputation and respect which can compensate the regrets inseparable from the privation of command" (The Board of Control's Collection, F/4/175, "To the President: Minute in Council, 16 August 1803"). By 1877 Lord Lytton was more blunt in his defense of spending a large sum to bring all the princes of India to Delhi for the great durbar to mark Victoria's assumption of the title of Empress of India. This grand event was justified as only "a few acts of liberality . . . [such as] the presentation of guns and banners [which] will, I believe, be much more effective than any political concessions" (Copeland 1982, 156).

On the surface, then, the British never claimed any personal need for involvement in such pageantry, but they admitted the sheer economic and political sense of trading a bit of pomp for real power. While the British native subject may have reveled in the pomp, the British presented themselves as disinterested spectators in a ceremonial rule necessary to their feudal-minded people. As Ian Copeland summarizes it, the British saw this pageant as a means of reconciling the princes by satisfying "their appetite for ceremonial" (156). Of course, the British admitted no such appetites of their own.

Evidence that the "native subjects" indeed reveled in the British pageant empire can still be seen in the streets of the old provincial capitals written in stone and bronze. Within a block of gold-gilded Gandhis sit those eternal Victorias and conquering British lords. The power of the pageant-queen over her Indian subjects is written into now faded but numerous lengthy traditional ballads composed by members of old Indian bardic families for the royal family. The Delhi durbar of 1877 inspired one such "Poolaver" (taken as a title adapted from classical Tamil, *pulavar*, poet), who was then working for the Indian Civil Service, to write of Victoria's assumption of the title Empress of India:

> Hail! Hail! Empress of India, mayst thou ever wield the sceptre of this land. Crowned heads and powerful independent Chiefs, from the eight points of the compass, robed in their gaudiest and richest attire, bedecked with diamonds and jewels most costly, surrounded by their armies of Cavalry, Artillery and Infantry most valorous, have assembled to welcome and reverence thee, in the person of thy Viceroy, in such immense numbers, on this occasion that they hardly find sufficient space for them-selves; and so crowded have they become, that their elbowing and jostling have divested them of countless diamonds, whose sparkling radiance, like that of so many falling stars, has sufficed to illuminate the darkness and render it bright as day. (Ramaswamy Poolaver 1877, verse 3)[1]

It was not difficult to defend the sheer practicality of maintaining a British pageant queen as a hedge against any native prince who might capture enough ceremonial charisma to turn "empty" ceremony back into political power.

The British rationale for their own pageant rule has essentially continued in retrospective analyses of the empire. As late as 1965, Percival Spear's standard *History of India* accounts for Victoria's ceremonial success in the Indian empire as the result of a regime that was "more personal, something which Indians liked." Of Victoria herself as an active instrument

---

1. For other examples of poems for Queen Victoria and the royal family in Tamil, as well as in Hindi and Bengali, see the list of manuscripts still extant in the British Library in "Modern Poetry: Panegyrics, Satirics, and Elegiac Poems" (Barnett and Pope 1909). Such poems were apparently a popular genre.

in this "imperial heyday," Spear can only comment that "by some esoteric magic of her own" she caught the imagination of her Indian subjects and that "without apparent effort, Victoria had captured the mystique of Akbar" (1965, 148). Other detailed analyses of the British use of ceremonial still support the thesis that the British fostered pageantry as a practical political tool necessary to bridge the gap between native needs and modern British polity. "Their philosophy was pragmatic, guided by the principle of workability" (Thompson 1943, 287). In his influential article "Lion Rampart," D. A. Low lists among the factors that made the rule of so many by so few possible, "charismatic qualities which, at all events in the early years, imperial rules have possessed for many colonial peoples" (1964, 247). Both these latter factors depended on the shrewd or sometimes simply intuitive use the British made of indigenous polity often based on familial or religious paradigms. Barbara Ramusack comes to a similar conclusion: "Anxious, sometimes consciously but frequently unconsciously, to justify their position as usurpers of political power, the British tried by a variety of means to acquire the veneer of legality and a moral basis for their rule" (1978, 10). The frequent use of terms like "magic," "unconscious," and "charisma" in this almost universally accepted picture of the practical British accommodating rule to native forms leaves a serious question behind. Why were the British unconsciously, intuitively, and magically able to play their pageant role so naturally and so well that their subjects took the game for reality?

For such practical men, the members of the Foreign Department serving at native courts took to ceremony with gusto. The Oriental and India Office Collections of the British Library preserves the careful notes and corrections made on the many printed programs for the British political ceremonies of installation and investiture and for the formal visits of British officers culminating in the durbar (see Residency Records, R2/50/894, "Installation and Investiture Darbars"). The care for precedent and the precision demanded in these programs is striking. For example, in a program marked "Confidential," concerning a viceregal visit to Mysore for an investiture ceremony, an Undersecretary to the Government of India dictated that "the Viceroy will receive His Highness within the Reception Room, at a distance of one pace from the threshold." The full program of the visit of the viceroy required seven printed pages and included a formal arrival ceremonial: "The First Assistant to the Resident in Mysore and the two principal officers of the Mysore State will meet His Excellency at Bangalore Station, and will accompany His Excellency to Mysore, their carriages being attached to the Viceregal train." On the next day, the "Ceremony of Mizajpursi," in which "four of the Maharaja's principal officers will call at the Viceregal residence to enquire after His Excellency's health," was to occur. The next day, the maharaja was to come to the viceregal residence with all his principal officers. A ceremony was to be held with all of the Mysore court seated around the viceroy "according to their rank." The next day, the ceremony was repeated with the viceroy then visiting the maharaja at the palace. On the final day, the investiture ceremony, through which the British Government of India formally both recognized and "invested" the maharaja with full administrative powers, took place. The details included the mandated gun salutes, the distribution of attar and pan, reciting of the maharaja's full titles, and an address by the viceroy, followed by a formal reply by His Highness during which "all present will rise and remain standing during the address, the Viceroy alone being seated" (The Residency Records. R/2/Mysore Temp. No.

13187-1. "Directive from the Foreign Department, Simla, 1902"). The concern for exact time and precise movements, and the care for space and place, makes exhausting reading, even for the modern researcher who might have previously assumed that the instructions in the Sanskrit Brāhmaṇas were the epitome of ritualism.

This penchant for ritual precision betrays far more than a dutiful stiff upper lip toward an unpleasant necessity. There is a pride here, and a passion expressed in the very terms that only the natives were supposed to understand instinctively. That the British civil servant enjoyed ceremonial, even thrived on this pageantry, becomes a serious thesis when officers like Lewin Bentham Bowring are considered. Bowring retired in 1870 from government service in which he was closely associated with the Native States, yet he remained in India to complete an amazing project. He quite independently decided to collect photographs, genealogical tables, hand-signed documents, seals, and banners from each of the extant and the extinct native states in India. He carefully cataloged his treasures, following the order of precedence established for the princes at the 1877 Delhi Durbar (Lewin Bentham Bowring Albums, "Handlist," Mss. Evr. G. 38/i-iv). No book of English heraldry could display more reverence, more sheer devotion, than those three volumes of carefully labeled artifacts, in which each photograph of a strange bejeweled raja is obviously as alive and real as any English earl for Bowring, and certainly more real than Tennyson's knights of old. The photograph of the utterly handsome maharaja of Marwar with his piercing eyes and broad shoulders must have titillated romantic notions far more potent than any Sir Lancelot. The maharaja was, after all, still quite alive and devilishly handsome (Plate 19). Similar to Bowring's visual enterprise, put in words, was Roper Lethbridge's *Golden Book of India: Genealogical and Biographical Dictionary of the Ruling Princes, Chiefs, Nobles, and Personages, Titled or Decorated, of the Indian Empire.*

In his acceptance of Indian rajas as noble personages, Bowring had good company. His Queen Victoria willingly took the deposed young Maharaja Duleep Singh into her court and her family. In a revealing work, *Queen Victoria's Maharaja,* the queen is quoted as answering a critique of her intense interest in the young man with "We accordingly treat him just as we do all Princes" (Alexander and Anand 1980, 54). Certainly Duleep Singh had converted to Christianity, yet that alone would not have legitimized the young prince's nobility in the queen's mind. She liked the intelligent young man whose princely stature *she* never questioned as simply native. Both Mr. Bowring and his queen were imperialists in the most striking sense: They lived not in England but in an empire whose princes wore velvet cloaks, but some also wore turbans.

The process that created the "Native Prince" within the British Raj began in the eighteenth century when the East India Company became involved with India as more than a trading partner. Very quickly, issues of the source of British power were articulated. On what model of polity were the British to rule? Their first claim was to achieve independence from "theology." Their rule was to be secular in every respect. The Indians were to be indulged in their own penchant for ritual, but the East India Company was to stand above (or rather behind) it all. It remains to be seen exactly how free of "theology" this model of rule remained. Two moments in the British involvement with South India will serve to make the contrasts between overt principle and covert theology.

Plate 19.   This photograph of Maharaja Jaswat Singh of Marwar (one of the largest states in India, known later as Jodhpur) is one of the most striking in Lewin Bentham Bowring's collection. The catalog from a recent exhibition of art from the Indian royal courts states that an 1880 painting of the same maharaja derives from a photograph (Desai 1986, 43–45). A comparison of Bowring's piece with the painting leaves little doubt of that. The painting fills in details and changes certain key features of the photograph. The table on which His Highness so effortlessly rests his arm is given a book and flower vase. His elegant Moghul shoes become the famous Jodhpur boots, and a long necklace modeled on jewelry the Prince of Wales might wear now hangs around his neck. The maharaja, like his counterparts in the smaller states of South India, commissioned images to please both Indian and British admirers. Bowring, a longtime resident in the courts of North India, would probably prefer this more martial and far more "native" photograph of a great warrior prince to the less erotic and more intellectual prince of the painting. (Courtesy of the Oriental and India Office Collections, The British Library.)

Maharaja Jaswant Singh of Márwár

Scene One. The Invisible Empire: The Early Days of British Rule

> It has been asserted that any great power based neither on a display of force nor on the affection and esteem of its subject races is bound sooner or later to topple under its own weight. . . . But I firmly believe that nothing of this sort will happen to it as long as it maintains amongst its troops the perfect discipline and the sense of comfort which at present exists, and so long as it does all in its power to make its yoke scarcely perceptible by permitting its subjects every freedom in the exercise of their social and religious practices. (Dubois [1816, 1823] 1906, 7)

The guns had just quieted in South India when the first comparisons of oriental and British polity began. By 1810 Mark Wilks had published his long history of Mysore introduced by a terse discussion of "the Despotism of the East." In 1815 Abbé Dubois's *Hindu Manners, Customs, and Ceremonies* began with a preface accounting for the "almost miraculous" fact that "a mere handful of men managed to coerce into submissive obedience a hundred million people . . . whose creeds, habits, customs, and manners of life are so absolutely different from our own" (4). Both Wilks and the old missionary acknowledged the challenge facing the British: They must create a government outside of the ancient religious-based polity of

The staunch ally of the British, the raja Vijaya Raghunatha Tondaiman, died in 1807 leaving two minor sons and an ensuing squabble over the management of this "zamindary" (the British never used the term "kingdom" and adopted "native state" much later). William Blackburne was charged by the government at Fort St. George to investigate the situation and recommend suitable managers for the governor's public appointment. He was directed to "impress on the minds of the managers the important nature of their duties," which specifically included the reduction of the late raja's debt and the "scrupulous care and education of the children of the late Tondiman and the importance of regulating their conduct on those principles of attachment to the British Government" (Board of Control's Collection, F/4/245 no. 5541, letter to Major Blackburne dated July 24, 1807). The resident interpreted this charge, correctly reading the coded meaning that he was in fact to quietly direct the management of the state. His reports of 1807 and 1809, sent first to Fort St. George and forwarded to the Board of Control in London, were received with praise and assurances that Blackburne had "laudibly exerted himself for the attainment of these objects" (Board of Control's Collection, F/4/277 no. 6188, letter dated August 2, 1809). Never did Blackburne openly admit to controlling the state. While Radhakrishna Aiyar, in his 1916 history of the Pudukkottai state, proudly credits him with assuming "the superintendance of the State" (345), Blackburne's own reports show him to be a masterful practitioner of invisible rule.

After the death of Vijaya Raghunatha, the guardianship of his sons and the official management of the state was assumed by the Western Palace Jagirar, the head of a collateral family line that was considered the successor to the kingdom should the primary line fail to produce a legitimate heir. This respected Jagirar died shortly after assuming office, and his son claimed the title of manager. At this point Blackburne quickly stepped in to protect "the rights of the sons of the Tondiman" and to prevent this young and "ambitious" Jagirar from becoming "an instrument in the hands of our open or concealed enemies" (Board of Control's Collection, F/4/245 no. 5541, folio p. 11). In a series of letters to London from May to October 1807, Blackburne argued for the appointment of two other managers, passing over the claims of this "Rajah Gopaul Tondiman." Blackburne spurned the "bold and daring" Rajah Gopaul for the late raja's son-in-law, "Maupillay Pullawarier," "a man of moderate talents and excellent character," whom he later describes as "mild, unassuming, and diffident" (35). To lend legitimacy to the office of manager, Blackburne also recommended "Tirmul Tondiman," the late raja's brother. Blackburne never directly describes Tirmul when suggesting his appointment, but earlier in the polemic against Raja Gopaul he speaks of the Jagirar's dangerous "nearness to the Throne, between which and him are only the two sons and the childless and imbecile brother of the late Tondiman" (9). This "imbecile" could be none other than Blackburne's nominee for co-manager. So Blackburne's great concern for the good government of Pudukkottai led him to appoint an "imbecile" and a "moderately talented man" to rule. Fort St. George, obviously reading the broad lines between Blackburne's solicitous report, heartily approved.

Throughout his 1807 reports, Blackburne openly set his goal as the establishment of a "just administration giving security and confidence to the Inhabitants" (37). He also admitted that "the present was the appropriate and probably the only time for making substantial reforms and establishing a regular and equitable system of government" (37). Blackburne never publicly—not even within the privileged language of his report—allowed that he and not the managers ruled. He reports his addresses to an assembly of state officers in which he "endeavored to impress upon them a serious conviction of the sacred nature of the important trust which had been committed to the managers" (37) and exhorts them to "discharge all of their duties." When the managers hesitated to make cuts in the budget necessary to liquidate the debt, Blackburne took upon himself "the odium of the reforms." Convening another assembly, he pointed out "those charges which appeared to me to be unnecessary or extravagant." He then "invited and encouraged objections" and like a good democrat did not act until "the opinion of the assembly was unanimous." Having "conceded much to custom and more to religious prejudice," this man of the Enlightenment cast himself in the image of the Unmoved Mover.

Blackburne's later report of 1809 is quite explicitly an explanation of "the principles which have governed my conduct." He expected that in this report the governor "will perceive the nature and full extent of the interference which I have exercised." Blackburne, that master politician, then promised to "regulate and limit the future exercise of it, if it shall be found that I have exceeded the spirit as well as the letter of his instructions" (Board of Control's Collection, F/4/277 no. 6188, folio p. 7). He then immediately laid open the logic of his actions:

> The instructions of the Government communication to me in your letter the 24th July, 1807, directed me to attend particularly to the conduct of the managers and to aid them with my advice. I determined therefore to leave the entire administration of the affairs of Tondiman in the hands of the managers ostensibly at all times and actually as also, except when my interposition should appear to be indispensable to the particular interests of the minor, to the welfare of the country and to the security of individuals from injustice and oppression, and it was my intention in all cases to regulate my interposition in such a manner that while it should be effectual in regard to the attainment of its object, it should also be as little as possible felt or known within the country. (7–8)

The British resident then contrasted his powerful unseen rule with the pompous quarrelsome managers whose interest in mere externals he makes obvious:

> I persevered in this plan eight months, during which period a large portion of my time was painfully occupied by Tondiman's affairs. The managers were on exceedingly bad terms and transmitted to me almost daily their mutual complaints and recriminations. The weakness and vanity of Trimul Tondiman induced him to display a greater degree of pomp and state than were proper, and his interested dependents very frequently persuaded him to issue orders and commit acts for their benefit utterly inconsistent with justice and propriety. On the other hand Maupullay Pullawier discovered a strong desire to be relieved from the embarrassment which his colleague occasioned, and to be appointed sole manager. He exaggerated all the defects of

Trimul Tondiman, treated him with disrespect, and excluded him as much as possible from the appearance of any participation of authority. The representations of both parties were seldom confined within the limits of truth, and neither of them hesitated at direct falsehood when it appeared necessary to extenuate his own misconduct or aggravate that of his adversary: much neglect and inconvenience to the public business were caused by this misunderstanding. (folio pp. 10–11)

These vignettes from Blackburne's pen draw a familiar picture. The British, setting aside the mere externals of appearance, quietly get the job done while the Indians' own vanity overpowers good judgment and justice.

In spite of this seemingly secular report, a Dubois-style condemnation of Hindu idolatry versus European monotheism lies, perhaps unconsciously, behind Blackburne's words. In Imago Dei of the West, Blackburne silently dispenses justice to a people who remain blissfully ignorant of the source of their own life and liberty. The people imagine that the pompous managers actually rule. These vain souls are likewise deluded into taking their pomp and passions for real power. "In vain are Hindu idols decked with rich ornaments," declares Dubois, for their ugliness cannot be "rendered thereby less agreeable" ([1816, 1823] 1906, 581). So too Blackburne's description of the managers reveals a tragic and yet comic scene of two simple men dressed only in the cloth of power, which is far too large to fit their puny being. Meanwhile, real power, heedless of all dress and vanity, quietly writes their script. For Blackburne and for Dubois, an unseen empire rules while the visible forms of India—its customs, manners, and its kings—play like noisy shadows empty of all but sight and sound.

Thus, both overtly and covertly, the British civil servant made peace with himself. The formula of invisible rule behind the undisturbed religious and social externals may have quieted the issues of how to be British in an Indian world. The forms could be observed, even if these were Hindu forms, as long as the heart remained enlightened as to the true nature of power. But the British civil servant had created an uneasy peace. One difficult question remained unasked: What was the relationship of this new invisible empire to the professed religion of England? As long as the confluence of theology and polity flowed beneath overt professions of faith, the British Empire could appear safely secular and yet wholesome to the Christian religious community in India and in England. But even Dubois began to sense a problem brewing. He speaks of many Europeans "being far from robust in their own faith" who, when seeing the great variety of creeds in India, end "by endorsing one of the favourite axioms of modern philosophy, namely, that 'all religions are equally agreeable to God and lead to the same good end' " (608). Dubois went on to firmly condemn rationalism, arguing that "some so called philosophers of modern times have maintained that the mind of man alone is able to conceive a just notion of the divinity. They have dared to attribute that which they themselves here conceived to be the efforts of their own critical faculties, as if this power itself had not been imprinted on their minds in the first instance by the Christian education they received in early youth" (609). It is significant that this condemnation comes at the end of Dubois's discussion of the "idolatry" in the Hindu temple. The accusation is clear: The rationalist is himself an idolater in his denial of revelation and his self-created religion of reason. The unbelieving British civil servant is therefore as much an idolater as the Hindu.

Abbé Dubois never moved his argument just one step further toward where the logic of his own accusations was leading. Was the empire, based as it was on reason and proud as it was of pure effort, in cahoots with the very ground of Hindu idolatry? At this point the very wall Dubois himself had constructed between the silent secular power of the British and the overt religious forms of the Hindu proved to be made of glass. There were those in Britain who were ready to throw the first stone as soon as rationalism itself gave way to new Christian piety.

Twenty years after his famous work on Hinduism was published, Dubois came under censure. "Most justly, too," explained an angered missionary, "for asserting that Christianity could not be propagated in India, unless it be allowed to bend to the prejudices of the natives, and to the usage of caste" (Read 1836, 137). As early as 1811, Claudius Buchanan had argued for "the Expediency of a Ecclesiastical Establishment for British India: Both as a means of Perpetuating the Christian Religion among our own Countrymen and as a Foundation for the Ultimate Civilization of the Natives." Buchanan associated both religion and "civilization" with "manners and institutions" (1811, 27). For him, religion was external form; rite or custom could not be separated from spirituality. Buchanan's early position became dominant by 1833, when the bishop of Calcutta, the head of the Church of England in India, forbade the observance of caste practices within any of his constituent churches. In effect, this order commanded Indian Christians and English clergy alike not only to believe like Christians but also to conform to all the ritual and social conventions of the church. Christianity, and with it all religion, once again came to be viewed as an external matter. In a sense, religious forces in England had forced the unseen God of the rationalists to put on his body, the church, and to appear clothed in all His majesty within the British Empire once again.

The new insistence on a visible adherence to Christian manners and customs affected the British civil servant as seriously as it did the small Indian Christian community. Buchanan's early memorial was primarily concerned that loyalty to the Christian church and to English institutions be "maintained in this remote Empire" among those Britons "in exile" from the homeland (26–27). Buchanan was voicing the growing suspicion in England that the East India Company had grown too Indian, or at least too tolerant of Indian practices. William Campbell's classic statement of this position, *British India and Its Relation to the Decline of Hinduism and the Progress of Christianity* (1839), bitterly attacked the company for its "zeal in support of idolatry and superstition" (39–40). Campbell directly opposed the long-standing "incontrovertible axiom that the progress of our religion among the natives is incompatible with the maintenance of our rule" (39–40). Not only were Hindu practices tolerated, but the company had refused to hire Indian Christians in their service for fear of offending orthodox Hindus. The attack on the East India Company's supposed anti-Christian policies intensified when the charge against them grew into a major accusation that the company not only hindered the growth of Christianity but actively supported idolatry by its inherited superintendency of the old royal temples within its domain. By 1845 a parliamentary investigation into "the connection of the Government of British India with Idolatry or with Mohometanism" was ordered (Parliamentary Paper no. 664, 1845 session). Church leaders strongly insinuated to the British public that the East India Trading Company would be willing to set up an idol of Mammon if it increased their trade or ensured their power.

The argument over the company's relationship with Hindu temples ended oddly. Arjun Appadurai, in his study of the changing relationship between the British Raj and temples in their South India dominion notes that by 1841 "in response to pan-Indian as well as domestic pressures, the court of directors of the East India Company decided to withdraw from 'all interference with native religious establishment' " (1981, 151). Here again the issue was stated as a problem in "interference" and not in active participation. The company's language essentially diffused the charge against them by reverting to their old "incontrovertible axiom" that interference with religion must be avoided. They no longer supported idolatry because they no longer would "interfere" with its practice.

By the beginning of the Victorian era, the East India Company in South India faced a complex problem with religion that reintroducing the concept of church made especially difficult. The company's early demarcation of power from status, and its later separations of the "unseen" from the "seen," had created a logical system that could account for both the theological and the political presuppositions of eighteenth-century man, which kept the following categories in separate and opposing columns:

seen	unseen
status	power
ritual	reason
idolatry	inner faith

By this logic the company could separate "civil" from "religious," but in so doing Hinduism itself had to be denied as a religion in the European sense. Hinduism belonged to that category of outer ritual and mere custom, while Europeans knew that true religion was realized in the mind's eye. At first, Blackburne actually classified the "civil" in both columns. The British dominion operated much like the biblical kingdom of God, ruling unseen in the right-hand column, while the Hindu sense of civil followed the logic of their religion and belonged to the "seen." The formula was destroyed, however, as soon as the logic of church and state had to be grafted on to this model. Appadurai argues that this was the case when the British were forced to define their legal relationship with the Hindu temples.

This was the paradox: How were church and state to be understood within the old model? The categories as delineated for the eighteenth-century mind did not fit nineteenth-century England—to say nothing of India. The English church did have form, institutions, manners, and customs that many a church member equated with the very essence of Christianity. Thus a new urgency arose to confront, not tolerate, the externals of Hinduism, which, oddly, now had to be taken seriously. To take part in ritual was to become affected by that ritual. Hence the new accusations of idolatry against the East India Company's long-standing practice of lending marching bands for temple processions and to police appearing in dress uniform at festivals. Some missionaries had tried to argue that Hinduism had no church in that "there was no such thing as a hierarchy of Brahmanical faith . . . fixed by certain tenets, and guided by an infallible head" (Buchanan 1811, 31–33). Yet the seriousness with which "nonexistent" Hindu institutions were taken confirmed their stark reality for the British. The East India Company was pledged to keep their distance from idol and temple. By this new logic, the *form* of both the British state and the English church was now crucial. Ironically, by the logic of the old system, that would put both in the same category as ritual and—idolatry.

The East India Company may have side-stepped the issue of its direct connection with Hindu idolatry by the policy on noninterference, but the nature of its own growing involvement in so-called "political ceremony" remained unarticulated. In his careful reconstructions of the development of political rituals by the British, Bernard Cohn argues that after the Mutiny the British "who had started as 'outsiders,' became 'insiders' by vesting in their monarchy the sovereignty of India through the Government of India Act of 2 August 1858." As soon as Victoria was queen over India and Great Britain, the full-scale "construction of a ritual idiom" began in which the British attempted to represent the nature of their authority and their relationship to colonial people (Cohn 1983b, 165). Cohn's work suggests that in order to understand this kind of ritual the modern historian must give up the idea that British ritual was mere "window dressing." He suggests a methodology that defines the British use of ritual as a "cultural-symbolic constitution" (1983b, 178): "It is about culture as defined as organized sets of meanings, it is about authority and how it was symbolized and how the British attempted to make it compelling" (Cohn 1975, 2). Yet the modern scholar must make this kind of analysis ex post facto. Neither in Cohn's articles nor in the earlier descriptions of the British rituals in this chapter did the British themselves ever confess that their ritual was anything more than pragmatic—a necessity in an oriental world, a concession to circumstance. Why the silence? Why the inability to invest their own ritual—or for that matter, Hindu ritual—with any ontological significance beyond "representation" or "symbolization"? What Pandora's box had the British opened when they put the first imperial feather in their hat and stepped into the Indian durbar halls? A second scene from Pudukkottai provides an interesting case of conflict over ritual that was disguised as an issue of fiscal responsibility.

Scene Two. Only a Bird in a Gilded Cage: The Last Days of Raja Ramachandra Tondaiman

> They have got a self-acting singing bird for sale. It is very curious indeed. I am very anxious to have it in my possession. You know my pecuniary difficulties. I shall really feel indebted to you if you would kindly direct the Sirkele to buy the bird box for me. . . . This will be purely a mark of kindness and favor from you towards me. I am laid up with rheumatic pains nearly for a month. I am unable to go to town. I am here only. (Palace Records, letter to the political agent dated September 13, 1883)

clearly saw Victoria as one of his models for munificence—and of true dharmic rule (576). The British seemed willing to reward his activities, until his bankruptcy changed their minds.

The raja of Pudukkottai in 1854 never pursued "enlightened" education, as did the young Ramnad raja forty years later. But Ramachandra Tondaiman was no stranger to British manners, at least to what he knew to be British. S. Radhakrishna Aiyar, in his *General History of the Pudukkottai State,* proudly quotes outside notice of the raja's fine manners and fluent English: "The present Raja of Pudukota is one of those princes who possess in a remarkable degree the power of producing the most favourable impression on outsiders. He speaks many languages, English included. This last he speaks with fluency, correctness and elegance, which I have not seen surpassed in the whole range of my experience of native princes. He also possesses most agreeable manners" (Radhakrishna Aiyar 1916, 435, quoted from a note sent to the chief secretary of the Madras Government). The raja's English and manners were cultivated in close association with John Blackburne, the political agent for Pudukkottai whose more famous brother, William Blackburne, had served as first British resident of Tanjore and Pudukkotai for almost twenty years. A collection of correspondence, apparently originally in English, between the young raja and John Blackburne has been preserved in Pudukkottai (Huzur Records, vols. 2, 3, 4). Raja Ramachandra always addressed the political agent as "uncle" and his wife as "mama." Two volumes of letters prove the Blackburne-Tondaiman relationship was not an example of mere oriental politeness. The volumes record the profits and losses in a joint venture of an indigo plantation between the Blackburnes and Raja Ramachandra's father. The Tondaiman family indeed had serious connections with the British and knew them quite well. Theirs was no case of backwoods innocence.

Here again in the case of the extravagant Raja Ramachandra is a prime example of the British admitting no involvement in actually pushing the raja to the very spending they found so distasteful. In the person of Political Agent Parker, the British Raj had cleansed itself of any guilt in the raja's seemingly reckless pursuit of splendor. They had lectured. They had warned. But the detailed records of the period between 1852 and 1853 reveal some interesting facts about British exhortation for economy. Not all requests for expensive rituals were denied. The lists of what the raja was allowed to spend are revealing. In 1870 Raja Ramachandra sent a plea for a special purchase. He wanted 1,200 rupees to buy a cheetah for hunting but was allotted only 600 rupees (Darbar Files, DD 11/1870). Yet the same year, a request for 2,000 rupees for new carriage horses was approved primarily because the sirkele had argued that the British governor's intended visit would require decent animals pulling His Lordship in the state carriage (Darbar Files, DD 32/1870). Similarly in 1867, the raja's request for 10,000 rupees for his daughter's puberty rites—very important rituals in royal Tamil households—was denied (Darbar Files, DD 2/1867). Yet in 1870 some 20,000 rupees was the amount sanctioned to allow His Excellency to attend a reception for the visiting Duke of Edinburgh (Radhakrishna Aiyar 1916, 428). In 1877 a grand durbar was held to honor the assumption of the title of Empress of India by Queen Victoria. Nothing in the records indicates any objections to these expenses in the midst of a serious famine in Pudukkottai. Again in 1877, the raja was permitted to purchase a silver throne for his use during the impending visit of the Prince of Wales (Darbar Files, DD 64/1878). Finally, no objection was raised to expenses for a grand durbar held to mark the resumption of his honors and a new title of "His Highness" conferred by the British in 1884. Yet again almost every year during the period from 1852 to 1884, the raja's initial budget requests for the important Hindu royal festival of Dassara were disputed by the political agent (for example, see Palace Records, document dated September 23, 1869). It seems the British command to economize for the welfare of the subjects of Pudukkottai never extended to rupee-pinching on rituals that directly touched on the relationship between Pudukkottai and the paramount power.

In 1878, under pressure from the British, a new sirkele was appointed by the raja. A. Sashia Sastri, a Tamil Brahman who had gained much favor with the British as dewan of Travancore State, began a series of "reforms." The story of the confrontation of this Brahman with the Kallar royal family of Pudukkottai will be central to the next chapter. Whatever economic reforms the new sirkele succeeded in bringing to Pudukkottai, it is clear that he also took pains to put on a good public ritual—or rather, a good imperial ritual. By 1884, although still in debt, the raja of Pudukkottai had his title restored. The sirkele easily had 2,500 rupees approved by the political agent, and there was no objection to more funds for coconuts, fireworks, shawls, and drinking water for the public celebration of this event. The clever sirkele presented his request for funds for these items after the fact, as "an after but a very happy thought since drinking gave the people great pleasure" (Darbar Files, DD 37/1884). Here the entire durbar is set in a different context. No longer are the "personal" needs of the raja at the fore—it is "the people" who are presented as gaining pleasure from the festival. Certainly 2,500-plus rupees is economical, compared with the 10,000 the raja was used to requesting for his Hindu royal family rituals. Nevertheless, the request seemed to work primarily because the need was presented in a mode more palatable to the British. Two years later, when the governor of Madras did formally visit the state capital, he remarked: "No Governor had ever before visited the little state . . . and I was naturally received with much empressement. At the fireworks on the night of the 3rd, there may well have been on to 30,000 men. Everywhere . . . it rained wreaths and nautch girls" (quoted in Radhakrishna Aiyar 1916, 444). In spite of the near sarcasm in this diary note, the governor officially recorded his satisfaction with the visit and with "seeing the agreeable relations, which had prevailed between this Government and his family, completely restored" (Radhakrishna Aiyar 1916, 444). Certainly the satisfaction could well have rested on those stated improvements in economy and concern for public welfare that the now Dewan Sastri had instituted (the title of "sirkele" was changed to conform to all-India practice). But as Vavi Varma's portrait of Duff reveals, the governor may have been as pleased with his ceremonial honor in Pudukkottai as he was with the new water system.

What actually did change between 1853 and 1884 that transformed the image of Raja Ramachandra Tondaiman from a vain spendthrift to "His Highness"? The British were well aware that he had not become less extravagant, yet they publicly honored him just before his death. Perhaps, from the beginning, this wily raja knew his goal: He knew the primary target for aggrandizement of his power lay in the sphere of ritual. Price has made that clear in the case of the raja of Ramnad. The movement from glory based on military fetes of power to glory based on ritual display appear common elsewhere in nineteenth-century India (for example, see Breckenridge 1978). In the case of the Tondaimans, the carefully preserved Huzur Records—a bound collection of the Tondaiman family's early correspondence with the British—shows this transition clearly. The volume entitled "The Book Containing Translations and Copies of the Letters in which the Services of the Ancestors of the Raja Ragooneth Tondaiman Behauder are Particularly Acknowledged and Approved by the Governor and Other Public Officers of The Honorable, the Company" ends with a plea by the then raja for a bestowal of honors by the company on the Tondaiman "as other princes." Raja Ramachandra's father asked for his "honors"—ceremonial regalia for use in public ritual—but still based his request on the history of the Tondaimans' "faithful services, which they have always rendered to the Honorable, the Company, at hazard of their lives." The final offer of services should "any troublesome event ever again occur" rang hollow in a pacified South India of the 1830s. Raja Ramachandra seems to have continued his father's quest for "honors" but knew full well that military fetes were no longer the price of glory.

In 1853 glory clearly meant spending money, but not on the old military retainer whose presence had been a traditional mark of the raja's power at court. Instead, the cards were now played in the suit of diamonds, not spades. Parker's correspondence with the sirkele in 1852–54 shows the raja spending a real fortune in the shops of British Trichinopoly on jewels, a whopping 38,000 rupees, and an equal amount for clothes and sundries. Parker's letters actually quote the palace budget for 1852 compared to 1851 (in rupees):

	1851	1852
Table expenses	7,000	16,366
Clothes	3,000	5,776
Feasts	4,500	6,351
Inam and Huzur expenses	5,400	24,091

Parker recorded his great concern that this increase in expenses related "entirely to the Raja's private gratification." The political agent bitterly laments the lengths to which this spendthrift raja will go "to indulge a fantasy or to gratify a favorite" while neglecting "his country, roads and tanks" (Pudukkottai Merged State Records, R Dis 1852, letter dated February 21, 1852). At this point Parker adopted the usual diagnosis that royal pomp and vanity were the source of the bloated budget.

Later in 1853, Parker began to ask more serious questions about the Huzur Establishment: "By the Huzur Establishment, the Political Agent understands the staff of menial servants of the palace and such as pertain to the Raja's state and dignity." But Parker now had requested an exact list of those servants and found the establishment inflated by "secretaries and munshis" and "a pandit on rs. 15 per month" (Pudukkottai Merged State Records, R Dis 1853, letter dated March 12, 1853). The raja apparently justified these new "servants" as necessary to keep him informed on the administration of the country. The political agent's observations that the Huzur Establishment had been bloated is confirmed by court records in Pudukkottai. A list of the raja's palace servants from the 1880s included tennis markers, gun peons, and drawing masters. Raja Ramachandra had clearly decided to build up his Dignitary Establishment. The "profuse gifts" to his servants mentioned by Parker were likely the means of gaining the absolute loyalty of this now-inflated court establishment. The raja also had apparently begun to give these people the most traditional form of "payment" for services rendered: land. Parker's concern over this inflation of what he assumed to be the raja's personal establishment was increased by his realization that "the Sirkele and Taluk Establishments were considerably diminished. By the Sirkele and Taluk Establishments must be performed the duties of regular administration of the country, and a decrease below the standard when Mr. Blackburne had charge of Pudukkottai State during the Raja's minority can hardly be consistent with the public interest" (letter dated April 5, 1853).

No longer holding accusations of simple vanity, Political Agent Parker stated his open suspicions to the sirkele: "When the Political Agent observed the immense number of jowabanneries and secretaries entered as Huzur, he cannot help but feel that the whole conduct of affairs is taken out of the hands of the agents appointed for the purpose and transferred to persons who have no ostensible responsibility." Later Parker asked "what share the Raja takes in the business of the country, and what are the duties that are really performed by the large Huzur Establishment? . . . He can scarcely doubt that such a double supervision and divided responsibility can be productive of delay in business." Then Parker offered his strong advice to the raja: If the raja needed to be informed of the business of his kingdom, he "should see the Sirkele at stated periods" (letter dated April 5, 1853). Parker's intention here is clear. The raja of Pudukkottai is asked to conform to a model of British constitutional monarchy. The prime minister should run the country, the raja should merely reign. In other words, the raja is told to get back to a ceremonial reign and leave the business of the kingdom alone.

Now here is a pretty state of affairs for the raja of Pudukkottai. On the one hand, he stands accused of vanity, of senseless spending for his personal gratification. On the other hand, he is told that the ceremonial and not the civil is the only sphere proper for his activities. Exactly who is advocating "empty" pageantry, or, as Dirks put it, "decontextualized rituals"? Raja Ramachandra moved his power to the Huzur Establishment, which he clearly saw as his only remaining base of operations. Further, he read the British better than they read themselves. He had only pageantry left, but he tried to put real power back into his own ritual establishment. The Huzur had always been exactly this—the center for royal ritual—a point that will be central to the latter part of this study. Raja Ramachandra was willing to accept pageant power as long as he was the center of that power and could use it to aggrandize his own royal "name and fame." But by 1884 the raja appeared to have learned a lesson. His clever dewan began to emphasize the rituals of the paramount power. Amazingly, this spendthrift now was received once again into the good graces of the British overlords. Perhaps Raja Ramachandra had learned that the British really had no objection to ritual. They even silently moved him toward proper pageantry. The British as the paramount power may well have openly praised the building of hospitals and schools, but they deeply loved a rain of garlands—as long as the flowers began to fall on them.

When those wreaths were offered to the British overlord, a significant change in the ritual idiom of Pudukkottai occurred. Just how significant the change was becomes apparent in the following chapters, but some of the changes are immediately apparent. The raja's earlier requests for funds had centered on rites within the family or on a series of rituals, such as Dassara, that had long been part of the history of his own house and of many other little kings like him throughout India. In these rituals, the circle of giving and receiving went no further than Pudukkottai itself. Even the Great Goddess lived quite literally in a temple not three miles from the raja's palace. Certainly the Moghuls in Delhi had already set the precedent for the giving of gifts from the far overlord to the local prince, but the British intensified the sense of distance the ceremonial encompassed. The space was now the whole empire, and the ultimate receiver of the garland was their royal lady in London. The British increased this space of ritual quite literally at the expense of the raja's own very domestic rituals. The change is important, for in a real sense the British never completely ceased to practice some of the tenets of invisible rule. Some power afar was always the ultimate receiver of honor. The governor was, after all, only the representative of the viceroy, who was by his very name only a stand-in for the queen-empress. As much as the British officers allowed themselves to be seen in massive rituals of display, they nonetheless were never to be seen for themselves. They exemplified British rule, they personified the presence of the queen, they symbolized power, but they could not admit that they had concreteness, that they were something in themselves. They had removed any ontological essence for the great position they occupied. They could not admit the corporeality of their ritual rule.

The British used a ritual idiom, but they were forced to empty it of any acknowledged religiosity—any power to move them in the way that it moved their supposed more gullible subject races. To have voiced their pleasure, their deep involvement, in such external forms would have carried them into much more murky waters. They had, after all, created these rituals. They were honoring an empire they had built. Who had crowned Victoria the Empress of India? Cohn records that Lytton's speech at the great Delhi Durbar named "Providence" as the authority that moved the British to now take up the regime of the Moghuls (Cohn 1983b, 205). But he also notes the charges made in England that this ostentation was not English and was a product of wild imagination (207). Perhaps it was not English, for if God had really ordained the power of the British, theirs was indeed a sacred rule, but such a possibility had already been eliminated from the game at the very beginning. The old regimes had fallen, the British told themselves, because they had confused theology with polity. The British had put themselves beyond such sacredness in favor of rationality. But playing with ritual can be dangerous. Perhaps the Indian empire had conquered its master as it had subdued many masters before with the seductive call to make "for themselves a religion more suited . . . to their own hearts," as Abbé Dubois would have put it.

The Victorians thrived in India at a time when their own religious convictions seemed most shaken and when their God both of rationalism and of revelation was being questioned. Houghton maintains that the new hero-worship and the renewed interest in legends of ancient Britain resulted directly from the demise of God, "for when God was dead, the Gods and heroes of history and myth could take his place and save the moral sum of things" (1957, 322). The Victorians, then, were fabricators, builders of much that could not be directly given the name of God because that charge of idolatry remained ever present. The whole hero-worship movement was termed "no better than any other idolatry" (Houghton

1957, 331). The British in India were caught between need and principles, between practice and theory. They needed to make gods—perhaps even to make themselves gods. But hush! That could not be said, for the almost-dead God of the Commandments might hear, or worse, the carefully constructed logic of their eighteenth-century minds might topple, thereby destroying the very rationality that was their pride and their one supposed distinction from the natives they ruled.

"Vanity, vanity. . . ." The age of *Vanity Fair* looked at the pomp and ornamentation of Raja Ramachandra Tondaiman and shook the finger of shame at him. Commenting now on the photographs of the once-glorious Nizam of Hyderabad, John Galbraith begins his foreword to *Princely India:* "The urge for a permanent pictorial legacy has always been especially marked among kings and princes. Vanity and the urge for immortality have rarely been lacking in these precincts" (Worswick 1980, 5). Yet the finger pointing to the vanity of the oriental prince in 1877 was already stretched from a sleeve made of gold brocade. The British had discovered that clothes do make the man. They simply could not explain why. While their words said "vanity," their fingers fondled the ivory hilt of their swords.

2

The Master of Ceremonies
Sashia Sastri Takes Charge in Pudukkottai

> The prickly pears, grown into enormous bushes sheltering venomous rep-
> tiles, . . . were flourishing . . . in close vicinity of the villages all over the
> State and threatened to swallow up the habitations. . . . The climatic condi-
> tions of the State unfortunately seemed too favourable for it.
> —A. Sashia Sastri

In the year 1877, Queen Victoria of England put on the title of Kaizer-i-Hind, Empress of
India. The great durbar in Delhi once again united status with power. Sight and sound
loudly proclaimed the British presence in India. But no sooner had the British constructed
their own gilded far pavilions than they forced the appointment of the Brahman A. Sashia
Sastri, a twenty-year veteran of their bureaucracy, as dewan of Pudukkottai. His mission
was nothing less than the reformation of the raja's too-lavish house. That reform did not
prove easy. The palace in Pudukkottai contained a queen whose beauty had dazzled the
raja (Plate 21) and whose sharp tongue and ready wit daunted the Brahman dewan.
Labeled early by the British as a "thoroughly dangerous and intriguing woman" (Darbar
Files, D90/1888, letter dated November 15, 1867), the rani led a fierce struggle that left
vivid evidence of life in the palace that makes it possible to look again into the raja's house
and watch the Brahman dewan with his buckets of orders trying to wipe out a system of
kingship that just would not come clean.

Plate 21.   Her Highness Janaki Subbamma Bai Sahib, by Ravi Varma, dated December 1879. The beauty of Raja Ramachandra's queen is revealed as the purdah curtain falls for the painter and for what must have become an admiring public. The portrait, which remains with His Highness in Trichinopoly, makes it easy to believe that this rani indeed ruled her husband's passion and his politics. The rani wears a sari in a very modern fashion, with the *palu* (the decorative end piece) casually thrown over her shoulder. She purposely reveals her gold ankle bracelets and toe rings, which mark her high status. A famous Tamil epic, *Cilappatikāram*, takes its name from a ill-fated gold ankle bracelet that belonged to a merchant woman. When the queen's duplicate bracelet was stolen, the heroine's husband was accused of being the thief while trying to sell his wife's anklet to raise needed cash. Ordinary women wear silver, not gold, on their feet.

The Taming of the Shrew

A raja hopelessly henpecked by his dazzlingly beautiful second wife, the Junior Rani Janaki Bai; Martanda Bhairava Tondaiman, the raja's young adopted heir; the Senior Princess Brihadamba Raja Ammani, the daughter of the junior rani and the natural mother of Martanda and his many siblings—these were the major occupants of the Pudukkottai palace when Dewan Sashia Sastri began to implement his long list of reforms. An unfinished and unsigned portrait now resting in a spare room in His Highness Rajagopala's palace in Trichinopoly still allows a glimpse of all these powerful characters as they sit together in a very domestic and, ironically (note the tea table and the chairs), very English pose (Plate 22). Only the rani and her younger daughter have been given the finishing touches by the artist (Plate 23, color section). Although the rani's earlier beauty, captured by Ravi Varma, had

Plate 22. This portrait is unfinished, undated, and unsigned. Despite the now matronly girth of the rani, the age of Martanda, leaning on his adopted father's lap, would date the painting no more than five years after Varma produced his ravishing rani. This painting presents a very domestic raja and rani sitting down, on chairs, to a nice English family tea. It is tempting to speculate why such an image was never finished and still remains in storage in His Highness's palace in Trichinopoly. Did the rani object to this less beguiling image as royal matron rather than royal beauty?

Plate 24.   In contrast to his queen, the raja appears simply dressed, although the artist may have intended more decoration on his now plain blue
coat. The raja's domestic pose, like that of his rani, seems to contrast with
his long-standing reputation as a wily spendthrift. His face wears the expression of a tired grandfather who has worked all his life for the welfare of his
family, whom he adores. The raja seems so ordinary here that his grandeur,
so evident in the durbar hall, seems to have vanished with the sparkle of his
missing jewels.

quickly faded, she still sparkles with jewels, while the raja (Plate 24) looks quite homely
hugging his adopted heir, Martanda. Martanda's mother, the senior princess, sits in the
background almost hidden by her many children. Her eldest son stands respectfully behind
his grandfather as his younger brother holds the limelight in the raja's arms.

The portrait seems peaceful, but its very domesticity is in sharp contrast to the bold durbar
poses of less than twenty years before. Why the raja would have commissioned this very
public display of his domestic life remains a question. Such family poses were not the usual
subject of portraits for the martial royal clans, whose women were expected to maintain
seclusion. Sastri, of course, had already exposed the raja's family to the brunt of his reforms,
and the raja's new domesticity is an inverse of the sketch Sastri drew of this family in his
many official reports. High on Sastri's priorities were "cleaning up" the palace along with
the capital, and those ever-present prickly pears housing venomous reptiles. Apparently for

Sastri, the palace and the prickly pears had a lot in common—the inhabitants of both knew how to strike back in kind. His intrusions into the life of the palace were serious enough to prompt the rani to make "a sacrifice of one hundred cobras hung by the tail over a fire which was kept up by a flood of ghee" to create just the right incantations to rid Pudukkottai of this "disagreeable minister"—or at least that is the way Sastri told the story (Darbar Files, D258/1892, "Conspiracy Against the Dewan Regent").

Sastri's public reforms in the capital and the outlying districts of the state were predictable for a twenty-four-year veteran of the British Civil Service. Hospitals, a college, widened streets, new tanks (reservoirs) for clean drinking water—all were duly built by the time Sastri retired from office twenty years later. But Sastri's reforms inside the palace had a special urgency for himself and for the colonial government. When set in the language of British administrative goals, Sastri ostensively performed a task here that was no more or less a matter of good "political" service than any of his other reforms. But the energy Sastri gave to his work in the palace, the force of the support the British political agent provided, and the fervor with which the raja's family fought the reforms again betray a struggle for power that the British in their own striving for ritual legitimacy did not dare to undertake openly. They left the purification of the palace in Pudukkottai to their trusted Brahman reformer who had already succeeded so well in Travancore State.

From 1878 to 1886, while Raja Ramachandra was still alive, Sastri began what would seem to be simple measures to end "corruptions" among the palace servants, to see to the reorganization of some "overstaffed" departments, and to put the palace buildings in good repair. After Sastri assumed the regency of Pudukkottai during the minority of the young Martanda, his interference in every detail of palace life was overt—mandated as his duty by his own sentiments *and* by the clear orders of the British overlords. After 1886 the rani indeed "left nothing undone" to bring about Sastri's departure from Pudukkottai. Not relying simply on her incantations, she hired a British lawyer and tried to argue in Sastri's own terms to save her remaining authority in the palace. Her voice was ironically preserved by Sastri in his own printed line-by-line response to her formal letter to the political agent, which he titled "Memorandum Drawn up by the Dewan Regent Stating Categorically the Results of Correspondence between Him and the Political Agent and Orders of the Government on Various Subjects alluded to and Allegations Made by the Junior Ranee Sahib" (Darbar Files, D90/1888). Her struggle with Sastri left the only negative voice yet audible in the garlands of praise that showered Sastri's efforts.

Sastri argued that much of the rani's objections to his rules of cleanliness in the palace, to his mandates for which apartments her daughter should occupy, and to the places where the minor raja should play were based on "superstition." But the rani's voice, transformed by her lawyer into British legal dialect, countered Sastri in a long letter to the political agent:

> To meet me with the plea that my objections are untenable because they are superstitious is a dangerous answer in the mouths of the representatives of the British government. It is but so much a slip from the domain of sentiment to the domain of religion. Yet could you expect obedience from me or approval from the government if you

were to turn a deaf ear to my objections against the proselytizing of my son on the ground that my adherence to my own creed was a foolish form of superstition?

Here the rani squarely argued that much of Sastri's reforms fell into the category of the prohibited interference into Hindu *religious* affairs. Her arguments were not accepted because the British, and their well-trained reformer, remained unable, or perhaps unwilling, to make that "slip" of the tongue—and here I take the rani's part—to admit the affairs of the palace into the domain of religion.

After a century of silence, why should the case against the rani be reopened? Her outspokenness and her actions in hiring a foreign lawyer on her own behalf hardly make her the perfect wife by the standard set less than a century earlier at the court of her native Tanjore.[1] Given her outspokeness, is there any truth to her defense that Sastri and the British were interfering in religious affairs of the royal family? It is interesting that Sastri never met her charge directly. In his line-by-line publicly printed response to her long letter of complaint to the political agent, Sastri dismissed her charges as a clever ruse to cover up her many plots to retain her financial and political power. Certainly no romantic sentiments should declare any innocents in this struggle. The rani was fighting to retain power. But so was Sastri, and so were the British. The question remains, however, why the British colonial government now wanted so desperately to reform palace life—something they had never before cared to "see" or to seriously understand.

Before Sastri, British records contain surprisingly little information about the inner workings of the palace in Pudukkottai or in any of the other native states. For all of their seemingly intimate knowledge of Pudukkottai, neither William Blackburne nor John Blackburne ever lived in the palace, nor in all their long correspondence did they provide eyewitness descriptions of palace ceremonials or of palace personnel. They had attended weddings and the many rituals at the palace, as did many European guests of the Pudukkottai royal family, yet they never described these beyond simply noting their attendance. Their official interest in the palace was bounded by economic concerns alone. William Blackburne began some palace reform by eliminating several palace watchmen to save money. His actions were serious to the "watchmen" and to the palace personnel who protested. But at least in Blackburne's eyes the issue remained financial. Even Political Agent Parker as late as 1854 still asked for information on the palace personnel in an attempt to economize.

After 1860, however, the British silence on palace affairs was no longer a matter of disinterest or perhaps of laissez-faire alone. Official records in Pudukkottai and other states after 1858 contained the same striking silence about palace affairs, but for some very different and sharply articulated reasons. In Travancore, which had received even earlier attention to reforms from a succession of British-trained Brahman dewans, including Sastri, the missionaries who usually provided some of the few glances into Hindu religious practice (see Mateer 1883) are silent about the palace, but clear as to why. An early letter from 1860 reveals a theme that was to be echoed in all British discussions of the "unmentionable"

---

1. For a translation and analysis of the *Strīdharmapaddhati*, written a century earlier by a minister at the Tanjore court to guide women in their role, see Leslie 1987.

palaces in the native states: "The present Rajah is a young man . . . who has kept himself much aloof, it is said, from the usual vices . . . of an Eastern Court" (Archives of the Council for World Mission, Travancore Files, Letter from F. Baylis to Dr. Tidman dated at Neyoor, November 20, 1860). Palaces were labeled as places of "corruption and vice"—as Sastri himself often wrote of the Pudukkottai palace—and certainly no place for decent people to go poking around for serious religious observances.

The popular three little carved monkeys with eyes and ears and mouths covered to the sights and sounds of evil characterized well the British attitude toward the palaces after 1858. The rani may have understood this attitude rightly. These later reforms were a kind of "proselytizing" carried out in the name of moral reform. And the interesting fact remains that all this urgency for reform inside the heart of the palaces on moral grounds cannot be traced further than the years just after the Mutiny and the East India Company's forced relinquishment of power in India to the British Crown. Victoria's famous proclamation of 1858 promised the rajas permanent security from any British expansion. Yet as the work of Bernard Cohn and the previous chapter illustrate, this was also the time of growing British involvement in the development of their own ritual and their own court life. The reforms of the palace might well have been as much a religious struggle as the rani claimed.

The rani's letter of complaint resulted in an interview with the governor that, instead of being a hearing of her grievances, backfired into a stern lecture on her behavior. As the dewan reiterated in his official answer to her complaint, the rani's "character" was already well known to the British. By 1868 her passion for jewels was officially cataloged as one of the factors leading the raja to the debt that supposedly triggered the 1854 rebellion. Reports of all past political agents portrayed her as the twenty-year power behind the throne in Pudukkottai. She and "her relations" and "two or three Brahmans, her special favorites" supposedly inveigled the raja out of the state seal and took control of the judicial process. In addition, "her Brahman Parasites" weakened the power of the former sirkele's (dewan's) office. Yes, in sum, Sastri can only point "to the disgrace and ruin she has been to the character of her late husband, and to the State." Thus branded, her voice had to be ignored as carefully as the sweet deadly calls of a Siren.

Undaunted, however, the senior princess took up her mother's cause, and we see her with new dignity in a portrait that still hangs in the royal palace in Trichinopoly (Plate 25). In a direct telegram to the governor, her only "father," she asked for protection from Sastri's animosity, which threatened her very life (DD 9/1888). The dewan-regent again framed his reply and sent it along with his printed reply of 1887 to similar charges by the rani. In another long and exacting memorandum, Sastri predictably claimed that all these "sensational" pleas were used solely as a means of "confounding, mystifying, and exaggerating matters, . . . forgetting that the British Government is above all things a Constitutional Government not easily moved by sensational telegrams" (Darbar Files, D9/1888, letter dated January 17, 1888).

This massive file conducted in full British bureaucratic medium has left little space for the palace ladies to speak on their own terms. Overtly, the issues the palace ladies raised do seem as trivial as Sastri claimed. The situation that roused the rani to assert her right to freedom of religion was, after all, only an argument over use of a playground. The senior princess's

Plate 25.   Brihadamba Raja Ammani Sahib, Senior Princess and the natural mother of Raja Martanda, by Ravi Varma, dated 1886. Still seemingly alive on the walls of His Highness's palace in Trichinopoly, the princess revels in her status as a respected Tamil matron. Unlike her mother, no woman of fashion is she. The senior princess wears the *palu*, the decorative end piece, of her sari draped around her waist in a very traditional Tamil manner. The sari itself is not imported Benares silk, but appears local in both weave and color.

wrath was incurred merely because Sastri wanted to move her temporarily out of her old apartments "to make them sanitary" with bucket, brush, and some fresh paint. The rest of the ill-will rose from the ladies' unwillingness to give up the company of "a band of notorious villains," which included a number of those noxious Brahmans, a group of unsavory playmates caught openly playing cards with the raja's brothers, and the very dangerous "dancing girls who were found in constant company with the Princess." Clearly, the beleaguered dewan-regent had only persisted in his duty, much against the sheer petty stubbornness of the palace ladies. Yet there is much here to decode in Sastri's British bureaucratese and the palace lady's "mystifying and confounding" language (Darbar Files, D9/1888, letter dated January 17, 1888).

For the sake of justice, let us inquire into at least one of the senior princess's foolish complaints—the matter of her apartments. By 1888 the palace actually had two separate *aranmanai* (houses of the king). The senior princess was occupying the eastern palace, and Sastri wanted to move her temporarily to a set of apartments in the older, western building. She refused, because these old apartments were "haunted." Sastri guessed, "I believe that she calls this aranmanai a haunted place since a pseudo-saint worshiped by her mother, the Junior Rani, is buried here" (Darbar Files, D9/1888, letter dated January 11, 1888). Today the palace grounds are standing, and it is possible to map out this struggle over place. No one in Pudukkottai ever mentioned the grave of a saint buried inside the palace—and that is something no one there would forget. There is, however, a saint much associated with the palace through the Dakshinamurti temple, which fronts the western palace building. The temple houses not the body of the saint but rather a casket containing the sand on which were written the sacred injunctions to the Tondaiman family by the saint Sadasiva Brahmendra. If the haunting saint is indeed Sadasiva Brahmendra, then the dewan-regent was either a blind fool or a very ambitious man indeed to dare to ignore the princess's objections to these apartments. Sadasiva Brahmendra, whose story figures prominently in a following chapter, was no pseudo-saint but the very preserver and protector of the Tondaiman dynasty. Of course, the descriptions of the exact garden location are too sketchy to know for certain that Sastri actually presented the patron saint of the Tondaimans to the British as just some personal fantasy of the Junior Rani and company, but the affair at least ought to arouse suspicion that at some level Sastri's reforms had an agenda unknown even to the British, at least not officially.

But there is yet more evidence on the side of the palace ladies. The affair of the expelled "dancing girls" invites inquiry. In his reports to the Government of India, the moral-minded dewan spoke with profound passion of this great "collision with the monster of the palace—vice":

> Next I found it necessary to nail up a secret door which opened directly to the apartments of the Senior Princess and allowing all sorts of characters at all hours of the day and night. Next I stopped the ingress of all dancing girls who were found in constant company with the Princess, and lastly, on information received of unspeakable things which had very recently occurred, I was compelled to prohibit some wicked and debaucherous characters from entering the palace where the young Rajah lives. (Letter dated January 17, 1888)

A door in the palace grounds (Plate 26) is still identified with that now-famous door. The "dancing girls" listed here along with all the unmentionable characters entering the palace were known by another important name, the *devadāsīs*. Of these women, much is still remembered in Pudukkottai, and much now has been written by Frederique Marglin and others about their importance in other royal states (see Marglin 1985). A princess of the Tondaiman family was until recently served by a devadasi. Rani Rema Devi explained that the devadasis served crucial functions for the palace ladies. At the turn of the century, the Tondaiman ladies were still expected to keep purdah. The devadasis who were free from such restrictions accompanied the ladies on all their visits outside the palace. They held up cloth screens to protect the ladies from the public eye as they moved from their palanquins. The devadasis' presence was essential in the vital life-cycle rituals for female members of the royal family. The education of the palace ladies also depended on the devadasis who taught the essential arts of song and dance. Thus deprived of the company of her devadasis, the senior princess would literally be captive in the palace—unable to go out and prohibited from fulfilling much of her ritual obligations. Was Dewan Sastri, son of a Brahman family that yet resided in the domains of Tanjore once famous for the perfection of its devadasis, really ignorant of this?

Plate 26.   This door, still padlocked, stands amid the ruins of the palace as
the last remaining evidence of the virtual war between the Junior Rani
Sahib and Dewan Sastri. While this may not be the actual door that gave
entrance to those infamous devadasis, several different guides in my explorations of the old palace did not fail to point out the door with a kind of
sardonic glee as they remembered tales of the willful rani's lone resistance
to the British. Here is a key visual element in a movie script waiting to be
written.

Then there is also the matter of the expulsion of the princess's "Puja Brahman," who was
also included among those aiding and abetting the general vice and debauchery in the palace
(Darbar Files, D9/1888, letter dated January 10, 1888). The expulsion is particularly puzzling because Sastri was a practicing Hindu who worked to repair temples in Pudukkottai
and whose first act after retiring years later was to repair, "greatly enlarge," and properly
reconsecrate his family temple outside of Kumbakonam for 10,000 rupees (Collected Letters
of A. Sashia Sastri, letter dated March 4, 1891). Yet here, Sastri seemed simply to parrot the
British disdain toward Brahman priests who served in royal courts. Recall that these Brahmans had long been cited as one factor contributing to Raja Ramachandra's disgraceful
debt. It was "Brahmans" that Parker saw swelling the ranks of the raja's Huzur Establishment, thereby swelling his debt. They were in cahoots with the rani. Sastri here sounds much
like the Travancore missionaries of 1860 who cite those Brahmans as the chief contributors

to the "vices of the Eastern Courts." Their full comments add evidence that is quite relevant to our Dewan Sastri:

> The first thing will be to keep the Rajah as much as possible from the clutches of the Brahmins, and both the Resident and the Dewan will, I think, help in this. The Dewan, it is true, is a Brahmin (Mahratta) but he has no liking for the Brahmins of the country or they for him. I believe they hate and fear him as an enlightened reformer and he despises them as a set of ignorant bigots.

This very dewan was Sir T. Mahadevan Rao, Sastri's "old school fellow" and his predecessor as dewan of Travancore. Could these two gentlemen from the new class of "enlightened" Brahmans have some special interest in removing from power another set of Brahmans who had no attachment to the British colonial power and whose sphere of influence clashed with their own?

There is enough circumstantial evidence now to bring an indictment. Sastri belonged to a group of Brahman reformers who set about the careful and knowing dismantlement of the religious structures that centered at the royal court. The motive—what was it? This hypothesis must be posed: The reforming dewan, and others like him, set out to restructure the locus of religious energy out of the court toward forms of religion less harmful and less rivaling to the growing centralized civil rituals of the British royal courts. Crucial here is the fact that this process of reform was an inside job—as much a Hindu as a British process. The changes these reformers effected are now enormously important to historians of religions, for their "reforms" altered much that we would see and all that we *could* see of seemingly "native" religion in India.

Out, Out, Damned Spot!

With the notorious lover of pleasure Raja Ramachandra Tondaiman now dead and a very young raja installed, the political agent and the Government of India were going to take no chance that history would repeat itself in Pudukkottai. The political agent, R. H. Farmer, declared his policy: The "home life" of the young raja was to be carefully regulated, especially his "indoor amusements" and the "character of his personal attendants." The political agent warned of the "vitiated atmosphere of the palace and its dangerous surroundings and of necessarily isolating the Raja as completely as possible from the effects of such influence" (Darbar Files, D90/1888). Mr. Farmer wanted to move the raja to the nearby British cantonment in Trichinopoly and to educate him there under his watchful eyes. Sastri disagreed, and proposed a compromise to keep His Highness in Pudukkottai for at least three years. Dewan Sastri gained official control over the "home life" of the young raja with the appointment of his own nephew as His Highness's "Guardian," a move that effectively took the raja out of the rani's control. The rani's protests that the new guardian was "practically a replica of the Dewan-Regent, a retailer of all of the tittle-tattle of the palace," were quoted by Sastri as a matter of pride to the political agent. Sastri promised the raja would be isolated from "vice" within the palace, with his nephew acting under Sastri's own superintendency. The dewan-regent's printed "Instructions for the Guidance of the Guardian of His Highness the Maharaja" satisfied Mr. Farmer for the present. These rules, however, were neither the British ideal nor hardly the rani's delight, but Sastri's own special formula for how to raise a king. The document is worth examining in detail.

The "Instructions" were as much a blueprint for the reformation of the palace as they were a means of isolating the raja from vice. On one level, they carefully echo the political agent's concern for selecting the raja's personal servants and regulating the conduct and duties of all other members of the palace establishment. Sastri's careful list of regulations included firm rules:

> —The company which His Highness is allowed to keep is a matter of great importance and should be strictly controlled; it should be perfectly settled who is to accompany His Highness in the drives, in the field sports and in house amusement.

> —A Register of attendance should be kept of all the personal servants of His Highness, their attendance to duty carefully noted, and all carelessness and misconduct should be summarily punished by fines or by dismissal as the case may call for.

But unlike the political agent, Sastri knew full well that the raja's home was not a house but a palace, and that the raja's "servants" were not hired employees but officers of the palace by inherited right. The people who accompanied the raja on state drives and throughout his daily routine inside the palace were defined by tradition. Sastri wrote with an eye to the political agent as if he actually had the power to hire and fire the palace personnel, but he could do no more than change the rules under which it operated. With the appointment of a guardian, Sastri added a bureaucratic head over what had never been a bureaucratic structure. The guardian was ultimately in charge of regulating the palace staff—an office and a role unknown in former times.

The penchant for rules and regulations and for bookkeeping and record-keeping characterizes Sastri's bureaucratic style. The "Instructions" announce his appointment of a Brahman "Private Writer of His Late Highness" to be the palace record-keeper who would "not only have charge of such Records of the Palace as may be put in his charge by order of the Dewan-Regent, but will generally act as the Chief Clerk of the Guardian." In addition, "the Guardian will examine all the Palace Records in Mallari Rao's possession elsewhere [and] prepare a first list of them and afterwards an index and arrange for their safe custody and ready access when necessary." As part of his general demand for clear records, the dewan-regent also ordered a complete list of the entire Huzur Establishment (the general name given to the complex set of "servants" who ministered to the raja within the palace), to include the exact title in both English and Tamil of each officer, their names, and their monthly allowances. The list, entitled "The Huzzoor or Palace Establishment, Etc.," is extant. Sastri intended to use it to begin yet another step in his palace reformation.

The careful regulation of the raja's "home life" was the first frontal attack on the old guard of the palace, the Huzur Establishment, which had been Ramachandra Tondaiman's carefully fortified stronghold against encroachment of the bureaucratic machinery represented by the office of the dewan. While Ramachandra Tondaiman enlarged his palace staff with all the wealth he could not afford to spare, Sastri began to make certain the palace was cut down to size. Specifically, during the year in which he wrote the "Instructions," the dewan-regent initiated "revision of the Huzur Establishment" as part of his lauded Inam Settlement of 1888. The full importance of this land settlement for Pudukkottai is carefully outlined in Nicholas Dirks's *Hollow Crown* (1987, 324–57). For the palace staff the settlement had special consequences. These measures on the surface seemed simple enough. Instead of payment for services through the unenfranchised gifts of land with rights to the profits of its cultivation tax-free, Sastri substituted wages for all the palace personnel and deeded their land to them permanently but subject to taxation. In addition, Sastri reduced the number of employees, arguing that corruption would be less likely with the larger wages paid to fewer persons (Darbar Files, Administration Report 1887–1888). Such changes might seem wonderfully fair to a British audience who were certain that unencumbered land ownership meant individual freedom and pride, but the measure had the opposite effect. The individual power wielded by the members of the establishment was curtailed if not ended.

"Title deeds" were issued to members of the Huzur Establishment during the Inam Settlement. These deeds were accompanied by a detailed description for each deed recorded in large volumes that are still available in the Settlement Office in Tanjore. Each record relates the story of how the *inam* (gift of land) was originally granted to the family and logs the inherited right of service in the palace that was also granted. Frequently the service is listed only as *araṇmaṇi ūḻiya* (service in the palace), with no exact duties specified but with the explanation that the grant was made for some act of bravery in one of the Tondaiman's successful wars. Clear examples of this can be seen in the grants made for the office of the court herald who announces the raja at the durbar, which was "granted for service in war" (Inam Settlement Faisal Registry, Title Deed 116); the beaters of the royal drums, who served the palace because their ancestors "gave their lives as a [human] sacrifice as soon as the Tirumayam fort was complete" (Title Deed 1424); the Chamaram-holder, who held the office of standing behind the raja with a yak-tail fan because an ancestor had shot a leopard in the forest (Title Deed 1047). Clearly, then, the service was not "work" but a coveted honor, a prize that accompanied rights to land. This was not an exchange of land for work, but a gift of land and rights of service. The title deeds point to an older system in which a person did not fit into the "job" but the "job" accrued to the person as a fact of his inheritance of "land." Recent analysis of the importance of the old land-tenure systems in India gives clues to the nature of such a system. Walter Neale argues that there was a distinction between the Indian traditional concept of land as a sign of power over people and the British concept of land as capital—an object to be worked. He argues that land traditionally first meant the right to rule, not the right to own, because, "accustomed to a system of local government based upon prestige and number of followers, the Indian employed the resources at hand in a different manner." Neale continued: "Since numbers were important to political power, it behooved the Indian interested in acquiring power to increase, or a least maintain, the number of his allies and followers" (Neale 1969, 9). The exact nature of the legends accompanying the grants of inams is explored later, but the fact remains that service in the raja's house was not the work of mere salaried employees.

Sastri was well aware of the exact names of and services performed by each member of the Huzur Establishment, yet he chose to officially reduce their importance from palace incumbents to palace servants whose position depended on their personal conduct. It seems absurd to speak of a person being morally fit to hold a yak-tail fan or beat a drum or announce the raja, but that is exactly the system of regulations that Sastri presented to the political agent as the plan for his reformation. After Sastri's reforms, palace records began simply to list the "palace menials" in the way a British house might list its various paid employees. The actual purpose and importance of the office was now glossed over by a vague category of "menial service," which kept the office but demeaned the officeholder. Paid servants were given money to do a job; they were given land that had to be used to make money to pay taxes. Now, as merely employees, they had no substantial connection to the land of the palace. When the interconnectedness of person to office was broken in the palace, the palace itself began to look on paper just like a well-regulated part of the general bureaucratic machinery of the state. All the traits of a bureaucracy were here: the intense concern for clear rules, the general manipulation of power now meaning manipulation of laws instead of people, delineation of exact duties, exact functions for each staff member, and the careful maintenance of records that would be "inspected" to ensure proper implementation of "policy." But for Sastri this process of "bureaucratization" implemented more than good government: It remained an important part of his formula for (re)making a king.

For all his flat political language, Sastri was never prepared to define his king as simply a good ruling chief. Why would a frugal administrator maintain the old establishment intact— including the shoe-carriers, the lace-makers, the gun-peons, the elephant-tamers, and the fan-holders? In fact, Sastri did more than keep the establishment; he actually planned to reestablish some of the older offices that had gone out of use. Later records speak of his intention to reestablish the position of Tamil poet laureate in the kingdom. In his carefully devised plans for the official visit of the governor to Pudukkottai in 1892, quoted earlier, Sastri subtly reminded His Excellency of the raja's own royalty with "a little nautch, . . . heralds proclaiming the ancient titles of the Rajah." His later letters to the maharajas of both Pudukkottai and Travancore after his retirement are written with the full flourish of a proud minister addressing kings he had helped to make great. The older maharaja of Travancore is "Your Most Gracious Highness"—words fit more for Her Royal Majesty than for an Indian native chief. To H.H. Martanda Tondaiman, Sastri recommended that a good Brahman jester be introduced into his court. He argued that all Asian and European kings had such a functionary at court. "No fault will be found in a prince who revives this time-honored institution," advised Sastri in a voice with very Shakespearean overtones. Indeed, in 1894 the same much-praised Sastri was reprimanded by the British authorities for his shocking use of the terms "royal" and "royal family" in connection with the "Native Chief of Pudukkottai." Sastri's slip was prominently cited in a British manual of proper ceremonial for expressing the relationship of the native chief to their sovereign lady. In his manual, Sir Charles Tupper made it clear that "the Rulers of Native States are not royal personages" (Tupper 1895, 1:1).

There is no evidence that Sastri ever denied the overlordship of Her Royal Majesty, yet this same Hindu Brahman was equally unwilling to accept the royal monotheism of a civil servant like Charles Tupper, who declared there was but one *royal* family in the empire. The bureaucratic Sastri must indeed have well understood the use of working in duplicate—the same act duly recorded for the political agent as the reformation of an unruly vassal also functioned to make a space within the British Raj where a native chief could be a king.

Bureaucracy, for Sastri, became a key method of remaking Pudukkottai into a righteous kingdom. The opening paragraphs of Sastri's own "Resumé of My Sixteen Years of Administration of the Pudukkottai State" begin like the simple recollection of a difficult administrative reform program, but end like the prologue to an epic war of righteousness. The document is worth quoting at length as an exhibit of Sastri's elegant style and his keen sense of storytelling:

> Moreover, the various courts and offices of the revenue department, including that of the Dewan, were scattered about in some anterooms of the Palace or corners of the Palace yard, and others in different parts of the town, whereas the effect of supervision was made difficult. In all of the offices from the Dewan downward, there was no method of transaction of business. There were no fixed hours of attendance or, if there were, nonobservance was the rule. The records of reference of several officers were stowed away in various places without order and without arrangement. The useless and the useful had all been thrown in a heap or bundled together without distinction.
>
> The town of Pudukkottai, which is the capital of the Raja, was in deplorable condition. While originally well laid out, all of the streets and lanes had been extensively encroached upon. Drains had been obstructed, and during the rains the side drains so overflowed that they were converted into streams or bogs. Neither were they well swept and kept clean. The ponds, so conveniently scattered over the town, had long been neglected and in the rains the water in them was muddy and dirty; and, in the hot weather, they became filthy and pestilent.
>
> The prickly pears, grown into enormous bushes sheltering venomous reptiles, had not only obstructed the path leading to the town and taken possession of bunds and their vicinity, but also had overgrown every available space around the town. They were flourishing, not only on the bunds of most of the tanks on the commons, but also in the close vicinity of villages all over the State, and threatened to swallow up their habitations. Hardly a year elapsed without the death of men, women, children, and cattle from snake bites. It is probably the only vegetation for which too much rain or water is death and too little a source of luxury and growth. The climatic conditions of the State unfortunately seemed too favorable for it.

This "resumé" of an old man has the quiet but yet familiar tone of an epic tale. In one breath the elderly dewan connects the disorder of the records office with the general unruliness of the very land itself. Sastri's struggle with the prickly-pears and snakes becomes the dominant image of his struggle with a magnitude of disorder that was not simply the result

elephant by his clever mind and by moving others to get the task done. Sastri introduced a new order into Pudukkottai—a holy rationalistic bureaucracy.

In a later letter to the Raja Martanda, Sastri called the righteous raja "the Viceroy of God" as he coaxed the raja to make a donation for repair of a temple near Kumbakonam. Sastri envisioned a clear line of command from God to raja and from raja to the people. His very language reveals the marvelous affinity of such a system of order with that of colonial rule. The queen has her viceroy, and the gods of Pudukkottai have theirs. The analogue between the two allows each their royal status. But this implies that politically the raja of Pudukkottai must admit to deriving his status as ruling chief from the queen, while he also derives his status as a divine viceroy from his Gods. The raja is then free to participate in a dual set of rituals—the British political rituals and the Pudukkottai religious rituals. It is important to note that, by 1938, this is exactly how the system of rituals is described in *Standing Orders of the Pudukkottai Darbar.* The raja's durbar is said to have two forms: "Political" and "Carnatic." The political durbar was British in form and purpose, the Carnatic was used to honor learned Hindu Brahmans at the time of the Dassara festival.

Thus Sastri encouraged and helped to create a kind of separation of civil and religious matters that suited the British fiction of the nature of their own pageants as pragmatic need. This meant that in Pudukkottai the palace could no longer be allowed to function as a ritual center in any profoundly religious sense. At best, the ceremonies of state were civil, and even lower than civil. By the 1920s, the entire palace establishment is described as "more or less domestic in nature" (Venkataram Ayyar 1938, 451). In place of the palace, Sastri encouraged increased use of the Tirugokarnam temple rituals as the focus for the religious side of the Pudukkottai kingship.

Ramachandra Tondaiman became the first of the Tondaimans to take the title "Brihadambadas," Servant of the Goddess. The title was confirmed officially under Sastri's tenure in 1881, after some objections by the British government that it was done merely in imitation of the practice of Travancore—a much larger and "more important" state and one the dewan had just left. The Darbar Office does list use of the title as early as 1869 (Darbar Files, R20/1869), showing that the process of the raja's intense involvement had begun before Sastri's coming, yet the tendency seems to have been fostered by the dewan. This may well be the only instance in which the rani and Sastri agreed. The raja's involvement with the Tirugokarnam temple appears to have been encouraged by the rani. Records show that she and the raja spent much on special ceremonies at Tirugokarnam. The palace women apparently had a tradition of association with the Lady of the temple—the women of the royal family often bore the Goddess's name. In one record, Janaki asked for funds to hold a special worship service there, just as her mother-in-law had done before her. Janaki lived in her own residence very near the Tirugokarnam temple, and the raja often lived with her there rather than in his own palace in the town. The rani may well have prefigured the dewan's own penchant for a temple-minded king, because both came from Tanjore—an important wetland area whose rajas defined and legitimized their rule through temple construction and temple worship.

There is no denying that the Tondaimans had a long and special devotional relationship to the Lady of Tirugokarnam. One of the Tondaiman rajas is credited with composing five beautiful devotional songs to the "Merciful Mother," which are still sung, and another

Tondaiman raja wrote a long poem in praise of the Goddess Parvati.[2] However, neither Janaki Bai nor Sastri fostered the Tondaimans' own genre of ongoing devotional tradition in Pudukkottai. If the Tondaimans loved their Goddess, it was as protector-mother and as "wife." She was their *nayaki,* their guardian lady, but that they were her "viceroy" is another matter. Although a full discussion of the Tondaimans' relationship to the Goddess must wait for another chapter, the fact remains that the founding legends of Pudukkottai do not credit her with the Tondaimans' rise to power. If the Tondaimans were temple-oriented, it was to the Dakshinamurti temple that their first loyalty came. This temple was built within the palace walls. The geography of the royal palace was never oriented toward Tirugokarnam, but rather to this Dakshinamurti temple, built directly in front of the raja's old outdoor seat of state.

The importance of the Tirugokarnam temple during Sastri's years as dewan soon overshadowed the Dakshinamurti temple. Very early records emphasized the importance of the raja's durbar in the palace, his daily rides in the open to show himself to his people, and the Dassara festival—all of which are explored later in detail. By the twentieth century all the major royal rituals were conjoined to the ritual cycle of the Tirugokarnam temple. The royal rides were gone. The Carnatic durbars took place only as part of the Dassara festival. And the king's public religious presence was now seen only as a part of temple processions when he, passively carried in a palanquin, followed the divine image of Brihadambal in her procession throughout the streets of Pudukkottai. But now that His Highness no longer officially rules Pudukkottai, the temple festivals go on without his presence in the procession. He simply receives first honors as the chief donor to the temple.

The relocation of the royal rituals from the palace to the temple did more than provide a new and acceptable sacred space in which the raja could function. Sastri made certain that the house of the Goddess, and the houses of all Pudukkottai divinities, would provide the raja no sanctuary from the process of bureaucratization. In his "Resumé," the dewan emphasized that the general dishonesty and disorder in Pudukkottai was capped by the squandering of the temple funds. "Temples themselves were falling into decay. Owing to running out of funds, the daily worship could not be kept up properly." The problem, in Sastri's usual gloss, appears only economic: More funds will allow full worship. For Sastri, however, keeping up the rituals properly and doing proper rituals were not logically distinct. Recall his careful mention of the proper consecration ceremony with which he installed Sri Aiyanar into a new house and his personal reconsecration of his ancestral temple. As part of this concern for proper ritual, he began to insist on the use of Sanskrit ritual texts as the guide for temple worship. Members of the old families of Tamil scholars protest to this day that at the time of Ramachandra Tondaiman a process began that ended the power and position of the Tamil poets at court and replaced these ancient scholars with Sanskrit-trained Brahman pandits. They charge that while traditionally the raja in durbar honored Tamil scholars and poets with shawls, those special gifts were later given to the Brahmans.

2. The "Pancharatnam," Five Jewels, were composed by Vijaya Raghunatha Raya Tondaiman, 1730–69 (see Radhakrishna Aiyar 1916, 403). The former court musician Tirugokarnam Ramachandra Aiyar continued to play these in Madras. The *Pārvati Parinayamu* (1769–89), by Raya Raghunatha Tondaiman, is the subject of a thesis by R. Lokaiah Naidu of Theagaraja College, Madras.

There are records to support these charges. Old inam grants list that most valuable gift—land—given to a devadasi for the composition of a dance drama and to other poets for their Tamil verse. In late records, the Carnatic durbar during Dassara became a ceremony to award shawls to young priests who had successfully passed their examination in the Sanskrit Agamas and selected Vedic texts. While Sastri did not officially mandate the use of Sanskritic scriptures in the state temples, the Brahman dewan who succeeded him in office moved immediately to establish a Sanskrit college and to hold the examinations during Dassara in his own durbar in order to award "Dasarrah Pandit" prizes. The 1895–96 administrative report contains an appendix in which Dewan Vedanthacharlu described how pandits "displayed wonderful feats in literature . . . and the Sastras." The 1937 *Standing Orders of the Darbar* finally mandated that all priests of the state temples must pass a test in the Agamas—the rulebooks for orthodox ritual practice. Sastri clearly set in motion the cycle whereby the rule of law and order would finally bring the entire Pudukkottai system, religious and political, into full conjunction with his bureaucratic ideal.

The final process of bringing all the unruly in Pudukkottai to the rule of law intimately involved the raja. The dewan's "Instructions," a seeming manifesto for the moral and social cleansing of the palace, was far more if read carefully. The guardian was to be the caretaker in the palace of the raja's "person," his "general health and comfort," and "His Highness's morals." Under section 5—later marked "the most important of all" by the political agent—Sastri listed the rules for "the guarding of His Highness's morals." It was to be the business of the raja's guardian "to see that the personal attendants of His Highness are well-selected, well-behaved men, neither too young nor too old and free from diseases of any kind, such as leprosy, and from all moral taint. . . . They should be always made to wash daily and be perfectly clean and wear clean clothes." Elsewhere in the document, Sastri especially charges the guardian with seeing "that the places and rooms for His Highness's study are clean and well ventilated, . . . as also the places where he bathes and takes his meals are also scrupulously clean. . . . Great attention should be paid to the clothes worn by His Highness—ordinary clothes once worn should not be worn again till washed." The list continues to commit the raja's chairs, sofas, beds, cooking vessels, and of course his "privy" into the cleansing care of the guardian. In one final blow for a truly clean king, the dewan-regent enjoins the guardian to make certain that "His Highness's driving carriages are all kept in perfect order, perfectly clean and no horses are used which are not thoroughly clean and perfectly free from vices." Thus, under the code for isolation of His Highness from all taint, the young king would never have his eyes or ears sullied by so much as an immoral horse.

There is another level to Sastri's moral sanitation of the palace that anyone familiar with the Dharma Śāstras, the Hindu religious codes, might point out. Sastri, true to his good Brahman heritage, was not just cleaning the raja but purifying him. The political agent heartily approved Sastri's rules, likely reading them as a scrupulous form of the Victorian adage that cleanliness was next to godliness. After all, the political agent had expressed deep concern for the raja's health as well as education. But Sastri's rules reveal a traditional Brahman councilor concerned for the very body of his raja. The Laws of Manu declare that a king is formed from the particles of the Gods and therefore "even an infant king must not be despised . . . that he is a mere mortal, for he is a great deity in human form." Following this declaration, the text enunciates rules for the king to maintain his own good name and, also implied, his good body. Compare Sastri's rules, for example, with passages on the proper conduct of a king taken from the Laws of Manu in an English translation published the same year and with the same florid style as Sastri's own injunctions:

> Hunting, gambling, sleeping by day, censoriousness, (excess with) women, drunkenness, (an inordinate love for) dancing, singing, and music, and useless travel are the tenfold set [of vices] springing from love of pleasure. . . .
>
> Drinking, dice, women, and hunting, these four (which have been enumerated) in succession, he must know to be the most pernicious in the set that springs from the love of pleasure. (Manu 8:47–50; Bühler [1886] 1964, 223)

Here again is that double reading of palace reform. Sastri obviously had a mandate for purifying his king that emanated from some far more ancient formula for the ongoing Brahmanic reformation of curiously constant royal vices. This older mandate exceeded the British call for moral reform. Sir A. Sashia Sastri, unlike any British counterpart, had no need to honor the queen's formula for noninterference in native religious affairs. In his "Instructions," he had done nothing more than appeased his right—to take control of the king's body.

Even the political agent seemed to understand that control of the raja's person was of first importance in the "reform" of Pudukkottai. That kind of control had been impossible in Raja Ramachandra's day, but this new raja was virtually a godchild of the British. The third son of the raja's eldest daughter was chosen heir by the right of adoption granted by Her Majesty after the Mutiny. In a beautiful portrait of the young raja (Plate 27), Ravi Varma captured an innocence and sincerity that Sastri and the political agent must have desperately hoped to maintain. However, shortly after Sastri won his battles with the rani for control of the palace and its prince, Mr. Farmer confiscated Sastri's prize. The young raja was removed from Pudukkottai to a bungalow near the British cantonment in Trichinopoly to be educated by an English tutor fresh from Cambridge and to be taught good social graces by the political agent himself. In a letter to his beloved maharaja of Travancore, the aging Sastri confided: "I am most anxious of what the outcome of this kind of education will be, and I am simply watching the results since it is useless to run counter to the Political Agent's opinion" (Collected Letters of A. Sashia Sastri, letter no. 48 dated August 23, 1890). The curiosity of this tug-of-war over the raja is that the political agent also wanted to control not only the mind but also the body of the young raja.

In his yearly reports on the progress of his royal charge, the raja's tutor, Mr. Crossley, mentions again and again the importance the political agent placed on scheduling the raja with "less time to the cultivation of the intellect and more to the body" (Darbar Files, Administration Report for 1888–89). While Martanda Tondaiman was still in the palace, Farmer had noted with concern:

> I am not at all satisfied with the position in which the heir apparent is placed. We have been able to do little if anything for his physical education. His increasing

Plate 27.   Raja Martanda Tondaiman at age 4, by Ravi Varma, dated
December 1879. The young raja's bright face still looks down from
the walls of His Highness's palace in Trichinopoly. Painted in the
same month as the portrait of his grandmother, who considered him
her son, as he was the adopted heir of her husband.

obesity gives grounds for serious apprehension as regards his health. He has a very
considerable intelligence and his progress in Sanskrit is remarkable. If his education
could be conducted elsewhere than Pudukkottai, he may become less of a pandit, but
he would become more of a prince. (Darbar Files, D90/1888, letter dated April 16,
1886)

Evidence of the raja's obesity is clear in a portrait of him as a young teenager (Plate 28), but
weight alone could hardly justify removing him from his ancestral home. The political agent
has thinly disguised his perhaps unconscious equation of royal power with the well-
functioning physical body under the guise of his concern for the raja's health. What was the
danger in a pandit-raja? Surely Farmer knew well the illustrious Brahman dewan's own

Plate 28. Raja Martanda at age 17 as he still appears in the painting by G. S. Van Stzydonck in the keeping of His Highness in Trichinopoly. MacQueen (1926) identifies the retainer as Mohammad Sahib. The royal court retained Muslims especially as royal bodyguards, but in this case the choice of a turbaned Muslim gives the raja a Moghul as well as an all-India air.

Sanskritic learning, but his barbs against Sanskrit and a pandit's life-style never lessened. Even Mr. Crossley picked up the theme in a later report as he recommended that the raja should know the language of his own state at least as well as he knew English: "I would suggest that the half-time given to Sanskrit, a dead language, be apportioned to Tamil" (Darbar Files, Administration Report for 1887–88, "Report on the Education of H.H. the Raja").

By 1890 the attention to body over mind was a daily fact of the raja's routine, which Sastri described in his letter to Travancore: "He nominally goes through a few lessons in English, Sanskrit, and drawing in the hot hours of the day and spends all the morning and all the evening in driving, tennis, golf, shooting, hunting in the jungles, playing chess, playing the banjo and the violin and billiards." Clearly from his portrait as a big game hunter, Crossley much enjoyed his role tutoring the raja as a man of affairs. And certainly Crossley's own public-school training, with its emphasis on sports and manliness, would now come in handy on these new playing fields of royal India. Much later, when he accompanied his shining prince in his ultimate journey to London, Crossley's own flair for style and his unconcealed pride in his own handsome body are apparent in two photographic portraits of

Sastri, one such British civil servant had expressed his delight at the preservation of an independent Pudukkottai, "our staunchest allies at a time when a contingent of Kallar matchlockmen and spearsmen were by no means to be despised" (Collected Letters of A. Sashia Sastri, letter to Sastri dated June 9, 1878). The British respect for the rugged fighters in India now matched their new respect for their own rugged sportsmen at home. Their opposition to the effete ritual-bound orthodox Hindus long had a history in the complex images the British formed of their Indian subjects as their own ideals changed over their two centuries of rule. The British rode a seesaw back and forth between their respect for the fighter and their own will to stop his lawless ways at all cost. Now the British again wanted a brawny prince, and not a quiet little pandit immersed in his dead languages. A robust and wholeheartedly Indian prince was now, perhaps, a satisfying romantic ideal rather than a dangerous fact. His Highness's revered Kallar spearsmen posed no real threat to anyone, including the British. Nevertheless, many British civil servants seemed to need this kind of robust little prince as much as they had needed the allegiance of his spear-wielding ancestors.

What an odd turn of events for the dewan! He had so carefully substituted the rule of law for the reverence of mere personality in Pudukkottai. He had sneered at the rani's emotional pleas to the colonial governor, confident that the British government was "above all things a Constitutional Government." In Pudukkottai he had even turned the ritual framework of the state to the rule of law and order. A clear hierarchy had been created in imitation, he thought, of the British model of power moving from the top to the bottom through a carefully constructed bureaucratic system. His Hindu king now stood in right relationship to both God and queen—he was the viceroy of both. More important, the little prince had been removed from the murky, earthy den of sensuality. The palace was "clean" now. The raja's body was no longer available for those cunning devadasis, and singularly unavailable to the ogling eyes of the public in Pudukkottai. Gone were the daily durbars of old; gone were the ritual drives through the kingdom; gone was the raja sitting in his alcove like some earthy Solomon judging his people face-to-face. But oh, what a cruel blow! The British simply took the dewan's program a thirty-mile step farther and removed the raja altogether from the dewan's own sight. The beloved Martanda was to return from Trichinopoly to Pudukkottai only for necessary ritual occasions. Who saw His Highness now? He rode daily in the cantonment—an ornament for the court of the political agent, or perhaps a jewel for the crown of Victoria.

Within three years after succeeding to ruling power in Pudukkottai, where had Martanda Bhairava Tondaiman been? "I have been to London to see the queen!" he could proudly say as he spoke to cheering crowds in Pudukkottai upon his return. On the podium in the center of the town, his new dewan greeted the returning raja:

> It was a source of great pride and rejoicing to us, as it was to you, that our Sovereign was going to pay respects in person to Her Most Gracious Majesty, the Empress of India. And doubly proud and joyful were we when we heard that you had fulfilled your long cherished object and obtained an honor not obtained by your ancestors but reserved for Your Highness. It was indeed a red letter day in the annals of

Pudukkottai when Your Highness paid your respects in person to Her Majesty the Queen-Empress. (Darbar Files, Administration Report 1898–99)

The raja had beheld the face of the queen. For the people of Pudukkottai, the raja's return was celebrated for the blessings he had brought back to them through—let's use the right term—his great *pilgrimage* to London.

Posing for his official portrait in 1914, H.H. Sri Brihadambadas Raja Sir Martanda Bhairava Tondaiman Bahadur, G.C.I.E., wore the state turban and a gold Benares silk brocade frock coat, but over his broad shoulders, almost hiding the coat beneath, the Oxford blue of his long knight's cape dominates his attire. In his hand is a pair of white gloves (Plate 31). Now the raja of Pudukkottai no longer spent money uselessly on palanquins, jewels for inveigling wives, or extravagant religious ceremonies. Thos. Cook & Son's *Information for Travellers*, and catalogs for fine leather saddles, silver teapots, tennis rackets, steamer trunks, and of course the latest prices for Rolls Royces are still among the artifacts of this gentleman-raja in the old palace record boxes. The political agent's careful training had paid off. But this perfect portrait of colonialism ended ironically. By 1917 neither His Highness's subjects nor the British could relish his presence; the lovelorn prince married an Australian beauty, much to the chagrin of his colonial keepers, who recoiled as he stepped too firmly into their world. This dramatic story of love and exile can be found in *Molly and the Rajah: Race, Romance, and the Raj* (Duyker and Younger, 1991). Martanda's life remains a script waiting for the right director.

The progressive reformation of the Pudukkottai rajas must be seen in all its glorious irony. The earnest Brahman dewan, virtually quoting Sanskrit scripture, carried out the most profound changes in the Pudukkottai ritual process. Pudukkottai became a country of laws and not men, as the raja was turned into the figurehead Political Agent Parker had envisioned as early as 1854. Yet the crowning irony must not be overlooked. When Political Agent Farmer took control of the young Martanda, his attempt to anglicize the raja actually worked on the oldest logic of the Tondaiman family—the ornamented king, shining in jewels, meant power. The "mission civilisatrice," as Ian Copeland calls it, demanded that the native princes conform to the rule of the British sense of propriety and good taste. A dewan like Sastri rightly defined this sense of propriety as the rule of bureaucratic exactness that was considered to bring the kind of order that nourished a moral life. But the supposedly pragmatic need to maintain a ceremonial life for the empire necessitated more than law and order. Live princes were needed to fill out the spectacle. Their anglicization did not take place as a truly British process. The crucial point is that the British anglicized their princes only to re-dress them in new ornamental garb that replicated a most Indian expression of royal rule.

The colonial government had captured the physical presence of the raja of Pudukkottai, but recall that the British had done this many times before. The presence of the nawab of the Arcot was required in Madras long after that lord's military power was gone. Similarly, the raja of Tanjore had been a kept man. In these cases the people of the Carnatic or of Tanjore did not see their ruler as much as the British themselves did when the seeming puppet princes

Plate 31. A popular painting of the raja rendered by Venkatarayalu Raju in 1914. His Highness was at the height of his popularity and success at this point in his life. The king-emperor had just conferred on him the title of Grand Commander of the Indian Empire to coincide with the celebration of his Silver Jubilee. The festivities in Pudukkottai were truly extravagant, with one thousand invited guests, a grand durbar, and a long list of economic and political boons to be granted by His Highness. This portrait also marks the last successful moment of the raja, who by 1916 destroyed his relations both with his British overlords and with his own people by marrying an Australian woman. The once-beloved Martanda died in voluntary exile in Paris fourteen years later. This painting of his last shining moment was reproduced on the memento distributed in Pudukkottai at his death (Plate 1) and hangs in the Pudukkottai palace in Trichinopoly.

were paraded during those "pragmatic" British durbars. Michael Fisher's detailed study of the British part in the imperial coronation of the raja of Awadh in 1819 confirms this practice of the British taking control of the ritual presence of the raja while at the same time subtly denying the people of his kingdom any part, even as an audience—or rather as a viewer-ence—to the proceedings. "The sole involvement of the populace was limited to witnessing this single excursion from the palace complex, itself intended less to display the new Padshah to the people even of the capital—he had not even been made into a Padshah yet—than simply to get to the Dar-gah and back" (Fisher 1985, 262). Thus, the British altered rituals in the native states in multiple ways. Within Pudukkottai, the British and their Brahman dewan decontextualized the royal ceremonials by first removing any substantial power from these rituals and finally by removing the raja himself from what was once a daily round of ceremonials. But in an amazing reversal, the British began to resubstantiate their own round of ceremonials with the living presence of that same raja.

Cohn's thesis that the British adapted traditional Indian court rituals to define, symbolize, legitimize, and "make compelling" the nature of their authority in India is very convincing (1983b). The issue now can turn to the more detailed questions about the exact nature of the rituals the British used as their model and the precise way in which they modified the structure and the functioning of those rituals. In his finely detailed comparisons of the British "ritual idiom" in both dress and ceremony with its Indian counterpart, Bernard Cohn makes use of the theories of F. W. Buckler, a bête noire of the English scholarly community during the 1920s whose work Cohn rediscovered. Buckler had argued the politically sensitive point that "oriental kingship," far from being despotic, functioned on the principle of "organic incorporation." The vassals of the king were made his "servants" through rituals in which the royal gifts of clothing and other articles incorporated them into the very body of the king. Buckler appears to be the first to suggest that the East India Company, in accepting the *khelat* (gift of clothes) from the Moghul emperor, had become part of this "oriental" logic of rule. In accepting Buckler's basic thesis in the context of the work of Ronald Inden on the ancient royal processes of "incorporation," Cohn accedes to the prime importance of the royal body in premodern India. However, he then goes on to argue that this very organic, physical, bodied quality of the ritual was eliminated by the British in their reconstituting of the imperial idiom. Describing the exact nature of the Imperial Assemblage of 1877, Cohn explains:

> By eliminating what had been rituals of incorporation, the British completed the process of redefinition of the relationship between the ruler and the ruled begun in the middle of the eighteenth century. What had been a system of authority based upon the incorporation of subordinates to the person of the emperor now was an expression of linear hierarchic order in which the presentation of a silk banner made the Indian princes the legal subjects of Queen Victoria. (1983a, 191)

In changing the Moghul rituals, the British eliminated the process of organic incorporation and created instead a procedure to sanctify contractual relationships within a carefully articulated hierarchy.

Cohn's model of the British disembodiment of royal authority contrasts with the case I have argued for Pudukkottai on one crucial point. The evidence from this little southern state places *both* the political agent and the Brahman dewan in the same field, battling for possession of one young royal body. The dewan cleaned the raja and emptied him of ultimate ritual power, but nonetheless desired his presence in Pudukkottai for purposes that have their ancestry well before the British period. The political agent also needed the raja's presence organically/physically at his own seat of power. But notice the reversal of Cohn's model that this suggests. The model of Moghul incorporation assumes that the imperial body is *the* body—one that can give real presence to those otherwise naked of power. The political agent's fight for the raja's presence seems to suggest another model of body-building in which the process of incorporation becomes, rather, the king collecting the right stuff inherent in the body of the "vassal" to build his own sacred power. Such a hypothesis now openly states what has been long implied in this narrative—it was the *presence* of the Indian princes "at court" in Trichinopoly, Madras, Delhi, and at last in London that turned the dowdy and faltering British monarch into a real queen.

Both the British political agent and the Brahman dewan operated with more than one definition of kingship. Sastri had his own version of an "orthodox" monarch in mind as he reformed the raja's untidy house, but that model was not free from contradictions. The British civil servants were inconsistent in their own attempts to raise a raja. On the one hand, both the Brahman and the British shared the same penchant for law, precision, definition; on the other hand, each coveted the raja's *presence,* his elegant, silk-clad, bejeweled body. In the intercultural situation of a British lord meeting an Indian prince, the British fascination with the royal body was left unvoiced but for that nagging concern with health and robustness. Notice that Sastri's near usurpation of royal power became most apparent in actions that were extant as "legends" or "reminiscences" and not in the official files so carefully preserved in the Darbar Office. The orthodox Brahman dewan was as keen to manage the royal body that he seemingly emptied of power as was the political agent. Their joint attempts at reformation ended only by producing an even more glittering and lavish lord. Did either really intend to give the voiced codes of bureaucracy precedent over their unvoiced desire to capture a body of power?

In a real sense, the royal body never ceased to remain a holy *thing* in Pudukkottai. For all the talk of morals and laws, the tug-of-war between the rani and Sastri was actually fought on the same terms as the later struggle between Sastri and the political agent: Who was to control the raja's body, who would feed him, who would dress him, who would have him near at hand. His Highness was a very valuable *thing* that the Raj—for all of its purposes and principles, for all of its concern with fiscal restraint—could not do without.

3

The Book's the Thing

The Comparative Study of Religion in the Imperial World

> If I were to indicate by one word the distinguishing feature of the Indian character . . . I should say it was *transcendent* . . . as denoting a mind bent on transcending the limits of empirical knowledge. There are minds perfectly satisfied with empirical knowledge, a knowledge of facts, well ascertained, well classified, and well labelled. . . . Our own age is proud of that kind of knowledge.
>
> —F. Max Müller

Accusations of love of the material over the spiritual have a curious history in nineteenth-century European scholarship on India. The reproach was thrown between the East and the West like a hot potato—whoever had it was wrong. First Abbé Dubois accused the Hindu of this terrible state of mind: "All they care about is to gratify their vanity and their extravagant whims for the moment." Dubois had warned that Europeans might fall prey to this disease of the spirit if they strayed from the path of true revelation. He reminded his readers of those crafty Brahmans who knew the falsity of idolatry but continued in their evil ways to make a quick rupee. In spite of these dubious exceptions, the prime charge of materialism stayed in the Hindu court well through the century, until Friedrich Max Müller tossed it back to the West once again. For Müller, the new scientific empiricism was ultimately centered in the love of the earth: "To us this earth, this life, all that we see, and hear, and touch is certain. Here, we feel is our home, here lies our duties, here our pleasures." Max Müller then introduced the Hindu as the paradigm for one who "sees beyond." "Of nothing he professes greater ignorance than of what to others seems to be the most certain, namely what we see, and hear, and touch; and as to our home, wherever that may be, he knows that certainly it is not here." By the end of the century, Müller had constructed an influential portrait of "India"—a model of spirituality to shame Britain's own smug materialism. Thus, in this zigzag of accusations, to admonish the lavish Hindu of the eighteenth century was, by the end of the nineteenth century, to admire his great otherworldliness.

Thus developed the supreme irony in Britain's long interactions with India. While the Raj became more and more involved in their world of display, scholars in Britain were ready to reject in theory the very world the British had entered in fact. Names like Friedrich Max Müller and James George Frazer are a crucial part of the empire precisely because the modern situation between Britain and her colonial people was presented as a radical dichotomy of cultures whose commonality could be found only in a shared, tribal, dark past revealed by exotic texts or remnants of strange ritual behavior. But there is yet another irony to this story. Just as the British civil servant, once eager to reform the lavish Hindu prince, ended up in his clothes, and just as Dewan Sastri could not reform the body of the king without slipping into his shoes, so too scholars in Britain could not free themselves from the very world of display that dominated the Victorian era. Their story is fully a part of the empire in which scholars, like reforming Brahmans or eager political agents, all shared in a common dilemma: an inability to put terms like "visible," "material," and "ornamental" in the same category as the divine—while they did precisely that in the world of their daily lives.

From the Visible to the Invisible

"Let me therefore explain at once to my friends who may have lived in India for years, as civil servants, or officers, or missionaries, or merchants and who ought to know a great deal more of that country than one who has never set foot on the soil of Aryavarta, that we are speaking of two very different Indias" (Müller [1882] 1934, 7). In the same year that A. Sashia Sastri began his reforms of Pudukkottai, Max Müller delivered the first of his famous "Lectures on the Origin and Growth of Religion as Illustrated by the Religions of India" at Westminster Abbey. The purpose of the series of lectures was to set before the public "really capable and honest treatment of unsettled problems in theology." Speaking from Britain's holiest church, the ancient ritual center for its monarch, Müller declared that the history of religions in India held the key to Europe's present theological problems. Everyone in that audience would have been acutely aware of the great proclamations issued in Delhi in which the British had claimed India for their own. India was now Britain's true "other," that Aryan alter ego lost for centuries to Europe. Clearly implied in the lectures was a novel justification for empire: Britain's conquest of India made a reunion of brothers, a meeting of materialism with spirituality, possible once again.

A few years later, in a preface to his published lectures to the candidates for the Indian Civil Service at Cambridge (*India: What Can It Teach Us?*), Müller declared: "If some of the young candidates . . . make up their minds . . . to show to the world that Englishmen who have been able to achieve by pluck, by perseverance, and by real political genius the material conquest of India, do not mean to leave the laurels of its intellectual conquest entirely to other countries, then I shall indeed rejoice" ([1882] 1934, xi). In this series of lectures to the future officers of the Indian Civil Service, he argued hard to convince his audience that the India before their eyes, the Europeanized India of the cities and of the towns, was not the real India. Into their hands he commended the task of finding that India of yore, that India worth taking, that India that was truly Britain's other self—the spiritual India. To do this, he had to exclude India's new industrial cities, as well as the stalwarts of the past that failed to pass his test of true Indianness. There was no room in Müller's India for either her ancient warrior lords or her modern princes.

By the time Müller delivered those lectures at Cambridge, he believed his audience would be initially hostile to his own loving picture of India drawn from the Vedic texts. He openly defended his right to speak of India "as one who has never set foot on the soil of Aryavarta," in contrast to the many who had lived and worked in India for years. For Müller, because the India of "today" was a transformed Anglo-India of urban merchants and industrialists, he and his "friends" in the Indian Civil Service were "speaking of two very different Indias." "I am thinking" he said, "chiefly of India such as it was a thousand, two thousand, it may be three thousand years ago: they think of India of to-day, . . . the India of Calcutta, Bombay, or Madras. . . . I look to the India of the village community, the true India of the Indians" ([1882] 1934, 7). Thus the borders were fixed: Modern India was not truly Indian; only the hoary past and the pristine present could reveal her. Müller was undaunted, however, in his hope of converting these future Indian civil servants to his own model of a scholar–civil servant. Invoking the revered name of Sir William Jones, Müller dared his young audience to "dream dreams" and once again meet the true India to be found in the study of Sanskrit. Somehow his young friends were to live in the midst of an Anglo-India they were daily creating and at the same time experience that true India in the life of the mind.

A first step in Müller's development of a new science of religion was to silence as utterly "incompetent" the civil servants, such as Mr. Farmer, who had reported the India they saw in front of them. Müller objected strenuously to the kind of writing most had produced. At points in his lectures, he virtually spews fire at many of the standard works of the civil servants. James Mill's famous *History of British India* is a "poison," "mischievous," and "responsible for some of the greatest misfortunes that have happened to India" (Müller [1882] 1934, 39). Mill's problem, it seems, was that "his estimate of the Hindu character is chiefly guided by Dubois, a French missionary, and by Orme and Buchanan, Tennant and Ward, all of them neither very competent nor very unprejudiced judges" (40). Only Colonel Sleeman's *Rambles and Recollections of an Indian Official* (1844), with its glowing picture of the Hindu character drawn from "untouched" villages, meets Müller's approval. Müller considered Sleeman's account "more trustworthy . . . than even so accurate and unprejudiced an observer" as Professor H. H. Wilson, because the latter had the misfortune to live in the heart of the "false" India—Calcutta. In the end, Müller leaves the impression that few civil servants in the unenlightened years of the early nineteenth century knew anything substantive about "India" at all.

For Müller to call Abbé Dubois or Thomas Orme "not very competent" must have been shocking when he first lectured, and it is shocking still. Abbé Dubois hardly confined himself to the British cantonments, and Orme's painstaking collection of the early history of the relationship between the British and their Indian allies is one of the most lively historical collections now housed in the Oriental and India Office Collections of the British Library. Müller's rancor against many in the civil service is directed at those who presented his beloved but never-visited country as a place filled with people who strove for wealth, who lied if necessary, and whose pragmatism in the pursuit of power rivaled that of the British. This certainly is revealed in Orme's firsthand chronicle of the Indians who followed the British into power. Abbé Dubois, also no stranger to practical politics, pictures the idol-loving Hindus as far more concerned with the externals of religion than the inward-seeking Christian. But for Müller's needs, such reports simply would not do. India had to serve other purposes.

Müller's real charge against Dubois or Orme must be seen in the context of his own religious epistemology. The civil servant and the missionary had reported only what they saw or what others had seen in contemporary India. Their image of India was judged a superficial view much opposed to the "inner truth" the "real" Indians loved. Müller gives away much of his own philosophical-religious biases in an aside that marked his transition from India as described in such accounts to the India of Sanskritic literature:

> We are all apt to consider truth to be what is found by others, or believed in by large majorities. That kind of truth is easy to accept. But whoever has once stood alone, surrounded by noisy assertions, . . . knows what a real delight it is to feel in his heart of hearts that this is true—this is *sat*—whatever daily, weekly, or quarterly papers, whatever bishops, archbishops, or popes, may say to the contrary. ([1882] 1934, 59)

The externals of daily living, and the externals of religion, pale equally before that inner light. And now it was Indian scripture that was to serve as a model for such truth-seekers.

Why had Müller reversed the standard civil servants' picture of Indians as amazingly pragmatic people with a ready eye to profit, religious or otherwise? Times had changed in Britain. Müller's own theological position forced him to search beyond a Christian model for "proof" of his views on the nature of religion. English Christians heard voices now that were unwilling to set the outwardly visible against the inwardly true. The High Church movement, still popular in Müller's early days in Oxford, was as concerned with the externals of faith as it was with a pure mind. In his autobiographical sketches and in his major theoretical works, Müller held to his opposition against church-based religion of all sorts. He bemoans his early childhood days in church—a real bore. He opines his inability to convince Hindu religious reformer Keshub Chunder Sen to create in his new Hindu religious organization, the Brahmo Samaj, a sense of worship freed from church, mosque, or temple ([1901] 1976, 17). Chunder Sen had argued in Müller's words that "the Hindu wanted something else, he wanted some outward show" (17). The outward display of the movement at Oxford equally received Müller's sigh of despair. In "wonder and amazement" Müller recorded his impressions of the Oxford men who actually took church service and "questions of candlesticks and genuflections" seriously (167). Of this Müller declared, "God has to be served by very different things, and there is a danger of the formal prevailing over the essential, the danger of idolatry of symbols as realities" (167). For Müller, true religion, be it Christian or Hindu, meant seeing behind surface display.

In India, Müller saw a perfect model for the human religious evolution from the mere externals of religion to that going-beyond the visible to the invisible, to the "Infinite" behind the veil of illusion. In this formula, Müller obliquely assumed what came to be commonly accepted by "both the secularists and Christian idealists on the one hand, and the philosophical idealists on the other . . . that the monism imbodied in Advaita Vedanta constituted the essence of Indian thought" (Inden 1990, 105). India was the other side of ourselves that offered a paradigm for real spiritualism as opposed to mere pragmatism. Müller's intended audience was not churchgoing Christians who had already found their spirituality at the expense of "objective" reason, or the idolatrous Hindus who had not yet reached the higher stages of their own great faith. Müller's search for the "invisible" was a thinking person's—a scientific person's—search. His was a scholar's religious quest. He made a space between retrenched Christianity, on the one hand, and a radical scientism, on the other, and called that space "India." This space was to become a safe haven for those who wanted to live in a worldwide context, who wanted to remain objective in their own eyes and yet who could not, as Müller put it, "part with the childlike faith of their heart."

If the educated and literate city Indian was already too anglicized, who then would speak for the ancient culture? Max Müller's glorification of village India might lead any reader to expect that the likes of a Rani Janaki Bai, or even His Highness Ramachandra Tondaiman, might finally be given a voice in the "real" India. In spite of his idealized picture of the village, Müller did not trust the "common" folk quite enough to seek their aid in a description of this India. What knowledge of religion the common people, even in England, had gave him cause for despair:

> But let us look at the facts, such as they are around and within us, such as they are and as they must always be. Is the religion of Bishop Berkeley or even of Newton, the same as that of a ploughboy? In some points, Yes; in all points, No. . . . Bishop Berkeley would not have declined to worship in the same place with the most obtuse and illiterate of ploughboys, but the ideas which that great philosopher connected with such words as God the Father, God the Son, and God the Holy Ghost were surely as different from those of the ploughboy by his side as two ideas can well be that are expressed by the same words. ([1878] 1964, 366–67)

In his search for a truly authoritative record of religion in India, Müller had no role for the Hindu princes, who were hardly "ploughboys." Müller never allows authority to any but the same kind of pandits that informed Sir William Jones. By a process of elimination, Müller restricted his information on India to text and to Brahmans untouched by the city who could speak for all the mute voices in the village and all the dead voices of the past. Such were the outlines of the faith set by the father of the comparative study of religions.

Max Müller began his study of the religion of India by asserting that Hindus were neither disorderly, nor liars, nor idolators. His lectures to the Indian Civil Service candidates were meant to prove the truthfulness of the Hindus. His *Lectures on the Origin and Growth of Religion* were ultimately devoted to illustrating how the Hindus were the first people to move beyond ritual and, most important, beyond idolatry—the false confusion of the infinite with mere matter. Thus, close to his mind were the ever-present issues of ritual as artifice in a world that now demanded a natural basis for all reality. The raja of Pudukkottai had of course been at the heart of the issue of artifice, and so was the glittering viceroy of India. Müller was doubtless unaware of Pudukkottai, but he was painfully aware of what can now be called the problem of religious materialism.

It is important to realize that Müller began his influential *Lectures on the Origin and Growth of Religion* by giving religion an almost organic base. He claimed that there is in the very nature of the human mind a category of perception devoted to perception of the "Infinite." He argued that no human can be without religion because it is patterned into the very structure of the mind. The idea that religious power resided somewhere within the human body was not new. Thomas Carlyle had already created a modern version of the human body as the temple of God:

> The essence of our being, the mystery in us that calls itself "I,"—ah what words have we for such things?—is a breath of Heaven; the Highest being reveals himself in man. This body, these faculties, this life of ours, is it not all as a vesture for that Unnamed. ([1841] 1904, 13)

But Carlyle's romantic image flirted with the risky theological proposition that flesh was itself divine—an almost idolatrous notion by Victorian standards. Müller moved beyond, and perhaps around, Carlyle by proposing the existence of an innate "faculty" in the mind for the *perception* of the "Infinite." Notice the care Müller took to avoid any confusion of this innate "faculty" with material substance:

> Faculty signifies a mode of action, never a substantial something. Faculties are neither gods nor ghosts, neither powers nor principles. Faculties are inherent in substances, quite as much as forces or powers are. We generally speak of faculties of conscious, of the forces of unconscious substances. Now we know that there is no force without substance, and no substance without force. To speak of gravity, for instance, as a thing by itself, would be sheer mythology. ([1878] 1964, 24)

Here Müller's argument was directed to the work of early anthropologists who concluded that the higher notions of God developed in a phylogenetic scale from fetishism to monotheism. Müller publicly worried about the logic of such a theory and asked: "Can spirits or gods spring from stones? Or, to put it more clearly, can we understand how there could be a transition from the precept of a stone to the concept of a spirit or God?" Here Müller obviously feared the hidden logic in this kind of theory, which could conclude that religion developed from a very natural process by which the human first "saw" God quite literally in the world and only in the world. Müller's formula for the definition of a "faculty" placed religion in the domain of the natural while affirming the traditional orthodoxy of God's independence from the material world. God, in Müller's system, became that "Infinite" which stimulates the "potential energy" of the innate "faculty" to realize Its presence. Such a God is at once divorced from the material world yet empirically evident through a special human faculty that perceives beyond what the simple senses reveal.

Müller's formula for an empirical science of the infinite ended not only the possibility that God could be equated with the material world but also the possibility that the divine was in any sense a product of human creation. God remained neither *made* nor *material*. Yet in Müller's system all was natural. The "function in the conscious self, for apprehending the infinite" ([1878] 1964, 26) was "ontogenetically and phylogenetically" in human beings. Even today's structuralists continue Müller's odd formula for a natural religion. They still assume that no one made religious structures consciously. Structuralists neither equate the divine with material nor dare to allow for fabrication. Ritual simply "wells up" from the patterns of the mind. Myth analysis assumes such a naturalness, as do anthropology's arguments for social structure. Joseph Campbell's long argument in his *Masks of God* (1959, 30–38) that myth has a biological basis reflects Müller's initial approach. As late as 1966 Louis Dumont argued that hierarchy is simply part of the human makeup and will "break out" no matter how much it is suppressed under the ideological formulation of egalitarianism. However, notice again that hierarchy and structure are not in any sense *things*.

Yet in spite of his interesting epistemological-physiological base to religious perception, Müller denies at every turn the concretization of the Infinite in any external object. Quite ironically and yet deliberately, he defines the evolution of religion as a movement from the mistaken perception of the infinite in the physical to the pure concept of the Infinite itself. But Müller argues that the only way this great movement could occur was with this first mistaken sense of the infinite in the tangible:

> We have thus seen, what I wish to show you, a real transition from the visible to the invisible, from the bright beings, the Devas, that could be touched, like rivers, that could be heard, like thunder, that could be seen, like the sun to the Devas or gods that could no longer be touched, or heard, or seen. We have in such words as *deva* or *deus*, the actual vestiges of the steps by which our ancestors proceeded from the world of sense to the world beyond the grasp of the senses. The way was traced out by nature herself; or if nature, too, is but a Deva in disguise, by something greater and higher than nature. That old road led the ancient Aryans, as it leads us still, from the known to the unknown, from nature to nature's God. ([1878] 1964, 214)

Here Müller has covered all his bases. Religion is "natural," yet it is not to be connected to matter in a gross sense. The Infinite is beyond this world, yet it leaves its imprint on the world without ever becoming of the world. The Infinite retains Its own form in some beyond.

Müller was desperately trying to solve the major problem for the emerging field of comparative religion in the mid-nineteenth century. The locus of religion still rested with the theologies that derived from an uneasy confluence of the old church system, the new scholarship, *and* the powerful evangelical movements that used the word of Scripture, but always as the stimulus toward an inner experience of God's power over mere externals. It is odd that the evangelical tradition both shrugged off the institutional externals of the church and yet embraced an experience of God that was far more tangible than any Enlightenment scholar would have accepted in the book of nature or in the Scriptures. In a sense, theology was also stretched between two poles: (1) tradition decreed religion was inscribed onto the surface of holy things and in the holy codes of conduct that marked one as a Christian; and (2) the surface of the church did not matter because only inner, invisible commitment was ultimately true. That commitment, however, was felt to be very tangible, making possible a closer walk with a perhaps invisible but certainly present God. So the problem remained: Does religion rest in the tangible, in the intangible, in the externals, or in the internals? Note that the problem is compounded by the new scholarship that decreed that what is real is organic but that the organic is skin-deep. Hence, if religion is to get its academic due, then religion must also follow the laws of history and be part of the organic nature of the world. But that would make religion a kind of *thing* rather than a kind of sign.

In larger historical terms, then, this is where Max Müller entered the scene with his new comparative study of religion. The evangelical movement, the Oxford Movement, and the plumed viceroy of India may have been moving toward a far more tangible sense of the divine, but none of these groups could meet the standards of a truly academic discipline. To give the study of religion scientific legitimacy, which certainly was Müller's goal, religion had to be forcibly returned to the right scholastic order of things, which had no place for the merely visible and tangible. For Müller's understanding of science emerged from the older humanistic discipline of philosophy, not directly from the study of natural science. Scholarship, as opposed to mere experience or observation, primarily meant disciplined thinking, and Müller could imagine no discipline outside of that scholastic world. Thus Müller created a scientific epistemology in the context of an old textual tradition, which he now expanded—much to his credit—beyond the Bible to his great editing of the fifty volumes of *The Sacred Books of the East* (1879–1894). Müller's bifurcation of knowledge from experience, then, was reminiscent of the Enlightenment program to transfer religion out of the hands of the "unenlightened"—priests with their rituals, and the churchgoing, genuflecting, even Jesus-seeing, Christians—and into the hands of the scholars, where it could be safely deposited as a new authoritative discipline that would permit, without embarrassment, a noble return to faith.

The faith Müller now defined was suitable for a world far larger than Europe. He hoped his program of study would invite all the enlightened of the world:

> When that time of harvest has come, when the deepest foundations of all the religions of the world have been laid free and restored, who knows but that those very foundations may serve once more, like the catacombs, or like the crypts beneath our old cathedrals, as a place of refuge for those who, to whatever creed they may belong,

long for something better, purer, older, and truer than what they can find in the statutable sacrifices, services, and sermons of the days in which their lot on earth has been cast; some who have learned to put away childish things call them genealogies, legends, miracles or oracles, but who cannot part with the childlike faith of their heart. ([1878] 1964, 377)

Müller's science of religion was a faith fit for an enlightened empire, and the empire did not fail to notice. Müller was much honored at Buckingham Palace.

Müller's new scholarly approach to India also became an important part of a movement within the Indian Civil Service that took descriptions of the "true" India as a formula for righteous rule. Perhaps Müller's passionate pleas to those young candidates for the service directly effected the change. Beginning in the 1890s, the Orientalist movement began. Ian Copeland describes the movement as a "retreat from reform" (1982, 182) because its precepts attracted those who no longer assumed India could be ruled by British principles. The policies of reform in the Native States, the Orientalists argued, had created rulers who had lost touch with the people. The British Raj had likewise grown too remote from the village level of Indian life. As Copeland puts it, "Within the I.C.S. [Indian Civil Service] there was a strong feeling that the Raj had grown too cumbersome and hidebound, too remote from the mass of the 'real' people and yet too susceptible to the wiles of clever lawyer-politicians in the towns" (187).

Here are Müller's same whipping boys—those city folk, both Hindu and British, who had ruined the real India. But, like Müller, the Orientalist Indian Civil Service officers did not presume to ask these real folk to describe themselves. Rather, the movement turned, again like Müller, to what Francis Hutchins describes as an "India of imagination" (1967, 157). This "India" was created on the assumption that an impartial and well-trained Englishman could know India far better than any Indian. The Orientalist civil servant's position was that the British alone could save India from its own modernist reformers. Note how closely Francis Hutchins's description of the Orientalist administrator's position parallels Müller's formula to find the "real" India, but with the native princes added to Müller's native pandits:

> Englishmen constructed a myth of their own omniscience, and a further myth which presumed to describe the "real India." Conceived as a guide for adapting British government to Indian needs, it served to convince many Englishmen that they were serving Indian interests and successfully winning Indian appreciation. This "real India" consisted of the ancient India of the countryside, and of the retainers and dependents of British power, of princes, peasants, minority groups. Indians who lived in cities, engaged in business and the professions . . . were designated "unrepresentative." (156)

If the Orientalists in the civil service saw their duty to preserve this real India, Müller believed his duty was to reconstruct what was lost. But for both, the "real" Indians had to be preserved and remade if necessary. Shades of this new Orientalism are apparent in Martanda

Tondaiman's Cambridge tutor, and in the political agent as well. Both wanted to create a really Indian king. Sastri, as a Brahman, also had his own Orientalist formula for reconstructing a "real" king in Pudukkottai. Like Sastri or the political agent, Müller never adjured the right of British imperial rule over India. His language retained the militancy of an imperial age. Müller called for the "intellectual conquest" of India and clearly assumed that the great white man's burden was now to re-create the foundations of a truer India in the face of that shadow world than Indians themselves had allowed their civilization to become.

Thus, Max Müller and the new Orientalist movement within the Indian Civil Service effectively muffled the voices of those inside and outside the Raj who might have asked whether India had any claim to a love of time, of history, and of the world itself. Müller glorified the Brahman seeker of the world-beyond, while the Civil Service promoted the need for a true oriental rule. Neither ever really asked the "natives" their opinions. Yet our main story of the dewan, the political agent, and the Hindu prince suggests that the actual rise of the Orientalists within the Indian Civil Service complicated, and disrupted, a far more intense process of orientalization that had long held the British in its grip. The new Orientalism gave Dewan Sastri's conscious formulas, drawn from Sanskrit scriptures, the last word. Thus, the drive toward a renewed orientalization of British rule, documented by historians of British imperialism such as Copeland and Hutchins, was only one kind of an orientalizing process the British had undergone. The characteristic of the period after 1890 was the open defense of the proposition that India should be, and could only be, ruled by truly Indian principles. However, the British had already ruled India by Indian principles long before. This earlier kind of orientalization continued to be evident in daily records, actions, and attitudes—the kind of data Müller forbade for his new scientific study of religion.

By 1890, however, the comparative study of religion had many new voices from the growing field of anthropology. Unwilling to submit to the authority of text alone, anthropologists insisted on using records of observations of religious behavior. Soon after the publication of *The Golden Bough* (1890), James Frazer emerged as a dominant voice in the study of religion. He shifted interest from ancient texts and otherworldly pandits to sacred kings. For a moment it looked as if scholars might poke into the dark corners of princely India and find traces there of Britain's own "natural" affinity for monarchy. Frazer did not find the origins of religion in an innate human affinity for the Infinite, but rather in an innate human lust for control of the material world. At the root of religion was magic, with its passion for power over matter, over time, and even over God. Britain shared this aboriginal materialism with the civilized and "uncivilized" people of her empire. There were no mystical havens from the mad human lust for pomp and power.

A Dark Shadow on a Fair Prospect

At this height of the British Empire in 1890, James Frazer introduced a startling scenario of kingship into an otherwise confident and seemingly well-ordered age. The central image that begins and ends the first edition of *The Golden Bough*, "a masterful example of Victorian purple prose" (J. Z. Smith 1978, 213), is the scene of a wild-eyed priest-king peering into the night to await the fatal blow from an attacker who would then succeed him, as he had succeeded the man he once murdered, as King of the Wood and the priest of the Goddess Diana. The first edition of *The Golden Bough* invited the comparative study of religion to step into darkness just at the moment that the sunshine prose of Max Müller seemed to have convinced his now-faithful followers that the dawn of a truly new imperial day was at hand.

Frazer appeared to be conscious of the distinction between his own theories and those of the then-celebrated Müller. In spite of Müller's status as a scholar at this time (Kitagawa and Strong 1985, 183–84), his name never passed through Frazer's pen—a tell-tale sign of the powerful latent presence of Müller in Frazer's work. In his original preface, Frazer began as if his study were to be an inquiry into "the primitive religion of the Aryans"—he was, after all, investigating a Roman practice. Nothing in his early mention of Aryans, however, prevented Frazer from citing evidence from such ethnically diverse groups as the Japanese and the Mexicans, who even in Victorian England would have required a firm push to be moved into the Aryan fold. This immediate reference to Aryans appeared as a thinly veiled critique of Müller's reliance on classical texts as a source for study of the origins of religion:

> Compared with the evidence afforded by living tradition, the testimony of ancient books on the subject of early religion is worth very little. . . . The mass of people who do not read books remain unaffected by the mental revolution wrought by literature; and so it has come about that in Europe at the present day the superstitious beliefs and practices which have been handed down by word of mouth are generally of a far more archaic type than the religion depicted in the most ancient literature of the Aryan race. (Frazer [1890] 1981, x–xi)

Within the first two pages of *The Golden Bough*, then, Frazer had planted a distrust of literacy, of pure rationality, in the intellectual heart of the empire—Cambridge, where just a decade earlier Max Müller had dared young civil servants to dream dreams of a new intellectual "conquest" of India. Frazer now forcefully introduced the intellectual British public to the importance of the unspoken and the unwritten in daily action. At first glance, it looked like the rajas and ranis of Pudukkottai might finally be given a voice in British scholarship.

The extent to which Frazer consciously intended his long "essay" (xiii) to contradict Müller is a point for future research, but the differences in the two general theories remain striking. For Frazer, the most potent source for understanding religion was the peasant—Max Müller's horrid ploughboy—whose "inmost beliefs" operated often in spite of any rational overlay. "Indeed the primitive Aryan, in all that regards his mental fibre and texture, is not extinct. He is amongst us today. . . . In his inmost beliefs he is what his forefathers were in the days when forest trees still grew and squirrels played on the ground where Rome and London now stand" (x). Between later civilized philosophy and early religion there was a gap—*something* continued to operate in spite of, not because of, literacy and rationalized thought. The same something had continued into the highly polished world of Rome and, as Frazer bluntly stated, was yet to be found in modern imperial Britain. The real history of religions was not Müller's pretty picture of a long road, with its innocent false turns into the trap of misunderstood language, that yet found its way to the threshold of the Infinite, but was, as Frazer later put it, a "melancholy record of human error and folly" (in Gaster [1959] 1964, 738).

Frazer's long descriptions of this hidden religion of the peasant threw cold water on Müller's elegant defense of religion as ultimately the unselfish pursuit of transcendental spirituality. Frazer openly followed Edmund Tylor's view that earliest forms of "religion" derived from the basic human desire to control the material world by manipulating the seeming impersonal power that gave it life. Humankind never let go of that will. When humans could not imagine themselves controlling the universe, they imagined a God who could. The piety of priests could disguise but never contain the wanton human will to control. In his most shocking blow to the scientism of his time, Sir James asserted that the very science of the modern world, the new rationality of his time, was a definitive return to these most primitive desires:

> Hence, when at a late date the distinction between religion and superstition has emerged, we find that sacrifice and prayer are the resource of the pious and enlightened portion of the community, while magic is the refuge of the superstitious and ignorant. But when, still later, the conception of the elemental forces as personal agents is giving way to the recognition of natural law, then magic . . . reappears from the obscurity and discredit into which it had fallen, and by investigating the causal sequences in nature, directly prepares the way for science. ([1890] 1981, 32)

Frazer, like Müller, portrayed the modern world as enmeshed in the love of the material. But by this new earthiness, modern humans had ironically returned to their most primitive roots. The folk in England and the less-civilized subjects of the empire practiced a "magic" that the polished society of England had refined into science. Yet this polishing had not removed any of the taint the old archaic system carried with it. Materialism had sinister ancestors.

It would not have taken a Sherlock Holmes to observe that the new scene of this ancient "crime" was no longer in the grove of Nemi but in England. The question of the true locus of an ever-resurgent barbarity at the heart of some great imperial civilization would not have needed a second guess in a society that for the last half-century had erected public buildings in the image of imperial Rome and made the grand tour of the ancient world de rigueur for even the middle class. The faraway *Theys* of the empire, the distant peoples of time and place, were now *Us* in a most shocking sense. Here, then, in the very last days of Victoria's reign, came the voicing of the suspicion that Britain was linked to its empire and beyond by some deeply shared experience of a primordial "crime." At points in his essay, Frazer insinuates that the more scientific Britain becomes, the finer grows the line that separates the vast complex of London from the wooded land and the barbarous people that was its foundation. Why Frazer was moved to introduce such an image into the heyday of the empire remains an important issue with as yet only a few suggested answers. But the image emerged in spite of its seeming incongruity with the age. Once the scene of a cover-up, of unvoiced motives, of hidden secrets, of murder, entered the repertoire of imperial self-images, the empire could not be seen in the same light in the twentieth century as it was in the nineteenth.

By 1900 Frazer ended his revised work with a more direct indication that the major issue of *The Golden Bough* pointed very close to home—to the relationship between science and religion. Between the disclosure of the true identity of the "Golden Bough" and his "fare-well" to Nemi, Frazer inserted a brief essay on the interrelationship of magic, religion, and science that must have shocked many of his readers. With the full flourish of his elegant prose, Frazer cast science, magic, and religion into the same gloomy portrait of the human condition. In spite of the vast hopes of science and magic alike to control the universe,

> a dark shadow lies athwart the far end of this fair prospect. For however vast the increase of knowledge and of power which the future may have in store for man, he can scarcely hope to stay the sweep of those great forces which seem to be making silently but restlessly for the destruction of all this starry universe in which our earth swims as a speck or mote. (in Gaster [1959] 1964, 740)

But where a reader might expect some comforting words about the ultimate ability of science to meet this challenge, Frazer introduced a jarring conclusion to his long-drawn picture of the human desire to control this seeming solid world of matter:

> Yet the philosopher who trembles at the idea of such distant catastrophes may con-sole himself by reflecting that these gloomy apprehensions, like the earth and the sun themselves, are only parts of that unsubstantial world which thought has conjured up out of the void, and that the phantoms which the subtle enchantress has evoked to-day she may ban to-morrow. They too, like so much that to the common eye seems solid, may melt into the air, into thin air. (in Gaster [1959] 1964, 741)

Not only is old Lady Magic a phantom hope of humanity, but young Science with its empirical, clear-sighted construction of the nature of this universe, has his eyes as clouded now as his mother did at the beginning of human history.

But Science and Magic were not the only victims of Frazer's own subtle murder-by-intellect. Like some God imparting the breath of life to his creation, Frazer built the holy body of the sacral king and then drew the very life out of his creation at the end of his labors. Throughout *The Golden Bough*, Frazer made it ever so clear that divine power was for the primitive and folk people alike a real and present fact within the physical world—a "super-natural energy which, like energy in general" followed laws of transformation and not the laws of morality ([1890] 1981, 242). This power could be transferred by contact with the king, evoked through royal rituals, or regenerated when the dead king's body was buried in the earth. Before Frazer, Tylor had already explained this kind of material divinity as a "confusion" of the primitive mind, but his descriptions were clear. For the primitive, divinity was an odd kind of physical power. At one point Frazer described the power of this kind of energy by arguing that the danger inherent in the power of kings "is no less real because it is imaginary; imagination acts upon man as really as does gravitation, and may kill him as certainly as a dose of prussic acid" (171). Yet in spite of such a defense of the literal power of his phantom, Frazer insisted at the end of his work that his sacred king was but a strutting, fretting wisp of thin air.

In the second edition of *The Golden Bough,* Frazer claimed to be part of a new movement to exorcise the superstition out of modern life by broaching "these venerable walls, mantled over with the ivy and mosses and wild flowers of a thousand tender and sacred associations" (in Gaster [1959] 1964, xxvi). He broke down the sacred walls by showing that all the patterns and motifs so integral to the institution of kingship and so tied to Western political and theological beliefs were only holdovers from an "outworn" system. It is clear that Frazer chose to describe a system of kingship so parallel to the "tender" associations of God and country that it could not be ignored. And yet something more than a confusion of the natural with the supernatural lingered still in Frazer's poetically drawn portraits of kings—kings put to death so the earth could live, kings bearing the "sins" of their people, or kings hedged and guarded by rigid ceremony lest the very life drain out of the community. With his deeply moving narrative of the "king," poised between life and death, the pomp of ceremony and the nakedness of expulsion, between sin and glory, Frazer moved this study beyond a bold revolutionary call to behead this king of the ancien régime and to execute with him all the mistaken hope pinned on both magic and science. The ancient king, scourged and humiliated before his ritual death, could not but conjure up those deep-seated biblical images of the Suffering Servant of Isaiah and the naked Jesus of Nazareth nailed to the cross with the ironic words above his head "This is the King of the Jews." Was Frazer really ready to take up the hammer and drive the nails into such a king? Sir James had clearly become, like Max Müller, a preacher as well as a teacher. But was he preaching for or against the holy text of Britain's ultimate king?

The power and insistent presence of biblical imagery in *The Golden Bough* needs no complex exegesis to be revealed, but ascertaining the purpose of that imagery—theological, anthropological, and personal—is difficult. When posed for Frazer personally, this question requires the kind of detailed study Robert Ackerman has long pursued for the illusive Sir James. A thorough analysis of the place of all biblical imagery within the structure of Frazer's opus should be set aside for a separate study. But Frazer's very particular biblical imagery that linked kingship to a primordial "sin" and "murder" cannot be consigned here to footnotes. Problems of life, death, and the will to power are so biblical and yet must have been tantalizingly suggestive to an imperial age proud of its accomplishment of world dominion both scientific and political. The coming of life and then death amid a seeming paradise begins the biblical narrative. And the Garden of Eden made the perfect backdrop against which Frazer could begin to reveal his "melancholy" tale of human folly as he sat amid the glory of the British Empire.

The first paragraphs that open Frazer's tragic tale—a tale meant to teach rather than inform—indeed seem to be "a product of Frazer's imagination" (Smith 1978, 219). Now, as it was then, the "fairest natural landscape," the woodland lake of Nemi, rests in sweet "slumber" and "stillness"—a place where the Goddess Diana might yet walk among "these woodlands wild." Yet here in this place of sweet repose was enacted "a strange and recurring tragedy." In the middle of the sacred grove that formed part of the sanctuary of Diana, "there grew a certain tree." With sword in hand, a mighty warrior guarded that tree lest any come there to slay him and take that power. This was the scene from which Frazer was to build his tale of *The Golden Bough*.

The resemblances of persons and places in Nemi to that other tale of human tragedy in the Garden of Eden already appeared more than coincidental. Here was the protected grove of trees, with that one very special tree jealously guarded by a powerful male. Immediately Frazer added the very necessary female character. Enter stage left, the "Goddess" Diana. Frazer gradually filled in details of her character, supposedly gathered from classical texts. Diana's cult image—Frazer later argued that such icons were thought to embody the living presence of divinity—had been brought there by Orestes and his sister Electra as they fled to Italy. This pair of matricides (Frazer assumed his audience knew this detail) had taken the image forcibly by killing its previous keeper, the king of an even fiercer people who had regularly offered human sacrifices to Diana. This Diana, now more tamed, satisfied her old blood lust in witnessing the ritual death of her priest at the time of his fall from power. The impetus for this orgy of death was the desire to "pluck" a branch, the golden bough, from this sacred tree. Yet this same Diana, Frazer quickly pointed out, was worshiped as a fertility goddess. Like Eve, Diana offered to a hapless male a fertile power at the risk of death.

Diana, like Eve, was supplied with a male companion—a mortal man whom she had convinced Aesculapius to raise from the dead and whom she now hid in her sanctuary as a forest king called Virbius. Aesculapius paid a heavy price for his ministrations. Frazer did not fail to include that "Jupiter, indignant that a mortal man should return from the gates of death, thrust down the meddling leech himself to Hades." Diana's man does not die, as did Adam, but someone certainly does pay the price of death for her passion. Thus the story at Nemi became the tale of a chain of death brought on at the behest of a woman's little passions for a tractable but greedy male.

Diana instigates the action in this play for mortal stakes, but the actors in the tale of Nemi, as in Eden, are men seeking something worth risking death. The Goddess's priest-kings risked their own death, again like Adam, to "pluck" that golden branch. (It is interesting that Frazer never used "break off" or "cut off," which would seem more appropriate for a "bough.") This great tree with its clinging vine, however, could not have been that first tempting Tree of the Knowledge of Good and Evil. The actual data of *The Golden Bough*, sandwiched between this imaginative beginning and Frazer's brief return to Nemi at the very end of his tale, become Frazer's long unraveling of the mystery of the identity of that "Golden Bough." Frazer ended his first edition with the supposed solution for the "crime." A murder was necessary to ensure a young and vigorous new guardian for the "Golden Bough"—finally identified by Frazer as the shining mistletoe that hung on the great oak as a repository of the effervescent power of the sun, of fire, of ultimate power for the Aryan people. This guardian was both the keeper and the embodiment of that power, "an incarnation of the supreme Aryan god, whose like was in the mistletoe or Golden Bough" ([1890] 1981, 370). Thus, like the Tree of Life guarded in Eden by an angel with a fiery sword, it offered not divine wisdom but divine life. It is this tree with its promise of eternal life that humankind, untempered by holy writ or the hopelessness of a real return to Eden, has nonetheless tried to pluck throughout history. Humanity could not resist the temptation to write its own sequel to the pious biblical version of the primordial drama in the Garden of Eden. Frazer told that melancholy tale in *The Golden Bough*.

Frazer continued to revise and enlarge *The Golden Bough* well into the twentieth century, and his solution to the mystery of the golden bough continued to expand. Jonathan Smith has suggested that Frazer gradually defined his tale as the hapless human search for immortality and for the ultimate control of nature. Frazer's early mention of the resurrection of Virbius, and also of Aeneas's own round-trip journey to the world of the dead, built the implied goal of deathlessness into the frame of the tale. Frazer's final revelation that the golden bough was none other than oak laden with English mistletoe brought the case for humankind's eternal yet fruitless search for immortality—the ultimate victory over the forces of nature—close to home.

In the biblical context evoked by Frazer, the power over death served only as a generalized definition of God's power in relationship to his creatures. In Genesis, God alone had the ultimate power to make his own world and set that world in motion for his once passive creatures. For Frazer, the real human "sin" and "folly" was humans' daring to create their own being or their own world. This interpretation is strongly suggested in Frazer's later, melancholy insertions into the end of *The Golden Bough*. What humanity has created with its magic and its science is but a phantom universe of imagination. Yet this universe, as Frazer also admitted, remains "real" for the unknowing beings who center their lives in their universe fabricated from "that ever-shifting phantasmagoria of thought." In a quick turn to Platonic imagery, Frazer defined this human world as "registering the shadows on the screen" (in Gaster [1959] 1964, 740). In the end, the "matter" of the world and the matter of humanity's own frail bodies is not ours to control, much less to make. Perhaps that is why Frazer's ultimate human "hero"-king, the one deluded into grasping for that "bough," was condemned like Adam to return to that low station, to death, and to the earth from which he had been involuntarily created.

This is the ultimate irony in *The Golden Bough*. Sir James Frazer, either deliberately or quite unconsciously, used the only standards for a critique of false religion that he could muster: the sin of the primordial garden and the shadow world of Plato. Thus "God" was never really exorcised from the human mind in *The Golden Bough*. A very ancient God found in Frazer a new Aesculapius to give Him life in the midst of a scientific and imperial age. This God said no forever to any human endeavors to remake the world in their own image. Thus Frazer opened the door to religious materialism and then quickly encased the contents in biblical injunctions and Platonic ideals. Like the Right Honorable Friedrich Max Müller, Sir James Frazer began with religion in the category of the visible, the sentient, but could not end with it there. Like Müller, Frazer denied the link between material and spiritual and ultimately condemned the "magic" of kings, their pomp and their ritual, as mere vanity. This kind of vanity in the Victorian world was a synonym for idolatry.

An Icon for a New Age

To allow Max Müller and James Frazer, the most celebrated scholars of the comparative study of religion in their century, to be defined by their theories alone would be equivalent to analyzing the Dewan Sastri as nothing but a good bureaucrat, or cataloging the many British civil servants in the Native States as simply good pragmacrats. These scholars were far from untouched by the world of display that they labeled as vanity at best and idolatry at worst.

But Müller and Frazer were not iconoclasts in all matters. Like Dewan Sastri, they exorcised one form of sacredness to replace it with a form that was far more palatable to an "enlightened" empire. Beyond the theories of the Müllers and Frazers of the empire was a style of thinking, no more than this, a style of self-definition, that reveled in the discovery of books and in the making of books. It could be argued that the interests of scholars were no less material than those of the British seated with the raja. However, it was not gold braid or silk jackets or jeweled elephants that they used to ornament their own and the British public self—it was the printed word. Describing his initial efforts to discover the real Sir James, Robert Ackerman presents another portrait, appropriately written and not painted, for our contemplation: "The wall of books bound in dark green just seemed to grow and grow and as it did it blocked any view of the little man behind them, working away tirelessly at his desk" (1987, 20). The only dominant portrait Müller created for himself is his monumental edition of the Rig-Veda. Putting the title page in Sanskrit, he "translates" his name as *Mokṣa-mūla-rabhatta*, "one grasping for the origins of spiritual liberation." Oxford became *Gotīrtha*, literally the "ford of the ox" but figuratively "the place of liberation." The issue is what sort of liberation Müller has in mind. He, like Frazer, liberated the past from those who had owned it. India's history belonged to the empire. The holiest source of its lengthy spiritual quest was liberated from priestly control and freely printed for all to read. It was now safely bound in a book.

Müller's publication of the Rig-Veda was a major trophy in Britain's ultimate conquest of India. His was the first edition and the first printing of this priestly collection of hymns. This new German Gutenberg provided many Indians quite literally with their first sight of this text. But Müller did more than this. Until this time, there really was no single Rig-Veda text, but rather a number of manuscripts in the hereditary keeping of certain priestly families. For many Vedic priests, the manuscripts themselves were really superfluous, because the Veda had been passed on by rote memory from a time measured in millennia. Müller actually turned a sacred collection of hymns that had been used orally as part of ritual into a book, a book published not in Benares or even in Calcutta but at Oxford. Later, when Müller threatened to take a chair of Sanskrit at Vienna and publish his new project, editing the various volumes of the Sacred Books of the East, outside Britain, there was an uproar in the highest circles of government. During the debate to offer him a comparative professorship at Oxford, many spoke of his importance as a scholar, but none failed to miss the fact that "the results of his labours so important to the Rulers of India should be published in England and in the English tongue" (Papers of Friedrich Max Müller, Dep d. 172, newspaper clipping). At the time of this debate, the Prince of Wales was journeying to India, taking with him copies of Müller's edition of the Veda as suitable gifts for the important personages he would visit. Müller had made his books of sacred scripture things of considerable national importance.

After Müller died, his wife took charge of his memory by editing his papers and sorting the material pieces of his life (Georgiana Müller, 1902). In addition to publishing many of his letters and essays, she produced for herself and the family a hand-decorated album of photographs called "Our Life." Her face is pasted inside the letter "O," and that of her beloved in the letter "L." This album of photographs presents the contrast, the alternate universe, to the ceremonial world that both Anglo-Indians and the rajas shared. Georgiana Müller's album of "photographs" contained no pictures of her late husband except that small face in the large "L" and a final photo of his gravestone, inscribed with the German epithet "Wei Gott Will." In between there is a series of postcards of unidentified places with dates and even times carefully noted under each. Many of the dates are clearly key moments in her long and poignant struggle to secure her father's permission to marry the young poorly paid German émigré (see Chaudhuri 1974, 145–76). The absence of Müller's face, however, remains significant. Georgiana preserved his words and published his letters and essays, but left no material image of him. That remained a memory for her alone. Gradually, in spite of the gossip about his vanity, Max Müller's face and form have largely disappeared from our box of memories. We have his books.

Robert Ackerman, in his new biography of Frazer, has reproduced a series of photographs from a family album. Finally we catch a glimpse of the man behind the wall of books. But the Frazer the camera sees never looks directly into the lens. His eyes, even as a child, dart to the left or right, looking at some world beyond his own eyes. Ironically, the only time Frazer stares at the camera is when he is blind. Yet Ackerman argues cogently that Frazer was not bookish in the usual sense. He had a "keen visual sense" (1987, 97) and was very concerned about the look of his publications. A gifted writer, Frazer painted graphic scenes of violence and struggles for his Victorian audiences, but he painted in words. Ultimately, he made books.

The raja and the British civil servants left us their images, and the scholars left us their books. There is a radical difference and yet a subtle similarity in these two traces of the long-dead. After Müller's publication of the Rig-Veda, the set of hymns from the great sacrificial rituals became food for thought. Young, educated Indians and Europeans alike began to search this book for clues of the origins and essence of Hindu culture. The hymns were to be read, not chanted, revered no longer for the numinous power of their sacred words but for the potency of their philosophy. Likewise, Frazer made ritual something to think about, not something to do. No one who read Frazer actually took up maypole dancing, but instead learned to analyze such familiar customs along with the more exotic rituals of the distant place or the distant past. All this greatly subjugated concrete ritual activity to abstract analysis. But again, like scholars today, neither Müller nor Frazer was rewarded for his abstract thought. Their books made their careers.

This is not a simple case of the power of ritual versus the power of abstract thought. True, Müller and Frazer distilled ritual into word, but then the portraits of Ramachandra Tondaiman stilled ritual into visual form. It would be a mistake to assume that the differences between the scholarly world and the world of court ceremonial were a simple matter of things versus thoughts, or doing versus thinking. As long as the books of Müller and Frazer are used as handbooks for analysis, this is a case of the rational world making sense out of a nonrational behavior. But paintings are a concrete thing, not behavior. And books are not thoughts; they too are also things. No one really reads Sir James George Frazer's multivolume study of kings as a text, but the green binding with the mistletoe motif and the striking engraving of the kings of Nemi by Turner on the frontispiece still make these a valuable set of books—lovely things. The great first edition of Max Müller's text of the holiest of Hindu scriptures, the Rig-Veda, published for the first time triumphantly at Oxford in 1848, still remains a useful text but also has life as a collector's item, great and valuable for its words but also for itself. Müller's Sacred Books of the East have now been reprinted in India with all lettering on the cover in gold foil, a set to be read but also to be displayed. It is odd that when the thoughts of these great scholars became obsolete only their books remain as things carefully kept in libraries acting as attics for now-unfashionable ideas or as beautiful items on a collector's shelf.

What we have left today of this world is the ascendancy of the verbal image and written word over the power of the visual image. For the rajas of Pudukkottai, and equally for the ceremonial-minded British civil servant, the concrete product of their ceremonials was the portrait that captured the splendor of the event at the moment when all characters were present and in their places. In postmodern terms, this was their "writing" of the event. This kind of inscription today has been exiled to the grocery-store magazine racks, where cover photos of Prince Charles and Princess Diana still attest to the power of the royal image. Now, in homes of the "educated" upper middle class, bound volumes of the world's great books in fine leather replaced etchings of the queen and other exotic princes as emblems of aristocratic tastes. At the height of the empire, gold-foiled book and gold-framed etching would have occupied the same parlors.

In the Year 1899, the Triumph of Ornament

In the last year of the nineteenth century, the governor of Madras posed with the elegant young Raja Martanda Bhairava Tondaiman for a formal portrait at the British residency in Pudukkottai (Plate 32). The governor was to lay a foundation stone for the town hall to be built in commemoration of His Highness's formal reception at Windsor Castle. At first glance, the portrait contrasts sharply with the opening image of Raja Ramachandra Tondaiman in durbar. Gone are the raja of Pudukkottai's plumes and necklaces; of the traditional Moghul court dress, only his turban remains. The members of His Highness's Dignitary Establishment, now dressed in livery that imitates the viceroy's own house staff, are barely visible behind large brick pillars. They, along with the old ministers of the Pudukkottai state, are introduced into this scene like women in old miniature paintings—they can be spotted only at second glance scattered in the shadows of the large portico of the Residency. Directly behind His Highness, and the governor—where the Dignitary Establishment should stand—are the raja's brothers and the governor's own personal staff, and Mr. F. F. Crossley. These Indians and British stand in near perfect symmetry: British, then Indian, then British, wearing uniforms very similar in style—ornate mandarin-collared jackets belted at the waist, worn over plain, straight-legged pants. One young British officer, wearing a brassard of mourning, nonetheless leans dashingly on his sword while his companion officer proudly holds his topee as if it were a badge of honor. The photographer has carefully

Plate 32.   Photograph of His Excellency Sir A. Havelock, Governor of Madras, taken in 1899 at the front door of the Residency. Seated on the governor's left is Raja Martanda Tondaiman. Behind the raja is the unmistakable face of his former tutor, Mr. F. F. Crossley. (The photograph is in the collection of Sri K. Sathiamurti Rao of Pudukkottai, who kindly made it available to me.)

directed the eye of his viewer, however, to the central image of this scene: His Excellency Sir A. Havelock. With the governor so sharply in focus, the viewer is invited to look closely at his face and the jewels, metals, ribbons, and gold gilt on his breast and plumes in his hat. Like the old-time props in a modern photographic studio, the governor now looks out from the hole once occupied by the face of that spendthrift, hopelessly lavish oriental lord.

And in the same last months of the nineteenth century, the Right Honourable Friedrich Max Müller, now a member of the Queen's Privy Council, lived his last days. Now as revered among young reformers in India as in Britain, especially in his later years, Max Müller carried on a lively correspondence with many Hindus who had read his books both in English and in the new translations in India's regional languages. Nirad Chaudhuri, in his biography of Müller, remembers hearing of Müller as a child in "the backwaters of East Bengal" (1974, 5). And indeed, the letters that are preserved at Oxford came to Müller from the larger cities and more remote towns of India. All these extant letters address Müller as a pandit, and some clearly expect him to play the role of a guru, teacher, in its full Indian sense. "I consider you as one of my spiritual guides and as such I expect from you some valuable teachings for my salvation if you have the time and convenience to do so" (Papers of Friedrich Max Müller, "Indian Letters of Interest," Dep d 173, dated February 1, 1900). A zamindar (princely landowner) of Bengal actually sent Müller a shawl to honor him as a pandit in the same way he had honored the Brahman learned men at the death rituals of his father. Müller accepted the honor in a long reply that he signed with his Sanskrit name, Mokshamularabhatta.

The most telling of these "Indian Letters of Interest" has been printed in part by Nirad Chaudhuri (1974, 4) and Müller's wife (1902, 2). It relates that, on hearing of his illness, three of his devoted readers in Madras had gone to the Sri Parthasarathy Temple to ask the priest there to perform a puja for Müller's recovery. The priest refused, on the grounds that Müller was not a Hindu, but "then we discussed with him the subject at length, and told him that Prof. Max Müller is a European by birth . . . but he is more than a Hindu." When those arguments failed, the offer of a handsome fee changed this priest's mind. The three Müller devotees then enclosed bits of the Prasadam, the blessed offering, in their packet to Müller with the instructions "You take it (I mean devour it) in the name of God." Professor Friedrich Max Müller, no longer bereft of the Prasadam in his hands or a shawl over his shoulders, died in 1900. In the eyes of many Hindus, he had become the holy pandit that his words created. Like the plumed governor of Madras or Her Majesty the Queen-Empress, India dressed Max Müller in the ornaments appropriate to the image he had created for himself. Georgiana Müller may have wished her husband an eternal life of the mind, but in India pandits who have drunk godly knowledge must also eat divine food and wear the outward signs of their mindful devotion.

4

The Disenchantment of the Raj

The Unresolved Conflict Between Precept and Practice

"But he has nothing on!" said the whole people at length. That touched the Emperor, for it seemed to him that they were right; but he thought within himself, "I must go through with the procession." And the chamberlains held on tighter than ever, and carried the train which did not exist at all.
—Hans Christian Andersen

Brahman bureaucrats, political agents, Oxford and Cambridge scholars, and loyal maharajas alike kept the imperial procession going through the late nineteenth century. An image of this unlikely confluence of cultures is still extant in the streets of Madras when deities ornamented like maharajas emerge from their temples during festivals, preceded by a band dressed in English-style uniforms (Plate 33) blowing trumpets and beating drums, closely followed by the dhoti-clad players of the clarinet, marching drum, and saxophone, later followed by the traditional players of the Nadhaswaram. A painting recently refurbished in the outer court walls of the Tirugokarnam temple in Pudukkottai depicts the same scene, with the Goddesses going in procession guarded by the sepoys in unmistakable nineteenth-century British uniforms (Plate 34). Nadhaswaram and trumpet, turban and topee, they all paraded together without really knowing who called the tune.

But that is the issue here. There is a sharing of parade, procession, and ornamentation between British political agent and Brahman dewan, between scholar and governor, but there is also a sharing of disquiet over what it all meant. Certainly the reader may not yet allow that, with his passionate pleas for the spiritual over the material, Max Müller belongs

Plate 33. Preceding the deity during a procession at the Kapaleeswara temple in Madras, these dhoti-clad players of European instruments still wear British-style caps. Behind them and not yet in the camera's sight, the temple staff carry an image of Lord Shiva bedecked like a Moghul prince. But like his bandsmen, the divine lord wears a dhoti beneath his velvet coat and jeweled turban. The Lord Shiva's palanquin is guarded by Madras policemen, whose uniforms have changed little since the last days of the British Raj. The photograph was taken during the Tye Pusham festival.

in the parade with the organizers of the 1877 Delhi Durbar. Is it enough to implicate Müller and Frazer in the construction of colonialism simply because the one had worn the emblems of the queen's Privy Council and the other the robes of a knight? Are they implicated, moreover, into the creation of the culture of ornamentation merely because their books became objects of devotion in both Britain and India? Does a Brahman like the great Sashia Sastri, with his own staunch support of the Hindu temple and maintenance of the Pudukkottai royal court, share the same road with Müller, who considered daily temple rituals a modern detour from India's ancient route to spirituality? And what can be said of Rani Janaki Bai and His Highness Ramachandra Tondaiman? This royal family shared the same space and time as those who insisted on reformation of the palace while tapping its ancient power.

The issue is tricky. I am not arguing that the succession of political agents to Pudukkottai, the reforming Brahman dewan, or the early British scholars of comparative religion shared a carefully articulated program to undo Pudukkottai at the same time that they usurped the power of its courtly ritual. Rather, I have argued that they shared a common *iconic* culture. The term "iconic" has been used loosely to this point to mean a culture deeply involved with decorative things rather than with decorous thoughts. I could also say that all these members of the empire shared a developing global "public culture," involved with the exchange of "commodities" (Richards 1990) rather than of overt ideas.[1] But I also want to emphasize that

1. The new journal *Public Culture: Bulletin of the Center for Transnational Cultural Studies,* explores global flows and exchanges of what would once have been called popular culture. But in the twentieth century, as in the nineteenth, such culture is far too important and powerful to label "popular."

Plate 34.   A renovated painting in the entrance hall of the Tirugokarnam temple in Pudukkottai. The painting depicts the Goddess Brihadambal as she would have appeared traveling in procession during the Dassara festival. The women painted in miniature at her sides are likely the devadasis, once an important part of the staff of this state temple. The only life-size image is the sepoy guard in early nineteenth-century British garb.

an iconic culture is indeed a *religious* culture because it cannot be separated from the central fact that when the raja sat in durbar he sat there as a "God." Certainly the definition of this sense of "God" is by no means simple or obvious and remains an important question. Yet any who came to occupy the raja's seat occupied a divine space in some important sense. There is far more in the choice of the term "iconic," which will unfold in the latter part of this study. At this point, it is enough to admit that while this unlikely group of "imperialists"—Brahman civil servant, political agent, governor, scholar—shared a common but unrecognized cultural space, they also shared a common confusion about what might be called the *theo-logic* of the royal rituals they had joined and yet disowned in places like Pudukkottai.

I introduce the term *theo-logic* rather than *theology* as a means of describing the ways South Indians in places like Pudukkottai—and the British who joined them—*realized* how divinity relates to matter, to life, and to humankind. I do not imply by the use of this term that this ceremonial lacked written texts. By the end of the nineteenth century, reams of paper tied with the inevitable faded red tape committed much of the ceremonial system to the typed page. There were orders of precedent and careful instructions printed for all major ceremonials of Pudukkottai and of the Raj. The system even developed its pandits: officers expert in protocol and procedures in the Political Department of Her Majesty's Government of India, and officers of the Pudukkottai palace whose major duty was to know and rule on ceremonial matters. But all the writing and the doing neither began nor culminated in theological texts, unless we are willing to classify *The Standing Orders of the Darbar* as a *śāstra,* a Hindu religious code. There were rules and procedures, but no treatises that openly named such activities as ritual or attempted to define its complex meanings. This fluent ritual system came to embody all the divinity that doth hedge a king but always remained a rose by another name.

But what is the relationship, if any, between the theo-logics of the political ceremonials and the traditional theological-philosophical systems of South India? A good Brahman pandit in Pudukkottai would have every right to argue that the Tondaimans settled Brahmans in many of their own villages early in their rule and made individual land grants to learned Brahmans well into the nineteenth century, to support the traditional class of priests and pandits (see Dirks 1987, 429–43). He might ask why the ancient keepers of such a vast Sanskrit theology did not provide a theology for this court. The answer lies in part in the very nature of the literal and figurative position of Pudukkottai on the borders of orthodox India (see Chapter 7) and in the history of the Tondaimans' patronage of religious institutions, learned pandits, and revered gurus (Chapters 6 and 8). But at this point the reader needs to know that the Tondaimans' patronage of learned Brahmans, or at least their pretension to such patronage, appears to have dwindled by the middle of the nineteenth century, in favor of promoting active and highly public state rituals and highlighting the grandeur of their own durbar in conjunction with the ceremonials of the Raj. Thus, the coming of the imperial British served to reenforce what I will argue was the indigenous position of the Pudukkottai rajas as hinterland kings vis-à-vis orthodox theology.

Radhakrishna Aiyar's *General History of the Pudukkottai State* gives special emphasis to the early Tondaimans' active support of Vedic learning, as might be expected of a Brahman principle of the H.H. the Maharaja's College, an extension of the British educational system into Pudukkottai. He tells us that Vijaya Raghunatha Raya Tondaiman (1730–69), whom we shall meet again, took spiritual instruction, led the life of a *sannyāsi* for a period, and remained intensely interested in Advaita Vedanta (Radhakrishna Aiyar 1916, 181). He documents the Tondaimans' liberal donations to temples, to poets, and to learned Brahmans to support Vedic instruction in the eighteenth and early nineteenth centuries (327–30). Such largess earned Raja Vijaya Raghunatha Tondaiman (1789–1807) fame as the Bhoja Raja, the Bountiful King. But after enumerating all these charities, Radhakrishna Aiyar notes that the brahmadeya villages (exclusively Brahman villages) did have the added advantage of getting motivated owners to clear new agricultural land and adds, "The Raja had, even in performing charities, an eye to business" (330). The Tondaimans never lost that eye.

Many of the land grants in the Inam Settlement Registry seem to confirm this picture of the early Tondaiman involvement with what Burton Stein and others have come to call "moral order" (Stein 1975, 86–87). During the medieval period, South Indian kings nodded to the authority of the Brahmans to constitute that "moral order" by establishing connections with Brahmanic learning through support of individual scholars and whole villages of Brahmans. However, as Stein proposes, the influence of such an articulated moral order never paralleled the power of the Roman church during the same period in Europe, especially in the hinterland states, where "the mass of rural folk and rustic Brahmans could not, in any case, be controlled in the manner of parish priest of medieval Europe" (87). Further, in Pudukkottai, the Brahmans were crucial to the state, not because of their pure minds but because of their purifying bodies. So although there are links to orthodox learning to support Radhakrishna Aiyar's image of the early Tondaimans as Bhoja Rajas, there is little evidence that the Brahmans supported were theologians in the manner of the great Vedic and Agamic scholars of the temple cities of Tanjore or Kanchipuram (Davis 1991; Mumme 1992; Narayanan 1987), or that the Tondaimans used their Brahmans as theologians at all. And the fragile link between the Tondaimans and orthodox theology, never very certain, snapped in the nineteenth century. Although there is growing evidence that the separation of articulated theology from ritual action was unnatural for many communities in South India (Davis 1991), such a separation did occur in Pudukkottai in the development of its court rituals. As Raja Ramachandra began to emphasize the temple as the zone to display his piety as the Goddess's servant, the palace rituals displayed him as a "God." Had paramount power remained in the old Chola royal families of Tanjore through the nineteenth century, little kings like the rajas of Pudukkottai might have imitated their liege lords and grandly patronized temple complexes as centers of theology as well as arenas of display.[2] The temple and not the durbar would then be at the center of this study. But in the new imperial world of the British, power—political and religious—was not written into texts but into durbars, processions, and programs for entertaining the British governor. The new Bhoja Rajas of the nineteenth century, who wanted to keep an eye to business, knew that the kind of Brahmans important to their rule were more likely to recite a manual of administration than to recite the holy Vedas.

Moreover, and more important, the very fact that *theological* space was left empty in the courts of Pudukkottai and other Native States actually made room for the functioning of a common British-Indian ceremonial in the nineteenth century. Because the power system in a place like Pudukkottai continued to function primarily in the mode of making/doing and not analyzing/believing, the British could learn to do what they might fear to understand. The ritual system of the royal court, the grand durbar, was a ritual that functioned in the realm of dress and ornamentation—in other words, of *artifice* and *fabrication*. Even for the nineteenth-century educated Brahman such a space need not be overtly acknowledged as holy—holiness came to be confined to the orthodox temple or to the Vedic text. The Indian durbar was certainly the last place British Victorians would have looked for "religion," although such exotica was the very thing that had attracted the British to India and had elicited their most blatant imitation. While only a few in Britain openly adopted the tenets of

---

2. On the relationship of temple patronage to kingly sovereignty, see Dirks 1987 (285–304). By the late nineteenth century, the state temple became the site of royal rituals and displays of royal power, but was never developed as a center of theology.

Buddhism or Hinduism, many homes were filled with traces of this royal world: brocade cloth, ivory boxes, "quaint" paintings of dancing girls, and photographs of maharajas in gilded frames. This was a theo-logical system the British could hold in their hands, put on their heads, or wear on their bodies, while British scholars safely searched the most ancient Vedas to discover what the essentials of religion in India might be.

The fact that the elements of the "political ceremonial" remained unrecognized as religious in England as well as in India allowed it to function for the overt Christian or Hindu, idealist or pragmatist, who shared its space. Theo-logics could coalesce in the nineteenth century, where theologies clashed. A quick review of the last three chapters will illustrate the complexity of the many overlays of overt rationales and functioning *theo-logics* that operated under the raja's sacred canopy. Never has there been such a case of concocting apples and bananas, or cummerbunds and kings.

The members of the Political Department, for all of their ornamentation and parade, continued to work as if the ultimate power of the Raj remained invisible. Major Blackburne clearly placed his power behind and apart from the pomp of the Pudukkottai court. He posed for his portrait not inside but just outside the durbar room. But even when later political agents and governors put on the fancy dress of lords, they look as if they are wearing costumes. Lord Havelock and Sir Mountstuart Duff are not wearing something they own; they are wearing uniforms as surely as are their staff. Uniforms are only signs, indexes of status in relationship to something else. This is best expressed by Lord Lytton, who thought of ornamentation as nothing but "bunting" worn only to command authority. Such authority always belonged to someone else, to a faraway queen and finally to "Divine Providence," who was evoked when there was no one else at the end of the finger to point away from oneself as the source of power. At one level, signs/uniforms were not an integral part of their beingness, but rather simply decoration to be put on and taken off at will.

By this kind of logic, if there is not enough money to afford fancy uniforms and jewels, economy would demand that a raja set aside such frills for the moment. Clearly this was not a message Raja Ramachandra could hear. In fact, the more the British nibbled away at his "secular" power, the more he spent on jewels, clothes, and lavish rituals. He seemed to cling to his ornaments for dear life. The British are assuming that all he need do is take off some of these excesses. They are also saying he could simply remove some signs and put on others. But that was not so easy for this lord. These clothes were not easy to pull off, and their removal implied more than a temporary embarrassment over finances. Ornamentation here is not a uniform, not a costume. It is something else.

There are indications, however, that as the British moved into the heyday of their imperial power they too began to take their own "uniforms" more seriously. Bernard Cohn suggests that the British consciously manufactured rituals as a means of expressing their natural superiority. Cohn's most recent work on clothing as cultural expression contains a very significant section on the relationship between the British form of dress and the overt physiological theories they used to explain it. Dress became a means of separating the ruler from the ruled, because the British body, it seemed, could not be clothed as the Indian body. The two were not created equal in the capacity to sweat, to retain heat, and to fight the cold. Thus Cohn explains that the growing scientism of the late nineteenth century began to demand a material explanation for all facts of life in the empire, including the old issues of the nature of British rule over the Indian people. This intense interest in bodies is clear in political agent Farmer and in Martanda Tondaiman's tutor, Mr. Crossley, who under the guise of concern for the young raja's health exhibited a keen interest in building his body. For them a prince was not a pandit or a principle but a robust lord. The uniform had now to cover a truly superior body. However, Cohn's thesis still suggests that even when clothing was related to the body by using medical language, the clothing itself remained an outward sign of an inner physiological superiority that could be seen in the outward signs of a robust body, a keen countenance, and suitable clothing (Cohn 1983a).

No "political" issue lives without an ontological/theo-logical shadow, especially in cases where the definition and control of power is at stake. The rituals the British contrived both at home and in India were rituals that literally clothed the empire with sanctity. They dressed and redressed their subjects and themselves. And if Cohn is right, they began to invest those very clothes with the ultimate legitimacy—clothing mirrored a state of nature. But notice that these rituals simply expressed for them the right order of things, "natural" superiority. The young Martanda's body must be made to show its natural superiority as a prince in the same way that the British body must also be groomed to bring out its preeminence. Even as the British political agents began to give bodies their due, they never allowed that clothing might actually make the man. They insisted that such grooming and such grand garments were only an expression of an order that had been ordained by Nature and by Nature's God.

Dewan Sashia Sastri, educated in a government high school in Kumbakonam, a longtime veteran of the British Civil Service, and later a Knight of the Empire, paralleled but did not duplicate the British in his own "theo-logic." This Brahman's obsession with cleanliness exceeded the British concern with hygiene but remained curiously within the realm of body talk. Not only his mind but also the young raja's body had to be protected from "vice." Recall that in his instructions to the guardian in the palace Sastri made no distinction between a clean room and a "clean" companion for the raja, or horses free from vice. Where the term "vice" is applied to a horse, ethics is not at issue. Coupled with his fear of the dancing girls, Sastri's dictum against horses with vice could only mean that the young raja should not be exposed to overt displays of sexuality—which horses, like the birds and the bees and dancing girls, are apt to openly display. A "pure" king clearly had to be guarded against his sexual appetites, against (over)using his body as an instrument of passion. But what would such a concern have to do with the good dewan's penchant for bureaucracy, his love of law, and his concern for economy?

The differences between a king controlled by vice and a king controlling his domain may well be the difference between the raja as the dispenser of law and a raja as a power in himself. Sastri as dewan-regent illustrated his definition of kingship by his own actions. The good king makes law and ensures perfect order. He controls beasts as he controls himself. He sets even the Gods in their proper place, the way Sastri got Lord Aiyanar out from under a tree and into a proper house. Here Sastri's concern for order and law does parallel the British, but for some very Indian reasons. In order to transform Martanda Tondaiman into such a king, Sastri had to empty him of vice and of passion in a far more organic sense than the moral-minded British would have imagined. There are clues in the very language of

Sastri's dictums for the royal reformation, which leaves a strong impression that this Brahman knew that "vice" in Pudukkottai went beyond morals and into the very heart of royal power. Yet like the British, his desire to remain near to such rajas and to live as part of their world leaves the impression that Sastri was attracted to the very things he labored to reform.

For all their affirmations of science, for all their great expansion of bureaucracy, for all their faith in rationality, and for all their love of morality, a significant *some* of the Victorians *some* of the time lived neck-deep in a "gilded age" of their own making in the empire. I say "neck-deep" because the British and their Indian cohorts did manage to keep their heads above these old "oriental" waters by redefining many of their cherished principles to permit them to participate in what appears to the naked eye as a thoroughly magical (reenchanted, as Max Weber would later express it) world. Their interest in the royal body became a concern for "health," a crusade for morality, or a matter of economics. They cherished proper form and structure, but they all were nourished by some power in the raja that, I contend, operated in spite of—or perhaps at the heart of—their own conglomerate world of peacocks and principles.

James Frazer and Max Müller were far from naive about this new "materialism" of their day. The scientism of the late nineteenth century had made the British conscious of bodies. The new empiricism of modern science meant using the eyes to examine the material world. This was the period when libraries gave way to dissecting rooms and microscopes. Moreover, this was the gilded age of capitalism, when consumer culture took hold among the new middle classes. Recall that both Frazer and Müller began their work with the common anthropological assumption that early religion belonged to the world of *materia* and not to *legere,* to matter not law. Furthermore, both linked the new nineteenth-century materialism to this ancient *religious* past that Britain shared unknowingly with its subject peoples. In a very real sense, both Frazer and Müller came very close to a description of a *religious* materialism.

However, when faced with two major dilemmas—the first theological and the second metaphysical—both Müller and Frazer backed away from any clear affirmation of such a materialism. Theologically, neither could assent to what Frazer called magic and what Müller termed idolatry: the notion that divine power could be "made" or controlled by humans. God, or as Müller put it, the Infinite, had to exist as a stable entity. Metaphysically, Frazer's sketch of divine kings, and Müller's depiction of the early earthbound Hindu devas, placed this divinity on the line between imagination and reality, between perception and conception, between mind and matter. Frazer argued again and again that the kind of magic he described must be understood as intensely "real" for its adherents. Müller never denied that the early Aryans did "see" their Gods in the world around them. Neither man was a nineteenth-century nominalist or rationalist in the eighteenth-century fashion. Yet neither could abandon the notion of a fixed yet "invisible" God with any more ease than the imperial civil servants were able to abjure the permanence of the imperial system. However, both came close to describing a world in which there existed a kind of *thing* that was neither purely imaginary nor purely real. They were indeed among the theological radicals of their day. Müller lost his bid to be named Boden Professor of Sanskrit at Oxford in 1860 after a "long and nasty" struggle because of his suspect theology (Gombrich 1978, 9), and Frazer raised more than a few ecclesiastical eyebrows in his time. But these imperial scholars could not quite resist the urge to bring their rich descriptions within the bounds of the grand theories that made India and the empire conform to theological and metaphysical axioms that ultimately ensured them an honored place among the knights and notables of the empire.

Closely allied to the scholarly rejection of materialism was the hidden factor of British and Brahman morality. Recall that, for Sastri, vice was an organic-ethical category. The same can also be said for both the British scholar and civil servant, but with a considerable twist. The British were very worried about the lavishness of the raja. They connected this tendency toward lavishness with licentiousness and general moral weakness. Here was another link in a chain that led to moral and theological destruction—idolatry itself. The early nineteenth century had already made the link between vanity and idolatry. The very popular *Essay on the Evils of Popular Ignorance* (1821) by John Foster declared, much like Abbé Dubois, that once the notion of one God was denied, human vanity ran rampant:

> This ignorance could not annihilate the principle of religion in the spirit of man, but in removing the awful repression of the idea of one exclusive sovereign Divinity, it left that spirit to form its religion in its own manner. . . . Depraved and insane invention took this direction with ardour. . . . The promiscuous numberless crowd of almost all shapes of fancy and of matter became . . . mounted into gods. They were alternately the toys and the tyrants of their miserable creators. (38–39)

Thus, at the root of immorality was vanity, which was rooted in the ultimate vanity—the assumption of the power of God by mortals. In this sense, all oriental splendor, all lavishness of the native Indian court, could be viewed as a sign of a deeper problem: an unwillingness to acknowledge the supreme power of the supreme lord. It is easy to see how the concept could apply as well to a native raja's unwillingness to acknowledge the queen as true author of his power, or God as his ultimate creator. A lavish lord tended toward "immorality," as Mr. Parker accused Raja Ramachandra, in spending on his "own gratification" and not on his people. Of course we have already seen that as soon as Dewan Sastri made it appear that the raja was spending both for the sake of his people and for the sake of the Raj, then all was well—the idolatry of self-ornamentation was over.

So behind the problem of ornamentation is a series of interlocking theological and metaphysical and moral issues that the British themselves understood as a unit. Vanity = instability = impermanence = invention = promiscuity = idolatry = vanity. Perhaps the pomp of the empire could be separated from vanity only if it signified some higher principle, only if it stood as a sign for a greater good, a higher purpose and the like.

But the days of imperial glory waned in India. The Tondaimans in Pudukkottai managed to outlast the theological and moral dilemmas of the Raj. Scholarship also moved beyond Müller and Frazer. The time for deconstruction of the empire now gives way to a reconstruction of issues of the discussed "divine kingship" as now posed in the twentieth century and as lived in Pudukkottai after the heyday of the empire. Such a process does not look between and behind the British toward the true India, but yet assumes that Pudukkottai was heir to more than nineteenth-century Anglo-Indian culture. Is there more to the "bunting," the clothes, the bodybuilding than spectacle for political expediency in the days of the Raj? What was so much at stake in the urgent telegrams, the endless reports, the fevered preparations for a durbar? What was here in practice that could not be expressed in words? And, most important, what was shielded under the royal umbrella that may well have engendered one of the first subsets of modern global culture?

Beyond the Age of Imperialism

With the empire in India long dismantled and the many effects of imperialism the subject of much recent study, Frazer's and Müller's portraits of deity in India might now be stated without the no-no of biblical and Platonic languages. Frazer did introduce a sense of kingship in which the royal body, and the divinity it held, underwent transformations in and out of bodies in a constant "tragic" flow between life and death. His arguments that the human world and its divinity is constructed from imagination empty of physical matter and yet "real" and visible in the world might leave a modern poststructuralist quite happy if Frazer could have resisted the temptation to judge his own description with a classical mind. The same might be said for Max Müller. Without his insistence on a "mistake" in language, the same types of divinity in India might yet be placed in that important space between word and flesh, between matter and spirit, between mind and body. The full story of the raja of Pudukkottai and his unconscious British heirs now demands a second look at the study of sacral kingship—another foray into the recent scholarship for outlines of those elusive "other" systems of theo-logic with their own rules about life in a body and the life of a divine body.

In the early pages of *The Golden Bough*, Frazer stopped his narrative to answer "in the negative" the suggestion that the king-priest of Nemi may have been some king of an urban center who had been stripped of political power and left merely to rule in the nearby wood. Frazer made it perfectly clear that he had set out to describe an ancient covert system of royal rule, not the later overt system. Frazer insisted that the evidence "hardly allows us to suppose that he had ever been a king in the common sense of the term" ([1890] 1981, 52). Such common-sense kings, the reader must suppose, were interested in establishing the rule of law and order, of overt political stability. The kingdom of Frazer's woodland lord was not of the written and the rational world.

When the study of sacral kingship so long buried was resurrected in very recent times as a *historical* entity in India, Frazer's suggestion of a dual form of kingship reemerged in the work of A. M. Hocart. Hocart proposed the existence of two archaic kings: a "law-king" of propriety and order (also called the sky-king) and a "second king" (the earth-king) responsible for war, the crops, and the enforcement, by violence if necessary, of tribal custom. The second king ruled no dominion but was called to duty at times of special need. The law-king was "passive" and permanent, the earth-king was "active" and yet unsettled (Hocart [1936]

1970, 163–79). This second king reflected much of the structure of Frazer's own dark lord of magic, a lord involved in carnal violence and uncertain power. Speaking in a very Frazerian/Freudian voice, Hocart described the demise of that second king whose active and yet unworldly nature went underground as history moved forward. This earth-king, Hocart guessed, reemerged in the spiritualized unworldly kingships of later religious reform movements—his references to the scorned Jesus and the wandering Buddha were obvious. "Thus an everyday institution, a petty sovereign entrusted with the regulation of tribal custom, perishes in the flesh only to be reborn in the mind as a universal ideal, a spiritual monarchy overflowing all national boundaries. The Man becomes an Idea" (173). Hocart assumed the transmutation of flesh to idea occurred early in the course of history. In a footnote, however, at the end of his major work, Hocart added that historically "the fate of the earth-king is obscure":

> It has certainly varied in different countries. Where sky and light and their impersonators, the first kings, have become identified with goodness, the earth and darkness with wickedness, it would seem that no one has aspired to be appointed devil. . . . Indian evidence, on the other hand, suggests he may be the Brahman, who has been transferred to the higher side of society, the side of light and life. A great deal of comparative work is required to settle this point. (292 n.)

Although Hocart felt unable to pinpoint the fate of the earth-king in India, he did outline the importance of "the people of the earth" who, like their king, had been assigned the role of the evil opposition in the sacrificial rites, the forces of "darkness" who fought the "light." Once merely honored players in this game of holy exchange of goods that "made" life, the people of the earth were later shuffled to the bottom of a static social system. They rule over the dichotomies of fertility and infertility, health and disease, life and death. Hocart had left significant room in India for Frazer's discredited underground followers of "magic."

Although much of Hocart's general theory was ignored or rejected (see Dumont and Pocock 1958), his hypothesis that a bipolar structure was inherent in the metalogic of Indian culture became the core axiom in the influential works of George Dumézil and Louis Dumont during the 1960s. Dumont spoke of purity and impurity, and Dumézil spoke of "force and sovereignty vs. fecundity." Dumont argued that India's caste structure was generated in the space between two ends of the dichotomy between being light and pure, dark and impure. Dumont admitted that impurity had strong physical content—close to the immediate sense of something "dirty." Dumont described the castes at the bottom of the system as enmeshed in matter and the material, while the upper castes were light, ethereal, and spiritual rather than fleshy bodies. Dumont argued that the orthodox Indian system did not grant this latter physical plane of existence a place in the realm of the sacred. Yet he did not deny the power of physical force and of material wealth to control human action. Even Dumézil, when he wrote of "fecundity," recognized this "third function" as closely connected to the dark, fertile, and hence powerful soil. Although the upper end of this bipolar system, then, has been characterized as ethereal, the lower end was seen as somehow physical, with overtones of Frazer's own description of dark yet fertile "magic." So ironically at the very heart of the theory of *structural* polarity, Frazer's old sense of a materialized power was at work.[3]

Dumont admitted that the system of purity versus impurity cannot fully explain the social organization on several points. Dumont pointed out that ranking the meat-eating king above the vegetarian merchant is illogical in terms of ritual purity. Dumont explained this anomaly as the system's accommodation of the facts of political life—the necessity to acknowledge and incorporate political power within the total system. The other series of illogical placements within the hierarchy, Dumont explains only in passing: the odd position of the untouchable sorceress in South India whose normally polluting saliva in fact purifies the Kshatriya, and the open acknowledgment of the kings as Shudras, lower castes, in the south. To both sets of "problems," Dumont answered that such anomalies are examples of how other groups always seem to enter the orthodox system at the level of untouchables or kings. Why such alternately high and low positions should be open to outsiders was never fully explained by Dumont. The reader is left only with hints that there may be another system or other systems integrated into orthodoxy at the king and untouchable level (Dumont [1966] 1970, 184–95).

Amid the mounds of Vedic texts and the pages of ethnographic observations is the remnant of a quite different religious system in India, much like that described by Frazer as intimately connected to both kingship and lowness. George Dumézil came close to making just such a hypothesis possible. In an interesting corrective to Hocart, Dumézil described "tripartite kingship" in a lesser-known work, *Servius et la fortune,* and in his better-known work, *The Destiny of a King.* Hocart hypothesized the existence of two types of king, each representative of the two aspects of order—law and force. Dumézil, then, offered a third type of kingship, connected to the third function: fecundity. As soon as Dumézil postulated the third king, he immediately freed the nature of kingship from the simple dualism of light versus dark as in Hocart. By doing this, Dumézil may well have described a kind of kingship unbounded by an ever-present division of good and evil, order and disorder, force and passivity.

In the mid-1970s, new versions of the existence of a subjugated, forgotten, or simply unnoticed form of popular religion began to emerge in modern Indology. The figure of the unruly earth-king was no longer central to these theories. A new group of scholars who specialize in South India pinpointed the sacrifice as providing the meta-logic that had made a cover-up of older, perhaps non-Aryan, systems possible. The old rift between Frazer and Max Müller over the importance of ploughboy versus bishop, peasant versus Brahman, was no longer considered the right way to frame the question of how text and practice have been linked in India. There are no either-ors, but rather, as Alf Hiltebeitel put it, a movement "towards a coherent study of Hinduism"—a description essentially undivided between popular and orthodox, between Brahman and peasant, and between ancient past and the living present. However, as soon as sacrificial rituals were seriously studied as the central link between popular and orthodox Hinduism, the figure of the outsider-king once again

---

3. See Marglin's discussion (1977, 265) of the problem of power and the organic in Dumont. See also Wadley's treatment (1975) of the complex meaning of Shakti.

appeared to be implicated in the violence and disorder that were soon discovered at the very heart of South India's paradigmatic ritual.

Madeleine Biardeau argued that popular religion "echoes" or "perfectly reflects" the system of Bhakti organized during the Epic and Puranic periods in classical literature. She adheres to the text and context theory, arguing at points that popular memory sometimes forgets the very origins of its rites (1981, 238). Within her methodological framework, Biardeau explains how the demonic/village/low caste has been integrated into the Sanskritic tradition. Beginning at the village level, she highlights the anomaly of the "good" demon—a royal yet evil figure who becomes a devotee of the major deity either after a glorious defeat by the deity or after the reformation of his own character. She argues that this transformation derives from the highly developed logic of Bhakti. In the late Vedic texts, the sacrificer was also seen as the victim transformed by death. In medieval times, defeat by a righteous enemy in battle could thus be transformed into an interior experience of purification. Biardeau therefore sees no sinister cover-up of the popular tradition, but rather speaks of the process of "englobing," which is not obscurantism but a process of theological and ideological development. At that point, as Alf Hiltebeitel put it, the demon-devotee theme has become an important part of the continuum that connects popular and Brahmanic Hinduism (see Hiltebeitel 1989).

David Shulman has also discovered this theme of sacrifice and self-sacrifice at work but in his *Tamil Temple Myths* he assumes that much of ancient Tamil tradition had to be subverted to fit into the orthodox mold. At the root of Tamil myth, the God (here Shiva) was the victim in an offering to the Goddess. Later this shocking fact was covered up even within the texts to protect the purity of God from the taint of death. A surrogate victim had to be found for Shiva: "(1) his bull, Nandin; (2) his devotee; or (3) an enemy, human or demonic" (Shulman 1980b, 132). Later the victim-devotee-demon came to share in the divinity of the God because that devotee was by nature a part of the God's own self-sacrifice, a part of the same cosmic whole. Shulman holds fast to the interconnections between orthodox Vedic and Puranic myths and the Tamil Puranas through the logic of the sacrifice. But he does not suggest that the connections took place naturally without the careful Brahmanic intervention in the process.

The tendency to view the sacrifice as the encompassing logic that integrates popular and orthodox Hinduism was not without its critics. In a retrospective of Biardeau's work, Hiltebeitel is not quite willing to give up the older debates over the differences between the Aryan and Dravidian traditions, between the overt and hidden systems of religions in South India. He suggests that Bhakti may yet be the product of "two abutting worlds" of Indo-European sensitivities and of the Hindu Goddess tradition. In the important Tantra and Shakti traditions, salvation depends on the principle of "sacrificing the sacrifice," of giving up orthodoxy for an even higher religious goal. In the myths of the devolution of Brahma and the subsequent union of Shakta with Shakti and the ultimate liberation of all beings, "the union of the Male with the Female takes on its full logic only if Brahma has in some sense been sacrificed, even if in one sense his sacrifice is that of the values of the brahmanically defined sacrificial world which he represents" (Hiltebeitel 1983, 211).

Kees Bolle, looking at sacrifice, points out that, in the village context, death and violence are crucial to the power and meaning of the sacrifice itself. He looks to an older theory that argued for two types of sacrifice proposed by J. Van Baal. The person-to-person sacrifice is comparable to a humble individual giving a gift to someone of high stature. A divinity can be like the latter, but as Van Baal argued, this is not the sort of relationship that is ultimately fulfilling, because "the longing for mystical union is a recurrent phenomenon in all religions" (quoted in Bolle 1983, 75). Bolle points out that during the ritual the participants seem to experience vicariously the violent death of the victim. In this sense the longing for union may be fulfilled in the experience of death via the bloody and much displayed suffering of the victim. Important in this thesis is Bolle's injunction that the transforming powers of death and violence cannot be ignored in the sacrifice. These, he claims, are central to the participants, *not* the social consequences or supposed "origins" of the ritual (see also Blackburn 1985, 272–73). Bolle, like Biardeau, sees a unity built around the sacrifice, not just a fragmented explanation or an attempt to trace the cause of the sacrifice or its social use. Yet here sacrifice is instead a rite of violent transformation that moves the body out of the flesh and into another state. Bolle leaves open the possibility that sacrificial language may be englobed by the larger category centering on the processes of *transformation*.[4]

Beyond these reevaluations of the meaning of the sacrifice in folk cults, new investigations have questioned the Vedic sacrifice itself. While others have often taken the Vedas at face value as a theological statement or a description of actual Aryan practice, J. C. Heesterman views the Vedic textual tradition as the product of an overt act of political and theological reformation—a reformation that indeed smothered "death and destruction, . . . the essence of the sacrifice itself" (1985, 85). In its initial use within the Vedic culture, Heesterman argues, sacrifice went

> far beyond the bounds of gift and reciprocity, of solidarity and participation. This stands out clearly in the fact that sacrifice always involves the destruction, through fire or otherwise, of part of the sacrificial offering, be it ever so minimal a part. In this respect, sacrifice is decisively different from the gift, which remains at man's disposal and will return by way of reciprocity. This element of destruction tells us that something dangerous is at stake in sacrifice. (1985, 84)

For Heesterman, this dangerous element was rooted out of the sacrifice, which "as it has been elaborated and systematized by the ritualists, has resolutely turned away from its origins and from popular practice as well" (87).

Thus if the popular religion survives as an extension of ancient Vedic culture, it does so only in that it has escaped the deadly disinfectant of the textual tradition. The actual remnant of Vedic culture exists now within the Vedic texts only as "the scattered and fossilized remnants of a lost and discredited world" (Heesterman 1985, 99). Here Heesterman's description of this priest-warrior conflict parallels similar conflicts described by Bruce Lincoln.[5] Heesterman, in a deconstructive move, suggests that "an earlier fundamentally

---

4. Note here Veena Das's list (1977, 120–26) of the dead who do not fit the sacrificial model of death.

5. For a summary of his position, see Lincoln 1981 (163–84). F. E. Pargiter ([1922] 1962, 58–77) postulated a similar conflict between the Brahmanic and Kshatriya traditions.

different state of affairs" can yet be seen "through the cracks, as it were, of the closed ritual system" (1985, 3). With the shadow of James Frazer perceptively sitting on his shoulder, Heesterman once again suggests that the keeper of this "discredited" violent system remained the king who had to rule over the realpolitik of daily India, "the lived-in order of society characterized by conflict and interdependence, . . . the protagonist of the mundane little tradition is the king" (9). The brand of legitimation, of any holiness, that the king retains "is not derived from a transcendent source but is rooted in worldly relationships. The king's sacrality is the exact opposite of transcendence" (156). Here Heesterman had set Dumont on his head. In the king's hands, daily life becomes the context of sacredness.

Heesterman's description of those textual and ethnographic "cracks" in the orthodox system remains limited, but it is just the kind of fissure into which a modern Frazerian would gladly risk falling. Adopting Jasper's concept of an "axial breakthrough," Heesterman describes the pre-axial period in terms similar to Frazer's age of the preliterate king. The pre-axial sacrifice was a raw physical enactment of the life-and-death struggle to "win" from the gods a world of health, wealth, and power—a world immortal not in the denotation of everlasting life but in connotation of the wholehearted wishes for long life. This kind of long life demanded a mortal risk of a bloody end in a field of battle where swords were not blunted for mere "ritualized" play. Heesterman's rich analysis calls to mind both Frazer and Freud in their contention that ritual before the age of reason was not symbolic or metaphoric but brutally real. Enactment meant action, not imagination-substituted-for-deed. There was nothing certain, nothing frozen outside of time in this "warrior's world."

> The tragic world of the warrior's sacrifice was certainly no Arcadia, but at least god and man were at one in the internecine strife for the goods of life. Even though the pitch of violence was raised to the breaking point, it was still one world held together by the nexus of sacrifice. Life and death were not irreconcilable but complementary, success and defeat not decisive but reversible, good and evil not absolute but ambivalent. Nothing is decisive and everything is liable to recall at the next round of sacrifice. (Heesterman 1985, 101)

Heesterman's thesis, in the context of Frazer's discussion of the continuing presence of make-do magic, is rich in implications. As long as there was a rival and an earthly field of battle, there was no individual psychology, no concern for inner logic, no space for "imagination." The axial age brought with it the rise of the individual, which in the context of India meant an internalization of the sacrifice into metaphor abstracted from worldly deed. The preclassical ritual program did not function as inner experience, but rather as the rules of a game for mortal stakes. Action here was sacred, not words. Even in the old verbal contests, words did not function aside from action, as Heesterman makes clear. To win was to win life. To lose, as in any battle, was to lose life. This preclassical tradition and its remnants worked in the mode of making/doing, not in the mode of thinking/imagination. The pre-axial age subsumed word into action, the post-axial age bifurcated action from word—leaving the desire for action its only compensation in the realm of imagination.

The temptation to take Heesterman in a deconstructive turn at this point is too strong to resist. The fragments of pre-axial India have been, in a Heestermanian sense, subjected to a second round of reductional analysis that began with both F. Max Müller and James Frazer in the heyday of imperial Britain. In the hands of the "modern" scholarship, the pen overcame the sword by once again turning the definition of a world based on action into a world defined ultimately as thought. Sir James Frazer and Sigmund Freud, and many who followed in their line of analysis, took under their wing the last remnants of the pre-axial age. Something fascinated them about these dangling edges left in world history. Yet they submitted that covert system to the logic of overt rationalism just as the ancient Brahmans wrote their own staid formulas over the bleeding body of the sacrificial victim. The modern scholar's immersion in their own axial breakthrough may have made the modern academic the most subtle enemy this discredited system ever faced. The first axial hammer forged a dual system that Biardeau, Shulman, Heesterman, Hocart, and Dumont agreed did not destroy the older system but englobed/covered/sublimated it. The second axial system may have, like the Pharisees, taken the keys to the kingdom of the "warriors' " royal world and forbidden entrance for themselves or for future generations of scholars. As with Frazer, the problem is in unconsciously adopting a critical mode that reenforces the Brahmanic rationalism already lying heavy on the text. Such a form of analysis ought to be declared unconstitutional as an act of trying the people of the earth twice for the same crime.

Dumont's "note" on "a strict implication" of the classical Indian system in his *Homo Hierarchicus* reveals an example of the inner judgments and assumptions of the logic of modern cultural analysis, not of India. Dumont accused "traditional" society in general of "transferring 'lived' reality to the plane of the eternity of thought" ([1966] 1970, 195), an interesting allegation from the Western sons of Plato. Dumont never suggested that historical action did not occur, simply that the pure actor could not "think," but only mimic the transcendental plane or move willy-nilly through history, thus condemning India "to political instability" (196)—again an ironic accusation from an imperial people whose early encounter with the rough-and-ready Indian rajas made establishing a fixed and quiet order its prime objective. How ironic that whenever some poor but lively straggler from the lost warrior's age has knocked on the door of Dumont's scholarly world he has been whisked away by the new Brahmans as a wish-fulfilling fantasy of a world lost in its own thoughts.

Indology continues to assume an evolution from action to thought without asking whether action ever had its own mode of evolution, whether the violence of sacrifice and of ritual battle ever settled into a "peacetime" mode that did not smother but developed its sense of "the material." The clues to such a reconstruction are already present in much of modern Indology. The expressed dualism between "force and the priests," in Dumont's terms ([1966] 1970, 196), if put in positive language, may well have created two sacralities that Frederique Marglin has recently seen as an interlocking definition of sacredness as *power* and sacredness as the power of order (Marglin 1985). This second system, if indeed based on power, may well view ritual as a process of alchemical transformation of the participant—a formula already suggested by Frazer before he sacrificed his ideas on the altar of the God of biblical theology. The sublimation of violence in the rationalized sacrifice becomes instead the transformation of violence into another state of being. "Instability," then, would be built into such a system, rendering Dumont's critique irrelevant for a system that depended on constant transformation of being within the daily historical world. Such transformation simply could not occur in the transcendent realm of the symbol, but must exist in history—where matter and nonmatter, time and no-time, contend for power. Of course, action does not write in words; it writes in the kind of "ritualized" gesture and movement Sigmund Freud described so well and then so neatly pushed into the category of the "omnipotence of thought" ([1913] 1946, 118–29). Perhaps all these clues point to a system that has its own version of a "breakthrough" from violence. Instead of sublimating violent action into thought, a special kind of "symbolizing" process may well have *transformed* violent action into a kind of ritual-*making* that created the royal sacred body. *Doing became making?*

So the problem turns full circle back to the very inhibitions that stopped James Frazer from a full affirmation of the religious materialism. How can a world of self-making and world-making be accommodated in either the Brahmanic world of traditional India or, ironically, the modern world of Europe. Both appear to share the common fear of a *making* culture. That almost perfect union of Sastri and the British has deep and mysterious roots that no essay of this size could hope to uncover in full (see Waghorne 1981). But this emphasis on thoughts and meaning, rather than on transformations and creations, has obscured the theo-logic and metalogic of the long-suspected second system from modern Indology. There has, however, been enough work in the last decade to begin again. Pudukkottai, with its Kallar heritage and the legacy of the irascible Raja Ramachandra, deserves a serious second look through the world of Brahman and British principles of the nineteenth century into the last days of the Tondaiman rajas, when they began to achieve independence from Britain not in politics but at least in ritual. Ironically, when India gained political independence, Pudukkottai lost its brief chance to reclaim and redevelop its ancient royal system as the state melted into the modern world of democracy.

A Parting Image

As the heyday of the empire waned, the images of the empire changed as the British gradually admitted that India would soon no longer be under their control. It is in this brief period, between 1928 and 1947, that the British began to wish themselves out of Pudukkottai, or at least out of the ritual and out of the limelight. A British administrator was in residency in Pudukkottai during much of this period, but the days of drums and jewels were over for the Raj. Thirty years after Max Müller's death, Müller's image of a spiritual India would incarnate in a near-naked Mahatma who pointed his thin finger at the British to shame their lavishness. At that point, the durbar scene in Pudukkottai would again reverse and leave a poignant parting image. A British administrator now attends the official installation ceremony in 1928 for yet another very young raja. The Britisher and his wife (Plate 35) sit with faces hardly able to hide their exhaustion and indifference. His uniform is a study in simple white—no braids, no metals, no gold. For such an important occasion, she dresses as if she were going out for a casual ride in the country. His Highness shines alone now in a far more

Plate 35.   Photograph taken at the civil installation ceremony that followed the Pattabhishekam (coronation) of His Highness Rajagopala Tondaiman. His Highness, looking very nervous, is seated to the right of the British representative of the Madras government (unidentified) and his wife. In contrast to earlier portraits of British participants in such grand occasions, this modern British couple seem to treat the whole affair with dutiful indifference. (From the collection of Sri K. Sathiamurti Rao of Pudukkottai.)

"Indian" dress of ornate gold brocade. The Dignitary Establishment stands in its place behind the raja once again, not merely insinuating but actually intruding itself into the picture. The face behind the British administrator's chair looks out boldly, not shyly, as the crowd of men and boys push close to their raja. Another great reversal has occurred as the British prepare to leave their house of ostentation to go as they had come, naked of the garb of royal power. As the British move out of the center of attention in the Pudukkottai court, the raja moved back to sit alone once again, providing a last brief darsan for new eyes—a last chance to look at the sacred space the British occupied so firmly but so blindly. Perhaps we shall see that the cycle the British experienced, from nakedness to ornamented power to nakedness, was ever so Indian, the shadow side of splendor that they feared to face for so long—a world of grandeur but also of impermanence, a world utterly visible but ultimately intangible, a world of images that reflected not Infinity but an immense yet fragile power.

Plate 4.   In this detail of Ravi Varma's 1886 painting of the durbar in honor of the visit of the governor of Madras to Pudukkottai, Dewan Sashia Sastri sits at the right hand of the throne just next to the British civilian officer in formal morning dress, who was probably the political agent. On Sastri's right are three British military officers, hats in hand. Sastri wears the traditional turban that marks him as the dewan. Like other Indian officials, underneath his British-style frock coat can be seen a gold-bordered dhoti instead of pants. The dewan's corpulence makes him a caricature of the later-lampooned "fat" Brahmans who assisted the British. In his time, however, no one laughed at this powerful master of syncretism.

Plate 8. This detail of the raja on his throne in Maistry's "miniature" shows scale-model chandeliers placed below the raja as a decorative element and next to two major emblems of royal authority—the horse and the elephant. The micro-chandeliers have become new marks of royal dignity. During this period, Indian rajas were quickly adding European decorative elements to their palaces as a sign of their good taste and of their power to own and thus impound the "paramount power" within the walls of their own domain, scaled down to manageable size as furniture, clocks, or even photographs.

Plate 14.   The court dress of the raja is an exact duplicate of the flowing robes he wears in the bold portrait Lewis painted in 1853 (MacQueen 1926, 3). In contrast, the raja wears a brocade coat with pants in Tripe's photograph (see Plate 6) rather than the robes of Lewis's durbar scene and earlier painting.

Plate 74.   The green skin marks this Goddess as Brihadambal, here seated as a lovely young princess. Her image in the sanctum of the Tirugokarnam temple also depicts the Goddess as a gentle, youthful girl. However, in the mural on the left of the sanctum, visible in Plate 68, the green hue of the fiery Goddess nearest the sanctum reveals Brihadambal as the *nayaki*, the fierce protectress of the Tondaimans.

Plate 77. Drawing closer to the silver images of Shiva and Ganesa, the viewer can see that the priest has dressed both as ascetics, in saffron robes.

Plate 78. Gajalakshmi, again with the royal Chowrie-bearers, is carved above this portal in the lower reception room of the Darbar Hall.

Plate 80. The tank at Tirugokarnam is formed from a natural stream that flows over the rock-cut temple. Called the Mangala Tirtham, the waters from this natural pond were used to sanctify the raja during his coronation in the Tirugokarnam temple.

Part Two

Splendor on the Borders of Orthodox India

Splendor is reserved for the monkey who reads the signs.
—David Miller

5

The King's House
The Palace in Pudukkottai

> And all these performances so that I can remain alone, mistress and assistant mistress of this house and of myself.
>
> —Jean Genet

This is his coronation day, November 19, 1928. His Highness Rajagopala Tondaiman, richly dressed in gold brocade and surrounded by his Dignitary Establishment, is still for the moment (Plate 36). This small boy, who has just been transformed into the raja of Pudukkottai, unknowingly will be the last of the Tondaimans to rule this tiny South Indian kingdom. Yet for now this child-king sits for his first durbar in the same secure pose that Raja Ramachandra assumed in Tripe's photograph seventy years before (see Plate 6). All the original signs of royal dignity are here, as they were in the past. Bards called out the young raja's praises as he entered to sit on his throne under a special canopy inside the pillared durbar hall. Members of his Dignitary Establishment carry royal emblems—perplexing regalia that seem to fully clothe the raja in majesty. The bearers of two gold "maces" directly flank the raja on his right and left. Slightly behind His Highness, and again on his right and left, stand the bearers of four "fly whisks," one pair made of peacock feathers and the other of swan feathers. Along each side of the "fly whisk" bearers are the holders of the two "fans" made from yak tails. Outside the canopy can be seen the first of a row of insignia bearers, who extend the "government rods" in their hands. Unseen in the photo, but clear in the memory of those who witnessed many such durbars, are the rest of the row of these rod-

Plate 36.   This photograph is part of an album of photographs taken at Ponniatus Studio in Trichinopoly on November 19, 1928, the young raja's coronation day. (From the collection of Sri K. Sathiamurti Rao of Pudukkottai.)

bearers, stretching from the two sides of the canopy. Also invisible to the camera are men on their knees in front of the entire scene undulating a long white cloth in accordion folds during the entire durbar. Quite visibly distinguished in the photo by their headdress and brocade sash and belts are the heads of two members of the palace establishment who "minister to the personal comforts, pleasures, and dignity of the Raja" (Venkataram Ayyar 1938, 450). The master of all such ceremonial, the Harikar, can also be seen with his hands modestly folded but with power clear in his stance. All the faces of those standing so near to their king wear the look of profound seriousness tinged with self-importance that tells the onlooker that no one and nothing present in this portrait of royalty should be overlooked. And yet, despite their sure countenance, a glance at the bare feet of these seeming dignitaries reveals their status as royal servants. On the feet of the seated raja alone are a pair of brightly polished shoes.

This was the royal scene par excellence that the British had romanticized in painting, brought into their homes as prints, and entered in fact during the heyday of the British Raj. The British civil servants are no longer present in this durbar, but the Raj is still close at hand. The members of His Highness's entourage standing in a semicircle around the bejeweled young raja are dressed in livery in respectful emulation of the viceroy's house. The Raj is also present in the very items so carefully held by these uniformed "servants." The two gold maces called Chobdar sticks were a gift from the British to an ancestor of this young prince who had helped establish the Honorable Company in power (Radhakrishna Aiyar 1916, 325).

In spite of so close a presence in this court scene over seven decades, the British made surprisingly little effort to understand or even to describe its structure, function, or meaning. While British administrators worked to understand the "native" system of land tenure and tax structures even for small places like Pudukkottai, they made no systematic study of the palace here or in any other princely state. But this British reticence about moving behind the glitter of the durbar and looking seriously at the palace structure is not mere oversight. Something about the workings of the Indian palaces excited, possibly threatened, the British but never moved them to overt analysis.

The Oriental and India Office Collections in the British Library contain endless documents on the Native States filled with detailed accounts of everything from the viceroy's hunting plans with this or that raja to suggested taxidermists to embalm the prize, but few detailed descriptions of the inner workings of any palace. Even as early as 1774, George Patterson in his diary begins to exhibit the tone that would characterize British attitudes toward the inner workings of the palace. On his long journey through South India under the auspices of the nawab of the Carnatic, who was already heavily in the power of the East India Company, Patterson carefully noted the architectural detail of several palaces recently captured by the nawab's forces. Although he reveled in the beauty of the ruins and noted architectural styles with sophistication and care, he divulged little information about the palaces' recent inhabitants, except when the tales were too titillating to pass mention. For example, he paused in his detailed description of the dimensions of the raja's bath in a palace at Ramnad to note:

> This we were told was the Rajah's private Bath where he used to enjoy his amorous inclinations with a variety of Women either in the Water or out of it as desire might prompt or the excess of voluptous caprice dictate.

When the raja died, Patterson continued, his favorite rani seized supreme power and happily continued the use of the baths with exciting reversals:

> In the Rajah's lifetime, one Man used to indulge his amourous caprice with hundreds of Women, but when the Rana succeeded to the Government one Woman appeared there alone and directed the motions of scores of the stoutest Men in the Country in all the extremes of the most voluptuous debauchery. She drank likewise to excess, and used to punish her Paramours with death when they fell under her displeasure. (Diary of George Patterson, 9:7–8)

Patterson willingly entered the captured and deserted palace as a romantic ruin, but he leaves his reader wondering whether any good son of the age of reason dared to venture into the halls of such despotism and debauchery when the royal occupants were yet alive.

As early as 1800, when the East India Trading Company had gained full control over the remaining princely states in the south, the resident at Nagpur adopted the vague language that would characterize official British reports from the palaces of Native States for the century: "The Resident attended the Rajah at the Festival of Dassara and made the customary Presents, having received the usual compliments" (Wellesley Papers/ADD 13589, "Correspondence of H. T. Colebrooke, report dated October 13, 1800). After this come detailed descriptions of the "character" of the raja's ministers, but little on their duties or function. Following a similar formula for reporting characters, but little structural detail, is "The History of Rewa with an account of the Raja and his Court" (1848) by James O'Brien (Wellesley Papers, ADD 30386). Colonel Tod's *Annals and Antiquities of Rajast'han* ([1829, 1832] 1972, 107–71) provides the most detailed and systematic description of the many royal courts in Rajasthan, but even this contains little information on the palace itself. The letters of missionaries to their home offices in London often mention attending such crucial palace ceremonies as durbars or even coronations, but a detailed description of Mrs. Smith's kind invitation to dinner usually follows a curt statement like "The Rajah was installed with much ceremony and visited the Resident the next day. I was present on both occasions" (Archives of the Council for World Missions, Box C, Neyoor, November 20, 1861, from F. Baylis).[1] Even the gazetteer for Pudukkottai, which included a chapter on the palace establishment, simply classified this enormous structure as "more or less domestic in nature." The British-educated Brahman author of the 1938 edition misidentifies the duties of several of the officers, whom he lists in a meaningless jumble of assorted titles, services, and functions in the royal household (Venkataram Ayyar 1938, 450–53).

Outside the circle of administrators and missionaries, an account of the palace in Pudukkottai comes from the eye and the pen of Henry Holiday, a Victorian artist whose paintings and sketches of his many travels made him famous.[2] Holiday came to South India in 1871 to see an eclipse of the sun and ended up the honored guest of the Raja Ramachandra, who invited him to set up his telescopes on the roof of the Residency of Pudukkottai. While intent on his scientific observations, the artist nonetheless described his first view of the town and the palace:

1. The coronation and installation ritual is briefly described along with other royal ceremonies in Mateer 1883, 115–41.
2. My thanks to Allan R. Life, an aficionado of Victoriana at University of North Carolina at Chapel Hill, for discovering the references to Pudukkottai among Holiday's *Reminiscences of My Life.*

The streets are broad, the houses painted, and in form suggest Aladdin and that sort of thing, but it was when we came to the immense Palace walls, high, smooth, and stretching away to a great distance, and reached a great archway in them, that I first perceived that it was really a palace we were coming to such as I supposed had no existence except perhaps in China. We entered this gate and found ourselves in a vast courtyard, with a palatial building . . . covering acres, on every side, and colossal painted idols along the facade, with other courtyards branching out everywhere. On one side was an enclosed space where six or seven elephants were pacing about. In the courts through which we drove were hundreds of the servants of the palace; and at length we reached that part where the Rajah himself was. Here we were conducted into a room where a billiard-table looked about as incongruous as it would have done in Solomon's Temple. (Holiday 1914, 205)

Could this be the same palace complex Dewan Sastri found so shockingly dingy less than a decade later? Holiday's trained eye gives some of the few glimpses into Raja Ramachandra's inner world just before Dewan Sastri's mandated intrusions. The artist's account of the outer walls of the palace and the many courtyards can be confirmed in Pudukkottai today and help fill in the missing brick and stone among much of the decay.[3] However, the scale of the palace—whose walls were no higher or longer than those of British-built Fort St. George in Madras, or the more familiar Buckingham Palace—hardly fits Holiday's excited tones. An Aladdin's lamp surely lighted this artist's eyes with such a romantic glow that again the beholder blurs the palace as much as the British civil servant or the Brahman dewan.

The British did not allow themselves to "see" the inner workings of the palace, because something there was either too holy or too wholly problematic to view with a clear eye. The British administrators more often ignored these homes of their "chiefs" almost in the same way that a conservative member of a Christian denomination might politely attend, but not really attempt to understand, a service in another church that only "claimed" to be a house of God. The Indian palaces perhaps seemed tainted—like the house of an "idol," not like the home of the true king in England. Even Holiday's glowing visions of oriental exotica or Patterson's earlier images of romantic ruin join the missionary and the civil servant in a commonly held opinion that these native palaces were, like all forbidden places, riddled with mystery and intrigue. For more than a century the image continued that the inner workings of the palace were permeated with sex and excess. Here is a rather blurred picture of a raja surrounded by servants who control and taint his very body, either in the Brahmanic sense of pollution or in the British sense of egging the raja toward uncontrolled lavishness or even debauchery. In a real sense the British pay the palace establishment the highest compliment: They assume that an enormous but unpredictable power resides here.

The first step of moving past the British world and into the royal world of Pudukkottai, then, is to take that first stride into the doors of the old palace in Pudukkottai. But the doors

---

3. The published account is listed only as an extract of Holiday's diary, which if extant may contain more details. Holiday mentions that he did several sketches of the interior of the palace that were also not reproduced in full.

to this sacred domain have been guarded for years by British inhibition as much as by the Hindu rules of purity that forbade entrance into the temple and the purdah rooms within. Reconstructing the workings of the Huzur Establishment—as the full staff of the palace was called—becomes an exercise in reading underexposed or overexposed images in some balanced form. No explicit logic or rationale for the system is provided either in British records or in the files kept in the administrative offices in Pudukkottai called the Darbar Files. Fortunately, the Palace Records, which were kept by the raja's own staff, are available although much disarranged. These record the expenses and often mention the duties of the various palace servants. The Rosetta Stone for this complex system is a handwritten list of the "Huzur or Palace Establishment" with both Tamil and English titles for each of the then 818 servants. Although undated, this list was probably written during the major Huzur reform in the 1880s. During the same period, the land settlement left descriptions of the duties of the palace staff. More than 2,500 of these inams were classified as *araṇmaṇai ūḻiya* for "service to the palace." Such settlement cases, handled individually, sometimes provide details on the nature of palace service, but they must be used with caution because the settlement officers were operating in a British administrative mind-set. Their own categories and questions adopted from the land "reform" system in British-controlled territories seem to classify Hindu mangoes as if they were British apples and ended with an overall tasteless explanation of the whole category of "palace service" by lumping it with all other service grants. Later manuals in Pudukkottai simply claimed all such grants were "so mixed together that it is difficult to draw a distinct line of difference between each" (Standing Orders of the Pudukkottai Darbar 1937, 2:189).

Fortunately the old court officials also remember details of the palace servants, but these memories are clouded because the unexpected merger of this ritual state into a modern secular government of India shattered the personal and social self-definitions of many of the former palace servants. Remembrance of the overall logic of the palace system seems lost in the shuffle and in the fragmented world that followed. The change was so sudden that even His Highness Raja Rajagopala, as late as 1947, did not expect the merger of the state. On the eve of Indian independence in the "Proclamation issued by His Highness Sri Brihadamba Das Raja Rajagopala Tondaiman Bahadur on the Occasion of His Twenty-Fifth Birthday," the raja announced changes in the administrative system of the state and ended his announcement with "May this new era, by the grace of Sri Brihadamba, bring happiness and prosperity to all my loyal and loving subjects" (Palace Records, pamphlet dated July 15, 1947). Less than a year later, Pudukkottai was merged into the Indian union without even the dignity of retaining its name as a single district. Forgetfulness was fostered as Pudukkottai was erased from the map as an anachronism in a new democratic state.

Such are the problems in both reconstructing and understanding the function of the raja's household. Yet in spite of the lack of clear information, the royal court remains at the center of much speculation about the nature of society and religion in India. Here in the structural organization of the royal servants is supposedly the very paradigm for caste (Hocart [1936] 1970). Even the origins of social life and divine worship are said to be hidden in these dark corridors of royal power. But the actual structure of such a court remains in bits and pieces, a puzzle whose overall plan must be reassembled. In this case, the structure of the personnel is so intimately related to the palace buildings that architecture will be the first clue to the anthropology of this sacred place.

The Old Palace

The lack of knowledge the British had of the palace was not due simply to their own reticence. While they were often invited to the durbar hall and to the other public audience halls in the palace buildings, many parts of the complex were simply not open to outsiders. The beautiful interior of the Dakshinamurti temple was forbidden to non-Hindus, and only now, by the kind permission of the royal family, could we photograph all of its rich interior detail along with the rest of the palace complex. It is one of the sad ironies that these photographs of the palace complex are perhaps both the first and the last witness that non-Hindus may have of these buildings. The palace is threatened with destruction to make way for new industry in this prime location at the heart of Pudukkottai city. In addition, there are several other extant photographs: an old photo that was part of Tripe's 1858 photographic views of Pudukkottai, and another set of pictures taken during His Highness's coronation in 1928 that display some of the structural details of the outer buildings. Come! The old palace is fully open to us for the first and likely the last time.

The old palace in Pudukkottai town is a network of buildings interconnected by corridors, courtyards, and winding staircases and encased by four stone walls. The whole complex stretches several square blocks and opens out into the city with a gate at each of the four cardinal directions. Entering on the south side at the Elephant Gate, one sees the ruins of the large stable complex on the right, and the remains of the elephant stalls on the left (Plate 37). The oldest administrative building, the Sirkele's Office (Plate 38), is directly ahead, with two enormous *yāḷis*—half-lion, half-elephantine creatures—sculpted in high relief at the two corners of the building (Plate 39, color section), which may be the objects Holiday took for "colossal painted idols." When one looks directly through the main corridor of this office, the upper story of the oldest structure in this palace complex becomes visible (Plates 40 and 41). Here at the back of this central portion of the palace is the L-shaped, two-story building that served as the royal living quarters. The upper story, with its round columns, was called the Ringu Valassam (Tamil, *reṅku-vilācam*) and served as the royal ladies' quarters. Downstairs was the raja's quarters. The eastern and western wings of this building were all too obviously seamed together (Plate 41). Here in a courtyard in front of the royal quarters and at the very center of the palace complex stands the Sri Dakshinamurti temple, where worship services are still conducted daily amid the general ruin (Plates 42 and 43). Inside the small temple is carefully preserved a box of sand upon which the silent ascetic-saint Sadasiva wrote the original religious injunctions that were to ensure the salvation and prosperity of king and kingdom. Facing the front of this royal temple is a multicolumn portico (Plate 44) probably used by the earliest rajas as a durbar hall and a court of justice. Behind this portico, now bricked in, are the oldest parts of the palace complex. These meandering halls and tiny courtyards once swarmed with servants but now ironically house only bats and bees. Con-

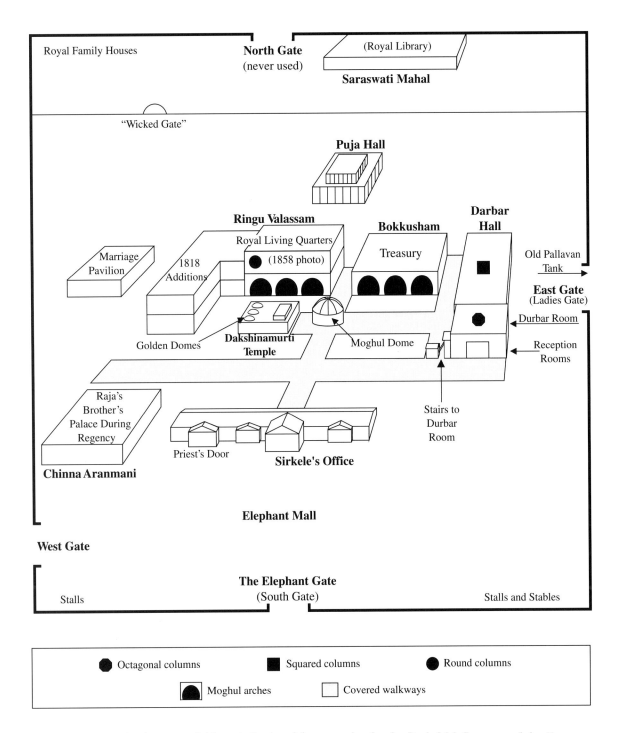

Royal Family Houses

North Gate
(never used)

(Royal Library)
Saraswati Mahal

"Wicked Gate"

Puja Hall

Ringu Valassam
Royal Living Quarters
(1858 photo)

Bokkusham
Treasury

Darbar Hall

Old Pallavan Tank

East Gate
(Ladies Gate)

Marriage Pavilion

1818 Additions

Golden Domes

Dakshinamurti Temple

Moghul Dome

Durbar Room

Reception Rooms

Raja's Brother's Palace During Regency

Priest's Door

Sirkele's Office

Stairs to Durbar Room

Chinna Aranmani

Elephant Mall

West Gate

The Elephant Gate
(South Gate)

Stalls

Stalls and Stables

⬢ Octagonal columns ■ Squared columns ● Round columns

◖ Moghul arches ▢ Covered walkways

Figure 1. The Old Palace in Pudukkottai. (Designed from my sketches by Rachel M. Bowman of the Center for Teaching and Learning, University of North Carolina, Chapel Hill.)

Plate 37.   Looking out from the front entrance of the old Sirkele's Office, the south
gate of the palace opens into the main street of modern Pudukkottai. The
Tondaiman rajas, a "lunar" dynasty, faced south rather than east while seated in
durbar, and thus the rajas exited and entered through this south gate, called the
"Elephant Gate," for major ceremonies. The ruins of the massive elephant stables are
visible here in the upper left. Just outside this gate is the grand Public Office Building, constructed at the turn of the century to house the modern bureaucracy that
outgrew the small Sirkele's Office. Notice, in the upper right corner, that thorny
prickly-pears grow again in Pudukkottai to guard the old fluted wall.

necting this old portion of the raja's living quarters to the back of the large building known as
the Darbar Hall, which stretches along the eastern side of the complex, is a columned portico
(Plate 45, color section) with very Moghul-style arches. The two-story Darbar Hall is a much
grander building, with massive ornate doors, carved columns, and intricate door lintels on the
lower story. The Darbar Hall, although connected to the royal living quarters by this Moghul
portico, was usually entered by turning right after leaving the Sirkele's Office (Plate 46). The
downstairs of the Darbar Hall functioned as receiving rooms. These rows of gilded columns
(Plate 47, color section) that once saw the comings and goings of British governors and Indian

Plate 38.   The Sirkele's Office, when added to the front of the palace, was still quite modest, but it did block a direct view and direct access to the raja's old living quarters. It still stands as an architectural proclamation of the end of the Tondaimans' direct rule of the state.

rinces now shelter tobacco workers but still retain their magnificence. On the sides of this long, columned hall were small rooms closed off by ornately carved doors (Plate 48, color section) that housed royal state jewels and family heirlooms. The upstairs of the Darbar Hall was reached by a covered staircase (Plate 49), which turned so it could be entered just behind the Sirkele's Office. The stair tread was tiled to form a grand entrance (Plate 50, color section) to the formal durbar room, with a polished mosaic-tile floor area once used for the palace dancing-women (Plate 51, color section). This tiled area directly faced the pillared portico, where Raja Rajagopala Tondaiman had been seated in such grandeur for his coronation durbar and where Tripe photographed Raja Ramachandra Tondaiman. This palace complex was never magnificent by the standards of larger kingdoms. Raja Martanda Tondaiman had a grander palace built away from the dust of the old town (Plate 52), but no royal rituals were ever held in the "New Palace." For the small principality of Pudukkottai, all the pomp and splendor of royalty was alive only in the old palace.

Field notes and photographs, old and new, helped produce the diagram of the palace in Figure 1. Without the photographs, the task would have been impossible. This diagram,

Plate 40.   This portico juts out from an earlier passageway to the royal living quarters at the back. Although the arches are not Moghul in design, the dome reflects a Persian architectural heritage. The covered passageway with the dome at its center divides what may have been a large courtyard into four quadrants, again echoing the design of Persian gardens. To the left of the dome is now the Dakshinamurti temple. The right leads to the newer Darbar Hall.

Plate 41. Left from the domed passageway, the upper stories of the royal living quarters are visible behind the lower roof of the Dakshinamurti temple. Notice that the portion of these quarters just behind the passage was once an open veranda with round pillars supporting a flat roof.

Plate 42. This west wing of the royal living quarters is the portion of the palace probably added along with the Darbar Hall in 1818. The arched windows still have their fanned glass panes in the last row on the left. The flat decorative squared columns on the surface of this building match the same motifs on the exterior of the Darbar Hall visible in Plate 56 (color section).

Plate 46. The long Darbar Hall on the right is entered by the covered walkway approached below from the public offices or at the door on the open upper gallery. The raja and dignitaries entered from below.

Plate 49. The squared columns in bas-relief on the stairway up to the durbar room echo the outside of the Darbar Hall itself.

however, reduces the real experience of the palace by giving it an almost artificial orderliness. The buildings are truly a maze, and my attempts to keep the many corridors straight only ended in utter confusion as I walked through these ruins. To be inside this complex is like being lost in the woods. Rows of columns, some ornate, some simple, stand like dense trees. Everywhere there are doors leading into some dark nowhere that surely must get somewhere at some time.

So while not forgetting the crucial experience this architecture creates, it is possible to step

Plate 52.   The "New Palace" now houses the offices of the Collector of Pudukkottai District. Raja Martanda Tondaiman built this grand European-style building to suitably entertain the British ladies and gentlemen in nearby Trichinopoly and Madras. Many in Pudukkottai also argue that this grand palace was designed to please the tastes of a European wife. Martanda married Molly Fink soon after his new palace was completed. (From the collection of Sri K. Sathiamurti Rao of Pudukkottai.)

back and begin to guess how this complex was created over several centuries. Unfortunately, there are few records available that can confirm these inferences. The palace buildings are a mosaic of different architectural styles. Clearly the upstairs portions of some buildings were added later. There are additions to older buildings, and everywhere staircases, covered corridors, and upper-story open walkways connect the complex. It is interesting that George Patterson, in his description of nearby palaces in 1774, already notes the eclectic character of the architecture. Writing of a recently captured palace of the Nayak dynasty of Madurai, he comments: "Although I examined it with the utmost care, I could not perceive that any regular plan had been pursued for the different buildings so as to make the whole a Complete Work; on the contrary it appears to one, that it has been built at different times and by different Architects" (Diary of George Patterson, 8:238–39). It seems that the palace at Pudukkottai followed the style, or rather the lack of style, of nearby royal houses.

For Patterson, the long colonnades, corridors, and variety of differing columns—in this case at Madurai and in the palace at Ramnad—also appear to be the major architectural features that catch his attention in the same way that they still caught mine at Pudukkottai. Patterson attempts to classify the columns and already notices the presence of "Grecian" style that is also apparent at the Pudukkottai palace: "The style is in some respects Indian;

but the Columns have much the appearance of Grecian. It is supposed that a Portuguese Architect gave the design of some of the Squares" (8:239). Later he included in his inventory of the Madurai palace other styles that he calls "something of the Doruk or Tuscan Order" (239) and "Moorish" (241).

The ever-present columns in Pudukkottai divide into very distinct styles as well. There are series of Moghul arches with short columns (Plate 53); plain squared columns (Plate 54,

Plate 53.   This graceful colonnade is in the oldest section of the palace related to the treasury. Although such Moghul influence in South India is usually associated with the period after the fall of the Vijayanagar empire, among the ruins of the capital of this last Hindu empire in the south, similar Moghul arches can still be seen (Fritz, Michell, and Rao 1984, 122–24).

Plate 55.　The stained-glass panes forming an arch over the simple door contrast with the ornate gilt columns that lead to it. Such squared-columned and arched thresholds are ubiquitous in the late eighteenth- and early nineteenth-century architecture of the former French colony in nearby Pondicherry.

color section; Plate 55) on the outside as well as on the inside of several buildings, including the back portion of Darbar Hall (Plate 56, color section) and the Puja Hall in back of the central palace complex (Plate 57); octagonal columns with very "Hindu" ornamentation found in the front portion of Darbar Hall both downstairs (Plate 58, color section) and upstairs (Plate 59); and round columns on the upper story of the major royal residence that I also would label Grecian (see Plate 41).

The very earliest period of Pudukkottai building produced exactly what its name implies—a new fort. Pieces of the stone wall of that fort still crop up within the town. I doubt that the present wall dates from that early period. A Tamilnadu government publication suggests that as late as 1754 an East India Company agent reported "There is neither stone nor mud wall" in the town, but that by 1813 the palace achieved its present form after it "arose phoenix like" from the fire that destroyed large portions of the complex (Raghupathy 1983, 6). I assume the Islamic areas within the palace complex were the first to be built, at the time the Tondaimans were considered vassals of the Muslim nawabs of the Arcot or perhaps earlier. Islamic architecture influenced South India significantly by the fifteenth century, and an innovative style combining Deccan Islamic architecture with older Hindu forms appeared in the domestic building of the maharajas of Vijayanagara, whom the Tondaimans claim as their first liege lords (Fritz, Michell, and Rao 1984, 122). The Moghul sections of the Pudukkottai palace are in the middle of the complex, and legend has always

Plate 57. The Puja Hall, once the center for an entire priestly establishment, has clearly been repainted so many times that the original features are difficult to see. The squared columns are unmistakable, however, and leave a series of unanswered questions as to why a Hindu raja would choose to construct his own prayer room in such European style.

claimed that in the old days the raja sat in durbar under one of these arches to judge cases in his realm. These arches match one of Patterson's sketches of the "Moorish" design and also closely resemble recent diagrams of a pavilion found at Vijayanagar (Fritz, Michell, and Rao 1984, 129).

The Dakshinamurti temple appears to have been constructed in the important area directly in front of these arched porticoes. If the temple were not there, the palace would be laid out in the typical Islamic pattern, adopted in South India, of squared, interlocking courtyards opening out to a main gate. If this were the case, the raja's portico would have originally faced a large courtyard filled with petitioners and courtiers who would have entered directly through the main South Gate.

The Dakshinamurti temple and the front portion, upper and lower stories, of Darbar Hall were probably the next addition, as the rajas of Pudukkottai were enjoined to worship this form of Shiva well after they assumed royal titles. The very and almost self-consciously "Hindu" columns are nearly identical in the raja's durbar room and reception rooms in Darbar Hall and the Dakshinamurti temple. These buildings probably date from the late 1700s, when British power was beginning to displace the Moghuls but before the Raj had become a serious cultural reality here. The fact that Patterson never mentioned such octagonal columns confirms this suspicion that the more-Indian style is actually later than the Moghul and perhaps even the Grecian. The back portion of Darbar Hall and the entire outside changes to a plain squared-column motif, a style that Patterson likewise never mentions. The same style is clear in the lower stories of the eastern half of the royal living

Plate 59. The columns in the room in the upper story, where the formal durbars took place, are comparatively plain and lack any overt iconic forms, such as the otherwise ever-present yalis.

quarters and in the Puja Kattu, the puja hall. Pudukkottai town, which had been mostly thatched huts, burned in 1812, at which time the raja apparently built a new palace west of the Pallavan Tank (Radhakrishna Aiyar 1916, 360). The style and location of the newer portions of Darbar Hall and the upper story of the western wing of the royal living quarters are probably these new structures, completed in 1818. The squared columns are neither Hindu nor Moghul. The British influence was probably written into the walls of Pudukkottai at this time. Tripe's 1958 photograph of the living quarters shows the upper-story Grecian columns (Plate 60), which could also be classified as "the Tuscan Order," in place over both the Moghul and the squared-column portions of that building. Whether these were also added in 1818 is unclear, but that they are distinct from the lower stories is obvious. The Sirkele's Office building, which covers the entire front of this complex, was certainly there by the 1870s, when Holiday noticed its painted "idols." The wood columns here seem to match the Chinna Aranmani, literally a small palace within the palace to the right of the office used by the rajas' close family, which may well date from the same period as the Dakshinamurti temple and the raja's durbar room.

The palace complex reveals several periods of development. The old Vijayanagar past left no building except the walls of the fort that gave this state its name. The late Moghul period provided the first durbar hall, which should be no surprise since *darbār* is a Persian word. The brief period between Moghul and British hegemony opens the door to a resurgent Hindu period. Finally the very halls and walls of the palace began to echo the British Raj. Where is the key to understanding the root logic of this massive complex? Perhaps this very

Plate 60. Colonel Tripe's photographs of the palace for the East India Company show that most of the structure was already in place by 1858. Shot from the upper level of the complex, the roof of the Dakshinamurti temple, with its five-pointed golden dome, is seen directly in front of the Darbar Hall. The palace was designed with upper and lower corridors. The upper halls are usually open, and the entire palace can be accessed via this network of walkways. From "Photographic Views of Poodoocottah." (Courtesy of the Oriental and India Office Collections, The British Library.)

layering of rooms in disparate styles, and the multiplication of rows upon rows of seemingly dissimilar columns, is the most observable clue written into the palace itself. The palace complex may well be its own metaphor for the logic of the kingship within: Row by row, layer by layer, nothing is discarded, everything is added to build this holy house. Did the Moghul and British overlords rule, or did they simply provide yet another layer to this ever-expanding space?

That question of the ancient origins of the royal system will require a return to Sanskrit and Tamil sources, but for now the process of mapping the palace must be extended to "mapping" the palace servants in their relationship to the king and to the palace. Here the same principles that created the architecture of the palace are equally at work in the architecture of the palace personnel: Each "layer" of the palace establishment builds upon the previous layer to create not a sacred building but a holy body—the body of a king. That argument requires a much closer look into the palace. It is time now to open the great South Gate and enter the king's house as it was years ago—not an empty shell but very much a beehive of activity, with its many corridors and halls filled with royal "servants" who at one time numbered more than one thousand.

Inside the Palace Walls

The various lists of the members of the Huzur Establishment in Pudukkottai contain a curious mix of "servants." At first glance some of these appear to be personal attendants to the king, but others seem to have official administrative duties. The same mixture of seeming administrators with personal royal servants has also been noticed in older Tamil sources. S. Krishnaswami Aiyanger, in his history of Hindu administrative institutions, notes that Tamil texts mention the eighteen councilors of the king, made up of two sets of five "ministers" plus one set of eight—the Āyam (Tamil, duties). The last set, however, is listed twice. "The first of these seem to recite only those in personal service constituting more or less the chamberlain and his staff, the men in charge of unguents, the men in charge of flowers and dress and so on. . . . The next recital has got much more of an official colour" (Krishnaswami Aiyanger 1931, 21). This second list includes palace guards, the commander of the army, members of the elephant corps, cavalrymen, and other supposedly "official" servants. It is interesting that this suspended mixture of officials and personal attendants parallels that same mix of the *ratnin*, the king's "companions" listed in Sanskrit sources. These ancient lists likewise place the "commander of the army" and the "village headman" next to the "keeper of the dice" and the "chamberlain." It was exactly this supposed confusion of personal services with a budding administration that led A. M. Hocart to conclude that the function of the king's court evolved from ritual services to the royal person to a general government administration. The same mixture of "servants" in the ancient royal courts has led other scholars to assume that the palace itself must have functioned at one time both as an administrative center and as a house for the king.

In Pudukkottai the overlap of palace service with administration was said to occur with services that were military in nature. Guidelines written for officers of the inam land settlement explain that the difference between the categories of "palace service" (*aranmanai ūliya*) and another category, "service in the state militia" (*amaram*), are difficult to understand (Standing Orders of the Darbar, 1:189; see also Rules for the Settlement of Inams). Supposedly the officer was expected to duly record the landlord's own designation of his tenure and not expect fully to understand such a system. Certainly in the records many landlords claimed to hold their tenure for an unspecified "palace service" and affirm that their tenure was originally awarded for an ancestor's bravery in battle or another deed of valor. Others, designated "palace services," seemed outright military and carried old martial titles like Sardar (frequently spelled Sirdar in old records). Palace service inams were also granted for *sannāk safāri mutali,* "escorting the king during his processional drives," a service that seems to duplicate one of the primary duties of the amaram officers. In his study of inam grants in Pudukkottai, Dirks points to this confusion between the palace service and amaram tenures but focuses his attention on the amaram system. He argues convincingly that the amaram system was the oldest administrative machinery of the state, gradually superseded both ritually and politically by an administrative system borrowed from a British model (1987, 168–91). If the palace military were connected to this early amaram system, the Huzur Establishment would have to be considered a hybrid institution—part personal servants and part budding administrators, a house divided within itself.

In spite of all these supposed functional divisions of the palace officials, a detailed examination of the Huzur Establishment in Pudukkottai reveals a unified body distinct from the early state militia or later administration. The first clear evidence of this unity is circumstantial but interesting. In the Inam Settlement Faisal Registry, the landholders do know the tenure category of their own grant. They clearly stated whether the land was held for "palace service." None seem to confuse *amaram* with *aranmanai ūliya,* and there appears to be no record of any protest when a tenure was recorded as one or the other. The substantial factor that does clearly distinguish the two types of tenure is the inclusion or absence of the "Biruthus" (*pirutu*) listed as part of the land grant. Dirks has found that many of the amaram tenures carefully designate the Biruthus granted with the land. The inam grant sets aside a portion of that land for the maintenance of those who bear the umbrellas, palanquins, and other honors for the landlord. A sampling of settlement cases for each type of palace service, however, reveals no instance of any palace servant who was granted Biruthus, "honors" lent by the rajas. This fact is corroborated by the later Darbar Files and Palace Records. There are no recorded grants of royal honors for members of the traditional palace establishment—even for weddings and funerals, occasions in which such grants were commonly extended even to such minor administrative officers as a clerk in the Darbar Records Office. Thus in the matter of Biruthus a Sardar listed as a "palace servant" was treated exactly as an umbrella bearer, not as a Sardar in the state militia who was an amaram landholder.

The clear distinction between the palace establishment and the military or even civil administration was revealed in the order of the raja's state procession and in the seating position of all officials in the durbar. The palace servants, even the palace military, preceded the raja while administrative officers and officers of the old state militia followed the raja.

When certain palace guards, who did bear the title Sardar, were given a place in the durbar, it was to stand at the side of the raja or behind him with other members of the palace establishment. The ancient military Sardars, however, always were seated facing the raja. Here in these important matters of processional order, and in the seating at the durbar, was revealed the following maxim: The palace is the palace, the administration is the administration, and never the twain shall meet—at least not while in Pudukkottai.

These ritual distinctions that demarcate the palace servant from government official reveal much about the function of the palace establishment as a whole. To borrow Dirks's terminology, the newer administration and the old military establishment were involved in a redistribution process, a sharing of the king's own power and authority. They extended his rule throughout the domain, and hence they "follow" the king, extending behind him in procession. They likewise share the symbols of royal power, the Biruthus, when they replicate his authority in their own outlying districts. The palace servants, in contrast, no matter how seemingly administrative their titles, did not replicate or extend royal sway. Thus umbrella bearers and palace guards focused their attention toward the king, not toward the kingdom.

All palace servants, then, minister to the royal person, as the gazetteers put it, to his "personal comforts, pleasure, and dignity." But clearly such servants could not simply be equated with the domestics of just any wealthy person. The members of the palace did not have administrative power. But however illogical it may seem, they wielded enormous power, which in several instances did extend to real government authority. In Pudukkottai the leader of the abortive insurrection against the raja in 1853 was a palace Sardar. Records of the period explain that this Sardar was not a "Sirdar of distinction" but a "common Sirdar—a slave of the court," a gatekeeper in the palace (Pudukkottai Merged State Records, R.Dis. 29/1853, letter dated March 4 from Sirkele to Political Agent). The ability to muster such political force might well be attributed to exceptional individual ambition except for the existence of some interesting comparative evidence in nearby kingdoms. Legend attests that a successful conqueror of Madurai, Kampana Udaiyar, was once a gatekeeper under a nearby raja (Mahalingam [1940] 1975, 1:40n.). In Sivaganga, an attempted coup d'état was manipulated by two brothers who had been the deceased raja's Adappakkaran, betel bearer, and dog boy (Rajayyan 1974, 66). In defiance of the more legitimate election of a raja without clear issue by the clan heads, these brothers almost succeeded in installing their own "puppet" king (Price 1979, 220). The evidence is still minimal, but it does suggest that the power of such palace servants was not to replicate royal authority but quite literally *to make* the king.

In political terms, the palace menials had a control over the king that arose neither from the personal influence that might have come from the intimacy of domestic service nor from the power of an administrative proxy. In ritual terms, the palace servants stood aside from the royal cycle of "pooling and redistribution," that model of polity based on the sacrificial cycle. Rather, the Huzur Establishment cared for the royal body in an intimate sense, yet their ministrations remained a public and not a personal service to the raja, because the body they guarded and groomed was not the physical body of a man but the corpus of a king, the body politic. However martial or even servile their titles, the key to the entire logic of the inner palace establishment rests in their duties to that royal body alone.

A very late list of the palace establishment (Palace Records, 1943, "H.H. Household, Personal Establishment") divides the members into two categories using the English terms "household" and "civil." The use of both terms provides an important clue to the first fundamental division within the palace establishment. By 1943 no one in Pudukkottai would have considered the term "civil" synonymous with administrative or even governmental. This term, like the phrase "household," reflected a very special understanding of the bifurcation of the Huzur Establishment into what could be termed the "outer" and "inner" circle of servants in the palace complex. Such a basic division was clearly implied in the earliest complete Huzur list by the order in which the more than eight hundred servants were grouped. This oldest list began, as did the late 1943 version, with the raja's "intimate" staff and then seemed to move outward figuratively, but also spatially, to the stables and the military guard that indeed operated near the outer walls of the palace. Servants termed "household" were in many senses "close" to the raja, while those who were "civil" seemed to have been "farther" from his person, although no less important to the state.

Much of the meaning of the Huzur Establishment can be discovered by mapping a kind of geography of persons in relationship to the king. Some groups were close, and hence "personal"; others were "far," and hence "civil." As in the processional order and in the positions in the durbar, the king's establishment surrounded him in the palace, forming concentric circles between his royal person and the outer walls of the palace. Identifying the duties and the positioning of the many titles of palace servants is at least one method of discovering the logic of what was once called a mere "motley group of persons." Fortunately there exists material for such a mapping. Many lists of palace servants by title were compiled for various purposes between 1880 and 1948. The order of the servants in each list and the constant relative position of each category vis-à-vis all others provide the outlines for such a map. Important lists from 1928 to 1929 and 1939 to 1940 catalog the exact liveries worn by each type of palace servant (Palace Records, dated August 9, 1928, and April 4, 1939). The type of clothing worn by the servants indicates the groupings and relative relationship of the various categories. Birds of a feather here were indeed meant to be grouped together. The Inam Settlement Faisal Registry, the Darbar Files, and the Palace Records also fill in the details. It will also be useful to notice the names of these palace servants at each of the layers identified. Some of the names will be clearly Tamil, but others are Sanskrit and many are Persian, indicating that the servants were layered over time as much as the buildings. Again the issue of the source of primary logic of the system will have to wait for the next chapter. The mapping process, then, can begin with the most central of the servants, that inner ring "closest" to their lord's person.

The Inner Circle

Beginning with the 1943 list, the inner circle or "household" included, by this time, the expected British-influenced additions of a "valet" and "butler" and the usual array of traditional servants—tailor, barber, cooks, and dhobi. Any wealthy person in India would have such a staff. But here in the list have survived two ancient service titles: the Pillayandan (page boys) and the Kodaikkar (umbrella bearer). Another undated list marked "His Highness's Personal Establishments" included the page boys and umbrella bearers. The lords of the Western Palace, a collateral royal line in Pudukkottai, were likewise granted what was considered a minimal royal establishment because they were next in line to the throne. Once again the page boys and umbrella bearers headed this list. Another document singled out these two classes of servants in the later establishment for special liveries (Palace Records, dated September 21, 1929). The survival of two such offices indicates that these servants formed an ancient core of the inner circle whose "care" of the raja was a ritual matter, not a domestic matter. Using the method of list comparison, the inner circle can be expanded. This circle appears to have included the following servants as basic to the royal dignity of the raja:

Adappakkaran	Betel pouch bearer
Pillayandan	Page boy
Kodaikkar	Umbrella bearers
Bokkushakkar	Treasure keeper
Bokkushamkaval	Treasure guard
Povandan	Head palanquin bearer
Bogi	Palanquin bearers

All these servants were mentioned in the Inam Settlement Faisal Registry and were always present in extant Huzur lists. In the Inam Settlement Faisal Registry, these were all classified as "regular service" in the palace, indicating that their services were rendered on a daily basis. A grant for Pillayandan service was dated as 101 years old at the time of the settlement (Inam Settlement Faisal Registry, T.D. 546); another, for Kodaikkar, was classed as one of "the oldest inams" (T.D. 547). The Bogis all seem to have taken the title "Povandan" as their surname, as if this service constituted their family "caste." The Faisal Registry shows that brothers jointly shared these duties (T.D. 853) and that, conversely, others unrelated as kin shared the same land and the same service like a joint family (T.D. 1521; T.D. 1167). Such services, then, were so ancient that they constituted a group relationship that in some cases superseded even caste and family ties.

This group of intimate royal servants is perplexing. Translation of their titles alone gives not the slightest clue as to why these particular services should be considered so very crucial for the dignity of a king. References to the specific duties of these officers both in the Palace Records and in the Darbar Files do begin to fill in details. The Bokkushakkar, the head of the "treasury," guarded and maintained the jewels, the gold-laced robes, and the royal turban, which constituted the king's state raiments (Palace Record, dated August 5, 1906). This "treasurer" carefully guarded not only the actual royal raiments but also the propriety of their use by the raja and other members of the royal family. He alone knew the precedents and protocol for who might wear each article and on which occasion. He kept careful records of the use of each of these articles (Darbar Files, R7/1886, "The Turban Controversy"). When Raja Martanda Tondaiman went to England to see the queen, his Bokkushakkar was ordered to "take and deliver" the state jewels to Madras for shipment to England (Palace Records, dated May 16, 1906, "List of Jewels to be sent to England for the use of His Highness The Maharajah of Pudukkottai"). The raja took his turban jewels (with more than 150 diamonds), his neck ornaments (with 50 emeralds), and his long coat, which had enough gold brocade to classify it as jewelry. The Adappakkaran was likewise indispensable for the dignity of the royal person. The betel he carried for the raja was used ritually to bind all formal relationships between the raja and his equals or his vassals. Here the people who chew together must by custom stay together. Likewise the Pillayandans had ritual duties in the upstairs apartments of the palace. They attended to the raja's royal appearance as dressers, a position later assumed by the valet. They held lanterns for the raja not simply to provide light but as a sign of his royal dignity (T.D. 1084). This duty of lantern holders was again later taken by a more specialized group of servants. The Kodaikkars, likewise, were classed with the servants who maintained the raja's most basic royal raiments, particularly associated with royalty. The raja had to be covered by an umbrella indoors as well as outdoors. The umbrellas were, then, not classed with the formal Biruthus worn only on state occasions, but were part of the raja's daily attire. The palanquins, also, were such a primary sign of royalty that they were in daily use. Moreover, the Bogis not only bore the raja in the palanquin outside the palace but also had duties inside. By custom, the raja had to be covered by a canopy when he sat in state, even inside the durbar hall. The Bogis constructed and cared for these canopies. Their head, the Povandan, had the additional duty of personally bearing the raja's food from the kitchen to the table (T.D. 1521). Only the raja and his immediate royal family were so served by the Povandan.

The entire set of servants was the heart of the personal establishment of the raja. Their duties were performed continually, with only occasional nods to changing times, from at least the late seventeenth century (as evidenced by the Inam Settlement Faisal Registry) to the dissolution of this small independent state. In addition to this core of inner servants, other specialized services were rendered in the inner palace but fell out of use. These were mentioned in either the Inam Settlement Faisal Registry or the earliest extant Huzur list (1880) but appeared in no later lists. Raja Ramachandra, chastised by the British political agent for extravagant expansion of the Huzur, may well have inflated the number of servants by the mid-nineteenth century by adding such people as tennis markers and lantern men. In addition to these "new" servants, the Inam Settlement Faisal Registry mentioned a few quite ancient "services" that had long been discarded even by the 1880s, such as tying the raja's turban (T.D. 769) and giving him oil baths (T.D. 2251–54; 2406). The stable inner core of servants, plus all the various officers discarded over time, did share the same function: direct service to the person of the raja.

The inner circle of servants cared for the raja's body, but here an important distinction must be made. These core servants did not minister to the raja's common physical body. Such common needs appear to have been the province of the nonroyal servants, such as the valet, the butler, the dhobi, and the barber, who did have ritual functions toward the raja as a Hindu but not as a king. Only the servants who held signs of royalty dressed and cared for the raja's state body. These inner-core officials handled the royal ornaments that were basic and inseparable from a truly royal body. These articles constituted intimate apparel for the dressing of a sacred lord. The "jewels" the Bokkushakkar guarded, the ornate turban, and the state jewelry could be worn only by the raja and in rare cases by his immediate family. The raja's own brother was forbidden to wear the royal turban (Darbar Files, R55/1875, "Royal Turban and Swordwearing Objection"). The status of all of these "clothes" as exclusive to the king becomes clear in the lengthy records of the honors the raja granted various administrative officers of the state. As a mark of respect and a symbol of shared royal status, many other royal symbols from the palace itself were lent to these administrators for temporary use during marriages or funerals. However, the state jewels, the umbrella, and the royal turban were never shared.

The inner core of servants, like the raiment they maintained, were never officially allowed to leave the palace, with one exception: The Bogis left the palace when they transported the raja, and they had to set up his canopy when he made state appearances outside the palace. The palanquins were also the one "intimate" royal article that was lent to administrative officers. But the head of the Bogis, the Povandan, remained an exclusively royal servant. The Bogis formed the transition to the next circle of servants, the first set of the outer "civil" establishment. Prominent in this interface between the inner and outer servants was the palace Head Harikar and the Harikars who served under him. Like the Bogis, the Harikars also linked the raja with the outside world. The Head Harikar technically was the palace messenger, but again he did not convey simple business notes. Instead, the Head Harikar carried the royal family's much coveted gifts of clothing to weddings and funerals. So important was this official that the royal family continued to employ him well after the merger of Pudukkottai into the Indian union. As late as 1978 the palace Head Harikar, then a very old man, continued to carry royal gifts for weddings and funerals of old state officers and members of the extended royal family. Still a very busy man, he stopped for a moment to pose for our camera in his official court dress just outside the Residency while on his way to perform his duties (Plate 61). These palace Vastrams (Sanskrit, *vastra*, garments) were another category of honor bestowed on administrators and family members. The Head Harikar carefully noted the precedents for such gifts (see "The Harikar's Diary"). The palace Head Harikar also supervised the lending of palace Biruthus for such ritual functions. The Harikar's diary was often consulted when disputes over rights to all such royal honors arose. The Head Harikar alone, like his counterpart the Bokkushakkar in the inner circle, knew the exact protocol for each royal honor and royal Biruthus in his charge. Unlike the Bokkushakkar, however, the Harikar maintained a different set of royal "raiment." In his care was the palace Dignitary Establishment—the first circle of royal servants that formed or bore the paraphernalia of state that constituted the raja's "outer" garments.

The officials in the inner core of servants, plus the Bogis and Harikars who mediated between the inner palace and the external world, were part of a very old ritual establishment that functioned when the hinterland rajas were still warrior lords. The Adappakkaran, the Bokkushakkar, and the Harikar appear together in a vivid description of the final preparation of a king for battle. The Kaṭṭapommaṉ Varalāṟu, an old Tamil ballad, describes the last battle before Kattabomman (here the hero) was captured by the Tondaimans. The ballad dwells in great detail on the final ritual preparations for battle made by Raja Kattabomman in his inner chambers. The hero first "sent" his Harikar to call his generals to join him. Next

Plate 61. The tradition continues as Sri K. Subramanian, palace Head Harikar, waits on the front porch of the Residency, at this time the home of Rani Rema Devi (His Highness's sister-in-law) and the late Rajkumar Radhakrishna Tondaiman (His Highness's brother). A wedding in the family has given the Harikar much to do this morning as he prepares to greet guests.

he commanded the Bokkushakkar to bring the treasure chest; taking the royal raiment from the chest, Kattabomman dressed himself for battle. He donned his "gold-laced turban fixed with pearls." From that box he also took rings for his fingers, gold chains, and massive gold earrings. His royal dress was completed with jeweled armor, a jeweled dagger, and garlands covering his heroic chest. Thus dressed, Kattabomman called his Adappakkaran, here described as a person selected by the raja for his "steadfast loyalty." This Adappakkaran was never to leave the king's side; he was the "royal shadow." The Adappakkaran brought Kattabomman his outer garments, the royal robes, and also distributed the betel that sealed the bonds of fidelity between the royal lord and his generals. Thus ornamented, Kattabomman strode out "in his royal way" to meet "his cheering people" and finally to face his enemy (Kaṭṭapomman Ūmaiyan̠ Varalār̠u, 28–30).

The long-standing associations of the Harikar and the Adappakkaran with the ritual of battle finds further corroboration in very early records of Pudukkottai (Huzur Records, vol. 1, entry dated Fasli 1214). Harikar is identified in several other sources as key to military operations (Rajayyan 1974, 34). Here the most ancient ritual function of the inner core of servants highlights their continued service as royal "dressers." The later care of the royal person whose warlike fire was long quelled by the Pax Britannia still bore the imprint of this ancient preparation for war—the ultimate public appearance. The peaceful Tondaimans were still bejeweled each day to face their public by the same ritual hands that had once prepared them for war. This inner core of servants remained the first level of the ritual clothing process.

The Semicircle

The Head Harikar, ruler of the Dignitary Establishment, held the keys to the next layer of the king's public body. The full Dignitary Establishment included all the servants who encircled the king with what might be called the "public" Biruthus—the emblems of royalty the king "wore" only when he sat in full state in the durbar hall or when he drove out of the palace in full procession. Such public appearances were more frequent in earlier times in Pudukkottai than during the twentieth century. Some of Pudukkottai's older citizens still remember their grandfathers saying that the raja used to drive along the street in state every night. Many attest that a king was expected to appear in state on a frequent and regular basis. The many old land grants made for *sannak safāri*, "accompanying the raja during state drives," substantiated these memories. It was the Dignitary Establishment that fully "dressed" the king for these public "appearances" that gave darsan, that beatific sight of the king.

The Dignitary Establishment included servants who held the Biruthus, the emblems of royal power that further aggrandized the royal body. When asked why the king always had to be surrounded by so many attendants, an old court musician aptly replied, "So he would look majestic, be the center of attention." The paraphernalia bearers were the first rays of this expanded royal majesty.

Listed next to the paraphernalia bearers as a part of the Dignitary Establishment were the court dancers and musicians. The nature of this musical establishment changed over the years, but their ritual function continued. The musical establishment further extended the raja's majesty into his kingdom. While the royal insignia bearers were never lent by the raja for public use, the raja did send his own palace musicians as another honor to administrative officers and family members for use during marriages and funerals. These palace musicians, like the paraphernalia bearers, however, still retained their status as personal servants of the king. They were part of his royal person and were in themselves Biruthus. The very first set of Biruthus earned by the Tondaimans included a set of bards and a troupe of dancing girls with musical accompanists.

On the border of the Dignitary Establishment were a group of servants called Dalayets, led by the Jamedar and the Daffedar. These titles are Persian and most clearly reflect the Moghul heritage. These two officers stood on either side of the raja during the durbar and flanked his coach during processions. But the Dalayets themselves did not have a formal place either in the durbar or in the processions. This group with their officers begins the first ring of the royal military guards. The titles Jamedar and Daffedar are taken from old military rankings (see Huzur Records, vol. 1, letter dated Fasli 1215), but their liveries and that of the Dalayets identifies them more as downstairs "office boys" than as military personnel. In the same group of semi-military servants were the Ondiyaruppu (night watchmen), the Madikaval (upstairs watchmen), and the Kavals (simply watchmen), old Tamil titles. These three groups of services are prominent in the Inam Settlement Faisal Registry. The Madikavals and the Ondiyaruppu have a place in the 1880 Huzur list, but all such watchmen were dropped from later Huzur lists. Only the Dalayets were retained in an official status. Here the Muslim term and the personnel attached to it clearly occupied positions as guards, but in a much elevated status from their Tamil counterparts.

The king's actual bodyguard was formed from a most unusual assortment of people. The categories mentioned in the Inam Settlement Faisal Registry have been so long discarded that no one in Pudukkottai today was certain what their duties were. The Registry, however, does clarify the basic structure of this bodyguard. The head of the king's own forces was the Ressaldar, who led two groups of guards: the Baragiri and the Razus. The Inam Settlement Faisal Registry also mentioned a servant called a Bangu, most likely from another set of guards who disappeared even by the 1880s. The most striking aspect of these categories of guards was their caste designation. The Settlement Registry identifies those classed as Baragiri either as Muslims or as Telugu Brahmans. One such Telugu Brahman took out his official vest and dagger and posed for our camera with his wife in front of his house, with proud memories of long ago clearly written on his face (Plate 62). The title Razu was both a caste designation and a royal service. The Inam Settlement Faisal Registry does mention a class of guards called "Sardar" (or Sirdar) and identifies these as Kallars (T.D. 622, 623, 1238, 1336, 1260). It is interesting that the 1880 Huzur list identifies the Baragiri as "Sirdars" but that none of the names listed are Kallar ones. Those palace "Sirdars," then, must have been the remnant of that older group of palace guards, the Servai, classified as "slaves of the palace." The Brahman warriors, Telugu clansmen, and Muslim royal guards must have been like Swiss bodyguards to the pope. They were outsiders to the regular state militia and even to the general populace in Pudukkottai. Such guards were truly royal servants and are important remnants of the origin of the Tondaiman's power both in the Telugu regions of the Vijayanagar Empire and in the more recent Muslim rule. Early records indicate that such a guard remained fiercely loyal to their royal lord (Tanjore District Records, R. 3516, letter dated January 27, 1813). The king's body alone was their charge, not the kingdom. However, the British resident understandably tried to dismiss them as "unnecessary palace servants" in 1815 (Tanjore District Records, letters dated October 12, 1815, and March 20, 1816). Nevertheless, these bodyguards remained in the palace until the 1880s, when a far more neutral and far less ritually loyal group of "sepoys" replaced them as the raja's "own" military establishment. The use of sepoys was inspired by the British Raj, who granted the native princes the right to maintain such small armies as a sign of their status as former allies.

In the palace and in the state processions, the raja's bodyguards functioned as a layer of skin around the raja's full public body. Their modern counterparts—the sepoys—marched just in front of the Dignitary Establishment but behind the state bands and the great jeweled elephants that always led the procession. The category of servants who preceded even the bodyguard were part of the large palace Stable Establishment under the charge of the Stable Superintendent. This officer, like his counterpart the Bokkushakkar in the inner household and the Head Harikar in the Dignitary Establishment, kept careful records and was an expert in royal precedent, for the Stable Establishment also was a crucial interface between the raja and the public. The stables were geographically closest to the palace's outer walls and functioned to bring the raja closest to the public at large. While the inner core of servants dressed the raja to meet the public within the walls of the palace, and the Dignitary Establishment "clothed" him to meet public gaze during the durbar or the processions, the Stable Establishment actually brought the raja into the streets of his domain.

Plate 62. In a portrait that might be called "Indian Gothic," Sri Sathiamurti Rao, with his wife standing proudly next to him, puts on his green vest and holds the dagger that once marked his family as the raja's bodyguards.

Going Outside

The stables were complex organizations that included several types of bands, tent lascars, an assortment of important animals, and a variety of vehicles. Such an odd mixture, which seems to combine a musical and transporting function, did make ritual sense. The band itself had military overtones and functioned as a "guard" (Darbar File 1258c/1900, "Marriage Honours"). The bandsmen appeared to guard the king's person ritually with music (compare with Hart 1975, 135). The function of the Nagarakhana Band was an excellent example of the ritual logic of the stables. The very special musical instruments that formed this band had to be carried on decorated elephants and horses. The instruments themselves were exclusive royal symbols, and this band itself was a mark of kingly status (Darbar File, DD 13/1867, "Nagara and the Dunka"). This Nagarakhana played each morning and evening at the gates of the palace, a practice that illustrated the dual function of the stables—to open royalty to the public and at the same time to establish its borders. An earlier version of the Nagarakhana may have been accompanied by uniformed guards as it played throughout the night, circling the borders of the palace. These uniformed guards accompanying the band were identified in an interview with the Baragiri. The purpose of this night band clarifies the root function of the Nagarakhana: to guard, to demarcate, and as one member of the royal family put it, "to let the people know that the palace is always awake." The bands, then, formed a wall of music around the king, a very ethereal wall that infiltrated the streets of the capital with its unrelenting sound, eliciting not forbidding public interest in the royal body within.

The stables also provided the transportation used when the raja rode out to his people in state procession. The oldest of such royal vehicles may well have been the elephant and the Kothal horse. Coach and horses, however, carried the Tondaiman in state during the recorded history of the family. Later, motor cars were listed along with the horses, and their fuel charges were simply added to charges for the hay and oats (see Palace Records, dated March 23, 1942, and August 27, 1933). All these vehicles remained important royal symbols. No one in the kingdom could use the same type of vehicle as the raja without specific permission. There is a hilarious case of an unfortunate stranger to Pudukkottai customs who was arrested and nearly jailed for daring to ride through the capital in a double-horse carriage, an exclusively royal vehicle (Darbar Files, R1174c/1902, R1219/1902, R560c/1908, R1334c/1906). In addition to the drivers of the royal vehicles, the Stable Establishment included the tent lascars, who set up any outdoor tents needed to shelter the raja when he had to attend functions outside the palace.

The bands, the vehicles, and the animals of the stables were the insignias of royalty the raja most frequently lent as an "honor" for use by the administrative officers of the state during their family weddings and funerals. The palace honor most often sent for marriage or funeral processions of minor state officers was the simple "one jeweled elephant." The next order of status usually merited "one jeweled elephant and a kothal horse with black kalki." The same animals led the raja's own state procession and hence were farthest from his person. A much higher mark of respect was the sending of one band or the lending of a coach and pair. But all these stable honors were granted far more commonly than the sending of the palace pipers from the raja's Dignitary Establishment, which marked the recipient as closer to the royal person. The stables provided, on the whole, the most generalized sharing of royalty both in the outright loan of vehicles and bands and in the most public presentation of the royal person in the streets of his capital and beyond. The Stable Establishment was like a centipede whose numerous legs stretched out from the palace and into the streets. When the Stable Establishment carried the royal body itself, their vehicles and their tents became a moving house for royalty, a palace in motion.

All those who served the king in his house did not care for his body in a simple secular sense. These servants were elaborately organized in concentric circles around that royal person. Each circle wrapped the king in yet another layer of his full public garments. The inner circle dressed the king's body in the most basic of royal raiment—the very clothes that seemed to turn the Kallar body into the body of a king. The full Dignitary Establishment added the first layer of his outer garments, the dress that made him fit for public sight and that extended his royal person well beyond the confines of his own physical body. The Stable Establishment further built his full royal body, giving it the power of movement. At each stage in the process, the king became more public, more visible, a sight to behold. As layer upon layer of royal dress built and extended his person, the king was transformed from that self which was naked of social power into the social being par excellence, for when the king was fully dressed, he was indeed the font of all social being. When the king was fully ornamented, his own royal body hovered over the kingdom, guaranteeing that civilization would pervade the domain.

Although the fully ornamented king symbolized human society in the realm, the king inside the palace was never totally defined by that bejeweled body. It is significant that the king was considered to be the lord and master but *not* the owner of his own house. The palace Head Harikar revealed this concept by explaining that the different parts of the palace "belonged" to various royal servants. Thus the lemons offered there to the king by the administrative officers as a sign of fidelity were "shared" by the Bogis as joint owners of this part of the palace. Likewise, when the king rode in procession in the royal landau, the garlands presented to him there "belonged" to the syces because these horsemen "owned" the carriages. Exactly how far this principle of ownership extended in the palace is not clear, but the principle remained: While the raja's servants were rooted in the palace, his own kingdom was not quite of this world.

The Huzur Establishment allowed the raja to share and redistribute emblems of his royal status. In this capacity, the palace was indeed the center of a pooling and redistribution process modeled on the ancient sacrificial model. But any analysis of these ever so important "menials" must recognize their sacramental function. They were at once priests who transformed the body of a man into the body of a God, and yet were themselves the raw matter in this transformation process. And ultimately, what was the palace and its multifarious inhabitants? In a mystical yet corporeal sense, these columned halls and the servants who inhabited them must answer together, "We *are* the king." Yet the king himself was more than the sum of these parts.

6

Beyond the Walls of the Palace
The Raja's "Other" Kingdom

The young raja of Pudukkottai sits with his Dignitary Establishment in the old photograph. Here His Highness reigns inside the walls of his "new fort," his *putu-k-kōṭṭai*. But earlier that day the young raja traveled in procession out of his palace with an even larger and much more mysterious entourage. Long rows of sepoys were followed by uniformed guards carrying two enormous metal birdlike creatures followed by others carrying spears. Outside the orderly rows to the right of this group marched the bearers of the kettledrum, the Dunka (Plate 63). The raja's coach and white horses came next (Plate 64), adding a note of London to this seemingly primordial procession. His Highness's coach is flanked with women on his right and men on his left, all bearing silver torches on their heads to light his way on the sunny streets. A careful eye can also spot the Brahman priests in white dhotis also flanking the raja's coach, but at some distance. Many other Brahmans can be seen far behind. Alongside the king during a portion of the procession, the Guruswami, the raja's spiritual adviser, was carried in a palanquin. The ancient drum sounded and the bejeweled elephants lumbered forward, leading their lord's procession around the city in a scene filled with the noise of drums and sights of spears, birds, and elephants more reminiscent of a forest than of a "fort."

An old Tamil folk song lauds a much earlier procession, when the raja of Pudukkottai rode not in a landau but on his own royal elephant. The poem may well be describing the last great procession of H.H. Sir Martanda Tondaiman, who celebrated his own silver jubilee on the throne in a style to rival Victoria. That moment was fortunately captured by the camera (Plate 65) and seems to be well described in the folk song:

Plate 64.   As the raja's coach approaches in the second frame of this series, the Dignitary Establishment attests to his immediate royal presence in this coach made in daring imitation of the British royal landau. Notice the Valaiyan torch bearers on the left of the photograph, and the Brahman priests on the far right.

directly served the Tondaiman rajas show that the only major caste distinction that marks these servants is a distinction between those who serve inside the palace and those who retain direct forest connections. In the Inam Settlement Faisal Registry, the caste of all who held land on tenure for the service inside the palace were listed for each case. Of those who serve the king as his own staff, the particulars of caste seem to extinguish before his royal presence. Muslims hold office in the Dignitary Establishment alongside Hindu Vellalars. Vellalars, supposedly landholders and farmers, serve as the king's tailors. Kallars, those fierce fighters, as well as the "farmer" Vellalars, both dress their lord and carry his food. Brahmans alongside Muslims and Kallars serve as various types of guards. The only clear associations of traditional caste with royal service are the Brahmans who serve specifically as priests for the raja, and the Valaiyan, a forest people who hunt and guard the forest preserves

Plate 65.   A photo album of the grand "Silver Jubilee" of His Highness Martanda Tondaiman captures a moment that would be his subjects' last glimpse of the ruler riding the royal elephant in all his glory. The album also contains a striking picture of this Indian prince as he entertained his British friends at a garden party foreboding the overpowering love of things European that would be the raja's ruin. Raja Martanda's unwelcome marriage and his ensuing permanent exile in France occurred within two years. (From the Residency Albums, with the kind permission of Rani Rema Devi.)

for the king. Thus, while a variety of castes can serve in a single category for most forms of service, "caste" remains fixed only at two points. The divisions, then, of the palace servants are:

Valaiyan————the people————Brahman

But once the duties of the Brahmans and the Valaiyans are explored, this threefold division quickly breaks down into a simple dualism that can roughly be described by such terms as forest/field and palace/jungle. The dualism, however, moves well beyond a simple connection between king and forest. The raja's very divinity feeds on his forest connections.

The Valaiyan were represented inside the palace by the head Vedaikari (literally, hunting man) who was attached to the palace storehouse and supervised the goods and services that

His Highness's forest subjects provided for their lord. The Valaiyan as a group, however, did not work in or even near the palace. Their home and their domain were the hunting preserves of the king. When the raja entered these forests, the Valaiyan served him there to beat the jungles for game. As late as 1932, palace records mention a special reward given to one hundred Valaiyan who aided the young raja during his first shoot (Palace Records, document dated December 13, 1932). The services of these forest folk went well beyond hunting. Inam Settlement Registers also record their services as supplying medicinal herbs for the raja's health and game meat for the raja's table (Inam Settlement Faisal Registry, T.D. 761, T.D. 381, T.D. 384). Late palace records include requests that these forest servants procure honey for the young princes and capture a spotted deer for the raja's personal zoo (Palace Records, document dated October 11, 1941). During Dassara and for other temple festivals, the Valaiyan were expected to procure from the king's forest the poles needed to tie decorative festoons in front of the palace and the wood for the bonfires at the important Maheswari Puja. This latter ceremony fittingly involved the forest people, since it marked the sending of palace offerings, *kāvaṭi,* to Palani and Viralimalai, temples dedicated to that other great wilderness lord, the ancient God Murugan, whose divine "palaces" the Tondaimans especially patronized.

The Valaiyan, then, cared for the raja's forest domain and brought into the civilized world things needed from the forest. But their tasks extended to even more important duties. Their ministrations stretched from care of the jungle to care of the king. The vital healing herbs, the meat, and the honey preserved the king's own body. And honey is no common fare. Lord Murugan is said to especially like this substance, and that divinity's image is literally bathed in this sweet ooze during worship. Meat, while impure for most castes, has been deemed necessary to the strength of the king even by orthodox Brahmans. Meat the forest provided seems all the more powerful. The Valaiyan appear to have been "feeding" the rajas, but not on the dull food wrought by the plow. The king did not live by bread alone.

Certainly the king, also, did not live on honey and venison alone, and like any other South Indian took his share of cooked rice and grains. But such foods did not have ritual value for the royal lord. There are indeed palace cooks for all the raja's meals, but no special farmers are granted land as *araṇmaṇai ūḻiya* to supply ingredients for these daily meals. Rice and grain were common food at court, although both were the chief ingredients in pure Brahmanic sacrifices, but while rice is a suitable food for the Gods, the corpus of the king required stronger substances.

The forest people, then, were building and maintaining a special body for the king. Though closely connected to the earth, this body was more than physical. The forest people seemed to maintain the king's presence in the forest domain, from which he derived his royal strength. They were in this sense in charge of the king's forest self, for while the king went out of the forest into the "fort"—the bastion of civilization—the forest folk maintained power within his initial domain. Tamil folk legend credits the forest people with generalized powers of healing and, beyond this, with many of the same powers classical myth and Pudukkottai court ballads had ascribed to the king. In the *Virālimalai Kuṟuvañci,* a drama performed during the festivals at this famous Murugan temple in Pudukkottai, a woman from the Kuruva clan (another wilderness tribe closely related to the Valaiyan) described the powers of the hunting peoples. She claimed the magical ability to predict the future, to capture tigers and tame them into pussycats, to catch deer without force, to frolic unharmed with bears, to make even a bitter substance taste as sweet as mangoes, to turn copper into gold, to make a stone float, and to cure even the diseases of the Gods. That ability to live innocently among the animals, to effortlessly tame tigers, echoes the powers of the jungle exploits of the Tondaimans and the mythical first Hindu king, Pṛthu, as we shall see.

Just as the forest people were linked directly to the palace by a representative, the Brahman community as a whole had its link to the palace in the person of the Guruswami. Individual Brahmans or special Brahman sects did serve in the court as Harikars, in the treasury as accountants, in the Saraswati Mahal (the royal library) as copyists, in the raja's own armed forces as bodyguards, or in the durbar hall as singers and musicians. Brahman services were used throughout the complex system of state-supported temples. But there remained one special service, initiated by the first Guruswami, which all Brahmans performed for the raja. During the Dassara festival, all Brahmans who so wished were fed a full meal at a special feeding house temporarily constructed and maintained by the king. By eating this meal and thereby accepting his offering, the Brahmans performed an important "service" for the raja: They allowed him the right to perform righteous charity and thereby expiate sins. The nature of this "service" was complex and defined the most important aspect of the king-Brahman relationship in Pudukkottai.

In 1738 the raja of Pudukkottai became the disciple of the saint Sadasiva Brahmendra. The naked guru had taken a vow of silence and wrote only two spiritual instructions in the sand for the earnest raja: a mantra to Shiva as Dakshinamurti (his form as the south-facing preceptor of the Gods) and an injunction to appoint Gopalakrishna Sastriar as Guruswami. All formal Brahman connections to the palace developed from this source. Thus the entire Brahman community that served the palace did so not in their capacity as ritual experts, as priests of the sacrifice, but rather by virtue of their connections to a naked forest-dwelling ascetic, Sadasiva Brahmendra. In other words, it is their asceticism and not their ritual expertise that marked their relationship to the king. They were as much outsiders to normal society as the Valaiyans. Both castes, in a real and a figurative sense, are of the forest and not of the field.

The new royal preceptor, the first Guruswami, later interpreted Sadasiva's sparse message and enjoined the regular feeding of Brahmans as the major form of expiation for all the Tondaimans' past sins. Here the Brahmans functioned as the most important figures in a continuous cycle of expiation that revolved daily, weekly, and then yearly during the Dassara festival. In their capacity as expiators, the Brahmans were both the closest and the most removed from the daily business of kingship.

The center for this continual process of expiation in the palace was the Puja Hall (Tamil, *pūjai vīṭu*), "the house of worship," and the Dakshinamurti temple. Here the cooks and storehouse attendants attached to the inner palace Puja Hall and temple provided for these daily and weekly feedings. The Brahman priests attached to this temple were always listed in a group as part of the official Huzur Establishment. Usually mentioned were two "Purohitas," two "Poojaikaru," and the "Joshier," who was the official palace astrologer. The name of the Guruswami usually heads the list (see Palace Records, Document Listing the

Budget for the Dignitary Establishment, dated February 15, 1912). Although the king's preceptor never served as a temple priest here, his very name associates the Dakshinamurti temple with its ancient purpose, the expiation of royal sin. Why the raja needed expiation is another part of this long story, which must wait for the next chapter.

In the oldest palace lists available, the Guruswami's name appears atop a long list of yet another kind of Brahman servant that was dropped from the Huzur Establishment after 1890 and reclassified as a state service. The former classification of these Brahmans as palace servants, however, provides a most important clue to the full cycle of Brahman services for the king. Here were listed the Brahmans who did *japam* (quietly muttered prayers) and the *śivapūjā* (worship of Shiva). These services were not performed in the palace but were regularly done in the homes and small temples of the outlying *brahmadeya*, exclusively Brahman villages in the state. These villages were a kind of "wilderness," a compromise between actually living in the forest as ascetics and living fully in society. A recent photograph of a Brahman employed to recite japam during a temple ritual in a neighboring state shows him seated on an antelope skin quietly muttering prayers in the midst of the hubbub with all the signs of his ascetic/forest connections surrounding him (Plate 66). The photograph well represents the position of the "Japa Brahmans" in places like Pudukkottai. They were aloof from serving as temple priests, yet they maintained the delicate connections between the asceticism and social duty.

Plate 66.   Seated on an antelope skin, this Brahman quietly recited japam throughout the Mahakumbabhishekam, the three-day ritual to consecrate the divine image of the saint Sri Thyagaraja, a famous composer of Carnatic vocal music. The chanting of the japam here continues the old tradition in South India for great events to be blessed by the reciting of continual prayer by Brahmans, whose ascetic life is represented here by the *rudraksha* beads around the reciter's neck and the pot of holy water at his side. Now that royal patronage for such priests is gone, members of the old japam Brahman families work in the modern world and serve only for such special events. This gentleman holds a position in the city police force.

The Inam Settlement Faisal Registry contains a number of land grants for japam in particular. According to these, the prayers were for "the welfare and prosperity of His Highness the Maharaja" (Inam Settlement Faisal Registry, T.D. 3246, T.D. 3248). These land grants were among the few categories of service for the state that were not enfranchised and were allowed to continue on the most ancient basis of "payment," the gift of land for service (T.D. 3245–3248; see also Venkat Row 1921, 370). These japams were chanted on a regular basis. Some were performed daily in the private homes of Brahmans, others weekly in front of the main deity of local temples. During Dassara the japams were chanted continuously in the Tirugokarnam temple and other major temples of the state. One undated document in the palace records, "List of Names of Persons Performing Invocations to Various Astral Bodies," numbers the japams recited at 185. Another from the Dassara in 1940 lists 91 "Japa Brahmans" whose prayers filled temples in the town of Pudukkottai and beyond (Palace Records, document dated October 2, 1940). Daily, weekly, and yearly prayers resounded for the raja. The land was alive with the sound of holy chants repeated so much, says an old Tamil poem, that even the parrots learned them (Śri Birakatampaḷ Pēril Canta Kummi, 41).

The Guruswami headed all phases of Brahmanic services for the raja: the feeding of Brahmans within the palace and during Dassara to expiate sin; worship conducted inside the palace for the raja; and prayers chanted at all corners of the kingdom for the raja's welfare. Feeding expiated the raja's "sins" but also kept alive the very Brahmans whose chants ensured his "welfare." The outlines of a transformation process are here, a process that was the inverse of the activities of the body-building forest people. The Brahmans took rice and grain from the raja. The Brahmans were fed by him; they did not feed him. But like the forest people, the Brahman villages were as isolated from mainstream society as the forest preserves. The Brahmans, like the forest people, held the raja's place and established his presence in another type of wilderness.

Unlike larger and older princely states in India, the Brahmans of Pudukkottai seemed confined as a priestly community to extrasocial affairs. They never gained a firmly established place in the kingdom as royal advisers until the British intervened with their selection of a Brahman dewan. A group of Brahmans in Orissa, Mysore, and Travancore, for example, formally served as a body of advisers for the king in the regulation of society. The Pudukkottai Brahmans never held such a firmly established social position. Even in the courts of justice where Brahmans long functioned elsewhere as experts in Dharma Sastras, the early Tondaimans apparently functioned alone as the final judge and mediator. Only quite late, sometime in the early 1800s, did the Tondaimans establish a system of Brahman-controlled courts—the Darmashanam (Darbar Files, "History of the Courts of Justice," by A. S. Sastri, in Administration Report for 1882). Certainly in their individual capacity as scholars, Brahmans had long been honored with gifts of land. In the early twentieth century, Brahmans who passed a state-sponsored examination in Sanskrit scripture were honored as a group in a special "Carnatic durbar" held during Dassara. However, there is evidence to support the claim made by learned non-Brahmans that this form of durbar had traditionally honored the Tamil poets called Pulavars. This turn of royal interest from Tamil poetry to Vedic discourse is said to have been a late development in Pudukkottai. Also considered late was the practice of seating the Brahman Vidwans opposite the Sardars when the "political" and "Carnatic" durbar forms were combined. All these formal nods to orthodox tradition in more-established states remained pro forma in Pudukkottai. There are no records even hinting that the king actually consulted the Guruswami or the established Brahman Vidwans who sat among the courtiers in the raja's durbar on types of legal or ethical issues on which Brahmans normally pronounced the final judgment. Only after Dewan Sastri's time were the Brahmans clearly consulted as pandits. The powers of the Brahman community in pre-British Pudukkottai in practical matters of government were limited. Their major function remained "spiritual"—they were important cogs in the wheel of prayers and charities that expiated the raja's seemingly endless store of past "sins."

The Guruswami was called the preceptor of the king, but like the Brahman community in general that sense of "teaching" was specifically limited to "spiritual advice." Various versions of the meeting of Sadasiva Brahmendra with the Tondaiman affirm that this raja was seeking "spiritual instruction" (Radhakrishna Aiyar 1916, 792). In one version, the Tondaiman took instruction from the guru for many years until "the ruler himself started his penances in a state of enlightenment" (*Catācivam Pirāmēntirār Carittiram*). In most other versions, the raja received his actual instruction from the Guruswami. A long document in the Inam Settlement Faisal Registry contains a detailed legendary account of the spiritual relationship between the first royal preceptor and the ascetic-minded Tondaiman (Inam Settlement Faisal Registry, T.D. 1033). Here the Tondaiman begged his Guruswami to initiate him into spiritual learning. Gopalakrishna Sastri refused, saying that if he gave the raja such personal advice his own limbs would become incapacitated. The Guruswami relented, gave the raja *upadeśa* (spiritual initiation), and as a result lost his eyesight. The raja then ordered expiatory services in several temples and established several brahmadeya villages. After these expiations, Sastri regained his eyesight. The Guruswami was then established at the king's expense in his own brahmadeya village and allowed to live a sacred life without any hindrance, and all facilities to lead a life strictly according to the tenets of Hinduism were afforded the guru. After such an exemplary life away from the strain of earning his daily bread, the Guruswami—here not the raja—attained enlightenment. His place of samadhi became a shrine supported to that day by the Tondaimans. By tradition, then, the office of the Guruswami represented the ascetic life within the borders of the worldly kingdom.

Although the associations of the Guruswami were with the ascetic tradition, all the Guruswamis were granted the royal Biruthus of an umbrella, a palanquin, maces, and two silver torches. Such honors were normally granted those who shared the king's authority and replicated his functions throughout the kingdom.[1] Here the grant of these Biruthus to the ascetic Guruswami makes sense only in the context of another ceremonial reserved exclusively for this royal preceptor. When the older Guruswami died, his son was installed in

---

1. These honors, as well as the land grants, were not resumed until the Pudukkottai Settlement of Inam Acts of 1956. See Office of the Director of Survey and Settlement, Board of Revenue, Madras, G.O.M.S., 1464, dated April 16, 1958, Report of the Special Officer, R. Thirumalai. The inam rules from 1888 to 1956 are recounted in this document.

office in the Tirugokarnam temple in a ceremony that closely parallels the raja's own coronation (Palace Records, document dated May 24, 1945, "Formalities Observed on the Installation of the Guruswami"). No other palace official was so installed. Even the most royal symbols, the ring and the earrings, were passed down in the Guruswami's family in the very same manner that the dying Tondaimans were said to have passed their rings and earrings to their chosen heir. The title of Guruswami, often also called the Rajaguru, is perhaps best understood not as the "guru of the raja" but rather as the "guru-king."

The Guruswami appears to have been the king's own alter ego in the "forest" world of the ascetic Brahmans. Gopalakrishna Sastri lost his eyesight, a vital part of his own body, when he gave the holy mantra to the king. Only after the king built Brahman villages and maintained Brahmans for prayers did the guru regain his eyesight. Clearly, the raja could replenish the yogic body of Gopalakrishna and yet keep the relinquished "holy word," which had drained the very body of the guru. Here again the raja and the ascetic guru are linked body and soul. The raja is himself now an ascetic-Brahman in that he shares the power of the Guruswami's holy Brahman body. The cycle of Brahman–ascetic–king relationships becomes instead a Brahman–ascetic–king transformation process. Each can interchange functions with the other. The Guruswami is a king. The king is an ascetic. And the Brahmans serve as the mediators of these transfers of force and form between king and forest guru. The prayers chanted in the brahmadeya villages and in temples throughout the kingdom were chanted not *for* the raja but more precisely in his stead.

At this point an outstanding anomaly to the orthodox system in India existed in Pudukkottai. Here a startling reversal of the supposed sacrificial duties of the Brahmans occurred: The Brahmans, and not the Untouchables, removed the refuse of a royal ritual process. The Brahmans removed the king's sins by taking a share of his wealth in the form of grain and land. These priests transmuted that substance into the holy prayers—the essence of the king's ascetic body. Day by day they chanted new power into king and country—expiating and building, washing clean and filling up unseen vessels with invisible words that poured new energy into both the royal and the ascetic body. By doing so, the kingdom and the king prospered.

Yet the kingdom and the king could not prosper without that other type of priest, the Valaiyan, for again in an odd cycle of reversals these uncivilized persons give to the king. They preserve and maintain his equally necessary body—that forest self which is the very source of all civilized life. And in the midst of the ever-present reminders of *both* these wilderness peoples stand all the palace servants who fed and clothed their lord in splendor within the walls of the palace.

The palace Head Harikar stated that the king did not "own" the palace, but the Huzur Establishment also seemed to "own" it in a very transitory sense. Like their royal lord, the members of the entire palace establishment all had at least one foot in the "forest." Brahmans and the Valaiyans most certainly existed close to the "forest," but even the servants who lived in the palace had caste genealogies that stretched back into the wilderness realm. While there was no correlation between caste and each category of service in the palace, the staff as a whole belonged to a specific set of castes within Pudukkottai—primarily Kallar, Ahambadiyan, and Vellalar, and secondarily Razus, Valuvadis, and Idaiyan, as well as

Muslims. An often-quoted Tamil proverb that links the first three castes in an evolutionary scale from near tribal to pure Sudra states that a Kallar may slowly transform into an Ahambadiyan, who may by degrees become Vellalar (Thurston [1909] 1975, 3:63). Here the Kallar is still seen in almost Darwinian terms as the primal emigrant from the forest. The latter three common castes of the palace servants also shared such near tribal roots. Valuvadis (Tamil, *valuvāṭi*) are in fact said to be refined Valaiyan. The Idaiyan (Tamil, *iṭaiyan*) were an ancient pastoral people who inhabited the fringe areas between the cultivated lands and the hilly regions. The Razus were a pure Telugu counterpart of the Kallars, and the Muslims, by virtue of their religion, lived on the edge of Hindu society (Venkat Row 1921, 178–95). The palace servants, as their king, were immigrants to the capital from the borders of society. They lived together with their lord in the center of the social world like those who "dwell alone in a forest in the midst of a garden land" (Micah 7:14). The story of this deep interconnection between king, court, and forest is not only written into the structure of the palace staff but quite literally written in the legend of the rise of the Tondaimans to royal power.

Tigers, Panthers, Elephants, and Kings

In Pudukkottai no one is the least surprised if questioned about the historical origins of the Tondaimans' rise to royal status. The question makes perfect sense here in an area where families could rise to royal power and fall back into commonness within a matter of decades. Royalty has a beginning and an end here, and stories of the rise and fall of just about everybody were the stuff that made folk legends in these arid regions of Tamilnadu (Waghorne 1989, 406). Missionary-scholar Caldwell suggested as early as 1856 that even the great dynasties of South India may have risen from the ranks of the "semi-barbarous chieftains, . . . like those of Ramnad and Puducottah in later times" (Caldwell [1856] 1961, 112). Stories explaining the end of Tondaiman power in 1948 are just beginning to take shape, but a complete cycle of origin legends exists in texts from as early as the eighteenth century and orally into the present. The basic scenario has remained stable, with varied delicacy and tone added in the different tellings. A person close to the royal family told the legend with great flourish:

> The Tondaimans were elephant trainers in the armies of the Vijayanagar empire who came south from Andhra Pradesh and settled in this region in a place they called Ambukkovil, "the place of compassion." They were chieftains at that time and began to gain good reputation for settling disputes wisely. One day the king of the Vijayanagar empire was traveling through the Ambukkovil area on a pilgrimage to the Ramesvaram Temple when one of his elephants turned wild and began to ravage the countryside. The king sent drummers to warn the people to get out of the way. When the drummers came to Ambukkovil, the Tondaiman asked how a king could be so weak that he could not tame his own elephants and keep them under control. The Tondaiman

went straightaway to complain to the king, who told the Tondaiman that if he could tame the elephant he would be granted honors and a title, but that if he could not he would be executed. The Tondaiman located the elephant and tricked it into flinging its tusks into a sandbank while he cleverly leaped on its back. The Tondaiman rode the elephant, now quite tame, back to the king. For this act, he was granted the title of *rāya* (Telugu for raja), a large tract of land, and the following honors: the right to have torchlights carried before him in the day; to wear a special sword; to have a lion flag as his standard; and to have an umbrella carried over him as he walked.

While telling the legend, Mr. Sadasivam dwelt with great relish on the battle between the Tondaiman and the elephant, which for him was the central act of the story.

The old Telugu poems Toṇḍamān Paḷegaru Kaifiyatu and the Toṇḍamān Vamsāvali, by court poet Nudurupati Venkanna (similar but with a genealogy is the "Toṇḍaman Paḷegaru Biradāvuli"), are still extant and give poetic versions of this story with considerable detail and flourish. Radhakrishna Aiyar, in his *General History of the Pudukkottai State,* fortunately summarized the old Tamil versions of the legend, "Rāya Toṇḍaiman Anurāgamālai" and the "Tondaiman Iraṭṭaimaṇimālai," the full texts of which are now lost (1916, 119–20; see also Brindadevi 1978, 53). These older ballads about the origin of the Tondaiman rule expand the story to include a long genealogy of the family. The capture of the Vijayanagar raja's own elephant is inevitably mentioned. These poems also give an exacting and bewildering list of more than twenty "Biruthus," honors bestowed upon the first Tondaiman raja for his valor: a copper image of the Gandabherunda (a mythical bird that preys on elephants), five-color flags, umbrellas, a horse with bells, a Bheri (high-pitched trumpet carried on an elephant), a horn made from white conch shell, flags with the emblems of a lion, fish, and Garuda (the eagle that carries Vishnu), special musical instruments, incense, a vessel containing special scents, good horses, a finely decorated knife, a large drum, a palanquin painted with a lion's-head emblem, the right to burn silver torches in the daytime, an elephant with a drum on its back, two white fans (Chamaram), bards, and a troupe of dancing girls, in addition to titles of honor. All these items were meant to be taken along when the new raja went in procession. In addition, these poems casually mention that the new raja was also given a tract of land.

Undaunted by the lengthy enumeration of these sets of emblems, the ballads relate the rest of the story of the Tondaimans' rise to power as if this were a long game of Biruthus monopoly. This first raja, Avadai Raghunatha Tondaiman (d. 1661), was childless, but after he prayed in a temple in his village, Shiva appeared to him in a dream and promised two sons who would be like precious pearls. These boys soon grew up and began to collect Biruthus on their own. The raja of Tanjore heard of the fame and beauty of these two young men and invited them to come to stay at his court. One version has the raja asking them to serve as warriors, but another hints that their good company alone was desired. The boys' chief exploit was to capture a tiger and a panther, for which they were awarded another set of Biruthus: a necklace with a coin bearing Rama's image, a sword called the Ramabhanda, more umbrellas, long coats with gold lace, jewelry, and a herd of elephants. When the Tanjore raja tried to force them to abjure their devotion to Shiva for Vishnu, the brothers returned home. Sometime later the Setupati (the title of the rajas of Ramnad) needed their services to catch some bigger game than elephants and tigers. He called them to help quell a rebellion of local chieftains. "Using kind words only," the elder brother talked the rebellious Tevars back into submission. Not to be outdone, his younger brother Namana returned to the more usual acts of bravery and killed one of the Setupati's own elephants, which had gone wild. Again the brothers returned home laden with more Biruthus, another tract of land, and the elder brother received the title from which he took his name, Raghunatha. As one final round of play, the two brothers served at the court of the raja of Madurai and tamed a rebellion of local chieftains to the south—this time by more bloody means. The Pandyan raja granted Raghunatha the right to use all his own royal titles. The longest and most classic of the Telugu poems continues the narration of war deeds in a staggering list of conquests from aid rendered to the Trichinopoly royal family to victory over the kings of Kerala and wars with former allies in Tanjore. By the time Raghunatha Raya Tondaiman (ruled 1668–1730) and his brother Namana completed their round of "services" in 1686, the raya was himself ruler of most of the territory called Pudukkottai. At this point the Tondaiman Vamsavali says that Raghunatha Raya worshiped the Goddess Brihadambal at the Tirugokarnam temple and built Pudukkottai, "a new fort," as the capital of what was now his kingdom. The tale ends as the Tondaimans entered history as the independent rulers of the new district of Pudukkottai in the year 1689.

This story of the Tondaimans was no doubt considered a truly epic tale. The Tondaiman Vamsavali adopts a grand tone for recitation at the court of a great monarch, and even the oral retelling was no less serious. Yet some of the most prominent figures expected in any epic are not here, and much of what is here seems trivial. Foremost in this cast of missing characters are the Gods who pour their blessings on the struggling hero. The Tondaiman Vamsavali traces the Tondaiman line back fourteen generations to one of Indra's earthly love affairs. The divine seed was long hybridized before the heroic deeds of Raghunatha Raya. Indra himself never appears on the scene. Shiva does intervene in the process of fertility, but again his presence hardly pervades the story. It is surprising that the great Goddess Brihadambal, the present tutelary deity of the Tondaiman, enters the picture only after the kingdom was won. Here other sources confirm that Raghunatha Raya indeed was the first Tondaiman to "pray to" the great Goddess, but he was not crowned in front of the Goddess's dais. Evidence is clear that the Goddess who viewed Raghunatha Raya's Pattabhishekam (coronation) was not Brihadambal of Tirugokarnam but the divine lady who resided in the nearby temple of Kudumiamalai.[2] Present opinion in Pudukkottai and older sources hold that this first coronation was done "in imitation" of the practices of the former rulers of the area and was not indigenous to the Kallar chieftains. It took centuries for the lady of Tirugokarnam to absorb the religious attention of the Tondaimans. The final admission that she was indeed vital to their rule came in 1881, when Ramachandra Tondaiman took the title Brihadambadas, "Servant of the Great Goddess." Again, opinion voiced in

---

2. From an interview with K. A. Panchapagesa Dikshitar, who read verses from *Sikāgirida Caritam*, a palm-leaf manuscript used in the last coronation ceremony held in Kudumiamalai in 1730.

official British records of the time tallies with present supposition in Pudukkottai. He did this in imitation of the practices of other, more major kingdoms (see "The Biruthus of the Tondaimans," 7). The Tondaimans, then, maintained good relationships with Gods of their kingdom, but the ultimate source of their power did not arise directly from such deities.

The story of the Tondaimans' rise to power presents another perplexing anomaly. The Tondaimans never actually gained Pudukkottai by conquest, as would be expected in such an epic tale. In fact, land is merely mentioned as one of the many rewards for bravery in those long lists of Biruthus. When Tondaimans perpetrated another heroic deed in Tanjore or Ramnad or Madurai, they were granted another piece of land near their own home village. The Tondaiman Vamsavali clearly disavows that land ownership makes a king. When young Raghunatha Raya went to the Tanjore court, the raja there asked him to be seated next to the throne, but the young Tondaiman modestly declined this public recognition of his royal status. The raja of Tanjore overruled his hesitation by assuring him, "Even though a servant possesses thousands of parcels of land, he will be a servant only. A king, even though possessing only ten villages, will always be called a king." Here the control of a tract of "land" was simply one sign of royalty—the size and location of this land was immaterial. This proved all too true for the raja of Tanjore. His own words prophesied his family's fate when a century later the rajas of Tanjore—along with so many other Indian kings, including Ramnad and Madurai—lost all land with the exception of the palace and "private" estates to the British. These rajas without kingdoms, now joined by the raja of Pudukkottai, remained kings nonetheless. It is interesting that when the new Republic of India annexed the remaining royal lands in India, the articles of succession stipulated that palaces, private estates, and all Biruthus or emblems of royalty could be maintained. The real tears of loss were not shed until 1972, when all these honors were also withdrawn. Only at that point was kingship in India legally abolished. The story of the Tondaimans' rise to power, then, was a tale of acquisition of royal power, not a tale of land conquest.

The audience for the epic tale of the Tondaimans' royal origins must have been expected to take seriously what the narration in fact makes surprisingly clear. The Tondaimans' rise to power was initiated by several bouts with two elephants, one tiger, and one panther gone wild, for which the family received an odd assortment of what were figuratively, and also even literally, white elephants. The Biruthus most certainly do not represent the basic necessities of life, but they are clearly basic to kingship. Both the blessings of the Gods and the control of the land were subordinated to these emblems as the primary sign—perhaps source—of kingship. Why should these very particular, even peculiar, objects "add" to the royal person? What exactly do they add? The Tondaiman legend at least offers an important clue: These Biruthus are directly related to a standard set of heroic deeds. The taming of elephants and wild animals and the quelling of rebellious chieftains are treated as formula episodes in all versions of the legend repeated whenever the Tondaimans take a new step toward full royal status. What relationship do tigers, elephants, panthers, and footloose clans have to the Biruthus?

The occupation of the Pudukkottai rajas with hunting tigers and taming elephants is an amazingly persistent theme in a variety of folk songs and court ballads in the district.

Martanda Bhairava Tondaiman, the sophisticated Edwardian gentleman of British training and education, was greeted during festivals by devadasis singing:

> Our king of Pudukkottai is His Highness Martanda Bhairava.
> If young ladies with spear-shaped eyes insist on it,
> He would fight and kill fearsome elephants and bears.
>
> (From a song sung from memory by Dasi Saraswati of Tirugokarnam)

Again a poet laureate of Pudukkottai praised the gracious exploits of the same royal gentleman:

> The king shot at the animals that came running toward him with their eyes wide with glee. People who heard the gunshots were frightened; they picked up their courage to go around the forest to see what had happened.
>
> Rutting elephants had died with begging screams; frightful tigers died out of fear; angry pigs fell dead; and tender deer fell like cotton balls.
>
> Someone ran shouting, "Look out!"; someone shouted, "Run!"; someone shouted, "Search!"; someone shouted "Assemble!"; someone ran joyfully and brought the pigs; someone danced and brought the deer; someone searched and became exhausted dragging in the elephants.
>
> The saints who heard about it became joyful; farmers heard about it and laughed heartily; ladies heard about it and danced; kings of other countries heard about it and feared for their lives.
>
> Everyone admired him; all were alleviated of their troubles and blessed him.
> (*Iyalicaippāmālai*, 13–14)

These poems cannot be viewed as simple statements of fact because in reality, by the twentieth century, the "forests" of Pudukkottai were inhabited perhaps by deer and a few bobcats but hardly teeming with elephants and tigers. For such game, the young raja and his English tutor had to roam over much of India in the name of education and of course good sport. The hunting expeditions of the raja were ritualized activities that the British ironically were happy to encourage because it tallied well with their own model of a country gentleman and with ancient traditions that to this day give Her Britannic Majesty exclusive rights over all swans and certain deer.

Teeming with animals or not, the forests of Pudukkottai were jealously guarded by the rajas as their private game preserves. Ramachandra Tondaiman, in the middle of the nineteenth century, carried on a heated correspondence with the British political agent over protection of his hunting rights against encroachment by a close relative (Darbar Files, D4/1869). The correspondence makes clear that when the raja granted villages, use of the nearby jungles was not automatically part of the gift. Such rights required special permission, because exclusive hunting privileges were considered a sign of royal status. Simple rights over land were granted by the raja to menial servants in his palace—to village blacksmiths and carpenters—but the hunting preserves of the kingdom touched far closer to his very royalty. In the poem above he was praised for doing what only he could do: kill the wild animals of the forest that encroached on farmlands. Clearly the control of those animals and their habitat was the exclusive domain of the king in a way that the cultivated land was not.

These strong suggestions of a special relationship between the Pudukkottai raja and the domain of the forest appears to be part of a broader South Asian motif. Nancy Falk explored the relationship of the wilderness to kingship in ancient South Asia through Buddhist texts, the Ceylonese royal chronicles, and recent practice in Orissa. She isolates "the wilderness pattern of kingship" in which conquest and pacification of the forest give the king control over the powerful beings and objects that reside there. The conquering king gains weapons, a new wife, and strong guards for the palace. In another scenario, the king acquires power by tending a shrine built within the royal capital that "is a kind of preserve, a presence of the wilderness in more civilized areas." This wilderness preserve often contains the royal seat of authority, a throne. Wilderness creatures and parts of their bodies likewise become "royal palladia" brought into the city and carefully tended by the king as primary sources of his authority. Trees, logs, and the ground surrounding a sacred tree form the major types of palladia (Falk 1973, 4).

The field research of Peter Claus on royal cults in Tulunad in Karnataka State confirms and expands Falk's textual findings. Claus argues that present aristocratic and past royal power in the area is based on a close relationship with a "spirit-king" whose realm is the wastelands and forests and the "dangerous animals and fierce spirits" that reside there. Claus points to continued mention of the "forest shrine" in both oral legend and ritual practice of the aristocratic Tulus. The deity of these shrines, which are located in a wasteland or forest, is housed in a palace-like temple and iconographically represented as a king. Claus develops an elegant model of the meaning of this dual royalty in districts of Tulunad. The human king, lord of the ordered civilized area, represented the realm of the productive and the realm of the living. The spirit-king presided over the "supernatural," "the realm of Maya" inhabited by the totemic spirits like the pig, tiger, buffalo, and naga (snake) and the deceased ancestors of the living. This forest realm is dangerous, but it remains the source of fertility for the living world. Claus argues that the primary priestly functions in this cult are held by those who mediate between the two worlds and who live symbolically and literally close to the borders between civilization and the forest. These low-caste ritual specialists include the oil pressers who prepare and carry oil soaked rag torches; the musicians; the carpenters who make the wooden shrine; and, the most important, the bard-mediums and dance-mediums, whose very bodies become vehicles for the forest spirits. All these low-caste priests entice the bodiless spirits into temporary bodies and carry them to a meeting place— the shrine—where aristocratic, royal family members, now also taking a priestly role, can propitiate those fearsome but necessary spirits (Claus 1978).

When the descriptions of the forest-king scenario in the research of Falk and Claus are combined, the outlines of a striking ritual pattern that parallels the raja–forest–Biruthus theme in Pudukkottai legend emerge. Of first importance here are the objects and people closely related to border areas and to the forest. These people and objects figure prominently

conquistador par excellence. His "servants" embody that forest power, but they stand at his command. Thus he is high, they are low.

Hart implies that this difference is clearly social and hierarchical. The king, the highest, is certainly not of the same class, caste, or clan as his necessary servants. Ironically, immediately after making this point, Hart was forced to explain "a curious phenomenon": Some poems clearly describe kings who freely eat and drink with their polluted bards. This anomaly in the whole hierarchical system shows that "the commensal taboo between high and low castes was not as universally observed as it is today" (Hart 1975, 125), but this explanation misses a crucial point. The poem Hart quotes to illustrate his point is dedicated to King Atiyaman, a chief of the Maravar, who were then and are now a wasteland people whose wild ways hardly classed them as solid citizens of a neatly ordered world.

Here, then, is the problem. The king's own body cannot always be neatly differentiated from the "forest beings" by caste or clan. In the case of Atiyaman, he is himself a son of the soil, a lord of forested and not solidly settled territory. The difference is crucial. The grandly bejeweled raja of Pudukkottai is also such a son of the soil, a Kallar. The Kallars, like the Maravars, are believed to be very closely related to the Kurumbas and the Vedar, ancient tribes that legend and history place as the "original inhabitants" of the forest areas in South India. In Tamil legend in particular, "the Kallars are never the migrating group, the aggressor, or the outsider, rather in every case, they are the settled group in the area 'brought under control' by the incoming group" (Blackburn 1978, 40). In the origin legends of the Pudukkottai Tondaimans, this distinction between a lord who tames his own people and a conquering outsider is clear. Here the fact that the Pudukkottai rajas never "conquered" the territory of Pudukkottai gains significance, as does that careful distinction between a landlord and a true king. The Tondaimans indeed tamed elephants and quelled rebellious Tevars, but again the language of conquest is never really adopted. In fact, the Tevars are Kallar clan chiefs, the southern branch of the Tondaimans' own people. Recall also that in some cases the rebellious chiefs and wild elephants are subdued "with kind words only," rather than with the sword. The Kallar Tondaimans followed the old rule and an older Tamil pun: "It takes a thief (*kaḷḷan*) to catch a thief." The Pudukkottai rajas, then, are part of a grand exception to the "conquering" model of the king-forest relationship. These sons of the soil— or rather sons of the forest—were lords over the very "forest beings" with whom they shared a common status.

Something in the very language of "conquest" and "ordering" of the forest, of pushing back the chaotic evil, does not quite fit the kings whose very bodies arose from the forest and who were kissing-cousins to those low, wild people who lived with the king's own clan within the forest regions. Much of the theoretical language used to describe the king's relationship to that dark power "the forest" embodies suffers from curiously mixed metaphors. On the one hand, the king "tames and controls" these dark forces as an overlord, while on the other hand he is said to "embody" or even "incorporate" them. Witness here the opening sentence of Hart's description of kingship: "The king was the central embodiment of the sacred powers that had to be present and under control for the proper functioning of society" (1975, 13). The key term "embodiment" would strongly imply that the king's own body was built from the same essence as those "low" forest beings whom he ruled and tamed. Yet to use the language of order and conquest is to see the forest from the outside in. But the Pudukkottai rajas and many other forest lords like them instead looked at the forest from the inside out.

The origin story of Tondaiman rule in Pudukkottai is not unique in this arid area of Tamilnadu. The most important of these forest-lord stories, however, reveals a sharp distinction between the forest-lord and the conquering king with more explicit metaphysical details than the Pudukkottai legends alone provide. This cycle of Tamil myth centers on the figure of Atondai (Tamil, Atoṇṭai), the first king of Tondaimandalam, the region the Tondaiman family calls its original home. The myth has several versions, and each reveals an interesting new twist to the relationship of this king to the forest people whom he "conquers."

The most-quoted version of the story of Atondai seems to present a simple case of the glorious warrior who subdues, and extinguishes where necessary, the aboriginal inhabitants of a vast wilderness. Unfortunately, the original text of this version collected at the turn of the eighteenth century is faded beyond use.[3] The following summary, preserved in English, comes from the *Manual of the Administration of the Madras Presidency* (1893, 3:907). Updating the now-arcane spellings of tribes and place names and the eighteenth-century grammar and punctuation, the summary is succinct and useful:

> After the deluge, the country was a vast forest inhabited by wild beasts. A wild race of men arose who, destroying the wild beasts, dwelt in certain districts. There were then no forts, only huts, no kings, no religion, no civilization, no books; men were naked savages; no marriage institutions. Many years after, the Kurumbas arose in the Carnatic country; they had a certain kind of religion, they were murderers. . . . Some of them spread into the Dravidian country as far as the Tondaimandalam country. . . . They ruled the country for some time, but, falling into strife among themselves, they at length agreed to select a chief who would unite them altogether. They chose a man who had some knowledge of books, who was chief of the Dravidian country, and who was called Kurumba Prabhu and the raja of Puḻal. He built a fort in Puḻalūr. He divided the Kurumbas' land into twenty-four parts and constructed a fort in each district. While they were ruling, commerce was carried on by ships. As the merchants . . . sought trading intercourse with them, the Kurumbas built the . . . forts for trade . . . ; whence, by means of merchants, . . . a commercial intercourse by vessels was carried on. Consequently, they flourished, and though they had no religion a Jaina ascetic came and turned them to the Jaina beliefs. The Jaina *bastī* [Hindi, a Jain temple] the Pulal king built after the name of that ascetic still remains, together with other temples and some Jaina images in different places; but some are dilapidated and some destroyed by the hatred of the Brahmans. They were similar to the Jainas of the present—shepherds, weavers, lime-sellers, traders. While living thus, various kings of civilized countries made inroads upon them, as the Chola and Pandyan kings and others; and being a wild people who cared not for their lives, they successfully

---

3. *Toṇḍaimaṇḍala Varalāru*. Several English summaries are available from a century ago. See also a long summary in Oppert [1893] 1971, 243–47.

resisted their invaders and had some of the invading chiefs imprisoned in fetters in front of the Pulal fort. Besides, they constrained all young people to enter the Jaina religion; as a consequence, [there was] vexation [and] a cry arose in the neighbouring countries. At length, Atondai of Tanjore formed the design for subduing them and invaded them; in front of the Pulal fort, a fierce battle was fought in which the Kurumba king's troops fought and fell with great bravery, and two-thirds of Atondai's army were cut up. Atondai retreated to a distance, overwhelmed with grief, and the place where he halted is still called Cholan Paid [Tamil, *paital,* grief]. While thinking of returning to Tanjore, Shiva appeared to him in a dream that night and promised him victory over the Kurumbas, guaranteed by a sign. The sign occurred, and the Kurumbas troops were the same day routed with great slaughter; the king was taken, the Pulal fort was thrown down, and its bell-metal gate was fixed in front of the shrine at Tanjore. A temple was built where the sign occurred, and a remarkable pillar of the fort was fixed there. . . . After more fighting, the other forts were taken and the Kurumbas were destroyed. Atondai placed the Vellalar people as his deputied authorities, having called them into the country to supply the deficiency of inhabitants from the Tulu country. . . . Some were brought from the Chola country and are still called Chola Vellalars. From the north he called certain Brahmans by birth, whom he made accountants. . . . He acquired the name of Chakravarti from rescuing the people from their troubles.

Encased in this story are two different definitions of a king and two distinct relationships between the king and the forest people. The first people, the Vedar, were "naked savages" who had absolutely no "civilization."[4] The Kurumbas, who followed them, had "civilization" of a sort. They elected their king, who built forts out of which simple manufacturing and commerce flourished. These Kurumbas were still called "wild men" and must undergo a second round of civilizing. At this point, Atondai comes, sees, and ruthlessly conquers, with the help of the Gods. He imports the Vellalar, a farmer caste, and the Brahmans. The land is now safe for the plow. Agriculture begins.

The same Atondai, however, has some legendary skeletons in his closet. Another manuscript, now in poor condition, names him as the bastard son of a king and a dancing girl (*Toṇṭaimāṉ Cakkiravātti Carittiram,* summarized by Oppert [1893] 1971, 250–52). Not able to inherit his father's kingdom, Atondai was given a tract of forest land that his father's cynical ministers called "Tondaimandalam"—which some interpret to be a cruel pun that could mean either "the land of Atondai" or "the land of the outcasts and slaves." Thus, in settling in the land of those outside the borders of pure social life, Atondai was simply joining his own. In this version, in fact, Atondai merely repeats the same acts as the Kurumbas king in the version above; he explores the forest, sets up a capital city, and brings in new inhabitants where necessary. There is no conquest, no pushing back of chaos. The first steps of "civilization" are taken inside the forest. It is interesting that, as in the kingly

4. See the similar description of the Veddahs in Sri Lanka in Pfaffenberger 1982, 121.

rule of the Kurumbas, the forest is not hewn for agricultural fields. Rather, "forts" are built as social, governmental, and trade centers within the forest.

The description of the Kurumbas kings emphasizes the slow transmutation of forest life into civilization. The forest people, once wild and naked, "each doing as he pleased," voluntarily came together as a civitas—a united body politic. The first version of the myth never acknowledges this as a valid social or political system. The second round of civilization is considered the only proper form of social organization. The Brahman priests and the Sat Shudras, pure caste farmers, make the forest safe for the endless cycle of growth and production—for agriculture. Thus while the forest lord rules over a body politic created out of a forest left intact and alive, the conquering lord clears the forest and thus resets the stage now for the farmer-Brahman hegemony, over which he continues to preside only as a protector.

While the forest lord remains outside an agriculturally defined society, the conquering lord is integrated into the agricultural cycle—the same cycle that defines the Brahman orthodox sacrificial system. Such a conquering king remains related to the indigenous powers of the forest, but the body-politic he protects is built by the Brahman and the farmer on another theological base. This entire mythic cycle reflects the much-quoted historical relationship that Burton Stein draws between two forms of polity in South India: the warrior rule and the polity of the "Brahman–Sat Shudra" coalition that ruled the areas of stable agriculture. A medieval "agrarian integration" was established, in which the warrior nominally protected those "nuclear areas" while also directly ruling newly settled areas in the forest (Stein 1969, 186–87). This fits Heesterman's recent description of the same integration of the ancient king of India whose domain was "outside" the village and the city but who, via Brahmans, came to be integrated into the stable agricultural social system of the village (1985, 123). Thus in this sense Hocart was right: Even the king and his court are related to the sacrificial order. Hocart, however, did not push his developmental model back far enough—back into the forest, when (as this Tamil myth-cycle claims) there was a type of king who ruled civilization as its first and only lord.

George Hart translated a Tamil Sangam poem that describes the inhabitants and the customs of the people who reside even beyond the pale of early Tamil society. In this forested wilderness, the *mullai* region,

> Except for the Tuṭiyaṉ, the Pāṇaṉ,
> the Paraiyaṉ, and the Kaṭampan,
> there are no clans.
> Except for stones worshiped
> because [men] stood before hostile enemies
> and blocked them
> and killed elephants with high gleaming tusks,
> and died,
> there are no gods worshiped
> with offering of paddy.
> (Hart 1975, 121)

The Pudukkottai rajas performed such deeds and lived; they controlled enemies and tamed or killed elephants. As in early Pudukkottai legend, no other Gods were worshiped but the power of the forest and those who lived passionately under it. And also, as in early Pudukkottai, there was no agriculture here or in those mythical forts of the Kurumbas lords. The tribes listed in this poem correspond exactly to the same bard (Pāṇaṉ) and drummer musicians (Tuṭiyaṉ and Paṟaiyaṉ) that called the tune for the Pudukkottai Highness. There are no Gods here, only heroes, only the king.

In conjunction with the origin myths of Pudukkottai, the Atondai myth cycle moves full cycle back into the forest and into another definition of society, of polity, and also of metaphysics and theo-logy. The basic outline of a religio-social system is here, a nonagricultural society centered on the relationship between the king and the very forest beings he rules. The only body politic is the king and his fort. But the vague shadows of this religious polity move back into myth but also forward into history. How far back into myth the pattern of the Pudukkottai and Atondai origin myths can be traced remains only a tantalizing question. Certainly Hart's description of the ancient mullai region fits neatly into the pattern. And the ancient Puranic myth of King Prthu is echoed here also. According to the Atondai myth, the forest people and their forest lord had "no religion." Their first conversion to an overarching religious ruler beyond their king was through a Jaina ascetic. This new religion was adopted by the king and supposedly imposed on the people. The king submitted to an ascetic, thus building a complex religious system out of this king-ascetic relationship, and not the king-Brahman relationship. Such an unorthodox religion had to be crushed by the conquistador bringing the rule of the Gods and of the temple to the forest. Yet something here in this description of the defeated "religion" of the forest begins to look and sound like the history of the Tondaiman family of Pudukkottai.

There may indeed be a pattern of "religion" in these various mythic images based on a synergy between king and forest-dweller. In Pudukkottai these images crystallize in the legends of the first raja of Pudukkottai, who mastered forest animals and forest people, dressed in raiment from the forest, and built a "new fort"—Pudukkottai. The legends of the second raja of Pudukkottai, the eldest grandson of the founder-king, established a pattern of connections with another kind of forest-dweller, the ascetic Sadasiva Brahmendra. That crucial second conjunction perfectly fits the term "synergism," which has been used in English both in a biological sense of two organisms that cannot function without the other, and in the theological sense of the necessity of both human will and divine grace. In Pudukkottai, the interrelationship between king and ascetic introduces a Brahman presence into Pudukkottai, but not, I argue, in terms of the ancient sacrificial system that eliminates the very divinity that rightly belongs to the king.

7

Those Unworthy of Sacrifice

The Royal Court as Ancient Outsiders

Ornaments, laces, through you I re-enter myself. I reconquer a domain. I beleaguer a very ancient place from which I was driven.

—Jean Genet

The Tondaiman raja sits in durbar. The seventy-five years that separate Raja Rajagopala from Raja Ramachandra brought British things to the heart of the kingdom just as the previous centuries of Muslim rule contributed clothing and ornaments to array their Highnesses. But this Moghul-British layer of splendor cloaked a far older set of ornaments, whose richness derives from the forest and whose presence has outlasted the new masters of the Indian soil. Never missing from the durbar scene are the two Chowries (yak-tail fans) and the four Chamaram (two fans of peacock feathers and two of swan). In addition to these persistent forest emblems, other marks of royalty remain constant. The raja always wears a jeweled turban, while the courtiers readily change their style of headgear. The raja sits on his throne under a canopy or umbrella, in his hand a sword ready for some unseen enemy. The members of his Dignitary Establishment are always barefoot, even into the twentieth century; His Highness always wears shoes. These potent royal emblems—fans, fly whisks, umbrella, throne, turban, sword, shoes—are mentioned early in the Vedic Brahmanas and were "directly and exclusively related to kingship" (Heesterman 1957, 50).

   Jan Gonda's description of the ancient king seated in *samalaṃkṛta* (or *samalaṃkāra*), "full state" or "fully ornamented" (1969, 77), makes this old photograph of the Pudukkottai raja seem like a case of déjà vu. The ancient paraphernalia or emblems of royalty were "a white umbrella, fly-whisks, shoes, turban, and throne. . . . In other sources the five are: the sword, umbrella, crown, shoes and chowrie" (37). In Pudukkottai the Biruthus appear to correspond to these ancient *ratna*, the objects that "by their very presence and qualities add to the power of their royal master" (Gonda 39). Further, just as in Pudukkottai, it was the fundamental duty of the ancient Indian king to appear regularly to his subjects in full state. The sight was said to have salutary effect on the viewer and a deep connection to the general well-being of the realm. Why this should be so is yet to be explained.

Clear in the texts cited and in this photographic image from Pudukkottai is the important fact that the actual emblems of the king are the persons who carry the paraphernalia, and others whose very selves were considered royal "jewels." These *ratnin* were powerful: "The theory underlying the practice of the ratnins and belief in the ratnas seems therefore to have been that the above persons, animals and objects by their very presence and qualities add to the power of their royal master" (Gonda 1969, 39). It is this ritual interconnection of the king and his court companions that Heesterman claimed was directly and exclusively centered on the king. During the ancient *rājasūya*, the coronation, the king was enjoined to go to the house of each of these "companions" to offer a sacrifice. The texts claim that through this act the ratnins are made to "bestow kingship upon the king" (Heesterman 1957, 39). But that same text also calls the ratnins impure and lists them among those "unworthy of sacrifice." Thus the most exclusive image of kingship was also the most paradoxical. It was as if the royal radiance had as its source a black light.

Thus when the Moghuls and the British occupied their own thrones in durbar, they sat in a very holy, a very exclusive, but, as we shall see, a very "hot" seat. For here in the cathedra of splendor the adage "All that glitters is not gold" was profoundly true. The king and his "jewels" were ritually potent but socially questionable, an irony in which the British participated as they tried to "reform" the royal systems they also imitated.

The Ratnins

It is not easy to decide how much of the royal court in Pudukkottai actually can be classified as archaic survival of the old ratnins, or even what such an analogue between the modern and the ancient might mean. The questions become important because much of modern Indology has used the ratnins as an important clue to the structure and functioning of the premodern Hindu state. The ratnins are closely tied to the issue of the confluence and/or contravention of modern administrative machinery with the "native court." Such kings as Raja Ramachandra may have tried to aggrandize their courts in the nineteenth century to counter the growing influence of the Dewan Sastris of the empire, yet the king's court has been called the precursor of late-medieval centralized administration, of the basic polity of the state, and even of the caste system itself. And amid all this debate, Jan Gonda has sounded the warning that in ancient India "the ratnins were no administrative council at all, but an especially constituted group of persons endowed with sacred qualities" (1969, 44). Although nothing has ever stopped government administration from enjoying sacred powers, Gonda's brief statement implies that the theological nature of the ratnin's sacred power may be an issue that should take priority over the nature of their administrative role in government. So too in Pudukkottai the king's court as an issue in polity cannot be separated from the king's court as a problem in theo-logy.

The complex lists of ancient ratnins should once again be reviewed. The concern of the early textualist to list carefully the ratnins indeed parallels the Pudukkottai administration's own production of registers of its royal "establishment" from Political Agent Parker's first demands for an explanation of the Huzur Establishment, to Dewan Sastri's own compilations, to the rolls of the palace controller that date to the last months of the Tondaiman rule in Pudukkottai.

The early lists of ratnins appear first in the Brahmanas in directions for the conduct of the rajasuya. The list varies from text to text and includes a bewildering array of servants whose individual and joint duties left the early translators of the texts perplexed because "the exact sense . . . is open to reasonable doubt, mainly as to whether public or private servants are meant, for the names are of uncertain significance" (Macdonell and Keith [1912] 1958, 2:200). Recent translators also initiate their work with similar cautions that "royal consorts, governmental or household dignitaries, and artisans are incoherently mixed up in the list" (Heesterman 1957, 49–57).[1] The ratnins include the royal prince, the chief queen, the favorite queen, and the neglected or barren queen, along with officials whose Sanskrit names listed with various translations yield an odd inventory for presumably holy figures:

purohita	Royal chaplain
senānī	Commander of the army
sūta	Bard and court chronicler
grāmaṇī	Village headsman, or governor of a province
kṣattṛ	"One who cuts or distributes," hence, doorkeeper or chamberlain or superintendent of the harem
saṃgrahītṛ	Charioteer or treasurer
bhāgadugha	"One who deals out a share or portion," hence, tax-collector, divider of food, head cook, carver, or bailiff
akṣāvāpa	Master of the dice
gonikartana	Slayer of cows or huntsmen
pālāgala	Courier
takṣan	Carpenter
rathakāra	Chariot-maker

1. A summary of the list is also available in Gonda 1969 (39–45). Eggeling heavily footnoted his early translation in the Satapatha Brahmana 5.3.1.1–13 ([1882–1900] 1972, 3:58–65).

Hocart, with his usual acumen, was the first to notice the crucial importance of the king's court, which he identified with the textual references to the ratnins. Using an elegant Darwinian model, he argued that this royal court was the last stage in an ongoing increasing centralization of the state. The courtiers, Hocart claimed, were once priests and bearers of divine power in their own right who gradually ceased to be independent and took the position of the king's servants ([1936] 1970, 102–27). In their proximity to his power, they were able to retain remnants of their own. By incorporating their power, the king in turn was able to rise to the status of sole repository of divine power. The royal court rituals in which the courtiers served the king became the last edition of the ancient sacrificial ritual that had formed the order of the state. Accumulating all power in himself, the king acted now, with the help of his "servants," to redistribute that power back to the country in the form of good government that increased the commonwealth. The royal court was so central to Hocart's theory on social structure that he claimed: "It is the popular version of the king's court that is best known to us under the name of the caste system" (114). As for the present courts of the world, Hocart bemoaned their fall into use as "a psychological device to enhance the dignity, and hence the authority, of the lord. . . . It becomes an empty pomp" (123). Apparently Hocart, no less than any British historian, believed that the royal rituals of his day in England or in the empire had no real power.

No modern historian would argue that the entire court of the Indian king had existed merely for pomp. Several of the ancient offices look enough like a budding administration to follow Hocart and classify the whole retinue as the core of a future social or bureaucratic structure (Saletore 1934, 255; Mahalingam [1940] 1975, 1:50). But early texts on the *ratnahavis* (ratnin offerings) during the rajasuya reveal much ambivalence about the ritual status of these most important royal servants. The text says that by making special sacrificial offerings in the houses of each of his ratnins the king is "thereby consecrated (or quickened)," and adds that by this sacrifice the king ensures that each ratnin will be "his own faithful [follower]" (*Satapatha Brāhmaṇa* 5.3.1.1; Eggeling [1882–1900] 1972, 3:59). Could the ratnin not be faithful if the ceremony were not completed? As Heesterman argues, the ritual text evokes the myth of the great creator God Prajāpati's falling-apart and reconsolidation throughout this long ceremony: "Like Prajāpati, the king integrates the dispersed element as the 'limbs' of the kingship, tying them together in his persons" (Heesterman 1957, 51). By this interpretation, of course, the king is actually taking back what once was his own.

In spite of the ratnins' seemingly high status as "king-makers," and therefore parts of the royal body, the Satapatha Brahmana exhorts the king to perform an expiatory ritual immediately after his contact with the ratnins:

> Now, once upon a time, Svarbhānu, the Asura, struck the sun with darkness, and stricken with darkness he did not shine. Soma and Rudra removed that darkness of his; and freed from evil he burns yonder. And in like manner does that (king) thereby enter darkness—or darkness enters him—when he puts those unworthy of sacrifice in contact with sacrifice; and he does indeed now put those unworthy of sacrifice— either Sūdras or whomever else—in contact with the sacrifice. (Satapatha Brahmana 5.3.2.2; Eggeling [1882–1900] 1972, 3:65–66)

Gonda does not comment on this passage, but points to another list of ratnins, which he offers as evidence that the group is associated with *tīrthas* and hence "are of pure conduct, possessing purifying power" (1969, 45). Ironically *tīrtha* is a sacred place (here, person) causing a holy transformation usually associated with washing away sin. If the ratnins were tirtha, their status could be high—such as the role the Brahmans play in the expiation of the king in Pudukkottai. On the other hand, their status could equally be quite low as the serfs and later outcastes in whose unholy hands the refuse of the sacrifice, its sins, are taken from the community. As for this ratnin expiation rite, it could be argued—as Heesterman does— that the rite was needed only to represent the Sudras as a necessary part of the whole community. Therefore not all the ratnins were impure. Yet a closer look at this list of ratnins reveals the difficulties with such an analysis. The translations and meaning of all the Sanskrit names may be debatable, but one fact stands out: Only the Brahman Purohita appears most certainly to be of pure caste; the majority are women, or worse. And considering Hocart's early suggestion that the Brahmans may well have once belonged to the dark side of the tradition, even the Purohita may be suspect. Robert Goldman's study of the Bhṛgus as a "race apart" highlights at least one group of Brahmans whose activities as described in Sanskrit literature have included "death, violence, sorcery, confusion and violation of class roles, . . . intermarriage with other varnas, and open hostility to the gods" (Goldman 1971, 5). The *kṣattṛ* and *sūta* and related occupations are listed among the mixed castes—in South Indian terms, "Tribe the Fifth."[2] Hunters, butchers, and carpenters can hardly be expected to remain in the ranks of the pure. Heesterman's later suggestion that the ratnin fit three categories that represent the three stages of the king's regeneration—the consorts, those related to the chariot, and representatives of the four castes—returns the discussion to the theo-logical matter of the ratnins' role in the making/remaking of the king's body. But the sheer numbers of impure castes listed along with women only invite more inquiry as to why the king's "makers" should be those on the borders of the orthodox social system.

The ritual system acknowledged as central to kingship returns again to a paradox: He who is supposedly foremost is yet most closely associated with the "low." In this image of the king in state is the far more astonishing fact that these "servants" make the king. Without them, the royal being is naked of the essential "parts" of his power. In Pudukkottai this becomes very apparent. The photograph of Raja Rajagopala with his Dignitary Establishment demonstrates the paradox of low-making-high. Look again at the feet of the king's Dignitary Establishment: They are "servants." In the palace records they are always called by the English term "palace menials." Quite literally in Tamil the word for royal paraphernalia, *rājacinnam*, means at its root "little bits" or "pieces." But the king needs these pieces, because without them he is naked of power. No one in Pudukkottai would derive the slightest blessing from a glimpse of the raja in his underwear. Only the king bejeweled with his paraphernalia bearers is powerful. Only the king fully decorated is God. Yet those closest

---

2. The full list of this "tribe," who are mostly artisan castes, as recorded in the Mackenzie Collection (General Section, Records of Baramahal 22:20–22), bears a striking relationship to the Huzur Establishment as a whole in Pudukkottai. Another Tamil document generated in the early nineteenth century lists the "left-hand" castes. Again many functionaries of the Huzur Establishment show up there, along with those who perform similar services for the Gods in temples (*Cāti Nūr Kaviyurai*).

to him—those who are his jewels, who bear his insignia—are once again closely associated with such terms as "servants," "menials," "pollution," and "darkness." Here once again, in text and living context, the "last" and the "first" seem to be linked in a zigzag of status reversals.

At this point a whole series of questions about the Sanskrit texts emerge, which are equally apparent in the living court of Pudukkottai. On the one hand, texts and their interpreters declare that the ratnins—the king's court—"make" the king. On the other hand, the entire scenario of the ratnin ceremony and the interrelationship of the court and the king is interpreted through the Vedic sacrificial ritual. Hocart readily acknowledged the position of the king's power-bearers as "servants" but then explained this as a by-product of the process of incorporation and its attendant loss of a pluralism of power. Hocart, however, was forced to accommodate two meanings of service in his theory. In the sacrificial model, "the servants" were those who freed their lord from the polluted residue of the sacrifice. Yet here in the court, according to Hocart's theory, the "servants" have a power that they share with the king. Are the king's men really "servants" in that old sense of ritual garbagemen? In this context, if the sacrifice is defined as gift-giving, the question "Who is the giver and who is the taker?" also arises. The Gods on high give; humans receive. The lords, the nobles, likewise give; the serfs receive. The gift-givers supposedly have what it takes in their own holy bodies. The powerful substance of life flows from the top to the bottom. The ratnin, however, presents a paradox to this theory. In the God-human and noble-servant exchanges, the raw elements are given by men to the Gods, while the Gods return food "transvalued, . . . filled with the divine natural substance," as Ronald Inden and McKim Marriott (1974) put it. The implication here is that the lower order has only raw substance to offer, while the higher has the inherent power to cause transformation of substance into holy matter. Yet with the ratnins and with the raja's Dignitary Establishment, who had the divine power *ab origine?* Who is the transformer? Who is the transformed? In the orthodox system, the king should have primal power, and indeed Heesterman interprets the king's role as Prajapati to be an act of the God-king taking back what he himself had given to his creatures. But is this the only model of transformation and transactions in the image of the bejeweled raja of Pudukkottai and the more ancient Indian monarchs seated in state dressed by their "jewels"?

Modern cultural historians of South India have continued to adopt the sacrificial model to explain the relationship of the king to his court and to the kingdom at large. In the new system, the actual Brahmanic ritual was replaced by the act of royal gift-giving. Nicholas Dirks theorizes that the place of the ratnin at the king's court seems to have been taken primarily by the petty military chiefs of districts, the Sardārs (*cērvaikkārars*) (1978, 20–33; see also Dirks 1987, 111–38). Dirks argues that these Sardars formed an extended family. They belonged to the king's own caste and were frequently his actual as well as symbolic kin. Between the raja and these once-removed Vedic ratnins a system of pooling and redistribution of power developed. The king gave them land, which included a share of his own power symbolized in the form of royal honors—the right to use some of the very same emblems, called Biruthus (*pirutu*), that signaled his own royal status. This term, "Biruthus," is the same term used to describe the king's paraphernalia. At this point, however, the nagging question returns: Who exactly were the ratnins, the "king-makers," his "jewels" in

Pudukkottai? If the old Sardars and their more modern counterparts in the twentieth century—the administrative officers of the state—were the ratnins, these should be the very people standing behind the raja bearing his Biruthus in that old crucial photograph (see Plate 36). This, however, is not the case. The Sardars were seated there at the durbar facing the king quite out of that old photograph. They march behind the king in the grand processions but were not classified as part of the king's own Dignitary Establishment. They replicated the king's power at the local level. They acknowledged his sovereignty during the durbar, and thus they served him. But the Sardar are never called his servants, nor do they hold the king's own jewels, or dress him, or serve directly in the palace. They are in association with his person only as a replica, not as "maker." Here in Pudukkottai those most closely paralleling the function of the ratnins—those who woke, fed, guarded, praised their lord— were not the king's kin once or even twice removed, but rather the "menial servants" who stood behind the king. That they were part of his own household and not state officers was clear in the earlier analysis of the structure of the palace. Power in Pudukkottai was curiously divided between the palace establishment, who decorate and hence add power to the king, and the Sardars and all administrative officers, who take that power and replicate it in all parts of the kingdom. The metaphor of gift-giving and redistribution of power does not quite fit the whole picture—the *religious* picture of divine power at home in Pudukkottai.

The sacrificial system as it had been adopted in Pudukkottai accounts for half of the royal system. This was the supply-side theory of royal sacral power, trickling—or rather, here, pouring down—from transvalued natural substance. In Pudukkottai there was another important side: the origin of the royal power the king so readily gave away. The legends of the founding of Pudukkottai and the tale of Atondai point to the forest as the origin of that power. Exactly what logic, what theo-logic, divides this "second" form of kingship, this earth king, from the orthodox world that encapsulates it? A Brahman like Dewan Sastri was only following in a long line of Brahman reformers of this ancient royal system. The orthodox Brahmans had long found something problematic, something "sinful," in the king sitting bejeweled with these ratnins, with his Dignitary Establishment, with all those unworthy of sacrifice. A series of odd connections of kingship with sin, with forest people, and with the destruction of the sacrifice appears in the legends of the very first Hindu king. The story is preserved within the Sanskrit tradition.

King Vena and the Suspension of the Sacrifice

The character of King Vena, "the evil anti hero of one of the major Hindu myths of kingship" (Shulman 1985, 75), and his "good" son Pṛthu appear in a cycle of myths that begin in the Rig-Veda and continue into the medieval regional texts. The tales have always been set in a thoroughly Brahmanic mode as the paradigm of the priestly duty to ensure a righteous, dharmic king for the state. The narrative of Vena's rise and fall from royal power is designed to teach the ongoing lesson of the proper relationship of sacrifice to kingship, of inherent evil in royalty, of the ending of violence by the sublimation of violence, and of the holy origins of social and theological orthodoxy within the Hindu state. In Heesterman's terms, this could be called the quintessential tale of the axial breakthrough in India and a very logical place to begin to read—and unread—texts for the "fossilized remnants" of a discredited kingship.

The story of King Vena has sparked the ardent scholarly attention that makes a close reading of this story possible. George Dumézil introduced King Vena to a Western audience in his early discussion of the three forms of Indian kingship. Wendy Doniger included a lengthy analysis of the Vena myth in her exploration of the origins of evil in Hindu mythology. Heesterman also invoked the Vena legend in his study of the "inner conflict of tradition" in India. With a poetic style that rivals Frazer's, David Shulman has most recently used the legend of King Vena as an entree to his study of the king and the clown in South Indian myth and poetry. Thus the "evil" King Vena has attracted the same kind of attention now that he had in the Indian classical era, as a paradigm—if not a paragon—of the natural caliber of kings unbridled by orthodoxy.

The legend of King Vena, as told in the Vishnu Purana in its most extended form, does not follow a clear sequence. Its abrupt changes invite those old suspicions—a là form criticism—that the myth may indeed have a multiple ancestry. The legend as it appears in that text must be summarized in detail to allow a close reading. An edition and translation that H. H. Wilson made during Raja Ramachandra's time is especially interesting here:

> When King Vena inherited the throne, he immediately ordered the end of all sacrifices to the God Vishnu, declaring that only the king is "the lord of sacrifice," and as such the only one entitled to oblations. He further declared that all Gods are "present in the person of the king." The sages, the king's advisers, argued that without sacrifice and without worship of the God of Sacrifice [Vishnu] "the world is at an end." When Vena paid them no heed, they killed the king by beating him with the holy grass used in the sacrifice. The people then informed the Brahmans that without a king "the world has become threatened by robbers." So the sages decided to produce a son from the childless Vena by rubbing his *thigh*. They rubbed Vena's thigh, and a dark dwarf rose up. This dwarf was driven off and his descendants came to be identified as the deprived inhabitants of the Vindhya mountains. "By this means the wickedness of Vena was expelled; those Nishadas being born of his sins and carrying them away." By rubbing the right *arm* of the king, the Brahmans then produced the good Prthu, "resplendent in person as if the blazing deity of Fire had been manifest." Prthu was then "invested with universal dominion" when the sky rained celestial arrows and a bow, the seas brought jewels and waters, and "all things . . . assembled" to perform his consecration ceremony." Immediately came a period of paradise, "the earth needed not cultivation, and at a thought, food appeared." Prthu then curiously underwent a second proof of his kingship: bards were produced from a sacrificial rite that is also said to have been the same rite that produced Prthu. These bards proclaim Prthu's glorious deeds (although he had done nothing as yet according to this section of the text). The deeds and virtues praised are typical of the ideal Brahmanic monarch: protection, performing sacrifices, giving alms. At this point the text adds a

seeming addendum to the already happy ending. The king was immediately approached by the people for help, because during the anarchy "all vegetable products had been withheld." The people begged the king to "grant us vegetables, the support of the lives of thy subjects, who are perishing with hunger." Taking up his bow, Prthu marched to "assail Earth," which had taken the form of a cow. Calling her [Earth] a "malignant being," the king threatened her death. Prthu declared that unless the unruly Earth behaved, "I will support my people by the efficacy of my own devotions." Earth submitted and requested the king to "give me that calf by which I may be able to secrete milk" and to prepare the ground for the first cultivation. "Before his time there were no defined boundaries of villages or towns upon the irregular surface of the earth; there was no cultivation, no pasture, no agriculture, no highways for merchants. All these things (or all civilization) originated in the reign of Prthu." The earth was milked by the good king, who took into his hands the milk that contained all the seeds for vegetables, and then graciously restored these to the people. Earth, now tamed and granted a new life by the king, received the patronymic appellation "Prthivī" (daughter of Prthu). (Adapted from Wilson [1840] 1864, 1:181–88)

The medieval South Indian offering of this tale in the Bhagavata Purana, central to Shulman's analysis, contains variants and adds details to this version. Vena is given a childhood as a vicious little hunter who kills even his childhood friends. Vena's ancestry as the grandson of "Death" on his maternal side and "Desire" on the paternal side figures prominently in the story. Later versions, made available in Doniger's work, dwell on Vena's salvation both through his son's own goodness but also in relation to the purifying waters of a Shaivite temple. Here Vena's relationship to the barbarians and forest and hill tribals, and his eventual elevation to a demon-devotee of the God, dominates. For Shulman, all these variants "sum up" into definable "main lessons": Kingship is thoroughly sacrificial, and the king is "faced with an avoidable evil, the consequence of the sacrificial violence." Vena's claim to "wholeness" as the "single sacrificer" causes him to amass an "unbearable burden of evil" because there is now no one else with whom to exchange and share both the pure and the impure, the good and the evil, burdens of the sacrificial rites. Once the sacrifice is restored as a process of interdependence between Brahman and king, this mutual dependency remains delicately balanced and always in danger of instability (Shulman 1985, 87–88).

Thus David Shulman reads the Vena story on the Brahmanic plane as a series of lessons for a righteous king bound to uphold the delicate balance of order within the kingdom and within himself. The sins of King Vena, in Shulman's analysis, are willful transgressions against the needful ministrations of the Brahmans. In addition, Vena exhibits an even more reprehensible egomania—the king "vaunts his divinity" (Shulman 1985, 87) as equal to the God's. At the end of *The King and the Clown*, Vena becomes Shulman's major example of what sounds suspiciously like the sin of idolatry:

Seen from below, from the vantage point of his subjects, the king's form masks the god's; the two figures, deity and ruler, seem to coalesce, to cast a single shadow. Their natures and attributes, even their interests, appear to be largely shared. But from the king's position, the distance from heaven still seems overwhelming—and a challenge. At this level, one is most conscious of the distinction, and of the urge to transcend it: there *is* divinity in kingship—what in South India is not divine?—but the essential relationship of the king and god is now an analogical one that is always in danger of being taken too literally (as in the case of Vena). (Shulman 1985, 405)

Although Shulman begins and ends his work with a sensitive description of the interior of the Chola temples of Tanjore, and in spite of his own finely detailed discussion of Tamil temple myths (see Shulman 1980a), he forgets the close connection between the daily process of worship of the divine icon and the myths South India has produced about kings. Even the Vishnu Purana bears the marks of a context of temple worship. For Shulman his last word on kingship denies the status of literal images not only to the king but also to the God, for in the great Chola temples of Tanjore,

kingship is seen at the edge, as the boundary of the real, enclosing and incorporating it, dissolving in it, serving as threshold. The true center is the dark *śivaliṅga* within encircled by these walls—the *liṅga* which is, as the name originally indicated, simply a "sign," a hint of the god, an ambiguous presence and absence, a suggestion of transition, a movement in stone. (Shulman 1985, 408)

India gives another lesson in the dangers of the man who dares to gain divine status, and even of an overly embodied God who does not fulfill that axiomatic definition of divinity as "the unseen" (Shulman 1985, 4), "the beyond" (5). All the recent evidence that the temple icon is indeed "literally" God cannot suppress the urge to ignore this aspect of the house of God (see Waghorne and Cutler 1985; Davis 1991, 119–20).

Shulman terms the righteous king "the icon" as a poetic metaphor to introduce the paradox of that unattainable status as a paragon on a pedestal to which the king nonetheless aspires. But there is an irony in Shulman's choice of words. The seemingly unrighteous king may have an ancient right to claim the status as holy icon in a quite literal sense. Within Shulman's rich materials are nestled details that bring King Vena into positive association with the divine image via his negative "son" Niṣāda and his own royal "sins." In both the Vishnu Purana and the Bhagavata Purana, Nisada is told to "take a seat" (hence his name) as the ancestor of the wild tribes of the hills and forests of South India. In the context, though, "Take a walk" or "Get lost" might make more sense. Yet "take a seat" is a rich expression frequently used in the context of installation of a king on his throne and the practice of placing a divine image on a seat, a small throne, as part of domestic and temple puja (see Courtright 1985, 40). Again, these covert references to the installation of king and of divine image among the unorthodox appear in Wendy Doniger's discussion of Vena and Prthu. In one text, Prthu seeks to save his father, who is living among the wild tribes. Prthu is told to take his father to a shrine associated with the Great Mother and the wishing-cow. The waters there wash Vena clean. Again in another reference to purifying waters, Vena is washed clean when a dog drenched in the holy waters of a Shaivite shrine shakes and thus washes away the king's sins. The references to the South Indian rite of Abhishekam—the ritual "bath" given to the holy icon or to the holy person—are difficult to miss here. The king's coronation, as in Pudukkottai, is a "bath" with purifying water just as it is in the Sanskrit texts (Gonda 1969, 87ff.). And, most interesting, the Pattabhishekam for the rajas of Pudukkottai uses the waters from the temple tank at Tirugokarnam—the Lord of the Cow's Ear—another temple associated with the holy cow as the vehicle (her ear) for the divine waters needed for Lord Shiva's own ritual bath. The washing away of sin and the process of installation of both king and God are to this day interconnected in the vernacular traditions of the same "barbaric" hill regions of South India.

For Doniger the myths of Vena and Prthu are important for the "wider and deeper concerns" that these reveal for "the problem of evil in relationship between parents and children" (1976, 321). Doniger does not disguise her Freudian interests, but inside the issue of parent and child, Doniger's fine detailing allows the unorthodox Vena to shine through. In addition to the implied analogue between the king and the temple icon, Vena's close association with the nonorthodox element of Hinduism is made very explicit. One of King Vena's apostasies against Brahman supremacy is his active support for mixed-caste marriages, a position that might have literally won him the right to "sit down" in Parliament during the heyday of the Tamil self-respect movement. In the myths, of course, this is a heinous crime, but the text allows Vena a stubborn pride in his position. The mixed castes he produces also produce the bards whose songs of praise confirm him in power. As we have seen, some of these mixed-caste classes are the same groups that continue to form the raja's court in Pudukkottai as in much of South India and even as far away as Rajasthan, where the Charans, bards, were held sacred (Tod [1829, 1832] 1972, 2:500). Not only do the myths of King Vena span the Hindu tradition from the Vedas to Bhakti, but his shadow seems to take visible form among the very people the texts so openly call his own.

Clearly the tales of Vena are not just lessons on royal morals; they constitute a sustained two-millennia-long theological and social polemic against the kind of kingship Vena represents. In his earliest references, Vena was not associated with deviation, and only later was his "character . . . blackened beyond recognition" (Shulman 1985, 76). That blackening has all the marks of an axial reevaluation of the very ancient royal "duties" enumerated by Heesterman—to hunt, to kill, to preside over the sacrifice of war and all other life-giving acts of death. Also present are Vena's upholding of what Hocart and Heesterman claim was the early interchangeability of all social-ritual roles. Caste had not then frozen the man to a role, as is clear in Vena's own insistence on *his* ability to play both God and man, Brahman and king—the giver, recipient, and chief officiant of his own sacrifice. And the king retained the right to play the part of both ascetic and king. With this in mind, a "deconstructive" reading of the myth of Vena in the Vishnu Purana is in order. The myth can be read, as modern Tamils have read the Ramayana, with the supposed evil king as the actual hero.

The legend of King Vena contains within itself two mutually opposed conceptions of the all-important relationship between the king and the earth's fertility. This is the first clue to the myth's dual origins in both the Brahmanic and that "other" world of kingship. Notice that the legend begins with the "sins" of Vena, his refusal to accept the sacrifice to the Gods as the supreme religious act. Vena, in fact, claims that the king is the essence of all divinity. The argument between Vena and the "sages" centers on the question "Is the earth's prosperity best assured in sacrificial cycle to the Gods or in the person of the king?" Accepting the Brahmanic position, when the good Prthu is installed a single emphasis on the reestablishment of sacrifice would be expected. Instead, the benefits of Prthu's official coronation and reign are defended in several distinct ways. First, his coronation instantly produces a period of plenty; second, he is pictured as the virtuous monarch, reinstituting the classical alms-giving and sacrifice; but third, he is seen as taking up arms and forcing the earth to restore lost vegetation to the people. According to the arguments of the sages, the reinstitution of sacrifice should have restored the earth's fertility with no further ado. But a "conquest" is necessary. A direct relationship between the king and the earth's fertility is thus drawn here *outside* the context of the king's position as the patron of the sacrifice and the sacrificial order. The king's power produces vegetables—the very element the paradigmatic myth of the creation of the world by sacrifice in Rig-Veda 10.90 leaves out of the list of sacrificial elements produced from the first sacrificial victim, Puruṣa (Doniger, trans. 1981, 29–32). In the Vishnu Purana, vegetation is consciously included in an attempt to bring these quite nonsacrificial elements back into the Aryan world of the sacrifice. This entire scenario between the earth and the king had to be pushed into the metaphor of social order = abundance, or sacrificial exchange = prosperity. At its roots, the scene builds on another set of crucial relationships that fundamentally alters the definition of good and evil in the king.

The king's direct control over the forces of agricultural fertility are made axiomatic in the myth. These forces, moreover, are both within the king's own body and within the earth.[3] This is clear when the king tells Earth that if she does not produce the vegetables he will do so from the force of his own "devotions." Here "devotions" refers to the vigorous techniques of bodily control through which the vital powers of the body are transmuted into a pure potential energy. The king is prepared, then, to transform this energy into the needed vegetative life. The king, then, can create fertility by intensely taming a primal power within himself as well as the earth—a crucial definition of the ascetic. His power to tame alone, and not the power of a sacrificial ritual, grants life to the barren soil of the earth. It is odd that the sinful claims for kingship for which his father Vena was executed were fulfilled in fact by Prthu: The king is indeed the lord of the world. There is no need for any other Gods, or for sacrifice as exchange. So in a real sense Vena's "sin" becomes Prthu's power. Prthu still has the power his father claimed, but now this "good" son gives loving lip-service to the royal virtues enjoined by Brahman keepers of the orthodox sacrificial system. He gives alms, and pays for the sacrificial feast, but these rituals are oddly empty of ultimate power.

There is more than a passing connection between the "sins" of Vena and the fertile power of his son. The veneer of "goodness" on Prthu is quite thin. His own body came out of his "sinful" father. His own brother, the first-born from his father's thigh, is the ancestor of those sinful tribal people, those wild men of the Vindhya mountains that mark the borders of the Aryan heartland. The thigh-born Nisada appears as an explanation of the shudra ancestry of the lords of the south of India. The arm-born Prthu is the perfected Kshatriya ruler of

3. Here Gonda argues that the king controls but does not contain these powers by nature. They are given to him at the coronation, after which his body functions as a conduit for the fertile powers of the universe. See Gonda's analysis of Prthu (1969, 128ff.).

the north. Yet this "good" king lives precariously close to the untamed, the uncivilized, and the uncultivated. Those very forces—alive in his father's flesh, which made his body—are the same forces nesting within the bosom of his "daughter," the earth whom he tames. But by his own admission these forces are also within his own body.

The king is therefore quite closely related to the mixed castes and to the lowest orders of society in form and in fact. As late as the turn of the century, when Edgar Thurston first began to collect the origin legends of the various castes in South India, there were still groups such as the Kurava, who openly traced their ancestry to Nisada ([1909] 1975, 3:445). In this version of the tale, Nisada is innocent of any wrongdoing; he is simply too ugly to be a king. When his handsome brother ascends the throne, Nisada takes a consolation prize as ruler over the forests. Thus the connection of the sons of King Vena to the south and to the low persisted through two thousand years. Here, then, is Frazer's same enduring king closely attached to the low, the outsiders, and bearing both "sin" and fertile powers within his own body.

Within the panegyrics of the good Prthu, the tension between the king's own power and that of the earth turns suddenly into a battle—a sparring with words backed up by the naked sword, and not a gentle "exchange" in the mode of the tamed sacrifice. An ancient model of a life-and-death struggle erupts here between the king and the earth: between forces of production and those of constraint. The earth has stored up her forces of fertility, and so has the king. In the end, the victor forces the release of his enemy's power while still retaining his own. This struggle of retention versus release, which also belongs to the Vedic tradition, differs considerably from the ordering-via-exchange process of the sacrifice. In another equally important and probably much earlier cycle of creation myths in the Rig-Veda, Indra, king of the Gods, "creates" the world by forcing the "evil" Vrtra to release the fertile waters the monster had either swallowed or simply penned up like cows. The importance of retention versus release, as in the later Prthu myth, seems to be unrelated to the supposed power of the sacrifice to produce plenty. The difference is not merely a variation on a theme, but a fundamental distinction in the very nature of the source of power in the universe. For the post-axial sacrificial system, the ordering process itself creates abundance. The polar opposites are brought together and set in right relationship to each other in order to create a whole. The retention-release process, however, centers on sacral power as a kind of energy with its own laws of flow and transfer. What is religious power? From whence does it derive, and how is it brought within the grasp of humans? These are the questions at stake here, not the genesis of social order.

That ever-lasting, ever-transforming King Vena may still have some tricks up his sleeve for those who would not let the Brahmans win a very ancient argument. The durbar scene in Pudukkottai can be read as continuing the dialogue between Vena and the Brahmans. There the raja sits at the center of attention enthroned in his own world. He sits as a self-made divinity, with the evidence of his success transformed into the very "jewels" that continue to build his holy body. The Tondaimans won each of those emblems by their own prowess. They made themselves. And even in modern times, that is the essence of their "sins." The British, in a very real sense, reopened this ancient debate concerning the power of the king to make himself with their own insistence that places like Pudukkottai "reform" and begin to acknowledge their place in a cycle of power that flowed, like the sacrifice, from a new "God" on high, "Divine Providence," represented in the person of the queen. In this system no persons dared call themselves God; rather, they were "viceroy." They were asked to represent, symbolize, imitate a power that was meant to be revealed in anything but metaphor. Like the reformed Brahmanic post-axial sacrifice, order was touted as the essence of the Raj, and the likes of Sashia Sastri in Pudukkottai carried on this same logic.

Brahmans like Dewan Sastri ironically represent a very ancient tradition—but in a very modern form, a form that suited the British need for a native ideology. Modern political adversaries of the "Brahman hegemony" in southern India point out that, before the British, Brahmans never had the kind of solid political power they acquired during the Raj. Max Müller's reintroduction of the Vedas into the discourse of the Raj may well have fueled the kind of unity between bureaucracy and a new vedocracy that Sastri so well represented. But Sastri was a reformist. To this day, Brahmans in Pudukkottai point out that the rituals there were never "*vaidika*," following orthodox practices, but rather were "*paurāṇika*," following local "custom." The customary place of Brahmans in Pudukkottai State was to play another kind of ancient-yet-modern role, that of the ascetics. They were expiators of the raja's "sins" and as such were thoroughly part of *his* system.

Something in the logic of a Sastri did not parrot but rather more naturally paralleled the British compulsion to "reform" native princes like Raja Ramachandra Tondaiman. And what did the Brahmans and the British want to reform? The king's "selfishness"—his spending on himself and not on his kingdom, his centering of power within his palace, his seemingly insatiable desire for ornaments. In short, Ramachandra's lavishness and fiscal irresponsibility in twentieth-century terms is Vena's heresy: a rejection of sacrifice for self-creation. Thus I am arguing that the palaces of "forest" lords, such as the Tondaimans, never redefined the sacrificial system in their own court rituals, as has so often been suggested. Rather than being englobed by the orthodox sacrifice, like the evil King Vena, they profoundly contravened it. As the Laws of Manu put it, "Through a want of humility Vena perished, . . . but by humility Prthu and Manu gained sovereignty" (7:41–42; Bühler [1886] 1964, 222). The Tondaimans, even when under siege by the reforming British administration, never really learned humility. In nineteenth-century Christian terms, both Vena and his southern sons, the Tondaimans, were guilty of the ultimate vanity: the sin of idolatry in its basest form—making one's own body into the body of God. The enigma of that great "idolatry" is hidden in the holiest part of the palace, the Dakshinamurti temple. Establishment of this temple during the early years of European hegemony in the area brought Brahmans prominently into the palace, but on terms that strengthened the king, *not* the coming bureaucracy.

8

The God on the Silver Throne

The Dakshinamurti Temple

Every day to this very day, an old Brahman priest and his assistants open the ornate door to the royal chapel, the Dakshinamurti temple. The Brahman enters the sanctum now barren of any permanent icon, removes a small silver image of Dakshinamurti from a metal box, and sets it in a wooden Mandapam (*maṇṭapam,* pavilion) on a silver throne just to the right of the sanctum (Plate 67). He then performs a modest puja, an offering of fruit, flowers, and incense (Plate 68). These are the last surviving rituals for the old royal regime in Pudukkottai. The kingdom no longer exists. The new palace has been sold, and the old palace will soon follow, but while His Highness still lives and as long as there is a Tondaiman heir, Dakshinamurti will be worshiped in Pudukkottai. This small temple is the heart of the kingdom and is the one public place in the palace that the Tondaimans never shared with the British.

The Dakshinamurti temple is not ancient, nor even the oldest part of the palace or the only important temple in the state. The official state temple is the Brihadambal temple in nearby Tirugokarnam, which the royal family continues to support. But the Brihadambal temple and other ancient temples in the district remain state temples. They are no longer under the exclusive control of the Tondaiman family. Only the Dakshinamurti temple retains that status, precisely because it was built by the Tondaimans and not simply acquired as a result of gaining control over the land. The Dakshinamurti temple, more than any other establishment, asserted that the royal family was Hindu in the face of both Moghul and British presence and as such is a product of modern times.

In the plan of the palace, this royal chapel stands directly in front of what is probably the oldest building in the complex. It appears to be set down intentionally in front of old

Plate 67. Behind this grand silver threshold, the sanctum with the holy seat empty of the permanent divine icon of Dakshinamurti is dark and dormant. Instead, the priest takes a small silver image from the box, clearly visible in front of the wooden shrine that now serves to carry out only the bare essentials of divine worship. The throne of the rajas of Pudukkottai in the durbar room above, and the divine seat of their ancient family deity in the royal chapel below, both remain vacant.

Moghul archways that were once used, it is said, for the raja's outdoor court sessions, where he sat like a Solomon judging his people. The only door of the temple faces that row of arches bricked in to form a solid wall. The lower half of that wall, as well as the outer walls of the temple, are painted with the red and white stripes that mark a Hindu temple precinct (see Plate 44). The red and white paint of a Hindu temple brushed over the remnants of those Moghul arches sends a message on these walls that seems to say "We are no longer this." The architecture of the temple inside and out, like the Darbar Hall that echoes it, remains uncompromisingly Hindu amid a palace complex that is otherwise wildly eclectic.

During a festival in the Kapaleeswara temple in Madras, someone once said to me that the early British allowed for a resurgence of Hindu temples when they supplanted Muslim rule here in the latter half of the eighteenth century. He was referring to the rebuilding of many temples, like the one in which we stood, that had been destroyed or damaged by the

Plate 68.   This puja to the divine image of Dakshinamurti consisted of an
offering of flowers, a bath conducted on the stand in front of the
mandapam, and a change of clothes.

Muslims. His point is important. Although brief, Muslim rule in the Carnatic disrupted
temple worship. There are stories in oral tradition and inscribed on temple walls that tell of
rajas who restored and reconsecrated divine images that priests had rescued from their
sanctums as Muslim armies approached (i.e., Jagadisa Ayyar [1920] 1982, 453). The historical accuracy of these stories is not nearly as important as their likely currency among Hindus
of the day. And indeed in this early period in the established British centers like Madras, the
East India Company's Board of Control in London and their servants in the field continued
to stress the very pragmatic need for the religious neutrality of their rule. Hindu resurgence
during this period, then, would not have meant an increase in home worship, which had
never been disturbed by the Muslims, but rather the renewed possibility of public display.

In the southern districts around Pudukkottai, the reign of Vijaya Raghunatha Raya
Tondaiman (1730–1769) saw first a period of civil war within the Hindu kingdoms of the
area, and then a war of succession among the Muslim rulers to which French and British
forces quickly allied on opposing sides. It was in these times that the second raja of
Pudukkottai met his guru Sadasiva Brahmendra and was said to have established the worship of Dakshinamurti in the palace. The present temple was probably built during this

important interregnum period when direct Muslim influence was scattered by several competing European military forces in the area. Ironically, the Tondaimans publicly, and apparently wisely, supported the British, who were politically allied with the more moderate Muslim ruler who claimed a clear sanction from the Moghul emperor in Delhi. Their astute choice left Pudukkottai as the only surviving Native State in the Carnatic. But the Dakshinamurti temple reveals a far less accommodating attitude, an attitude that took full advantage of a break in the clouds to build a space for what could now be defined as *Hindu* rule.

In these tumultuous times, a succession of Telugu Brahman ascetics came to be recognized as saints. Sadasiva Brahmendra was the third such saint in this Kaveri Namasiddha movement. This movement, according to William Jackson, was an important response by the "Hindu communities trying to survive or keep their way of life afloat as the tides changed with invasions, famines, demands for tribute and other sources of insecurity" (Jackson 1988, 5). The Brahmans as the keepers of tradition had responded differently. While many Brahmans found the new "professional and bureaucratic life-styles agreeable," as clerks and administrators in the Muslim and later British administrations, other Brahmans did not. These continued to look to the orthodox Hindu tradition but were nonetheless creative in their responses accommodating folk worship and folk traditions and remaining essentially nonsectarian in their practice and teachings (Jackson 1988, 5–7).

Of the five saints, three including Sadasiva were closely associated with kings in the Kaveri river basin, which included the Pudukkottai district. While these saints may have signaled a turn to the transcendent in the turbulent daily life of the populous, as Jackson concludes, the saints in their relationship to the kings remained important players in the very earthly matter of integrating the sometimes nonorthodox winners in these wild days of freebooting into more-sanctioned forms of kingship. At least in the case of Sadasiva, the relationship established between the ornate raja and this naked ascetic (re)established an order of kingship that affirmed both the king and the ascetic in a position that was far more "folk" than it was orthodox but that nonetheless began to speak more fluently in the idioms of the high tradition. The Brahmanization and hence Hinduization of Pudukkottai in religious matters therefore parallels the growing influence of the rajas and their support of those contenders for power with the strongest claim to political legitimacy, which in this case derived from the established imperial Moghul rule.

It is interesting that the relationship between king and saint is a religious idiom that transcends Hindu-Muslim boundaries throughout India. Muslim rulers appear to be as much involved with Muslim saints during this period as the Hindu kings were drawn to Hindu saints. Thus the saint-king relationship could well be studied as an all-India phenomenon. But in the case of the Pudukkottai raja and Sadasiva Brahmendra, this relationship affirmed a form of sacral kingship that no Muslim and no Britisher could possibly affirm if they had understood its full significance. Again, no matter how Sanskritic it may have looked to more-established kingdoms, such as nearby Tanjore, no matter how familiar to Muslim rulers, and no matter how innocuous to the British, the Sadasiva Brahmendra and Raja Vijaya Raghunatha relationship was a powerful statement of a form of Hinduism that was very public and concrete. It was, in fact, closely related to that very regeneration of the temples that my chance informant in Madras so astutely educed. The story of this relationship is written in and on the walls of the Dakshinamurti temple.

Inside the Dakshinamurti Temple

A priest stands at the door of the Dakshinamurti temple flanked by two stone devadasis carved on the ornate entranceway (Plate 69, color section). They wave the royal Chowries, bidding us to enter with camera in hand to visually chart this place once hidden from British eyes. Walking down a short corridor, we see that the side walls are filled with line drawings in blue that seem unfinished. The corridor opens into a single large room with two doors at each end. One door with an elaborate tooled silver frame reveals a sanctum with a small throne now unoccupied (Plate 70, color section). The empty throne faces east. Directly across from this sanctum, facing west, is a plain red wooden door with a solid brass padlock (Plate 71). That simple door is painted a deep red, as is the entire interior of the temple, with the exception of the columns highlighted in silver. Painted on the walls in that court are columns perfectly mirroring the architectural style of that interior but created in two dimensions. The ornate finials of these phantom columns form arches that open into "sanctums," each painted with an enthroned deity. Several of these spaces frame luxuriant sketches of what must have been well-known stories in early Pudukkottai.

Plate 71.   A servant of the Dakshinamurti temple blows into the conch to demonstrate its use as portrayed on the door to the small cache that holds it. The conch was sounded before major festivals. Next to the servant is the blood-red door to the chamber said to hold the sand on which the saint Sadasiva Brahmendra wrote the holy mantra that initiated the Tondaiman rajas into the worship of Dakshinamurti.

The murals declare beyond a doubt that this is a royal chapel. To the right of the main sanctum, a bright-red Ganesa with gold and green dhoti sits in state with two members of his divine Dignitary Establishment waving the Chowries at his sides (Plate 72, color section). To the left are the three major Goddesses (see Plate 68), differentiated by their emblems but also by the tone of their skin. Lakshmi's complexion is appropriately the color of gold, Saraswati is white, but Durga is not her usual black or red, but colored green. The green of this later Goddess is not a matter of artistic license. In Pudukkottai the Great Mother, Brihadambal, who resides in the state temple in nearby Tirugokarnam, is usually portrayed as a lovely young girl with green skin, like the goddess Meenakshi in nearby Madurai, recalling the time

Plate 73.   In a *kummi* (folk song) dedicated to Brihadambal, who resides at the Tirugokarnam temple, the Goddess is called "the Parrot that
prattles always" with her husband and lord, Shiva (*Śri Birakatambāl
Pēril Canta Kummi*). Here Brihadambal assumes the form of a parrot as
an expression of her perfect devotion to her lord. In this mural she actually takes the parrot form, while in other murals only the color of her
skin reminds the viewer of her wifely reverence. Next to the Goddess is
the cow who at the risk of her own life brought water each day in her
ear from the Ganges to bath Shıva at his temple here in Pudukkottai.
The cow and calf became the temple's namesake, Tiru-go-karnam,
"Lord of the Cow's Ear."

she took the form of a parrot to worship her divine husband Shiva. A mural on the wall to the right of the three Goddesses (Plate 73) refers to the gracious acts of Brihadambal as told in the legends of the founding of the Tirugokarnam temple. However, in her form as Durga she sits in her less-benign form as the mistress of war and death. In another corner of the temple, opposite this sanctum side, Brihadambal can be seen in her gracious form seated on a cushion and worshiped by a Brahman priest waving an *ārati* lamp (Plate 74, color section). On that far side, the green Goddess again appears as Parvati riding with her husband Shiva on their familiar great white bull (Plate 75). However, here in this royal chapel the divine couple ride as a royal pair with the bull decorated as if it were a kingly horse. Two Chowrie bearers run at their side. The only portrait that seems to jar these sumptuous royal scenes is now damaged, but still recognizable as a naked ascetic who stands next to that very plain red door on the wall facing the sanctum (Plate 76). This is Sadasiva Brahmendra, the ascetic that initiated the Tondaiman to the proper worship of both Shiva and the great Goddess, and thus (re)created the links between king and God in the mid-eighteenth century.

The selection of Shiva in his form as Dakshinamurti as their patron deity was not the Tondaimans' choice. In 1738 Vijaya Raghunatha Tondaiman met Sadasiva, who was under a perpetual vow of silence. The great yogi wrote the Dakshinamurti mantra in the sand. It is this precious sand that is said to be kept behind the padlocked door. This mantra, and the injunction to take a certain Brahman as his court preceptor, were the only religious instructions the yogi gave to the king. In spite of the brevity of the great yogi's meeting with the raja, the Tondaimans credit that moment with the beginning of their prosperity and blessings as Pudukkottai's rightful lords. Fortunately the many versions of the story of this famous meeting, when combined with these fragments on the temple walls, can provide a fuller understanding of this mysterious and yet central relationship between king and ascetic.

The story of the meeting of Sadasiva Brahmendra and Vijaya Raghunatha has many oral and written variants. S. Radhakrishna Aiyar's *General History of the Pudukkottai State* (1916) told the tale in considerable detail. He explains that even though the ascetic Sadasiva Brahmendra renounced the worldly life, he could not renounce his love of talking. The strong advice of his guru led Sadasiva into a lifelong vow of silence. Naked and utterly silent, the story went, he wandered through the forests of South India "and lived in the innermost recesses of forests for months together, and [was] once . . . in a state of trance (*samādhi*) for two or three months with the flood of the Kaveri running over him all this time and brought back to his senses when somebody who was digging near the spot casually wounded him and drew blood from his body. He often acted as a madman. . . ." Radhakrishna Aiyar continued the tale:

> In 1738 or just before, Vijaya Raghunātha Rāya Tondaimān had the good fortune to receive spiritual instruction from Sadasiva Brahma. It is not definitely known where the meeting took place between the ruler and the Yogi. Some say that the Tondaimān met him in the forests near Sivagnānapuram, a little to the southeast of the Pudukkottai town where the ruler often lived. . . . The Tondaiman must, immediately on seeing the Yogi, have known him to be a great sage, and made obeisance to him requesting spiritual instruction. The sage thereupon wrote on the sand by his side the

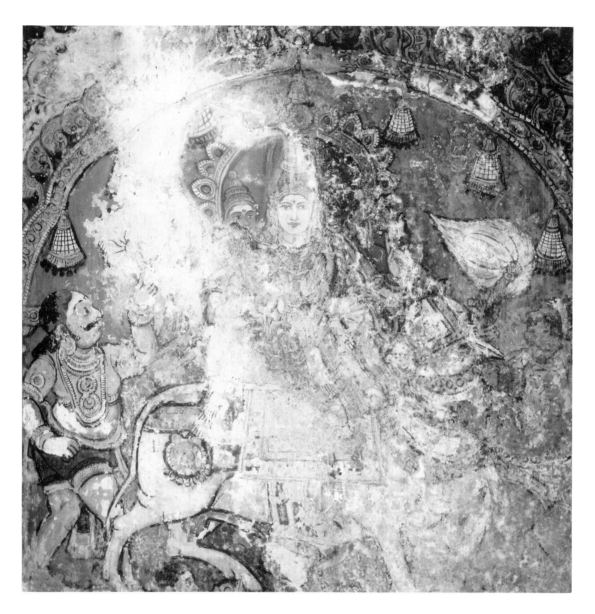

Plate 75. In this badly damaged mural, the more familiar forms of Shiva and Parvati ride on their bull. The image emphasizes the royalty of the divine couple, with the Chowrie-bearers prominent to the left and right of the bull. The bull is so ornately decorated that he resembles the royal Kothal Horse rather than a bovine beast of burden.

Plate 76.   Only the face of the saint Sadasiva Brahmendra remains clear in this portrait. There is no doubt that his body was nude, as he is always depicted. The theme of the nakedness of asceticism and the ornamentation of kingship is literally written onto the walls of this chapel in the sharp contrasts between the saint Sadasiva and the silver images of Dakshinamurti and Ganesa as ascetics, on the one hand, and the royal images of Ganesa, Shiva and Parvati, and Brihadambal, on the other hand.

Dakshināmūrti Mantra, i.e. the prayer to Shiva in his form as the *south-faced* preceptor of the Rishis, and also a direction that the Tondaiman should have as his spiritual Guru Mahābāshyam Gōpālakrishna Sāstriār, a class-mate of the Yogi in his boy-hood.

Gōpālakrishna Sāstriār was sent for, was made the Palace Guru. . . . The Tondaiman was required by the Guru, for the expiation of his past sins and for the security of the future welfare and prosperity of the State, to institute the worship of Dakshināmūrti in the Palace and to arrange for the annual conduct of the *Navarātri* or Dassera festival, when Lakshmī, Durgā and Sarasvati were to be worshiped and a large number of Brahmins were to be fed and given doles of rice and money, etc., and for the distribution of *Svayampākam* (rice and other articles required for a Hindu meal) to a number of Brahmins every day and to all girls that might apply therefore on Friday. . . .

Sadasiva Brahma, after the incident referred to above, again wandered where he liked and ultimately sank into eternal repose at Nerur near Karur. A few days before he closed his earthly career, he . . . asked the inhabitants of Nerur to have a pit ready for his Samadhi, in which was to be buried a *bāna lingam* (a white stone representing the essence of Shiva). . . . A temple was built by the Tondaiman over his tomb, which was endowed with two villages in the Tirumayyam Taluk by the Tondaiman. (176–78)

All these charities and festivals were maintained until 1945, when the celebration of Dassara was cut back in the name of both reform and economy. Many people in Pudukkottai blame this rash action for the loss of the state's sovereignty just three years later.

Certainly this story aims at the all-important religious legitimation of the warring Kallar Tondaimans, which is also written on the walls of the Dakshinamurti temple and into the architecture of the palace. The Puja Vidu building was constructed for these ritual feedings of Brahmans and young girls. The three Goddesses to be worshiped during the Navaratri (Dassara) festivals are prominent on the chapel walls, and the Dakshinamurti temple itself testifies to the Tondaimans' faithfulness to their guru's instructions. Much like the tale of Vena/Prthu, this story on the surface tells of the purification of a fierce warrior-king now settling into righteous rule. There is now established between the ruler and the Brahmans a clear interdependence that is usually the mark of the raja accepting the basic premises of Vedic authority—the primacy of the Brahman as ritual intermediary. In good classical form, the Brahmans relieve the king of his evil by accepting his food as expiation for his sins. In oral versions of the story, the king's sins are related to his self-polluting but necessary acts of killing. Vijaya Raghunatha had emerged as raja of importance after a fierce succession dispute and after years of war. As an act of expiation, the raja builds a temple to Dakshinamurti—the most Brahmanic of all of Shiva's forms, for here he takes the form of the preceptor to the Gods. In this form Shiva is himself the rajaguru for all other deities, and thus a powerful choice as lord and "teacher" for the Tondaiman raja. With such a divine master, who could now question the Kallar king's own purity? He can now feed Brahmans on a regular basis and honor pure virgin women. The Tondaimans could now conduct the most royal of rituals in this part of India—the Dassara festival, which began to replace the patronage of Vedic sacrifices as the mark of kingly authority during the late Vijayanagar empire (see Stein 1984, 302–26).

But this is only one level of the story. The roles of the purifying God who grants salvation, and of the righteous Brahman who accepts the king's gifts, are eclipsed by another more important personage. Sadasiva Brahmendra the yogi actually writes the script. His asceticism is hardly quiescent. Although a Brahman, he acts primarily as an ascetic, a powerhouse of energy—the kind of creative energy that Frederique Marglin has classified among the forms of divine "power" in India to which each person "has access by actions in this life" (1977, 267) and not by right of caste birth. No longer bound to caste or any other fixed role in society, the yogi established a series of analogous relationships between king, Brahman, and ascetic, and the Gods in which roles are shared, swapped, and even duplicated among both human and divine participants. Thus here the naked ascetic, by being silent, cannot talk; he must act, and he acts not simply like an ascetic but like a king, like a Brahman and like a God. He played each of these roles and left both king and God to do the same.

Like a king, Sadasiva Brahmendra wields power through action rather than words. There is a Tamil version of the story that has Sadasiva worshiping the Goddess at Tirugokarnam with flowers and a gift of gold beads (see "The Legend of Bakaulavaneswari"). Anyone can properly worship the Goddess with flowers, but the mention of gold beads immediately puts Sadasiva in a special category of devotees. The care, feeding, and especially the dressing of this very special Goddess was a royal duty. Usually only the king would offer the Goddess jewels. It is interesting that on the wall mural near Sadasiva's portrait on the Dakshinamurti temple walls, Brihadambal sits in her benign form being worshiped by what we would assume is a Brahman priest waving the arati lamps. The mural may well be making subtle reference to the legend of Sadasiva's own similar worship. At the same time, Sadasiva maintains his role as a Brahman priest. He also maintained his Brahmanic role as royal preceptor. His caste friend substitutes for his presence as the raja's teacher. It should have been the guru himself that attended the king at court, but he is there in the palace by proxy while he remains in the forest as an ascetic but is also seen in the temple caring for the Goddess as a king and a priest. This single actor plays the roles of "Brahman, King, and Sanyasi," which Veena Das has defined as the key to the conceptual order of Hinduism (1977, 18–56).

But Sadasiva Brahmendra is not alone in his capacity to wear these many garbs of power. Even the Lord Shiva, as preceptor to the Gods, is the perfect analogue to Sadasiva's own position as Brahman, ascetic, and king. Shiva's own asceticism is confirmed by his position as guru to the Gods and by his separation from female divinity within the sacred geography of the capital city of Pudukkottai. In his small temple placed inside the palace, three forms of the Goddesses are there as paintings on the wall. The Goddess is also present in the colors chosen for the temple. Red is the color of Shakti, silver is always associated with Shiva. Thus the red columns tipped with silver speak of the union of God and Goddess. However, the divine consort of Shiva was not present in the sanctum in iconic form; instead, Shiva lives here with Ganesa, who also is associated with asceticism. At the end of his daily puja in this temple, the priest dresses Shiva and his son Ganesa in the orange robes of ascetics (Plate 77, color section). The Goddess Brihadambal, the great Shakti, lives in a temple several miles away. In the palace, Shiva rules alone as ascetic master.

In the great Tirugokarnam temple, the relationship between God and Goddess is reversed. Just as Shiva really sits alone in his sanctum in the palace, the Goddess dominates the state

pattern—the king continually sins, yet the expiation of the king's sin equals prosperity—is repeated in temple legends and in stories about the origins of festivals (for example, see Jagadisa Ayyar 1921, 299).

Here once again the relationship between the king and the ascetic is central. The contrast is especially sharp in the paintings of both Sadasiva Brahmendra and the raja who benefited directly from his grace. Sadasiva always appears naked with a round little belly, while the raja is always elaborately dressed. The raja—with his luxurious dress in close relationship with his direct opposite, the naked ascetic—creates the kingdom's fertility, which flows from naked ascetic to the splendidly dressed royal "sinner" and from king to the kingdom at large. Such sins appear almost material in nature—a kind of base ingredient necessary to very substantive blessings. Such sin clings to the very flesh that royalty is heir to. Sir James Frazer rides again—well, almost.

The process of transmutations and transformations, then, dominate the issue of the king's purification and his "evil" in Pudukkottai. Two key relationships define the processes of transformation: the "sin" → energy model, and the energy → icon model. For Frazer, the issue of "idolatry," the man-made body for both God and human God, may well have forced his abrupt exit from his search for the metaphysics of divine kingship. He certainly was willing to go as far as the equations sin = energy and energy → bodies. His shadow play of Adam and Eve evokes this issue. Eve leaves the garden a fallen woman, but one who now has the secret of how to make more human bodies. The Bible soundly condemns the activity and carefully confines human bodybuilding to this one stolen power, and then only if those new human bodies exactly duplicate the plan of the Great Creator. Adam and Eve do not gain God's own divine body or remake themselves in their own image of divine power. Frazer argued that the culture of "magic" has always planned to do just this—build a divine body for humanity. But Pudukkottai, with its seeming pre-axial audacity, can make the final set of equations: sin → bodies, and human bodies / divine bodies → icon bodies. When viewed in the context of the myth of the legitimation of kingship, the story of Sadasiva Brahmendra and the raja, the transformation process becomes a process where both human-body and God-body come to take the same form. The catalyst is "sin."

The stories of King Vena reveal the shadow of the king's shared icon-body with God. Those references to the temple icon in many of the texts are confirmed in the context of the living royal tradition of Pudukkottai, that home beyond the Vindhya mountains where a Shudra family has long reigned as kings. The Sadasiva Brahmendra story assumes this connection of king/God/ascetic/icon and associates it with a "sinning" king. The exact connection between sin and body-making remains unclear. The secrets of this "magic" must again be searched in the shadow of text and finally in the light of practice.

Sin Builds Strong Bodies

There is general agreement both in text and in casual talk that the Dassara festival in Pudukkottai expiated royal sins, but the stories of the exact nature of these sins vary. These narratives form three basic scenarios: (1) The raja, while hunting in the forest, had accidentally killed a Brahman. (2) The raja, while hunting in the forest, saw a sleeping sage with insects swarming in his ears. Feeling pity, the raja applied a medicinal herb to kill the vermin. The sage awoke and accused the raja of committing the sin of disturbing his meditation. The sage then softened his anger, took pity on the raja, and granted him the boon of family prosperity if Dassara was instituted (as told to Nick Dirks, personal correspondence dated April 14, 1980). (3) The raja had sinned by causing the death of a famous rebel against the British, Kattabomman. The raja falsely promised him sanctuary in the forests of his realm. After luring the rebel there, the raja turned him over to the British for trial and execution. To this day, Tondaimans are condemned for this act.[2] This last version of the royal sin is the most widely accepted in Pudukkottai today, although the raja who founded Dassara is not the same Tondaiman ruler who captured Kattabomman.

The sins, then, seem to be varied: (1) killing a Brahman, (2) disturbing the meditation of a sage, and (3) causing death by false promise. All these sins are inherently paradoxical. The first was accidental, the second was a well-meaning blunder, and the third was an evil act that saved the independence of this tiny state through an insightful alliance with the later victorious British. Pudukkottai remained the only Tamil kingdom to escape annexation into the British domains because of this early treaty of alliance. All these sins were inevitable—either as a necessary evil or as an inescapable act that bound the hapless king to sin.

In addition to the specific types of "sin" cataloged in the variant Dassara legends, the king remains tainted by that excessive need for pleasure: the spending of far too much time and money on music, dancing, hunting, and gambling. These excesses are not condemned as mortal "sins" but appear in the excited gossip of the wish-it-were-me variety. In this gossip, the king is the star of an endless "As the World Turns." But he is caught in this role as surely as he is caught in his family's original sins. His power seems to demand that he must be sensually excessive in the way that the popularity of any film star rises rather than falls by excessive behavior that would be condemned in any other person.

The rajas' excesses were essentially sexual in a broad and specific sense. Before the "reforms" of Dewan Sastri, the king maintained his own devadasis, as was his royal right. The right to maintain these dasis, a fundamental sign of the raja's royal status, was granted to his ancestors by their imperial overlord. After the reforms, a group of dasis attached to the Tirugokarnam temple were assigned to serve the king during state functions. They were called, in Tamil, *araṇmaṉai-māṇikkattāl*, "the jewels of the palace," and continued to serve the living raja much as before the reform. There is no doubt that he was at liberty to have sexual relationships with them.

Music and dance are not overtly sexual in South India, but these arts are associated with the positive arousal of strong passions either for romantic love or for the spiritual devotion that became the medium of divine-human relationships in Bhakti. The rajas of Pudukkottai, as well as nearby lords, were much involved with the arts as the subject, the creator, and the patron. There are interesting ballad songs from the same part of South India in which the

2. A recent Tamil retelling of the story of Kattabomman has a chapter entitled "The New Snare of the Pudukkottaiyans" (*Vīrapāṇḍiya Kaṭṭabommaṉ*, 96).

king is praised as the romantic dream for all the women of his kingdom. One ballad claimed that the king was so virile he could satisfy fifteen women in one night, and that every woman in the kingdom naturally pined for just one night with their lord (see *Valḷi Pāratam*).

In the most general terms, the raja of Pudukkottai, like the evil King Vena, is next of kin to both *kāma* and *karma*, "sensuality" and "action." He is bound to his creative tasks by two basic facts of life: He must act and he must be sensual, even though both activities force him outside ideals of the perfected life espoused by post-axial Brahmans intoning the injunctions of Manu. But the rajas of Pudukkottai share this ironically necessary sin even with the Vedic Gods themselves, as a careful reading of Wendy Doniger's *Origin of Evil in Hindu Mythology* reveals. The task here can only be to relate the rajas of Pudukkottai not to the general problem of evil but only to that odd creative power that "sin" engenders. Why is "sin" related to making *bodies,* and what kind of *bodies* does sin effect? Why do the rajas of Pudukkottai—and the earth-kings in general—have the power, unlike the God-pecked Adam and Eve, to create the types of bodies beyond the endless duplication of the human form that is produced by good, clean reproductive sex?

In his *Destiny of the Warrior,* George Dumézil pointed out this important paradox inherent in the functions of the warrior class in the Indo-European world: The warrior must sin (1970, 53–105). Special attention here falls on Indra, the warrior king of the Gods in India whose sexual excesses and moral duplicity make the sins of the Pudukkottai rajas look like mere misdemeanors. Dumézil carefully reviewed all the myths and legends of Indra's sin and classified them into three major offenses: Brahmanicide, breach of contract, and adultery. The sins of Indra as cataloged by Dumézil are shockingly parallel to the variant sins committed by the Tondaiman rajas: Both are excessive in sexual passion, commit a breach of contract, and kill a Brahman. The remaining sin of the Tondaiman rajas—disturbing the meditation of a sage—is also shared by Indra. In the texts analyzed by Dumézil, the crime of Brahmanicide is made to appear especially hateful because it was committed while the Brahman was meditating.

The resemblance of the Tondaimans' sins to Indra's scandalous activities may be quite intentional. In a legend that mirrors a more general story of the origins of the Kallar caste, the Tondaimans trace their ancestry back to one of Indra's sexual adventures on earth with an attractive young maiden whom the passionate God simply could not resist. In this ballad poem written by a Brahman court poet, Indra's uncontrollable desire is blamed on a trick of Kama, the God of love, and is sanctified by marriage (see *Tondamān Vamsāvaḷi*). The child born of this divine-human love was the ancestor of the Tondaiman line. The original Kallar caste legend is far more bawdy (see Thurston [1909] 1975, 3:62–63; Shulman 1985, 349). It traces the ancestor of the caste back to an illegitimate son born from Indra's original sin with the wife of a Brahman sage. So while Dumézil fits Indra's sin neatly into the context of the strong Indo-European sense of order and balance in society, the same sins of Indra in the Pudukkottai context are used instead to account for the divine yet low status of the Kallar royal house. They are the incarnated fruit of Indra's sexual desire permanently stationed outside proper society. And their heredity runs true: They are indeed sons of their father doing on earth as he does in heaven. The rajas of Pudukkottai, then, have more than one ancestor among the old Vedic catalog of sinners.

An important but brief description of Indra's sins occurs in the Aitareya Brāhmaṇa as part of a description of the rajasuya—the coronation, or, literally, "the ceremony that sets the king in motion" or "begets the king." It is no coincidence that the ceremony that "makes" a king becomes the vehicle for relating the tales of the God-king Indra. Although the rajasuya is recounted in several other texts, the Aitareya's version remains unique. Indra's sins occur in the middle of a complex discussion about why the king must not drink real *soma* (a hallucinogen), the forbidden fruit of the sacrificial ritual reserved for Brahmans (Aitareya Brahmana 5.7.27–5.7.34; Keith [1920] 1971, 314–18). Instead, the king is admonished to stick with a kind of grape-juice communion. The introductory section of these preliminary rituals for the rajasuya then relates the strange legend of Śunaḥśepa, told to expiate the king from "his sins" before any coronation ritual can begin (Aitareya Brahmana 3.7.19; Keith [1920] 1971, 309). All this preliminary material is set in the dual context of the sin inherent in royalty and their exclusion from the full fruits of the great Vedic sacrifices. This text deals with a central issue of post-axial Indian kingship: Why is the king, the lord of all creation, excluded from the fullest participation in the central rite of the orthodox religious world?

These early sections of the rajasuya as set forth in this Brahmana offer one simple answer to this question: All kings are excluded because they inherit the original sins of Indra, which justified the divine king's own excommunication. But the exact list of sins here emphasizes that Indra's conduct was particularly odious because his warrior's wrath was directed against Brahmans: "He hath misused Viśvarūpa, son of Tvaṣṭṛ, he hath laid low Vṛtra; he hath given the Yatis to the Hyaenas, he hath killed the Arurmaghas, he hath contended with Bṛhaspati" (Aitareya Brahmana 5.7.28; Keith [1920] 1971, 314; see also Doniger 1976, 102–13, and Dumézil 1970, 74–81). All the people and groups listed here are classified as Brahmans, albeit of rather unusual sort. Earlier in the text, the recounting of the rajasuya begins with a story of a primordial antagonism between the kings and the Brahmans over control of the sacrifice (Aitareya Brahmana 4.7.19–26; Keith [1920] 1971, 309–13). The text divides the whole society between what it terms "holy power" and "lordly power," defined initially as those who eat the sacrificial oblations and those who do not. The text concludes that only the holy power can control the sacrifice, that the king whose only power is in weapons must come to the benefits of the sacrifice through the ministrations of the Brahmans. Yet Indra's fights with the Brahmans and this rivalry of the lords and the priests seems settled in a very uneasy truce. Here Heesterman's pre-axial and post-axial cultures seem openly pitted against each other.

This rivalry between lordly power and holy power has cosmic proportions. The text sets the entire story as a cosmogony, a story of the origins of life. First, the primal creator Prajāpati created the sacrifice and then created both lordly power and holy power. From each came a separate set of offspring, two orders of human existence, which both contended for control of the sacrifice. The holy power, whose offspring were the Brahmans, gained control. But the rajas did win an odd second-place prize: They have access to lordly power in a set of sacrificial rituals reserved for the king alone. These rituals, interspersed between the stories of this antagonism, appear to either tame or placate that potentially explosive royal power with both a hand-me-down share of the sacrifice and an odd substitute soma.

The first of these royal rituals is an unusual ceremony indeed. The king is made a Brahman so he can share in the sacrifice, but the text does not let him really eat the oblations that are handed over to the Brahmans who eat them on behalf of the king. The second ritual, which closely follows the first, solves the problem of what the king should eat by offering fruit-juice communion in lieu of the sacred soma. The proper food of the king is literally a punch made of five different fruits from a variety of trees. Each separate juice confers a vital ingredient of lordly power on the king. The whole cocktail confers ultimate greatness. Both rituals preserve some ancient sense that in spite of the Brahmans' claim to be sole "eaters" of the sacrificial oblations, the king has a direct claim to his own quite special share. While the rest of the class of "those who do not eat" continue to go hungry, the king is singled out as one who somehow must "eat"—must be directly related to the sacrificial ritual.

The fruit-juice communion the king drinks is said to grant him special royal power. It feeds him the sacred chemicals that within the caldron of his own body become lordly power. The second-hand communion confirms and protects those lordly powers by carefully realigning the natural powers in the royal body to the general and freely moving lordly power and holy power. This is accomplished when the king freely sets aside his lordly power during the ceremony in which he is made a "Brahman." The king gives his lordly power into the hands of the Gods with whom it originated. Then he is given holy power by another set of Gods. He soon returns this holy power to the Gods in favor of his own lordly powers. Chanting "I am who I am," the king receives his own lordly powers back into his body. This entire ritual, like the fruit-juice communion, centers entirely on the king's body, in which lordly power is made, released into the world, and then absorbed back from the world. The two substitute communions act like a reversible reaction in chemistry that both releases and reconstitutes this lordly power. In both instances, the king rejects the holy power as one that is not his own. The rivalry between king and Brahman centers not on political power but on metaphysical power.

The argument over control of the sacrifice is about the kind of divine power that will control and thus define the sacrifice. Here, in the early part of this brief cosmology, "the sacrifice" is the definition of life itself: Everything was created as a part of the sacrifice, including human society. Both lordly power and holy power were given a chance to "catch" the sacrifice. Using Hocart's terminology here, the two sides are fighting over the source of life. The king expects weapons to win the right to make life on his own terms; the Brahmans use their own priestly skills at the ritual to win the same right. The Brahmans win. Clearly, had the king won, the very nature of sacrifice would have changed. "Life" then would not emanate from ritual but would be "won" through the king's own strength and skill. Notice how the boasts of King Vena, given reality by Prthu, are openly denied. Prthu's winning the right to make life by his conquest of the earth, thus circumventing the ritual aspects of sacrifice, should never have happened, according to this text. The king's skills are, after all, the skills of death. Whether justified or not, the king kills to make life, while the holy Brahmans chant to awaken life. This deep connection of lordly power to the act of killing is unmistakably clear in the Sunahsepa legend, which introduces this entire section on the rajasuya.

The story of the sacrifice of Sunahsepa by his self-seeking father in the Aitareya Brahmana was "so revolting," according to Max Müller, that he was tempted to "recognize in him a specimen of the un-Aryan population of India" (Müller [1859] 1968, 377). Paralleling the famous stories of the sacrifice of Isaac in the Old Testament, this ancient legend tells of a frightful contract a king desperate for a son made with the God Varuṇa. The son is granted on condition that the young prince be offered as a sacrifice when the God asks. Each time Varuna asked for this promised sacrifice, the king stalled through one ruse or another, explaining why the body was not yet fit for sacrifice. Finally the boy fled for his life and wandered in the wilds of the kingdom searching for some father willing to substitute his own son in this sacrifice for a royal sum. Finally a very poor Brahman ascetic living in the forest agreed. This substitute sacrifice was deemed worthy, but none would kill the Brahman boy, Sunahsepa. Finally his own father, like Abraham, took the knife, not out of utter obedience to God but out of greed. The boy, seeing that the end was near, prayed to and was rescued by none other than Indra, king of the Gods. Sunahsepa then asked the protection of the officiating priest, Visvāmitra, who—it is interesting—was not a Brahman but a Kshatriya. Visvamitra adopted the boy as his son and heir. Visvamitra's other sons were then divided over the rightness of this intercaste adoption. Those accepting it became blessed, and those who rejected the adoption were exiled to the south of India to be ancestors of the hill tribes there. The story ends with the puzzling statement that when a Brahman tells this story to a king "not the least tinge of sin will be retained in that king."[3]

Thus a direct connection is made between the expiation of royal sin and this once-upon-a-time tale of a human offering in a sacrifice that established lordly power. The reader is left with the sense that the king must be cleansed of a kind of original sin that has cleaved to royalty since the primordial event in which the king shed this special human blood. Sigmund Freud would be most content with this attempt of the Hindus to "remember" that archaic event. Here the sacrificial ritual is redefined as an act of killing initiated paradoxically by the king's own desire to beget a son. Killing and the act of procreation here are intertwined: Birth demands death. The king receives the fruit of this sacrificial cycle but also bears its stain. So many of the theories of sacrifice offered by Heesterman and others seem well confirmed. Heesterman cites the story as an example of "the terror and contradictoriness of the confrontation with the transcendent in the sacrifice" (1985, 85).

One piece of this puzzling paradox remains unexplained. The king's sins both in Pudukkottai and in the case of Indra are related to desire and to death. But this kama-karma cycle has a context broader than the sacrifice. The relationship of the king to an ascetic remains central, even to the Sanskritic texts. This is the broadest context of the Sunahsepa legends, of the catalog of Indra's sins in the Aitareya Brahmana, and of another longer narration of Indra's sins in the Mārkaṇḍeya Purāṇa (5.1–26; see Dumézil 1970, 72ff.). In each of these brief dramatic episodes, the sage and the ascetic figure prominently. Indra kills his Brahman victims while they engaged in meditation. The enraged father of one victim is himself pictured in the garb of an ascetic.[4] In the Sunahsepa legend, the king moves Varuna

3. Another version of the story is summarized in Dowson 1961, 308–9. Max Müller also offers a summary [1859] 1968, 376–82.

4. See the summary in Dumézil 1970, 74. Pargiter claims that before the sacrifice "the chief pursuit and main exercise" of the "original" Brahmans was *tapas* ([1922] 1962, 308).

to grant him a son by the power of his asceticism (Heesterman 1985, 84). The king's son wanders in the wild like a homeless ascetic, and the son of an ascetic becomes his substitute in the sacrifice. But the relationship between king and ascetic takes on divine proportions when Indra, king of the Gods, guides the wandering prince in the hinterlands by appearing as a Brahman ascetic. Indra warns the prince, "Evil is he who stayeth among men. Indra is the comrade of the wanderer" (Keith [1920] 1971, 302). And at the end of this Markandeya Purana episode, Indra, whose vital energy has become incarnated into five princes, is identified as a yogi. The text assures the reader that "the great *Yogis* can convert their body into many" (5.26; Dutt 1896, 23). So as the prince in the Sunahsepa legend is an ascetic for a time, so Indra, himself the kingly killer of ascetics, is now the comrade of the wanderers. Kings, divine and human, oppose the ascetics in one form yet join them in another. The king is caught in still another great paradox, described by Wendy Doniger in *Asceticism and Eroticism in the Mythology of Siva*. The king, bound by kama and karma, is equally bound to asceticism—the stilling of all movement and the retention of all desire.

So the paradox thickens now like the matted hair on the ascetic-king's unkempt head. The king forever remains on the edge of order, entrapped by his impurity. He has blood on his hands and desire in his heart. His evils are necessary for the creation and maintenance of life, but should he choose to cease "sinning," to cease the cycle of karma and kama, he is pushed even farther from the ordered world deep into the forests. The breach between the king of the earth and the world of social and cosmic order is then absolute. Inside his palace, the king lives outside the bounds of purity and balance. When he leaves for the forest, he rejects his palace life not for balance but for the extreme simplicity of the forest. For this earth-king, unlike Shulman's Brahman-tamed kings, there is no golden mean, no sense of poise and balance, no careful compromising of sensual needs for the sake of duty. The king is forever out of bounds, with too little or far too much.

Yet the sources of life the king controls are in the extremes of the forest and the opulence of the court. The king who sins at court is forgiven and blessed by one from his own forest. The ascetic in the Pudukkottai legends transmutes the king's sins into prosperity. The king, when he joins those in the forest, gains, like Indra, the power of transmutation. Indra, as the yogi, has that power of converting his body into many forms. The king's entrance into the forest is an entrance into potential, unformed, and raw power. And these very sins that bind the king to the world also free him completely, for as Dumézil points out, Indra's sins release his royal powers into pure energies, which are then free to take a body once again. Indra, the royal sinner, is Indra the ascetic. The cycle of sin begins the cycle in and out of bodily life.

Sin, then, starts the process of release and reembodiment: A death releases the power to create a life. In ancient ritual terms, the killing and offering of the sacrificial victims buy life from God. In sexual terms, the desire to have a son begins the death-life cycle that is human history. In terms of ancient South Indian culture, "power comes from the taking of life" (Hart 1979, 15). Asceticism within the warrior tradition reverses the process: The embodied powers are disembodied and become untamed energy once again, to be reused as another kind of embodiment. And that may be the key to the relationship between "natural" sexual production of bodies and those "engendered" by the release of energy by an ascetic and by a warrior king. In Pudukkottai, it is Sadasiva Brahmendra who effects the changes that make the king into an icon. It is the king after his ascetic period during Dassara who can then provide Sadasiva, and the other Gods of his kingdom, with an icon-body and a temple home.

Asceticism, in the context of kingship, has the power to transmute reproductive energy into something more than the production of more human bodies. The ancient texts and the Pudukkottai story taken as a whole do not separate the king from normal sexual processes, but they do emphasize his part in another system of reproduction, defined by his ascetic self. The tales of Indra contain a subtle distinction between two kinds of body-making. When the normal processes of getting a son fail, there is recourse to the creation of a human body out of another conduit for power. The distinction between these two reproductive processes is the difference between what I will call *fabricated* bodies versus *natural* bodies. When the king sits in durbar, ornamented by his entire court, his body can no longer be defined as "natural." The nature of his iconic body is key to understanding the very power at the heart of the durbar—a power connected to ornamentation, to dressing, to the very royal opulence that the British so reviled but nonetheless came to share.

9

The Iconic Body of the King

The old photograph of His Highness Rajagopala Tondaiman's coronation durbar is a paradoxical image of royalty. This raja clothed in majesty sits in the durbar room just above the Dakshinamurti temple and its ever-present reminders of the ascetic life. The same photograph is filled with living souvenirs of the king's forest self. There is nothing solid, nothing stable, about this picture. Even the raja's royal dress is so ornate, so intensely glittering, that it appears surreal. If this king were the center of society, the nature of that very society would be a study in relativity. If this king were divinity, that form of divinity would have no solid being on earth or in the heavens. And if this king, as Hocart claims, were life, that very life would exist neither in the raw flesh of the body nor in some solid soul substance. Neither flesh nor spirit, this royal being sits quite visible to the eye, surrounded by music once audible to the ear—a sensual being without a solid body. He remains a most interesting theo-logical proposition.

The nature of the king's royal body remains to be seen and understood in this little kingdom of South India. The analysis of the king's Huzur Establishment and the study of his relationship to the wilderness provides the basic theo-logic of this form of sacral kingship. The legends of the Tondaimans' rise to power likened the acquisition of royal status to a slow process of getting dressed, becoming ornamented with the visible signs of kingship. The same broader series of legends also linked the process of socialization to an act of getting dressed. The mythic paradigm for the movement from forest to fort came to be expressed as a transformation from the naked forest person to the dressed man in society. It is notable that the word used for the king seated in state, *samalaṃkāra*, quite literally means "fully ornamented." Contrarily, the king's place in the ascetic wilderness was held by the naked guru Sadasiva Brahmendra. The Huzur Establishment "dressed" the king to "make" his royal body from his naked forest spirit. That transformative process from forest-to-fort-to-wilderness was marked by acts of dressing and undressing—an interesting metaphor for a metamorphosis.

The act of getting dressed and of dressing others was the primary ritual act at court in Pudukkottai. Not only was the palace establishment busied with ritually dressing and displaying the king, but the king himself "dressed" others. The royal honors the king bestowed on officers of the state were forms of clothing—the king's sharing of his own ornamentation. Each year during his birthday celebrations, the raja would sit on a carpet inside the Dakshinamurti temple and distribute gifts of clothing to the religious and civil officers of the state (see "By Sri Brihadambal's Grace"). The personal gifts the king gave the bride or groom at a wedding were always clothing, Vastram. In addition to the general feeding of Brahmans during Dassara and other feasts, poor Brahmans individually applied for a Dampathi (Sanskrit, *daṃ-pati*, master of the house), a specific gift unit that included food and clothing from the lord to his "servants." The letters of application for such grants beseeched clothing in particular—for example:

> Respected Sir:
>
>   There is no one among Brahmans of this state so poor as myself. Up to this year, my wife used to wear, after drying, one Jinnudi sari given to pitiable me as "Dampathi Pudavai" [a "cloth" from the master of the house] during last year's Navaratri by the Maharaja. Even that sari is torn by good wear and tear. So, without a sari to wear, my wife is very shy now even to come out.
>
>   (Palace Record, dated September 3, 1925)

Such pleas of near nakedness were not the exception but the rule. Unless the entire Brahman community indeed did not have a thing to wear, these petitions must also be read figuratively. To be clothed by the raja was to be truly dressed. This was felt by state officers and "poor" Brahmans alike. Likewise, poets and scholars also competed for gifts of royal shawls bestowed at the special "Carnatic" durbar during Dassara. The raja was the clothier, and not the clothed, for those whom he made by extending his power through them.

Yet when the raja himself acted as a "servant" in relation to the deities of the realm, it was he who clothed the Gods much like his own palace servants dressed him. The great Goddess Brihadambal was particularly well dressed by the king, as the legends about Sadasiva Brahmendra were well aware. It was the raja who brought the Goddess jewels to wear during her own public appearances at temple festivals (Palace Record, dated February 21, 1948). Other deities of the state were likewise "clothed" by the raja. Images in the state and private temples applied for and were granted "honors" for their festival processions in the same manner as administrative officers. But records also show that the rajas had new articles made especially for them (see Palace Record, on the purchase of an ivory palanquin for a temple image, dated August 14, 1923). Earlier Tamil ballads praise the Tondaimans' lavish gifts of jewels for the image at Virālimalai (*Virālimalai Vēlavar Kātal*, 5). It is doubtful that in these king-deity relationships the deities were seen only as an extension of the raja's rule. Rather, the logic of dressing the Lady of Tirugokarnam was a perfect role reversal of the raja's position in the palace. While in his own palace, his servants dressed him. In her palace, when he acted as "servant" of the Goddess, the raja supplied the Goddess's clothing.

Thus the ritual act of clothing functioned on two levels. When the king extended his power, he gave clothing as if it were his own, a kind of Prasadam, a sharing of his own power. But when he dressed the Goddess, he did so as a servant in replication of the model of ritual dressing in the Huzur Establishment. Yet this process of getting dressed spotlights the royal person as the glass of fashion and the mold of form. The logic of dressing seems to have originated in the palace and then extended into the Tirugokarnam temple when the Tondaimans officially declared themselves the Goddess's "servants."

The meaning of this ritual process of dressing so permeated life in Pudukkottai that it touched the individual subject in a very personal and deeply religious sense. Certainly on one level, "getting dressed" was a social ritual that publicly announced rank and status in society. Nicholas Dirks's study of Pudukkottai well demonstrates this social level of the ritual. Yet the ritual process of "getting dressed," and its concomitant of "going naked," was an act shared by all living beings in the kingdom. The primary honor granted by the raja was a jeweled and therefore "dressed" elephant, and a Kothal (plumed) horse. The Gods likewise also shared this process of getting dressed.

At this point in the discussion—after this long look at the palace, at the king, and at the court—this complex process of dressing can be understood in a broad theo-logical sense. Dressing is indeed a form of fabrication. Dressing makes "bodies." But why is this process of ornamentation also associated with the ascetic process of un-dressing, of going naked? The end of such a discussion is the appropriate time to look closely at an ancient creation-myth that, when read in the context of kingship in Pudukkottai, provides the last clues to the paradoxical nature of the divine royal body created when the bejeweled raja sat on his throne in durbar fixed in the south-facing position of Shiva, the passionate lord of ascetics. Here in the cycle of myths about Prajapati, the lord of creatures, is the ontological link between asceticism and the lavish ornamentation of the king: Both king and ascetic share the ability to create fabricated bodies.

Prajapati and the Fabricated Body

Prajāpati engendered the living world out of a primal passion to reproduce and create life. This cycle of myths encompasses the better-known Puruṣa myth and presents a concept of the universe that expands beyond the limited world that springs from Purusa's divided corporal substance. In the arch-myth of the origins of the sacrifice, Rig-Veda 10.90, the body of the dismembered cosmic "man" Purusa is used to make the male humans, goats, cattle, horses, and the holy hymns needed to make this world work. But the Prajapati myth, retold at length in the later Satapatha Brahmana (6.1.1.1–6.1.2.20; Eggeling [1882–1900] 1972, 3:143–61), encases the Purusa myth and gives the earth more than an Aryan world of men, cattle, and horses.[1] This myth cycle has deep significance for the study of kingship, for as J. C. Heesterman, Jan Gonda, and Ronald Inden each point out in their studies of the rajasuya, when the king is raised to cosmic proportions through the ritual he primarily becomes Prajapati, lord of the living world (see Heesterman 1957, Inden 1978, and Gonda 1969, 79ff.).

Prajapati, like Purusa, is the primal source of the universe; but unlike Purusa, Prajapati, even in the earliest extant references to him, appears to include more than "being" within himself. Rig-Veda 10.121 calls Prajapati *hiranya-garbha*, which standard translations have rendered as "the golden germ" or "golden embryo." But the word *garbha* means both the embryo and the womb in which the fetus grows. Hence, this hymn presents Prajapati in the typical Vedic style riddled with double meaning: He is the source of himself. Prajapati is that which is beyond the chicken-and-egg question. He is both embodied existence and that which generated it. His epithet in the Vedas is Ka, "Who?" and in the Brahmanas he is identified with a God, Ka, "Who?" and is also worshiped as Ka-ya, "Who-ness"—a fact that Max Müller reported with considerable dismay, pining the loss of a genuine speculation turned into a substantive creature for "artificial ceremony" ([1859] 1968, 393). Yet this is exactly Prajapati's nature. He creates and lives in a universe larger than merely what-is. There is room enough for what-is-not, what-could-be, or even what-is-no-more.

The ritual and speculative uses of the Prajapati myth in the Brahmanas and the Upanishads well illustrate Prajapati's position as the God always on that fine edge between existence and nonexistence. Prajapati creates the living world by instigating a long chain reaction. Things are produced which in turn reproduce. The process begins through Prajapati's desire. The desire is defined as the urge to "make a second"—to propagate and thus to begin the infinite chain of divisions that makes the universe in general but that primarily characterizes the reproductive system in organic beings. Prajapati remains always separated from the chain—he is its "life" but not necessarily its body. His primary contact with creation remains his "desire"—and that desire appears to be built into the system as the push and shove of embodied life. But Prajapati's desire clearly has metaphysical status—a reality somewhere between substance and nonsubstance.

The Satapatha Brahmana draws out the narrative of this process of creation in great detail. Here Prajapati is first "created" by the "vital airs" embedded in the nonexistent. The *asat*, that-which-is-not, has metaphysical status. The vital airs are kindled by desire, the first urgent fire of creation, and coalesce into the seven parts of the body of Purusa. But the vital life-sap (*rasa*) of all seven parts is then concentrated in the head. This Purusa + life-sap becomes Prajapati, who then begins the process of reproduction by making both the waters and the egg. This chicken-and-egg cycle then generates the living world. The major narration of the creation ends with Prajapati "falling apart" from complete exhaustion. The text uses the story to explain the true purpose of building the fire altar, which is identified with rebuilding the body of Prajapati. Here the real purport of Brahmanic ritual becomes the regeneration of that which

---

1. The place of the female in the term *puruṣa* is an issue. Doniger sees a female principle of creation in the figure of Virāj, and female "fluids" present in the process of regeneration (1980, 1–33). Yet women as such are not mentioned as in so many other myths in which the world parents, male + female, create.

is worn out by time—both human life exhausted by death, and the natural life cycle worn out by the passing seasons. The process of creation is a cyclical movement from the building up and the wearing out of living beings universalized as the cosmic Prajapati. But even this Brahmanic text appears to know that the process is reversible. There remains, after all, those original vital sins and the life-sap still in Prajapati that can move creation back past the building and rebuilding of Prajapati's body and into the time before it all began—that period of *asat*. This reversibility is explicitly developed by the mystically minded Upanishads, which dwell on this same story of Prajapati. The Bṛhadaraṇyāka Upaniṣad 1.2.1–1.6.3, repeats all the versions of this Prajapati creation cycle, each time forcing the reader to identify with the primal wholeness that, on the first retelling, is the body of Purusa but by the last stanza becomes breath—the primal vital air. The Upanishads ends by declaring that "breath is the immortal, name and form are the true [here *satya*, 'beingness'] by them the immortal is covered" (1.6.3; Macnicol 1963, 57). Prajapati, after manifesting himself as substance, can also reverse the equation and transmute his substantive body back to the vital essence, breath (*prāṇa*), that flows between "being" and the pregnant power of nonbeing.

In the Satapatha Brahmana even Prajapati's creation of the substance-universe has two distinct forms. First Prajapati creates the earth, then he "clothes" her with "clay, mud, saline soil and sand, gravel [pebble], rock, ore, gold, plants and trees" (6.1.1.13; Eggeling [1882–1900] 1972, 3:147). This first creation is engendered by an autosexual model of life-making that is based on ascetic *tapas*, the practice of "austerities." Prajapati "toils and practices austerities." His vital energies flow forth as "foam," and from these he makes the earth and "clothes" her. Once the earth is made, Prajapati then unites with her in the prototype of sexual union (6.2.1–18; Eggeling, 3:148–50). From this heterosexual union come the more familiar elements of Purusa's stable world: the wind, sky, moon, and speech, the Gods, and the mortal creatures that inhabit the stable geographic, theological, and social divisions of the Aryan world. Thus there are two divisions of "being": the one produced from Prajapati's single-minded and single-bodied austerities, and the one produced in union with a second. The heterosexual model here is encompassed by an autosexual ascetic model of reproduction.

Prajapati's creative activity then begins and returns to a nonsubstantive life-essence, the initial creative energy. This primal energy is desire, which is transmuted into the basic essences that begin the reaction that will result in name, form, and bodies. The primal essences are conceptualized as such ethereal materials as heat, particularly as *tapas;* fire; air; breath, *rasa;* or often as semen, clearly seen here as a kind of liquid energy. In the Satapatha Brahmana, when Prajapati "falls apart" his life essences "flowed along this [earth] in the shape of his life-sap" (6.1.2.28; Eggeling, 3:154). While his body parts retain their substantive character, the life-sap flows shapeless and free. The choice of words here is important. Rather than using the term for semen to describe this liquid energy, the text uses the term *rasa*, which in early medical texts means the juice or the sap of plants, and in later texts came to be used as a term in aesthetic theory to describe the emotion of feelings aroused by poetry, music, and drama. Rasa combines the characteristics of all the terms used for the primal life-essences. Like kama (desire) and tapas (the heat generated from the rigid control of that fiery desire), rasa stands midway between emotions and substance. Like air and breath, which generate the poetic word, rasa is the essence of the aesthetic emotions. The Satapatha Brahmana, which of all the early ritual texts takes the greatest interest both in the Prajapati myth and in the king's coronation ceremony, ultimately chooses rasa to describe the material essence that remains closest to nonbeing.

Rasa, the life-sap of Prajapati, does not materialize as part of all elements in the created world. The Satapatha Brahmana specifically states that when Prajapati flowed along the earth in the form of his life-sap, he was absorbed into the earth's surface. This story of the earth's creation from the hardening of Prajapati's conceptive foam is repeated in other texts. The Satapatha Brahmana repeats this same separate creation story in another ritual context, the *agnihotra*, the "homage to the fires" (2.2.4.1–18; Eggeling, 1:322–27). In this version, Prajapati needs to clothe the barren earth because there was as yet no food available to offer as sacrifice to the primordial Fire except his own dear self. The earth was "quite bald; there were neither plants nor trees." Acting fast as Agni opened his mouth to eat him as the only available food, Prajapati rubbed his hands and obtained milk. But the milk was polluted with hairs. He disposed of this in the fire, and it was transformed into plant life. Here again the clothing of the earth, the elements nearest to the earth's surface, are products from that which flowed directly from the creator's body. But the last version of this myth adds an important tone to this act of creation—the plants arose from the liquid energy that was polluted and unfit for the proper sacrifice. Those plants, the earth's first clothing, then receive the direct but tainted juices of Prajapati's first creative act. Thus once again impurity has entered the world associated with the earth's very special clothes.

Prajapati's close association with the "clothed" earth does not end with his acts as a creator. Prajapati himself must be re-created from the same things that are so often listed as the earth's garments. Here is an interesting theological twist on the biblical Genesis. By a larger sense of meta-chemistry, Prajapati has no body of his own after creation. He has been "worn out" and exhausted of both form and substances and must be "built up." This is the ultimate context of the Satapatha Brahmana's longest retelling of the Prajapati myth: The fire altar must be built in order to remake the lost body of the primal lord. Each brick of the fire altar is said to hold Prajapati's rasa (6.1.2.13–36). Each type of brick is named as the fire altar takes shape as a great bird:

> Now surely the first brick of clay is this earth—whatever is made of clay he places on that (altar) that is that one brick. And when he puts thereon the heads of the animal victims, that is the animal-brick. And when he puts the gold plate and man, when he scatters gold shavings thereon, that is the golden brick. And when he puts on two spoonfuls (of ghee), when he puts on the mortar and pestle, and the fire-sticks, that is the wood-brick. And when he puts on a lotus-leaf (petal), a tortoise, sour curds, honey, ghee, and whatever other food he puts on, that is the fifth brick, the food. (V. 30; Eggeling, 3:155)

Prajapati's new body of clay is not made from the stable elements created via sexual union but, as might now be expected, is created from the earth's mud, from gold, from the dead body of a tree (wood), and from the potent head of that victim of sacrificial violence. Even the definition of food belongs to the wild things that are not really part of the fixed social and agricultural world; they are also self-made, not sexually made, products. The God-ascetic now has a body of clay produced from the elements he made in an act of austerity. Here the old Max Müller-inspired axiom that there was no image-making in Vedic times seems contradicted by this making of a clay body for a God whose natural body was literally sacrificed in the process of creation.

The recipients of that first stage of the materialization of Prajapati's primal desire form a clear set within the logic of this far-reaching cosmology. The drama of creation presented in the Prajapati myth cycle has cast many other Gods in the starring role as the creative sinner, yet when the excesses of their sins are poured out upon creation, the same set of elements absorbs that overflowing desire. Wendy Doniger relates the story of the overflow of Shiva's excessive sexual energy, a common motif borrowed from Indra, whose creative sins fall into "fire, the waters, the grasses, trees, and the *apsarases* (heavenly female dancers)" (1971, 283) or on "trees, rivers, mountains, birds born of heads or blood, earth, fire and women" (283). The excessive flow of Indra's sin falls likewise in later Puranas on "trees, saline soil in earth, menstrual blood in women, . . . and bubbles in water" (Doniger 1976, 157). To this list can clearly be added that last element, the *asuras* or demons later so often identified with the tribal or even the outcaste peoples. The outcastes are, by the definition given earlier in the legend of King Vena, those who inhabit the forest and the mountains.

Those elements, enlivened by Prajapati's life-sap and later used to make his image-body, are paralleled in lists of pure and impure castes found in the Dharma Śāstras. The impure castes are those resulting from an improper mixture, a wrong-minded sexual union of members of different castes. The Laws of Manu are quite specific in the lists of social groups who result from mixed marriages of the castes (10.1–73; Bühler [1886] 1964, 401–18). The text carefully delineates specific groups resulting from various degrees of mixture that create men of greater or lesser degrees of impurity. The list, however, taken as a whole, seems a motley lot of strange occupational groups, such as hunters, herbalists, elephant drivers, snake charmers, spies, messengers, butchers, reed musicians, sorcerers, animal trappers, bards, eulogists, boatmen, leather workers, cane workers, iron mongers, carpenters, and cremators of the dead.[2] These groups are clearly defined by occupation. It is interesting that many of the groups listed are in tribal groups associated with specific trades in the larger Hindu society. Some of these tribal groups are also cataloged as emerging from the sins of King Vena and from the undutiful sons of Visvamitra. The list of mixed castes in Manu again connects the outcastes to those who live in or work with rivers, trees, and the forest. The occupations of those mixed castes are also in closest association with the surface of the earth: Ore, rock, and gold are mentioned as direct products of the conceptive foam of Prajapati.

Women, Earth and her "clothing" (trees, rocks, and soil), and the outcastes remain the common holders of that first materialized product of desire: the universal prime elements of fire, air, and water, or the more abstract energies, such as tapas, rasa, or another important

2. My translation of the Sanskrit caste names provided by Bühler in his translation of the text ([1886] 1964, 403–6).

power, *tejas*. These latter terms are at once both alchemical and biological and appear in many diverse Hindu sources as the primary ingredient in plants (rasa) or in women (tejas). The Aitareya Brahmana, as part of the Sunahsepa legend, traces the origin of women to the Gods who brought together "luster" (tejas) and thus formed her as a partner for man (3.7.13; Keith [1920] 1971, 300). The great Goddess Durga is said to have been formed from the tejas, the luster or the splendor of all the Gods—here in close association with beauty (see the Devī-Māhātmya 2.10–2.18; Coburn 1991, 40–41). In sources seemingly far removed from the Sanskrit tradition, the connection of the outcastes to these same ethereal materials remains fixed. In South India, caste groups from the same occupations trace their origins quite consciously from energies that flowed directly out of the creator's body. In these legends, the impure castes are created often out of or from the God's anger or other divine emissions always associated with excess energy or emotion.[3] This is the nature of tapas, tejas, and rasa. All are strongly connected to sexual desire or the more abstracted "passions," and all are conceived as materialized energy—a kind of liquid action that flows as a fundamental partner of desire.

The powers especially associated with ascetic austerity and with forest beings, and with certain "outcaste" groups, are therefore also the same powers that can create very special bodies—bodies without stable substance, bodies whose only "substance" is their "clothing," the ornamentation that gives their vital energies visible shape and form. It is no coincidence that these same groups were so very prominent at the court in Pudukkottai, where like shadows from this ancient myth of Prajapati they went about their own work of (re)constructing yet another divine body. Witness the importance of women—ranis like Janaki and the ever-present devadasis, who, we must remember, were among the first Biruthus won by the Tondaimans. The hunters, herbalists, elephant drivers, messengers, butchers, reed musicians, sorcerers, bards, and eulogists can all be found there in the palace listed among the "menials." And the most important forest-dweller of all was always present in the palace in the person of the Rajaguru. Sadasiva Brahmendra, the master ascetic, was the font of Vijaya Raghunatha Tondaiman's legitimacy or, more precisely, the designer of his royal body. Like the priests who regenerated the fire altar as Prajapati's new clay body, the palace members were fabricators not of natural bodies but of "icons," "images," or in the more common term, "idols." Their product was the central icon seated in ornamented glory, the raja of Pudukkottai in durbar.

The prime body-builders of the king's person were the Brahmans, the Valaiyans, and the Huzur Establishment that functioned in the palace and in the wilderness areas of the realm. While the Huzur Establishment literally dressed the king, both the Brahmans and the Valaiyans maintained his "naked" body in the wilderness by acting out his role in the forest world. The ritual ministrations of both forest and court to the kingly body continued daily, monthly, and yearly. But there was another important ritual context in Pudukkottai in which the king was given a body: the coronation ceremony, the Pattabhishekam. Here in this

---

3. For example, see the origin legends given for "Tribe the Fifth" in the Mackenzie Collection, vol. 23. The "Bhurtoowarus" (Bhatturazus), the court panegyrists, trace their ancestry to a drop of sweat from Shiva's forehead (pp. 162–75). See also Doniger 1971, 271–73.

temple ritual the same process of dressing the king was set in an unmistakable theo-logical context. In Pudukkottai, this royal Pattabhishekam occurred only once at the initial investi-ture of power. Unlike many other kingdoms in India, this single temple ritual appears to have initiated the process of building the royal person, which was then repeated in a ritual calendar in the palace and not in the temple. Thus, in this rather remote state the activities of the palace were given a broader theo-logical context, not through abstract theory but through the unspoken analogy of ritual action that conjoined the temple with the palace.

The Tirugokarnam Temple and the Pattabhishekam

No single definitive text directed the Pattabhishekam in Pudukkottai. The rite was always performed by the Rajaguru in conjunction with the Brahmans of the preeminent state temple. The earliest coronations were held in the Kudumiamalai temple. A palm-leaf manu-script kept in the family of the pandits of that temple contains a brief account of this ancient coronation ceremony as it was last performed in 1686 (*Sikāgirida Caritam*). The coronation dais (Plate 79) still stands in front of the Goddess's image in that temple. In 1730 and thereafter, the coronation was held in the Tirugokarnam temple. The only text that had figured in this ceremony was the *Śāntiratnākara*, classified by Brahmans in Pudukkottai as "Jyothisa" (Sanskrit, *jyotiṣa*), a class of texts relating to the astrological sciences concerned with individual fate in the cosmic flux. However, only the mantras from this text were used.

Plate 79.   The ancient coronation dais is located in front of the sanctum of the God-dess in the Kudumiamalai temple, the state temple of the Tondaimans before 1730. Like Tirugokarnam, the temple at Kudumiamalai predates the Tondaimans' rise to power by almost one thousand years.

Brahmans in Pudukkottai classify the entire Pattabhishekam form as *pauraṇika*, a term that in this context they translate as "popular." The coronation, then, in Pudukkottai was not *vaidika*, "orthodox," as the Brahmans freely admit.

The ceremony itself does appear to have had some continuity in its major features over the years. Fortunately, the former state Agama Sastriar, the formal authority on all matters of ritual, was present at the 1928 coronation and remembered much detail of the ceremony. His account, written with the help of K. Lakshminarayanan, then curator of the Government Museum in Pudukkottai, and clarified by later interviews, remains the primary source of an analysis of the ritual. The following is the priest's account as prepared for me:

> The new raja for his Pattabhishekam at Tirugokarnam Brihadambal temple started his procession through the western gate of his palace (the old palace). In that procession first came a state Elephant with a golden howdah on its back. Another with a silver howdah on its back came next. The third elephant came with the Hanuman Dwaja (Hanuman, the monkey God, flag), which is the state flag. A cavalry of eleven horses followed the three elephants. Next to the cavalry came three groups of musicians in the order of Military Band, Palace Band, and Carnataka Band. Then came the officials of the state. As a climax, the new raja came in a special chariot of four horses.
>
> The procession thus started in the west Main Street of Pudukkottai town and turned west. Toward Tirugokarnam, at the cross of North Main Street and 6th, which is the approach to the temple, the new raja was led to the temple tank, the Mangala Tirtham. There he took his bath in the tank water and wore a new set of clothes. There he sat before the twenty-one Kalasas (pots with mango leaves, coconuts and water) for performing the rituals.
>
> Of the twenty-one pots, twenty were silver and the other one was gold. These pots were filled with the water collected from the temple tarn at the top and from the Mangala Tirtham tank and wrapped with threads. On the spout of them were placed mango leaves upon which had been kept a full coconut. The twenty-one pots thus prepared were kept up on layers specially prepared for them.
>
> First, on the ground, paddy was put. Upon it a plantain leaf was spread. On it rice had been kept, upon which again another plantain leaf had been spread. On this leaf had been put Ulandu (Black-gram dhal) and El (sesame seeds) respectively.
>
> The priests chanted mantras for the pots, some verses from Santi Ratnakara. . . . The portions of the mantras chanted at that occasion were (1) Mahanyasa [Sanskrit, *mahānyasa*, planting] (for one time); (2) Rudram; (3) Thamagam [error for the Tamil *camakam*] (both for eleven times); and (4) Purusha Suttam [Sanskrit, *puruṣa sūkta*] (for one time).
>
> After the completion of chanting mantras, the king took another bath with the water from the pots. Before this bath, the Royal Priest's wife [Rajaguru's wife] poured oil on the king's head. After the bath, the king wore another set of new clothes and went to the sanctum of Sri Brihadambal, his family deity. There the new king was welcomed by the chief priest of the temple and other temple authorities with Purana

Kumbam [Tamil, *pūraṇakumpam,* ritual pot of holy water] and Pari Vattam [Tamil, *parivaṭṭam,* the deity's own vestments tied on the devotee's head as an honor].

Special ablutions and decorations with flowers and jewels were made for the deity. Prayers were made by throwing flowers and chanting names and the glory of the Goddess, with camphor lighting. After this, the temple's chief priest handed over the State Sword, which had been brought from the Palace for this purpose and kept under the foot of the deity for receiving her blessings. After obtaining the state sword from the priest, in the sacred place of the sanctum, on the promise that he would rule the country according to Hindu Dharma for the welfare of his subjects, he returned in procession with all pomp to his palace and held a special durbar.

The Pattabhishekam was carefully sandwiched between the crucial palace rituals: the processional display of the raja and the public viewing at the durbar. The durbar itself in such small kingdoms could function alone as an investiture ceremony. Pamela Price relates an instance in nearby Ramnad when the Maravar chiefs simply called "a durbar where they selected a new, Maravar king, and showed him royal honors" (Price 1979, 220). A rival group then had its choice for king installed in a ritual at the royal state temple. A similar succession dispute in Pudukkottai sent a rival group scurrying to arrange a shotgun coronation at the Tirugokarnam temple. Even in a more stable Pudukkottai, the durbar followed closely on the heels of the Pattabhishekam. Moreover, at least in the last edition of the ritual, the coronation was integrated into the basic ritual logic of the procession and the durbar.

In this Pattabhishekam, dressing the raja continued to be a vital part of the ceremony. At each crucial stage of this Pattabhishekam, the raja changed his clothes. In the procession to the temple, the pieces of his full regalia were paraded, but he was separated from them by the officers of the state. Here the usual order of the procession was reversed. The administrators that usually followed the king preceded a royal body who was not yet fully dressed. At the temple tank, the raja took his first bath, shedding his nonroyal clothes and covering his clean body with a set of temporary garments. After the Abhishekam, he donned his royal robes for the first time and finally took his rightful place in the return procession, now fully ornamented. The entire ceremony then could be viewed as yet another variant of royal dressing set here in the context of the temple rather than the palace. The temple setting, however, provided such strong theo-logical overtones to the palace activities that "dressing" was extended beyond the social realm and into the metaphysical.

The Pattabhishekam was held in the special coronation Mandapam (Plate 80, color section) added to the temple for this purpose when the Tondaimans adopted Tirugokarnam as their royal temple. The pavilion extends from the side of the main hall of the temple and faces the temple tank (reservoir), which provides a source of water for the central ritual, the *abhiseka,* the "besprinkling" of the raja with the contents of those twenty-one Kalasas (Sanskrit, *kālaśa*) (Plate 81). The coronation Mandapam bears many of the ornamental details of the raja's own Darbar Hall. The Gajalakshmi can be seen over the door lintels (Plate 82), and the columns are carved with images of Indra riding his elephant in his form as king of the Gods. The royal yalis appear next to Indra (Plate 83). The Mandapam seems a royal home away from home, but unlike his wooden palace, this house is made of stone. For

Plate 81. Directly in front of the Mangala Tirtham stands the coronation pavilion, constructed for the coronation of the Tondaiman rajas. In the door at the inner entrance to the pavilion is a window that legend says was used by Raja Martanda Tondaiman to see the sanctum of the Goddess after his marriage to a non-Hindu barred him from actually entering the temple.

Plate 82.   A profusion of royal emblems are carved into the columns in the coronation pavilion at the Tirugokarnam temple. Here the style of this Gajalakshmi recalls the same figure on the portals of the treasury rooms in the downstairs anteroom of the Darbar Hall.

their coronation, the Tondaimans come, for the moment, into the timeless world of the Gods.

Just as the Mandapam declares that the Tondaimans are kings in the ancient line of India, the "besprinkling" rites of the Pudukkottai closely parallel the unction in the ancient rajasuya. Like the Vedic rite, the contents of the "pots" were primarily "waters." In the more modern Tirugokarnam ritual, the waters were taken from only two sources: the temple tank and a natural spring within the temple compound. The temple tank is located just in front of a special coronation Mandapam. To reach the natural spring, priests would have had to climb the ancient stone stairs (Plate 84) that lead up to the outer rock that covers the oldest portions of this cave temple. Here the spring flows in a deep crevice over the temple (Plate 85). In the earlier rite performed at the Kudumiamalai temple, the waters were drawn from nine sources: river water, five different mountain springs, and three different wells in the temple (*Sikāgirida Caritam*). The latter compound of waters quite closely follows the collection of unction "waters" stipulated in the Satapatha Brahmana (5.3.4.1–17) and in the Taittīriya Saṃhitā (7.8.11–16). Even the explanation of the meaning of these waters given in these Vedic texts seems to fit the Pudukkottai rite. The Satapatha Brahmana explains that the "waters" are like the embryonic fluids from which a child is born (5.3.5.19; Eggeling, 3:85). The Taittīriya Saṃhita calls them "the caul of kingly power, . . . the womb of kingly power" (1.8.12; Keith [1914] 1967, 1:123). The Vedic abhiseka, like the Pudukkottai

Plate 83. Another pillar in the coronation pavilion of the Tirugokarnam temple is replete with royal signs. The face of a yali resides next to Indra, the king of the Gods, riding his elephant.

counterpart, was immediately followed by the king putting on new garments interpreted directly in these texts. "And as to why he makes him put on the garments—he thereby causes him to be born, thinking, 'I will anoint him when born': that is why he makes him put on the garments" (Satapatha Brahmana 5.3.5.24; Eggeling, 3:87). Again the Vedic texts seem only to reinforce the entire birth-by-dressing rituals in the womblike palace and suggest that the Pudukkottai temple rites ritually restate this entire process.

The Vedic texts and the Pudukkottai ritual affirm that the king indeed received a new body out of the abhiseka waters. But when the question arises as to the exact nature of that body, the Vedic texts and the Pudukkottai rite part company. The Vedic unction, according to Heesterman, was carefully placed into the context of the *śrauta* sacrificial cycle. Relying on this sacrificial context, Heesterman and others have concluded that, in the unction rite, the Brahmans poured fertile fluids into the king's natural body and thus transformed it into true substance—the solid essence of the cosmos (see Heesterman 1957, 222–27; Inden 1978, 28–76; and Gonda 1969, 87–93). These *śrauta* sacrifices, Heesterman explains, were agricultural rites. It could be argued, then, that as agricultural rites the srauta ritual defined the human life process on the analogy of the life cycle of cultivated plants and domestic animals. "Life" was defined as a cyclical process of birth and death, of sowing and reaping. In this context the king's body was "born" and "died" in a cycle of annual rites. Thus the abhiseka had to be repeated yearly. In Pudukkottai, however, the Pattabhishekam was not a

Plate 84.   A dramatic stairway cut into the rock leads from the sanctums of the Tirugokarnam temple to the surface of the rock above. The oldest part of the temple, the sanctum of Shiva, is a cave.

Plate 85.   A stream of holy water flows over the Tirugokarnam temple,
which is cut into solid rock below. The many pillars of the temple are carved
out of the rock. Later in the eighteenth and nineteenth centuries, an outer
gate and larger entrances were constructed in front of the original opening to
the cave temple.

cyclical process and, most important, was not set in the context of sacrificial, hence agricultural, rites. The fact that the Pattabhishekam was classified not as vaidika but rather as
pauranika becomes crucial at this point. As a pauranika rite, the Pattabhishekam was not
merely a "popularized" or watered-down version of the Vedic rite, but rather a rite set
outside the context of the vaidika definitions of life and growth.

The pots in the Pudukkottai abhiseka contained water only. They were not filled with
other fluids like ghee, honey, or milk, as in the Vedic rite. In fact, the contents of the pots
were not even called "water" or "fluid," but rather "Tirtham" (Sanskrit, *tīrtha*), an important word with broad implications and use in temple worship throughout India. Diana Eck
has recently explored the broadest context of this term. She points out that *tīrtha* has the

primary meaning of a ford across a river as well as any watering or bathing place. Figuratively the term also came to mean "to surmount, to fulfill, to be saved." In its fullest meaning, *tīrtha* is not "water" at all but the name given to any place where salvation occurs—a ford "where caste and sex, sins, sickness, and death and even samsara itself may be transcended in the crossing" (Eck 1981, 344). The unction pots were filled with such Tirtham in Pudukkottai. Unction "waters," then, were more theologically complex than the simple agricultural metaphor of the substantiated seed fertilized by the (uterine) waters.

The dual meaning of tirtha as both affecting a transition and cleansing the body of all the accumulated sinful residue of daily life—sex, sickness, death—can also be seen in the general use of Tirtham in Pudukkottai. Here the Tirtham constitutes one of the important honors given by the temple to the royal family and other important donors when they visited the temple for public worship. On these occasions, the "holy water" was taken by the king in a golden cup and presented along with garlands, holy ash (Tamil, *vipūti*), a red powder (Tamil, *kuṅkumam*), and flowers (Darbar Files, R6c/1909, "Respects Shown to the Royal Family at Tirugokarnam"). The fact that the Tirtham was categorized with these other four items is significant. The garlands, red powder, and flowers constituted part of the Goddess's toilette, items that minister to her icon body and invigorate and purify it but do not feed it. Her food as Prasadam was offered later to the king. By analogy, when the devotee, here the king, took the Tirtham and the other items offered with it, his own body was purified and invigorated. During the Pattabhishekam, when the king's body was literally bathed with the Tirtham, that royal body was treated exactly like the icon body of the temple Goddess. The Tirtham both cleansed and invigorated, and this is the meaning temple priests still give to "water" in general—that which both purifies and invigorates.

Tirtham remains a medium through which a transition is effected. The "waters" wash away the old and stimulate that which is about to be created. The pot that holds these "waters," the Kalasa, then, is the caldron for this transition. Like the Tirtham, the Kalasa remains a familiar ritual object throughout India. Resting on a base of paddy, black gram, and sesame seeds and topped with mango leaves and a full ripe coconut, the Kalasa presents an image of life-in-transition. As Susanne Hanchett concluded:

> The ritual element . . . is the liquid, and transformations are expressed in the sealed closure of the whole coconut, the temporary closure of the vessel, and the filling and emptying of the vessel. . . . And the ritual object becomes in itself a veritable conversation on the subject of mortality and immortality with some suggestion that life (or soul) is flowing through many vessels in its various transitions. (Hanchett 1978, 48)

The pot filled with "water," like Tirtham, speaks of transitions and defines such continuing transitions as the very nature of life.

The Kalasa, also called Kumbam in South India, is more than an image of bodily transition in a gross physical sense. The Kalasa appears in particular during temple rituals when it is used as a temporary body for the temple deity during periods when the image has been removed from the sanctum to be reinstalled into the bronze processional image before it is used for open public display (Waghorne 1992b, 9–11). The Kumbam also functions as a transitional body for any deity, before that God has accepted the *arcā*, the icon, as a more permanent body. The initial installation or the reinstallation of a temple deity is commonly called the Mahakumbabhishekam (Tamil + Sanskrit, *māhā* + *kumpa* + *abhiṣēkam*). The closest ritual parallel to the Pattabhishekam is not the Vedic unction in the rajasuya but rather this Mahakumbabhishekam—the embodiment of deity within a sculpted image.

In 1987 I observed a wide variety of these installation rituals as part of a study of new temples in Madras. In spite of many differences, the Kumbam was always the central feature, and the ceremonies always climaxed with the pouring of the Tirtham in these pots onto the new body of God. The Mahakumbabhishekam for the white marble image of Saint Sai Baba of Shirdi, held at the Sai Mandir on March 22, 1987, not only paralleled the Pudukkottai Pattabhishekam in structure but also included many of the royal emblems as part of the ceremony. The devotees of Sai Baba had worshiped their saint in the form of a painting when they felt the time was right to install a marble image. Sai Baba, a modern ascetic saint, is considered an incarnation of God. The ritual began by chanting mantras into 108 Kumbam (Plate 86). At the end of this long and complex ritual, these pots were carried by priests and devotees in a grand procession from the ritual hall to the temple. The procession was led by the head of the temple carrying the main Kumbam, considered the aniconic body of Sai Baba, with the royal umbrella at his side (Plate 87). Earlier in the ritual, the Chowries stood at the "seat," a clear throne, of the God-man (Plate 88). When the contents of these pots had been poured over the marble image, Sai Baba was awakened to live in his new body and greeted by his devotees as lord and God (Plate 89). The confluence of ascetic, royal, and

Plate 86.   The Kumbam, holy pots, are the central ritual vessels in all forms of consecration. For the Pattabhishekam, their contents anoint the king. For the Mahakumbabhishekam, the pot's holy waters enliven the image of the Gods. Here the Kumbam await infusion of divine energy from the many mantras chanted by priests in this consecration of a marble image of Shirdi Sai Baba.

Plate 87. The close connection between kings and ascetics continues today in many ritual contexts. Here the emblems of royalty are processed, with the Kumbam holding the divine presence of the ascetic saint Sai Baba during the consecration ritual. In addition to being accorded the royal emblems of umbrella, crown, throne, and Chowrie, the ascetic heads of South India's Hindu monastic centers are still addressed as "Maharaja."

Plate 88. The chief priest at the installation of the new image of Sai Baba garlands the portrait of the saint which was once the center for worship here but was preempted by the new marble image.

Plate 89. This is the crucial moment of darsan, when the devotees see the divine image for the first time. Wearing a crown of flowers, the divine saint sits enthroned like a king ready to grant the wishes of his beloved subjects.

divine emblems in this ritual is especially striking because it occurs in the context of creation of an icon body.

The nature of the theo-logic behind the Mahakumbabhishekam is verbally expressed in one version of the ritual kept in the notebooks of a priestly family of the Mylapore area in Madras City. The notebooks provide enough of the basic outlines of the ritual to initiate serious comparison with the Pattabhishekam. The procedure for the ritual was summarized as follows in a translation typical of the English used for the many non-Tamilians who come to the temples in this urban religious center:

> Place layers of sesame seed, raw rice, wheat and black gram dhal on the ground. The sesame seed stands for Brahma, the rice is Vishnu, wheat is Indra and black gram is Yama. Put twenty-six pots in a circle in these layers, with one pot in the center. The Purohita should then fill the pots with river water poured through a filter as he chants a mantra to the Ganga river. Cardamom spice and camphor powder should be put into the pots. Margo leaves are then put on the openings and covered with a large coconut. A sacred thread is tied around each pot. The Purohita then recites five mantras over the pot: the Rudra, the Camakam, the Purusha Suktam, the Busuktam, and the Panchasanti.

The resemblance to the Pattabhishekam becomes immediately obvious. Here, however, interpretation that helps confirm the meaning of this procedure with the Pattabhishekam is added. The Gods mentioned as corresponding to the layers of raw seeds bridge the full gambit between life and death. Brahma, the eternal creator, and Vishnu, the eternal preserver, are paired with Indra, the God who creates by an act of killing, and Yama, the God of death. Here the ritual is literally built on layers of immortality and mortality.

The waters in the pot, then, are not associated with that unidirectional cycle of material birth and death. The Tirtham effects a transition beyond what this system views as *samsāra*, mere bodily rebirth. The transition of this royal Abhishekam then cannot be viewed as the simple exchange of one physical body for another. The new body that emerged in Pudukkottai from that now-purified Kallar body left the realm of the purely physical. The Tirtham indeed allowed the raja to cross over the "sin," over perhaps his natural body, into the body of a king. But the entire image of the Kalasa here suggests that this new royal body was not corporal, but rather analogous to the icon-body of a God. The icon body of a God is molded from the substances of the earth—metal, stone, clay, or wood—and made by the hands of low-caste artisans (see Preston 1985, 10–12; Inglis 1985, 95–101; Huyler 1988, 21–28), much in the same way that the raja was "made" in the palace by his lower-caste "servants," whose ministrations turned his natural body into the ornamented body of a king.

The king's royal body was not corporal, but neither was his forest-self or his ascetic-self. This remains the most complex aspect of this metaphysical system. The Pattabhishekam clearly speaks in body language. The entire ritual process was an act of giving the king his royal body. Considerable theoretical refinement is necessary to understand the nature of such a body. The seemingly clear metaphor of the water in a pot seems to make perfect sense as a symbol of soul substance passing through the many vessels that are the human body. Such an analysis leads to the conclusion that while the body, the vessel, may be an insubstantial shell, the inner fluid must be real—the divine matter that creates many a body. But evidence proves the contrary. The contents of the pots remain as ephemeral as the vessel itself.

In the Pudukkottai Pattabhishekam, the Kalasa contained only "water." When questioned, the Agama Sastriar remained adamant on this point. There were no substances in the Kalasa, although the ritual process did focus on the content of the pots. Twenty-one Brahmans chanted mantras over those pots, which in some sense have effected a change within those metal vessels. The mantras were taken from the royal Abhishekam ceremony enjoined in the Śāntiratnākara. While the Pudukkottai ritual differed in many aspects from this Abhishekam, the chanting of mantras over a golden vessel does have an exact parallel in this Jyothisa text. Although the text of the Santiratnakara is difficult at this point, the royal ritual described appears to include two different Abhishekams. In the first, a clay figure of the Goddess Lakshmi is to be placed in the northeast corner of the coronation site. On the side of this image is set a golden Kumbam filled with water. The priest then "invites" Lakshmi to "come into the waters" by reciting the mantras:

Oh, one with golden color,
Attracting all minds
With your gold ornaments
Pleasing to everyone,
May you come here.

The Goddess is then "invited" by another mantra as the priest sprinkles water on the pot. These invocations are then repeated with separate offerings of sandal paste, flowers, camphor smoke, and a burning lamp. Finally, when Lakshmi's presence is certain, food is offered and then taken as Prasadam. Using a lotus flower as a ladle, the priest then bathes the new king with the contents of this golden vessel. The golden vessel in the Pudukkottai Pattabhishekam, then, can be considered analogous to this same vessel that holds the "golden one," Lakshmi. Frederique Marglin's analysis of a similar use of a golden Kalasa in the Abhishekam of the raja of Puri confirms this strong interconnection between the vessel and the Goddess. Her further insight that the vessel is an aniconic representation of the power of the Goddess, śakti, adds another dimension to the Pudukkottai ritual (1982a, 161–62).

The Pattabhishekam ended with the firm establishment of a relationship between the Goddess Brihadambal and the raja. The final confirmation of his coronation occurred in front of her sanctum, where he received from her the sword of state. What is explicit in the latter part of the ceremony, apparently is implicit in the Abhishekam itself. The golden vessel appears to have been as much an aniconic image of the Goddess as an image of the king's own body in transition. Both the king and the Goddess are "golden"; they both shine with the glitter of their ornamented form. That mantra to Lakshmi in the Santiratnakara reads much like the popular ballads that praised the raja's own shining self in Pudukkottai. But the full logic of this analogue between the king, the Goddess, and that golden vessel creates some paradoxical conclusions. The king would seem to be the Goddess's own body because he came to be invigorated by her sakti, present in those Kalasas. The easy equation, however, that the king = the body, and the Goddess = the soul, fails to fit the full logic of the Kalasa imagery. The king's body is no more solid, no more substantive, than the sakti that filled it. And that sakti itself must be understood within the context of the term "Tirtham." These "waters" of the Kalasa only effect a change, provide a transition, cleanse, and invigorate. They are not a fluid soul-substance like the sticky mixture in the Brahmanic pot of the Vedic rajasuya. The king, the Goddess, and the aniconic pot mix together in some other logical framework that leaves behind such substantive language borrowed from the sacrificial cycle.

A myth related as part of the *sthalapūraṇa*, stories about a sacred site, of the Tirugo-karnam temple explains the relationship between the Goddess Brihadambal and her husband, Shiva ("The Legend of Bakaulavaneswari"; see also *Tirukkōkarṇam Kōyil Varalāṟu*). The story is told as a parable on the relationship between what the myth terms "power" (the Goddess) and "action" (the God). The myth on a mundane level simply relates why the Goddess is now given precedence in this temple over her husband, whose image stands behind her own sanctum. The myth relates the familiar tale of the sacred cow Kamadhenu who was exiled to earth to do penance. She undertook to perform a round of rituals that exhausted her and threatened her death and the death of her calf. The heavenly maidens of the eternal Goddess pleaded with her to intervene to save Kamadhenu. Rather than taking action herself, the Goddess stepped aside, allowing her husband to save the cow and gain the glory of such a deed. The myth ends with the explanation that because of that singular act of submissiveness by the Goddess, Shiva decreed that "all mortals should pay their respects to her before they worshiped him." The story ends with a metaphysical epilogue:

> There is no action without Power (*śakti*), but Power manifests itself in all its glory when it is subordinated to action. The might of action speaks of the Power that impels it, thus multiplying its importance manifold.

This myth is as much a metaphor for the relationship of the raja to sakti as it is for the relationship of Shiva to Brihadambal. During the Pattabhishekam, the raja was given a body of "action" impelled by the "waters" of the golden vessel. The aniconic Kalasa, sakti without a visible body, was poured over the raja. Following parallel logic of the Kumbab-hishekam, the raja stood there like an icon awaiting the invigorating splash of water that would awaken his bejeweled royal body to activity. Here the sakti of the Goddess has found a body in the king! Sakti is formless; the king's body has form.

The king's body indeed has form, but by the very same logic of the full Kalasa, that royal body cannot be identified either with the gross matter of the vessel or with the raw flesh of the king. The king's body, rather, is best defined as that-which-can-act. And it is significant that this is the exact literal meaning of the term *sam-alam-kāra:* "to be made" (*kāra*), "fully" (*sam*), "able" (*alam*). The very ornamentation, samalamkara, then is the king's royal body, and it is this ornamentation that makes him a king and enables him to act upon the kingdom. At this point the activities of the priests during the Pattabhishekam fully confirm the function of the daily ministrations of the palace servants. During the durbar and the great royal processions, the forest chieftain whose valiant deeds confirmed the presence of power is displayed in the clothes of a king. During the Abhishekam, the raw power in that royal forest-being is installed in the icon body of a king—a garment-body that clothes power in a form fit to rule. The "clothes" have made the man.

Ornament as Ontology:
A Conclusion

His Excellency the Raja Ramachandra Tondaiman remains seated in durbar like a pressed flower marking an important page in a now-unopened Victorian book. While the empire existed, such a photographic image had a worldwide significance. The popular "art unit" created by Victorian ladies around the beloved fireplace moved such images into the everyday life of the modern middle-class wherever the fashion of the empire reigned. As exotic as they may have seemed, India's native princes were not strangers in the Victorian house. They entered as "decoration" in an era that loved the decorative. As the Indian princes adorned their palaces with glass chandeliers, their own stilled images decorated many a Victorian "castle" as they rested on the hearth in the heart of the middle-class home.

This remains the most enduring—and most telling—image of the Indian maharajas, their place on the mantelpiece of the Anglo-American home. Here they were "merely" exotic decoration, but in Pudukkottai—we must not forget—the raja's holy body was no less "decoration," *alaṃkāra*. And, like the Victorian lady decorating her home, the empire's political agents in the Native States also took to this world of buttons, bows, and bunting and created their own "art units" with themselves at the center. Thus I end not with another photograph of the durbar but with two curious snapshots of Mrs. Bossom's living hall and fireplace, Boston 1912. Here the most serious possibilities and problems for the recovery of *religious things* sit neatly on a shelf—visible if we begin to look with an eye that has seen durbar halls and palaces and temples of Pudukkottai and is ready to bring it all home.

Mrs. Bossom's Living Hall

The Victorian living hall was a very public space. This enlarged entrance hall, eliminated from domestic architecture immediately after this gilded age, served as a parlor when the formal parlor was too fragile and beautiful to expose to common use. The purpose of the hall was to impress, to make a statement, to invite a neighbor into the publicity of one's life. It is the closest that domestic architecture ever came to a royal anteroom. Mrs. Bossom followed custom perfectly by hiding her actual living and dining rooms behind a closed door and a drawn portiere while exposing much of herself right inside her own front door (Plate 90).

Plate 90.   This photograph is filed as "Room in Mrs. Bossom's House" and has already served as the cover illustration for *The Tasteful Interlude: American Interiors Through the Camera's Eye, 1860–1917* (Seale, 1975). The layout of Mrs. Bossom's house and her eclectic decor was actually quite typical for suburban Bostonians at the turn of the century. My own interest in such living halls stems from a ten year project restoring a similar Victorian house in Boston. (Courtesy of the Prints and Photographic Division, Library of Congress, LC-C801-118.)

I know nothing of Mrs. Bossom that her living hall does not tell, and perhaps that is as it should be. Obviously from a well-traveled family, Mrs. Bossom has collected artifacts from several different Eastern countries, but India dominates her motif. An American flag leans casually on the stair, as if to reveal her patriotism in spite of overwhelming evidence of her love for the foreign (note the leopard skin on the handrail). The art unit around her mantel (Plate 91) brings together with amazing acumen various emblems of Indian royal life. Swords that might have been seen at the sides of a raja's courtiers hang now under and over her mantel interspersed with antelope horns. Just above the raised shelf at the center of the mantel stands a photograph of what appears to be a village chieftain and his noble folk. Above to the right is a photograph of man who, if not a prince, poses in princely fashion. On the upper mantel from left to right rest a large incense urn, two bronze elephants, a laughing Buddha, an intricate (possibly carved ivory) vase, a two-bladed axe, a brass bucket, a butterfly, and another large vase. The main mantel holds an embossed plate with the image of what looks like a Moghul emperor. Mrs. Bossom has draped *rudrākṣa* beads, the sign of asceticism, at the base of this medallion. Similarly around the subsequent photograph of an obviously much revered man she has placed rosary beads. Another brass plate, a glass vase, a larger ornate vase, several photographs of young women, and a snapshot of a naval officer follow. At the end of this mantle, Mrs. Bossom has set sticks of incense in a miniature holder. Thus both on the right and on the left of the mantel are signs of spiritual India like bookends to the martial world held between.

This art unit would, by any other name, be called an altar. It is astonishing how close Mrs. Bossom has come to including the key emblems of Indian kingship here: the antelope and leopard, the ascetic's beads and the warrior's swords. The fact that she chose to place at the center of her "altar" an ornate vase in the shape of the ultimate aniconic image of deity, the Kumbam, must be put to sheer coincidence of the uncanny variety. I would guess that the vase was her most valuable piece and thus placed at the center of her collection. Even more astonishing is the simple fact that His Highness Martanda Tondaiman, reigning in Pudukkottai in 1912, would have felt quite at home in her living hall in spite of its modest proportions. The house built as his actual residence near the British cantonment in Trichinopoly was furnished much the same way. His present Highness maintains this room with swords, axes, and trophies of hunting (Plate 92) on a scale that befits the difference between a prince and a middle-class Bostonian. Yet on the other side of the globe from princely India, Mrs. Bossom made her home in the shared space of imperial decorative culture. Like our opening portrait of Raja Ramachandra, she too has her ornaments and willy-nilly mixes, cut glass and porcelain with swords, miniature elephants and leopard skins.

However, a significant difference between "East" and "West" remained. In the greater empire, decoration was given the ardor, the passion, frequently reserved for divine matters, but not the name. Ultimately James Frazer and Max Müller would reserve the term "Religion" for the "Infinite" which was beyond, behind, beneath surface display. They, as scholars who followed them, dismissed both idolatry in India and "materialism" in England as the tragic vanity of their time. In doing so, they not only bifurcated religion from magic, material from spiritual, but also alienated Mrs. Bossom from her would-be prince charming

Plate 91. The photograph is cataloged as "Mrs. Bossom's Fireplace." (Courtesy of the Prints and Photographic Division, Library of Congress, LC-C801-113.)

Plate 92. I pose for a portrait amid the many trophies of the Tondai-mans in His Highness's living room at his permanent residence in Trichinopoly. Members of the house-hold staff told me that most visitors picked this spot for a snapshot.

by sequestering the spiritual from the decorative. Already her art unit betrays a move toward the modern, with neatly framed photographs and vases and few of the handmade laces and "fancy work" that would have been omnipresent a decade earlier. The more "educated" Mrs. Bossom became, the more she would have replaced her "clutter" with good books on dusted shelves.

Middle-class Indians also read Max Müller with great passion, but they never "read" him with the logic of the Anglo-American world. They devoured his books, praised his grasp of the spiritual, and then sent him shawls and Prasadam. This is because in places like Pudukkottai outward signs are not signs at all. The "spiritual" is coterminous with the very outwardness that the nineteenth-century scholar assumed must give way to some inner truth. In middle-class India, Mrs. Bossom's art unit would indeed be an altar. At its center might have been placed *Jñāna* Saraswati, Goddess of learning, like the small house version one sculptor made for me in Kumbakonam on a model of a larger piece commissioned by a university in Tanjore. This divine lady's buxom bronze body is etched over with intricate carving that creates the jewels and the clothing that bedeck her. With book in one hand, the holy *rudrākṣas* beads in another, and a small pot of tirtha (holy water) in the third, her fourth hand makes the sign of wisdom. The holy book, holy tirtha, and holy prayer adorn her body like the jewels in her crown or the flowers etched into her feet. She teaches openly what Mrs. Bossom intuited and what Raja Ramachandra "knew": The spiritual body is not inside or underneath the fleshly body, it is layered on top of it.

To acknowledge this difference in the "location" of the sacred as exterior and not interior, as surface and not inner reality, as ornament and not essence, would have demanded that Protestant Europeans radically reform their perceptions of sacredness in the nineteenth century. Ironically at the very time that the comparative study of religion began, the goal of the new and very sincere academic enterprise of Max Müller was to legitimize the religions of the East by making them look outwardly different but inwardly compatible with basic Victorian values. Müller built an image of India as more committed to the frequently acknowledged Christian goal of inward spiritual development. Frazer introduced much of the logic of "magic" and argued passionately that this ancient attempt to control matter was at the heart of modern science. Then, instead of affirming the fact, he denounced the whole enterprise as vanity quite in keeping with the age of *Vanity Fair*. In a very pragmatic sense, Müller and Frazer had no choice. As scholars of religion, their supporters were frequently drawn from the ranks of reformist church leaders and religious scientists. Certainly, ardent rationalists and the coming positivists and Marxists were not likely to join hands with a discipline that asked the public to take religion seriously as religion. To openly name Mrs. Bossom's art unit, the raja's durbar, or the ceremonials of the Raj as "religion" would have forced the fledgling discipline into a confrontation both with church leaders and with sympathetic scientists. The former would have been shocked at the idolatry, and the latter might well have objected to the loss of a safe corner for religion that would remain compatible with but essentially outside the stricter empiricism of their scientific world. Such a confrontation would have ensured that a Max Müller or a James Frazer, rather than joining the ranks of the British Empire's academic nobility, would have ended in obscurity. To relocate religion at the surface of things, in the ornamental, would have forced Müller and Frazer to embrace much of the very "vanity" and "foolishness" they condemned.

Such a relocation of sacredness, however, is possible now in these times of poststructuralism, postmodernism, and the general willingness to revise the study of religion in a post-Imperial and perhaps post-Marxist world. The time is right to return to the original thesis of this study. The late nineteenth century in places like Pudukkottai, the residences of political agents, governors' mansions, and even Mrs. Bossom's living hall, came to share a common but unvoiced culture—a culture of ornament, fabrication, and grand display. But now we can confront the central *mystery*—and I now apply that term much as it was used in the Catholic church—of this ontology that was revealed within the raja's world in Pudukkottai. *Ornament/display/fabrication is about materialism, but not about matter. It is about bodies, but not about the physical form.* There was no need for the comparative study of religion to retreat from its initial insistence that there existed a sense of religion that was intimately connected to the visible world. The discipline need never have discarded the notion of "mana" or "animism" to embrace, as Eliade put it, "the sign of logos," if they had only been willing to admit what has been called the "excluded middle" into their own ontology (Derrida 1982, 79; see also Derrida [1967] 1976, 30- 44). This middle is a point between matter and the immaterial, between subject and object, between existence and nonexistence.

That excluded metaphysical middle is the world of the iconic—the location of beingness not in the essence of things but in their *pūrṇa*, their fullness, their overflow into image, into form that exists in full view of the human imagination.

I have also suggested throughout this study that iconic culture in Pudukkottai and in the imperial world was sometimes "reformed" and at other times simply co-opted and thus silenced by those who preferred order, bureaucracy, permanences, and solid rationality to what seemed a spendthrift, immoral, and dangerously chaotic world. Giving voice to the iconic world would have produced more than an academic conundrum. The iconic is deeply implicated in the world precisely because it is by its very nature *historical*. The "icon" is eminently visible and at the center of power. The king or God in this bodily form is power incarnate, and that power is sustained by his very existence as an icon. That is why the study of this sort of theo-logy cannot be accomplished outside of history. It belongs ontologically to history.

Thus iconic culture implies its own sense not only of the *space* that "sacredness" occupies but also of the definition of *time* in relationship to that "sacredness." I do not employ the familiar terms "the Sacred" or "the Holy" here because such a sense of ongoing permanence, of independence of both space and time, is also quite inappropriate to the system. But it is equally inappropriate to continue to describe "iconic culture" in overly generalized language at the end of what has been a detailed study of a fifty-square-mile area in South India. Yet the system in Pudukkottai, and the more general turn toward the ornamental in the empire, demands explication in more general terms of what the system implies for the very categories that the study of religion has developed as scions of Frazer and Müller. A systematic study of iconic culture belongs to future work and is in many respects already in progress in new work on the body, on "public culture," on performance theory, on dress, on the changing definition of "text" in literary criticism, and so on. A careful review of all these new theories, as well as the ongoing theories and arguments about the nature of religion developed in the last hundred years in the field, would be more appropriate for the introduction of such a new study than for the conclusion of this one. Moreover, this is not a study of anthropology, or of art, or even of history but a study of theo-logy. I offer, then, four general observations on the ontology of ornament in Pudukkottai and in the decorative world of the empire that, if given a voice in the history of religions, might in some small way have altered the dimensions of God in the modern world.

1. The Material, the Spiritual, and the Natural

The notion continues in textbooks and in almost all basic introductions to Hinduism that much of India shared a belief in *māya*, "the illusionary nature of the phenomenal world and its corollary, skepticism about the physical world and a desire to find truth beyond the material" (Huntington and Huntington 1990, 88). Little could be further from the truth in Pudukkottai, which reveled in material things and even used such things to create a body for divinity. Yet there is no denying that the Tondaimans were deeply involved with the ascetic tradition and honored as their great guru a naked saint. What was the relationship between spiritual and material in this little kingdom?

The problem of the material versus the spiritual as formulated by Max Müller and repeated in a thousand different ways over the last century is a misunderstanding of the nature of "materialism" in a place like Pudukkottai. There is nothing natural, nothing physical, about the king's ornamental body. There is equally nothing "physical" about the palace or the temple or the great Gods that inhabit these structures. Yet all divine things here are visible, audible, and even tactile. They are fabricated: matter once-removed, twice-born, re-created. *Religious things* do not gain their holiness by coming "fresh from the Creator's hand," as Mircea Eliade put it ([1957] 1963, 65), but by being remade by the hand of a human being. They are "spiritual" because they are the art-ificial product of ritual—ritual war, ritual hunting, ritual dressing. The Tondaimans, in fact, become royal because they tamed the "natural" power of wild elephants and tigers and make of them a glittering world of seemingly frivolous decoration.

But how can the naked ascetic fit into such an explanation of the "spirituality." Surely he has turned his back on the material world. Indeed, Sadasiva Brahmendra openly ignored the physical world, but that does not mean he did not value his "body." Yoga, in South India, should not be interpreted via modern psychology as a form of inner transformation. Yoga is an exercise to transform the body. The yogi needs no clothes because his very body has become "dress," a glittering body re-created from flesh. Sadasiva, like most saints in South India, was not cremated when he died. Instead, he was buried, and over his samadhi the Tondaimans are said to have built a temple to house his new icon body. Such a theo-logic may not apply to all yogis or to all parts of India, but certainly in Pudukkottai and I suspect much of South India the yogi-saint belongs most firmly with the king in a common mode of material beingness that transcended nature while existing firmly in the world.

Where did scholars like Max Müller and Frazer go wrong? Anthropology began by noticing the materialism of religious phenomenon. The young discipline fed from notions of "mana." Max Müller's *Lectures on the Origin and Growth of Religion* began as a brilliant argument for applying Kant's critique of pure reason to the study of religion. Müller used the term phenomenon and distinguished between nomen and phenomenon. He did not mistake religion for science, as some of the early anthropologists did. Yet at the end of the same ground-breaking lecture, he lost his footing in Kant and introduced the concept of a "mistake" of language to dismiss the interconnection between Gods and nature in India, and in doing so to dismiss contemporary "idolatry" in India as well. That was his own mistake of language. Whatever the relationship of Gods to "nature" in the Vedas might have been— and the question needs reconsideration (see Brian Smith 1989)—the Hindu icon is not an extension of any such nature mistaken for God. It is its own category of beingness.

South India clearly has a multiplicity of theo-logies and ontologies. Because Max Müller and others diverted attention toward their own version of Advaita Vedanta as the essential theology of India, a vast storehouse of texts and ritual practice in South India has gone unstudied and uncataloged even among academics in India. Those years of neglect are over, as the pioneering work of such scholars as H. Daniel Smith, Guy Welbon, and Fred Clothey in the United States, and S. S. Janaki, N. R. Bhatt, and K. K. A. Venkatachari in India,[1] allow an emerging new group of scholars, like Richard Davis in *Ritual in an Oscillating Universe: Worshipping Śiva in Medieval India* (1991), to expand definitions of the subtle relationships between matter, soul, spirit, and "nature" available in India. I suspect that as more of the Agamas and related texts become accessible, the theo-logic of the royal icon in Pudukkottai will have richer analogues in many of these theologies. Although as a hinterland such a state was not, and will not ever be, defined through any single system.

At this point in what will always remain a work-in-progress, the study of the royal body in Pudukkottai provides an alternative theo-logic to much that has passed for near axiom in the study of religion. Here I suspect that what is unreal is not the physical world but rather the very familiar European "naturalism," the belief that there is a stable entity called Nature with immutable laws that even God cannot disrupt. In Pudukkottai the material world is either "raw" or "cooked," to borrow from Lévi-Strauss—that is, matter is untransformed or transformed. Untransformed matter is "natural" but *not* valued as a sign of God's fixed laws. The physical is valued because it is capable of transformation. Neither ignored nor denied, certain kinds of matter are the substance needed to form the divine. In Pudukkottai the forest is the best source of "raw" matter from which to make the royal body precisely because it is raw—never touched by agriculture and therefore the base metal needed to create gold. Thus the forest is neither chaos nor cosmos, but serves the divine much as it serves humans as an inexhaustible source of the unhewn, the unpolished, and the undressed.

Thus in Pudukkottai the only *really real* is not real at all—it is artificial. No subject of the Tondaimans would be impressed by Hans Christian Andersen's bright little boy who could not "see" the king's magic clothes. Of course they knew the king was naked, for underneath his glittering clothes was an ascetic's form. But that form too was also "dress" for the ascetic's naked body, and is not his natural body anymore than the king's royal body is "natural." So the categories of material and spiritual do not work in an inverse relationship, but rather function in the same way that materials matter to the artist. Once re-created, feathers or rocks or gold become more than the sum of their parts. They are a new construction with an ontological status "beyond" matter but not beyond the sensual world.

As a theological postscript to this discussion of the spiritual and the material body, it is important to remember that the perception of the physical body as raw material for the spiritual, rather than as its prison house, does have antecedents in early Christianity. There is at least one major exception to the usual Western notions of the body and soul that scholars of the Victorian era never mentioned, perhaps because it remained as "absurd" to their scientific world as it did to the philosophy of the Greeks. That exception is the doctrine of resurrection. In the First Letter to the Corinthians, the apostle Paul explains resurrection in these terms:

---

1. Examples of this work can be found in two excellent volumes of collected articles published in India: *Saiva Temples and Temple Worship*, ed. S. S. Janaki, includes essays by Bhatt (1988, 24–45) and Janaki (1988, 122–81); *Agama and Silpa*, ed. K.K.A. Venkatachari, includes work of Bhatt (1984, 14–28), H. D. Smith (1984, 50–68), and Welbon (1984, 69–102). Clothey's work is best seen in *Rhythm and Intent: Ritual Studies from South India* (1983).

It is so with the resurrection of the dead. The body is sown in decay. It is sown in humiliation, it is raised in splendor. It is sown in weakness, it is raised in strength. It is a physical body that is sown, it is a spiritual body that is raised. If there is a physical body, there is a spiritual body also. . . . It is not the spiritual that comes first, but the physical and then the spiritual. (15:42–47)

The resurrected body of Christianity's kingdomless king, like the royal body and the ascetic body in Pudukkotai, had flesh as its raw matter, and then through a process of transformation—death, in the case of Christianity—took on a transfigured, splendid, but very visible form. I do not know how much more could or should be said about this analogy between the resurrected body and the iconic body, but the issue might well be traced in the Eastern church, which preserved the term "icon" for the modern world.

2.   A Variation on Sacred and Secular

Although sacred/profane has become the modern map of religious consciousness, this dichotomy assumes the same worn dualism, material/spiritual, that reentered the new "academic" study of religion a century ago. The daily world is, as Max Müller put it, "but a dream," or, as Eliade put it, "the never-ceasing relativity of purely subjective experiences, . . . an illusion" ([1957] 1963, 28). The irony is that Max Müller and later Mircea Eliade took most of their material, and later even their language, from India to further this discussion of the dichotomy of the commonplace and the sacred world.

But where is this dichotomy in places like Pudukkottai or, for that matter, even in Mrs. Bossom's living hall? Clothes, vases, pots are the decoration of daily life just as they are the ornaments that make a king. The line between fashion and holy ornament, between an ever so lovely hat and a crown, between a flower vase and a holy Kumbam, between a chandelier and an oil lamp, between a clock and a holy calendar, between an incense burner and a nosegay, is thin and meant to be so. That is why the religiosity of ornament can be so difficult to recognize but so easy to experience and to share.

In Pudukkottai no sharp line demarcates the sacred from the profane. Even the king's house is designed as a link between the ordinary and the extraordinary rather than as a haven/heaven in the middle of an otherwise tainted world. But this is not to say that everything is sacred here, but rather to suggest that dichotomy or demarcation is simply not the correct imagery to describe this sacredness. That which is sacred did not drop from another world, but rather was transformed from this world. It is an elaboration on the simple, a dressing of the undressed, a crafting of the unhewn.

The sacred in this sense is not a noun or even a verb, but an adjective, as Ananda Coomaraswamy argued in his now-famous essay on ornamentation. Adjectives elaborate but also specify, turning the common noun into the specific, the real. His point that "a person or thing apart from its appropriate ornaments . . . is valid as an idea, but not as a species" (1938, 252) places the accent on the right syllable in Pudukkottai. Ideas, abridgements, sketches, and generalizations are equated with the common, the mundane. The sacred here is not the essence apart from the material, or the core without the fruit, or the bone without the flesh. The daily becomes sacred as it fills out form, dots the "i," crosses the "t," and then turns mere letters into art.

3.   The Value of "Sin"

The rajas of Pudukkottai were glorious "sinners," but the nature of that sin is far removed from the notion Frazer first introduced of the king as scapegoat, the bearer of the sins of his people. "Sin" in Pudukkottai derives from a source other than contagious magic. This is the "sin" of second birth—the very deed that could have made Adam and Eve into heroic figures had the biblical editors chosen to tell their story without a monotheistic overlay. Adam and Eve give up simplicity for complexity, naiveté for enriched sensitivities, and nakedness for dress. They leave an enclosed, formed, static world to live in an incomplete world that they must "create." The Tondaimans' world was just such a patch of thorns, a "fort" in the midst of endlessly potential forest. The Brahman pandits, such as Sastri and the accountants of the empire, wanted to make them a garden land to fence in their willful desire for self-creation. But the Tondaimans, like the biblical progenitors of the human race, broke down the fences, broke through their natural place in the universe, not to become *like* God but to do what eluded Adam and Eve—to *be* God.

This is indeed the original sin that even a Frazer had to condemn in its modern form: the arrogance of humanity assuming that now, through science, it had won the power to remake the world. Fifty years later, Mircea Eliade would not have his *homo religiosus* transgress on this one grand commandment. In his description of archaic man's attempts to re-create the world through the repetition and reenactment of creation myths, Eliade stopped to make certain that "we must not suppose that *human* work is in question here, that it is through his own effort that man can consecrate a space. In reality the ritual by which he constructs a sacred space is efficacious in the measure in which *it reproduces the work of the gods* ([1957] 1963, 29). As long as the Gods provide the blueprint, the holy order, then humanity can reproduce. Any other mode of creation is what? Idolatry? Vanity? Sin? If this is the case, then the *homo religiosus* in Pudukkottai were the master sinners. And joining them in this "sin" were the British civil servants as they sat down with the rajas in durbar, the empire builders as they made an empress out of a queen, and a legion of Victorian housewives as they fashioned a world for themselves out of the plethora of the empire and the work of their own hands.

The "idolatry" of the Raj and the "idolatry" of Pudukkottai were not false charges from those who would equate the Sacred with a predefined order that forbade any tinkering with Its perfection. Why should the academic study of religion convolute the theo-logic of any iconic culture in order to defend it as serious and worth consideration? The rajas built their own divine bodies. The British politicals were likewise self-made men. Each sought legitimation in a world that had no language for their type of sacredness and indeed would not even have given it the name. Yet when the religion of India, or of archaic peoples or any such "others," was ardently defended, the "sins" were washed away and the whole of Hinduism came out looking like a white sheet of otherworldliness. Pudukkottai rajas challenged basic religious *and* academic values in the same way that they infuriated the political agents and exasperated the Brahman Dewan Sastri. They *were* Kallars, they never denied their cattle-raising and cattle-lifting past. They were extravagant. They were self-willed. They were disorderly, spendthrifts, and ardent materialists. And that is precisely why they were divine!

4.   History as a Theo-logical Category

There are historians who see history as the place where pragmatism rules over idealism, where the struggle for power, money, and status frequently makes a mockery of supposed higher values. History is said to prove that everyone is after Number One, and such statements are supposed to shock the sensitivities of those in the humanities who would argue for right over might, and justice over self-aggrandizement. But such logic works only as long as history is the domain of the expedient, the makeshift and made-do, while the realm of religion is the ideal, the should-be and must-be. But this dichotomy, like many others, does not do justice to the complexity of Pudukkottai. If divinity must have a body, and bodies are built out of the world and for the world, then *certain* processes of history—the wars, the conflicts—are indistinguishable from ritual. This was the point Heesterman so boldly suggested. Events are processes of transformation that for "pre-axial" cultures, are experienced as ritual. The Tondaimans' rise to power is both a ritual and a historical process. Their actions within history garner the emblems they need to build their royal bodies. Taken to perhaps legitimate extremes, the argument over axial and pre-axial civilization could be extended to claim that ritual merely replaces "the real act" when consciousness and rationalization demand *play* where there was once *deed*. The parades that accompany all important rituals in the Pudukkottai state bear a striking resemblance to the vivid scenes still part of our film heritage of the triumphal marches of the legions back to Rome. In each case the captured emblems of the enemy were displayed often with the now-naked vanquished enemy in tow.

Beyond these suggestions of history as transformative deed is a theo-logical issue. The "Western" God acts in history, as biblical theologians so often stress, and thereby sanctifies actions that otherwise would have remained profane. Discussion of the basic differences between East and West often cited these acts of God in history as fundamental to the West's affirmation of the world. A recent textbook still teaches students:

> Eastern religion is basically world denying. . . . In contrast, the religions of the West understand God to be active in nature and in history. Nature and history have not been abandoned by the Ultimate; nor *are* they ultimate in some mystical way. Rather, they are the arena in which God acts. He is separate from them, but works with them.

So instead of denying and withdrawing from them, one looks for God within them. (J. F. Wilson 1982, 66–67).

Again what is missing here is the excluded middle. The "West" has a God separate from but active in history. The "East" is forced to deny history not because it radically separates God from history but precisely because it makes no distinction between God and the world and thus so ties divinity to the world that God has no space in which to act. The East ends up in a mystical muddle, denying the very world that its theology would seem to affirm. While the West, giving no sanctity to the earth or to history, affirms the world because its transcendent God deigns to act there. Never is it allowed in this closed logic that in India history is holy because the Gods' very bodies are created within and by its processes. The Prajapati myths present this connection between rebuilding the world and rebuilding the God's body on a grand scale. The processes that involve Prajapati might be described as "natural," but the processes that made the Tondaimans were thoroughly historical even by biblical standards— acts of war, of conflict, and of peace.

When the Pax Britannia stilled the ritual process of war in India, the political processes of fighting for rights, of court "intrigues," of legal battles (see also Price 1991, 110–12), even of begging and clever borrowing, and buying, secured the rajas of the hinterlands a steady supply of new ornaments to sustain their royal bodies. A gilded songbird "won" by cajoling the political agent might have been a trophy in its own right. Certainly Raja Ramachandra annexed clocks and chandeliers into his own domain as signs of his incorporation of a world that thought itself his superior. Even the daily banter of this time of "peace," the constant exchange of memos and minutes swinging back and forth from bureaucrat to king, marked time in the raja's steady aggrandizement of power. The records of this "history" are as much part of a new ritual process as the Tondaimans' deeds in war. The ties that bind the Tondaimans to history are the ties that bind human to divine. There is neither a God above history nor a God below it, but slow process whereby history itself becomes the agency for the embodiment of God.

Raja Ramachandra Tondaiman in durbar, then, displays a complex theology for those with eyes to see. The photographs and the painting of this durbar became the writing that stilled this ever-flowing event for those of us accustomed to immobile data, to muse over the scene. Iconic culture has no "writing" other than the very world that it creates. This scene is its own event and its own inscription of the event. This ultimately is a system without abstraction, without an outside plan. It sits squarely in time, for it is made by time constantly adding new players and new emblems and even new Gods. It was a glorious play that even the British were invited to join as long as they brought more things to fill up a space that was never satiated and never complete. It is this holy consumerism that ultimately linked the raja to the Honorable East India Trading Company and to a European world that learned to revel in the very same process of venturing out amid danger—be it the dense forest, the high seas, or High Street—taking/winning/buying *things* to decorate a world of one's own fabrication. Victorian domestic architecture remains unrivaled in its sheer fancy, its abundant space meant to capture the bounty of a trading world within the bosom of the home. The materialism of Pudukkottai matched the growing consumerism of middle-class Britain, and we are left to speculate how the two meet and marry in the heyday of the Empire.

The term "material" has as its simplest meaning "cloth" or "fabric." Even the pejorative use of the term "materialism" refers to the growing worldwide shopping spree of late nineteenth-century Europe, which began in the fifteenth and sixteenth centuries when oriental textiles and other ornamental wares sparked an appetite for fashion. If Chandra Mukerji is correct in her history of the patterns of modern materialism, the British built their own great industrial enterprises not to establish secure and sober heavy industry, as Weber claims, but to produce cheaper versions of the coveted textiles, teapots, and numerous other trinkets that even the lower middle-class British began to demand for their homes (Mukerji 1983, 1–29). Mukerji doubts that there ever was a period of "this-worldly asceticism" in Europe. From the start of its trading and manufacturing, the Occident shared with the Orient a mad love of *things*. Consumerism fueled the industrial revolution as surely as it sent European ships to the far corners of the world in search of sugar, spice, and everything nice.

Scholars like Max Müller rose up in his day to denounce such materialism and thus began the long crusade by the academic humanities to educate modern people back into more-stable values through a reconstructed and revived Jesus, Socrates, or Buddha who were portrayed as the earliest fighters against materialism. Thus began the myths of Israel as the first nation to denounce Mammon in the West while India lighted the path to asceticism in the East. His Excellency Raja Ramachandra with his ever wily face would have smiled at all this. The life of the mind is not a home. Human beings, as even the Bible makes clear, must live in the space they have created, wear clothes they make, and tend this barren earth until it bears fruit. Ornaments mattered to the raja, to Mrs. Bossom, to the British governors, and even to Max Müller so elegantly dressed in his cummerbund, because ornaments confer actuality, vitality, and life.

Bibliography

Finding the Historical Records

Because the status of the princely states of India in the empire was complex, records remain scattered over two continents. Their present placement has a logic that satisfied what were once delicate political issues, but innocent researchers in the history of religions who expect simply to look up sources on sacral kingship or other religious issues will suddenly discover that they are forced to reconstruct that complex political logic before even the most ubiquitous manuscripts can be induced to come out of hiding. Some explanation might be useful to them and to others in the field of religious studies who want to supplement their study of texts or who seek new resources for the study of religion that now wait, literally tied up in fading red tape, for an appreciative eye.

Before 1948, when the Native States were incorporated into the Indian union, they held an odd status in India—somewhere between British possessions and independent foreign states surrounded by British India. For the purpose of government organization, they were classified during the rule of the East India Trading Company as quasi-independent states to which the British sent a "Resident," who was much more than an ambassador but much less than an outright administrator. In this early period, issues relating to the princely states were *usually* settled by the ruling authority of the nearest British provincial capital—either Bombay, Madras, or Calcutta. However, princes in the early days of Company rule often felt justified in appealing directly to the British monarch or in seeking redress from Parliament. Likewise, the Board of Control appointed by Parliament to oversee the activities of the East India Company maintained a keen interest in these states because the issue of their status vis-à-vis the British Crown was never clearly settled. Were they simply bound in treaty to the East India Company, or did they, as independent states, maintain some direct connection to the Crown? Issues on religious topics in India did find their way into Parliamentary debates and direct correspondence between the Indian princes and the ruling British monarch. Most records before 1858, when the East India Company's rule ended, are now in records offices in both London and India. All the correspondence for the Board of Control remains in the Oriental and India Office Collections at the British Library. However, early records sent to and from the provincial capitals are divided between Indian state archives and the National Archives in New Delhi. In the case of Pudukkottai, therefore, early records are in the Tamilnadu State Archives (Madras), the National Archives, and the Oriental and India Office Collections at the British Library.

All this is complicated by the changes in the governmental system after the British assumed direct control of India following the Indian Mutiny in 1858. Each of the old "Residencies" for the Native States was put under the control of a "political agent" who was usually the chief administrative officer—the "Collector"—of the nearest district in British India. The political agents were under the direction of a branch of the Government of India, the Political Department. The old records of the previous Residents of the Native States were then transferred to the district office to become part of the District Records, while directives sent from the capital in Calcutta (later Delhi or Simla, the summer capital) are now housed either in London (before 1920) or in the National Archives in New Delhi (after 1920). In the case of Pudukkottai, the definition of which was the nearest district changed, and the little state was transferred back and forth between Madurai, Tanjore, and Trichinopoly districts. Fortunately many early district records pertaining to the Native States have been transferred to the Tamilnadu State Archives as the Merged States Records.

In addition to these British-generated records, some princely states maintained official record offices, which contain both early and late material. Often the raja kept a private library or a separate record file within the palace, as was the case in Pudukkottai. In Pudukkottai, there are three such sources: the Darbar Files, the official records of the administrative offices; the Palace Records, which kept correspondence that went directly to the raja and his own palace staff; and the Huzur Records, which have the very early letters, now housed in the Government Museum at Pudukkottai. The Darbar Files and the Huzur Records are in good condition, but the Palace Records suffered because they were no longer deemed government property and therefore were not protected (see Plate 93). To summarize the case for Pudukkottai, *official* records for the state before 1858 are found in the Oriental and India Office Collections at The British Library in London, the Tamilnadu State Archives in Madras (Merged States Records and Tanjore District Records), the Palace Records, and the Darbar Files in Pudukkottai.

In addition to official records, there are collections of private papers and private collections of folk stories. Indians and British—who worked and visited this part of India as missionaries, civil servants, or educated travelers—left diaries and letters now found in British libraries but also in private homes

Plate 93. Working with the Palace Records was as much a matter of archeology as textual reading. With the kind permission of Rani Rema Devi, I sift through the documents rescued at the last moment before the present tenants moved into the Old Palace.

in South India. An important source of information is the folklore collections, both official and private. In South India the bardic tradition remained strong. Musician-poets sung many events and personalities into local memory. The early East India Company recognized the importance of such folk stories and sent Colonel Colin Mackenzie to their newly acquired territories to "survey" the people. His collection of the tales told to his many workers by various caste communities became the famous Mackenzie Collection, which is now divided between the Oriental and India Office Collections at the British Library and the excellent Oriental Manuscripts Library of the University of Madras. Collecting ancient manuscripts and folklore was not confined to the British. During the late nineteenth century U. V. Swaminatha Iyer amassed a marvelous massive collection that is now housed in the U. V. Swaminatha Iyer Library on the coast of Tamilnadu just outside of Madras. A similar fine collection of folk and classical music is in the Tamil Isai Sangam in Madras and in many private homes of enthusiastic collectors. Two other fine libraries in Madras are sources for manuscripts and early printed works, especially in Tamil and Tamil Grantha (Sanskrit written in Tamil script): the Maraimalai Adigal Library in Madras City, and the Adyar Library on the grounds of the Theosophical Society in suburban Madras. A full bibliography of all works cited follows, organized as archives, indigenous-language documents, and printed works.

This bibliography follows the usual practice in South India not to consider titles of caste affiliation to be a surname. Such titles include Aiyar, Ayyar, Aiyangar, Sastri, Row, Poolaver, and Pillay. Thus, for example, S. Radhakrishna Aiyar is listed as "Radhakrishna Aiyar, S."

Archival Documents

Aiyaswamy Folk Song Collection. Collection of Tamil folk songs in the private library of the late R. Aiyaswamy of Madras. Before his death, Mr. Aiyaswamy kindly helped me find poems on Pudukkottai in his important collection.

Archives of the Council of World Mission. Housed in the library of the School for Oriental and African Studies, University of London.

"Biruthus of the Tondaimans of Pudukkottai." Palace Records. Handwritten document with no date, but found among the Palace Records. Judging from the handwriting and paper quality, the document is probably from the 1920s.

Board of Control's Collection. Oriental and India Office Collections, The British Library, London. (The Board of Control was the regulating body that supervised the governmental functions of the East India Company.)

 F/4/245, No. 5541. "Arrangement for the efficient management of the Zemindarry of Tondiman on the death of the late Manager." 1807–1808.

 F/4/277, No. 6188. "Report from Major Blackburne on the subject of the administration of the affairs of the Minor Tondiman's Zemindarry." 1808–1809.

"By Sri Brihadambal's Grace." A description of the royal festivals in Pudukkottai by palace Head Harikar K. Subramanian, handwritten in Tamil, dated February 21, 1979, and June 30, 1979.

Collected Letters of A. Sashia Sastri, numbered and bound in separate volumes. Kindly lent to me by Tiru A. R. Seshia Sastri of Kumbakonam, the famous dewan's grandson.

————. "Resume of My Sixteen Years of Administration of the Pudukkottai State." Privately printed by A. Sashia Sastri and bound with the Collected Letters.

Darbar Files. Darbar Office, Pudukkottai. "Darbar" is the term used in the nineteenth and twentieth centuries for the bureaucratic government that functioned under the control of the dewan. These files are still in use and are housed in the Office of the Sub-Collector of Pudukkottai in the Public Office Building. The records contain files marked DD/(number)/(year), indicating "Darbar Disposal," which filed daily correspondence and orders, and others marked R/(number)/(year), indicating records usually on a specific topic. A few files date from 1836, but complete files begin in the 1860s. In addition are Administration Reports for each year from 1867 onward.

Diary of George Patterson, 1772–1773. 9 vols. European Manuscripts E379. Oriental and India Office Collections, The British Library, London. George Patterson worked for the nawab of the Arcot, who ostensibly ruled much of South India at the time the East India Company was consolidating power. The nawab sent him on a diplomatic mission throughout the newly pacified districts in the south, and Patterson recorded all his experiences in rich detail.

"Harikar's Diary, 1934–1936." A handwritten 92-page document in Tamil, found in the Palace Records, in which the head of protocol for the court recorded daily decisions and plans for all ceremonies.

Home Miscellaneous Series. Oriental and India Office Collections, The British Library, London. Contains early records of the East India Company, particularly on the wars with the independent chieftains (the Poligars) of South India from the 1750s to 1800.

Huzur Records. Government Museum, Pudukkottai. Correspondence of the Tondaiman family in the late eighteenth and nineteenth centuries. Copied and collected into six bound volumes. The subjects, quality of paper, and style of writing would place the date of compilation between 1830 and 1850.

"Huzzoor or Palace Establishment, etc." Handwritten document dating from the 1880s listing titles of palace officers and servants in both English and Tamil. Now in the keeping of the family of Sri K. Sathiamurti Rao,

Pudukkottai, who kindly permitted me to make a photographic facsimile.

Inam Settlement Faisal Registry of 1888. Sub-branch Settlement Office, Pudukkottai. These records in bound volumes detail the history, the required services, and the present status of each claim for land under *inam* (gift from the raja). In 1979 these records were moved to the Settlement Office in Tanjore.

"The Legend of Bakaulavaneswari (Brihadambal)." Manuscript, dated September 13, 1980, 2 pages. Collected from the Agama Sastriar, former chief priest of the Pudukkottai State, and kindly translated by Rani Rema Devi.

Lewin Bentham Bowring Albums. Department of Prints and Drawings, Oriental and India Office Collections, The British Library, London. Compiled 1870–1910. Includes "Handlist of the Lewin Bentham Bowring Albums."

"Like Heaven Above." Selections from the diaries of U. V. Swaminatha Iyer, translated by Professor A. Rama Aiyar of the Dr. U. V. Swaminatha Iyer Library. Tiruvanmiyur, Madras. The typed manuscript was kindly made available to me by Mr. M. K. Raman, former Honorary Curator.

Mackenzie Collection. European Manuscripts. Oriental and India Office Collections, The British Library, London.

General Section. "The Hindoo Collection—Memoirs and Pieces of the Ancient History of the South, the Chola, Chera, and Panyan Mundalums, Collected and translated for Major Mackenzie or communicated by his friends and correspondents" (1810).

Records of Baramahal and Salem Districts. "Inhabitants—Tribe the Fifth," vol. 23.

Napier Papers. European Manuscripts, The British Library, London.

ADD 30386, "The History of Rewa with an account of the Raja and his Court," by James O'Brien, 1848.

Office of the Director of Survey and Settlement. Board of Revenue, Madras. These records contain proceedings on continued disputes over land ownership, particularly those arising from old royal grants.

Orme Collection. European Manuscripts, Oriental and India Office Collections, The British Library, London. Early "Country Correspondence." Collected by Robert Orme. These are mostly letters from the 1750s, when the East India Company began to act as a serious player in the political struggles of the period.

Palace Records. The Residency, Pudukkottai. These were once housed in the Sirkele's Office in the Old Palace. When the palace was leased for commercial use, the records were saved at the last minute, collected, and kept in the Residency. Much was lost, and the rest was disarranged.

Papers of Friedrich Max Müller, 1823–1900, and his wife, Georgiana Adelaide Müller. Modern Manuscripts Collection, Duke Humphrey's Library, Oxford University.

Parliamentary Paper no. 664 of session 1845. Ordered printed by the House of Commons, August 1, 1849. "Communications in Relationship to the Connection of the Government of British India with Idolatry or with Mahometanism."

"Photographic Views of Poodoocottah." Oriental and India Office Collections, The British Library, London. A portfolio of photographs by Linnaeus Tripe produced by the order of the Madras Presidency, East India Company, 1858.

Pudukkottai Merged State Records. Tamilnadu State Archives, Madras. Contains records of the correspondence of the British Resident with the rajas from 1845 to 1857.

Records of the Crown Representative (R-1). Oriental and India Office Collections, The British Library, London. Files generated to and from the central British authority in India and the British Residents to the Native States.

Residency Records (R-2). Oriental and India Office Collections, The British Library, London. Files and daily records of the British Residents at the courts of the Native States.

"Rules for the Settlement of Inams." Darbar Office, Pudukkottai. A guide for settlement officers, published as a State Gazette Extraordinary in 1888. The guide outlines exact information needed to settle the taxes and ownership of each former land grant from the Tondaimans.

Standing Orders of the Pudukkottai Darbar. Darbar Office, Pudukkottai. A compilation of rulings and orders on the complex administration of the state and the temples, printed at the Brihadambal State Press in 1937.

"Statistical Account of Pudukkottai (1813)." A palm-leaf manuscript in Tamil housed in the Government Museum, Pudukkottai. The document was likely generated at the bidding of William Blackburne. Pandits in the museum transcribed the document under the direction of Mr. K. Lakshminarayanan, who has undertaken a translation. The document is indeed statistical and would be of use to economic historians. I have the 500-page typed Tamil manuscript in my library.

Tamil Journal Collection. U. V. Swaminatha Iyer Library, Tiruvanmiyur, Madras. Selection on Pudukkottai from the rare printed Tamil books and journals, compiled and copied for me by pandits at the library in January 1979. 125 pages. Contains Tamil poems on Sadasiva Brahman and the deities of the Tirugokarnam temple. Also included are descriptions of the Dassara.

Tanjore District Records. Tamilnadu State Archives, Madras. The major records here are the Residency files from Pudukkottai from 1830 to 1844, which ended up here after 1947, rather than in London or New Delhi.

Wellesley Papers. European Manuscripts, The British Library, London. Collection of

papers from the family of Arthur Wellesley, 1769–1852, better known as the
Duke of Wellington, whose career began in India.

    ADD 13589. "Correspondence of
H. T. Colebrooke, October 13,
1838."

    ADD 13657. "Papers on the Poly-
gars." 1799–1802.

William Blackburne—A Collection of Letters
from Tanjore to the Raja of Poodoocottah. European Manuscript D 812, Oriental and India Office Collections, The
British Library, London.

Works in Tamil, Telugu, and Tamil Grantha

Catācivam Pirāmēntirār Carittiram (The Story
of Sadasiva Brahmendra). Pudukkottai:
Neroor Sadasiva Bramendra Sabha,
1950.

Cāti Nūr Kaviyurai (An Extended Poetic Trea-
tise on Caste). Tamil Manuscript D 643,
Government Oriental Manuscripts Library, University of Madras.

Iyalicaippāmālai (Plain Songs for Ordinary
People). Songs in praise of H.H.
Martanda Bhairava Tondaiman, by R.
Ulakanadu Pillai. Pudukkottai: Puduk-
kottai Kamala Press, 1937.

Kaṭṭapommaṉ Ūmaiyaṉ Varalāru (The History of Kattabomman Umaiyan). Tamil
Manuscript R 5649, Government Oriental Manuscripts Library, University of
Madras.

Kaṭṭapommaṉ Varalāru. Edited by T. Chadra-
sekharan. Madras Government Oriental
Manuscript Series No. 67. Madras: Government of Madras, 1960.

Pārvati Parinayamu (Poem on the Goddess Parvati), by Raya Raghunatha Tondaiman,
1769–1789. Telugu Manuscript 151,
Government Oriental Manuscripts Library, University of Madras.

Śāntiratnākara. Sanskrit in Tamil Grantha

Lipi. Edited in the Santra Sanjeevam
Press, Madras, 1913.

Sikāgirida Caritam, by Gotra Swamidikshitar
and Siva Rama Dikshitar. Tamil Grantha on palm leaf. Manuscript in the
keeping of Sri K. A. Panchapagesa Dikshitar, Pudukkottai.

Śri Birakatampāḷ Pēril Canta Kummi (Rhyth-
mic Dance Song on the Person of Sri
Brihadambal). Composed in the time of
Raja Ramachandra Tondaiman by the
poet Chidambara Bharati. Printed in
pamphlet form by "Tamil Kadal" in
Tiruvidaimarutur, Pudukkottai District,
1959. (Translated by K. Lakshminarayanan, Manuscript, 1979)

Tirukkōkaranam Kōyil Varalāru (History of
the Tirugokarnam Temple). 34 pages.
Tirugokarnam: The Temple Devasta-
nam, 1979.

Toṇḍamān Paḷegaru Biradāvuli (The Genealogy of the Tondaiman Polegar). Telugu
Manuscript D 2621, Government Oriental Manuscripts Library, University of
Madras.

Toṇḍamān Paḷegaru Kaifiyatu (The Tale of the
Tondaiman Polegar). Telugu Manuscript
D 2620, Government Oriental Manu-
scripts Library, University of Madras.

Toṇḍamān Vamsāvaḷi (The Family History of
the Tondaimans), by Court Poet
Nudurupati Venkanna. Telugu Manuscript D 295, Government Oriental
Manuscripts Library, University of Madras.

Toṇṭaimāṉ Cakkiravātti Carittiram (The Story
of the Emperor Atondai). Tamil Manuscript D 3097, Government Oriental
Manuscripts Library, University of Madras.

Toṇṭaimaṇḍala Varalāru (The History of the
Tondai Country). Tamil Manuscript D
3102, Government Oriental Manuscripts Library, University of Madras.

Vaḷḷi Pāratam [*Vaḷḷi Bharatam*] (The Dance
Drama About Valli). A manuscript
housed in the library of the Tamil Isai
Sangam, Madras.

Virālimalai Kuṟuvañci (The Drama Told
About the Viralimalai Temple). Tamil

Manuscript R 5340, Government Oriental Manuscripts Library, University of Madras.

Virālimalai Vēlavar Kātal (The Story of the Viralimalai Temple). Tamil Manuscript R 5340, Government Oriental Manuscripts Library, University of Madras.

Vīrapāṇḍiya Kaṭṭapomman (About Virapandyan Kattabomman). Madras: Pirema Piracuram, 1958.

Books and Articles

Ackerly, J. R. [1932] 1983. *Hindoo Holiday: An Indian Journal.* 2d ed. Middlesex: Penguin Books.

Ackerman, Robert. 1987. *J. G. Frazer: His Life and Work.* Cambridge: Cambridge University Press.

————. 1991. *The Myth and Ritual School: J. G. Frazer and the Cambridge Ritualists.* New York: Garland Publishing.

Adams, Henry Brooks. [1907] 1961. *The Education of Henry Adams.* Reprint. Boston: Houghton Mifflin Co.

Aichison, Charles U. 1909. *A Collection of Treaties, Engagements, and Sanads Relating to India and Neighboring Countries.* 14 vols. Rev. ed. Calcutta: Government Press.

Aiyaswami, R. 1979. "Folk Literature in Tamil." Manuscript. Kindly given to me by the author.

Alexander, Michael, and Sushila Anand. 1980. *Queen Victoria's Maharajah, Duleep Singh, 1838–1893.* London: Weidenfeld & Nicolson.

Allen, Charles, and Sharada Dwivedi. 1985. *Lives of the Indian Princes.* New York: Crown.

Andersen, Hans Christian. [1889] 1983. *The Complete Illustrated Stories of Hans Christian Andersen.* Translated by H. W. Dulcken. London: Chancellor Press.

Appadurai, Arjun. 1981. *Worship and Conflict Under Colonial Rule: A South Indian Case.* Cambridge: Cambridge University Press.

————. 1990. "Disjuncture and Difference in Global Cultural Economy." *Public Culture* 2 (Spring): 1–24.

Appadurai, Arjun, and Carol Breckenridge. 1976. "The South Indian Temple: Authority, Honour, and Redistribution." *Contributions to Indian Sociology,* n.s., 10(2): 187–211.

Archer, Mildred, and Ronald Lightbrown. 1982. *India Observed: India as Viewed by British Artists, 1760–1860.* London: Victoria and Albert Museum. The catalog for an exhibition organized by the Library of the Victoria and Albert Museum as part of the Festival of India, April 26–July 5, 1982.

Arunachalam, M. 1976. *Ballad Poetry: Peeps into Tamil Literature.* Tanjavur: Gandhi Vidyalayam.

Babb, Lawrence. 1975. *The Divine Hierarchy.* New York: Columbia University Press.

Bagehot, Walter. 1867. *The English Constitution.* London.

Barnett, L. D. 1931. *A Supplementary Catalogue of the Tamil Books in the Library of the British Museum.* London: Trustees of the British Museum.

Barnett, L. D., and G. U. Pope. 1909. *A Catalogue of Tamil Books in the Library of the British Museum.* London: Trustees of the Museum.

Barton, Sir William. 1934. *The Princes of India with a Chapter on Nepal.* London: Nibet & Co.

Bayly, C. A., ed. 1990. *The Raj: India and the British, 1600–1947.* Published for the exhibit at the National Portrait Gallery, London, from October 1990 to March 1991. London: National Portrait Gallery Publications.

Bhatt, N. R. 1984. "Saiva Agama." In *Agama and Silpi,* edited by K.K.A. Venkatachari. Proceedings of the Seminar Held in December 1981. Bombay: Anathacharya Indological Research Institute.

————. 1988. "Development of Temple Rituals." In *Siva Temple and Temple Rituals,* edited by S. S. Janaki. Madras: Kupuswami Sastri Research Institute.

Essai sur la fonction sociale de louange et de blâme sur les éléments indo-européen du cens romain. Paris: Gallimard.

——. 1970. *The Destiny of the Warrior.* Translated by Alf Hiltebeitel. Chicago: University of Chicago Press.

——. 1973. *The Destiny of a King.* Translated by Alf Hiltebeitel. Chicago: University of Chicago Press.

Dumont, Lois. [1966] 1970. *Homo Hierarchicus.* Chicago: University of Chicago Press.

——. 1985. *A South Indian Subcaste.* Edited and translated by Michael Moffatt. New York: Oxford University Press.

Dumont, Louis, and David F. Pocock. 1958. "A. M. Hocart on Caste: Religion and Power." *Contributions to Indian Sociology* 2:45–54.

Dutt, Manmatha Nath. 1896. *A Prose English Translation of the Mārkaṇḍeya Purāṇa.* Calcutta: Elysium Press.

Duyker, Edward, and Coralie Younger. 1991. *Molly and the Rajah: Race, Romance, and the Raj.* Sylvania, Australia: Australian Mauritian Press.

Eck, Diana L. 1981. "India's *Tīrthas:* 'Crossing' in Sacred Geography." *History of Religions* 20:323–44.

Eggeling, Julius, trans. [1882–1900] 1972. *The Śatapatha-Brāhmaṇa According to the Text of the Mādhyadina School.* 5 parts. Vols. 12, 26, 41, 43, 44 respectively of The Sacred Books of the East. Reprint. Delhi: Motilal Banarsidass. (References are to part numbers not volumes.)

Eliade, Mircea. [1957] 1963. *The Sacred and the Profane: The Nature of Religion.* Reprint. New York: Harper & Row, Harper Torchbooks.

Falk, Nancy E. 1973. "Wilderness and Kingship in Ancient South Asia." *History of Religions* 13:1–15.

Fisher, Michael H. 1985. "The Imperial Coronation of 1819: Awadh, the British, and the Moghuls." *Modern Asian Studies* 19(2):239–77.

Forster, E. M. [1953] 1977. *The Hill of Devi.* Reprint. New Delhi: Arnold-Heinemann.

Foster, John. 1821. *An Essay on the Evils of Popular Ignorance.* 2d American edition. New York: William B. Gilley.

Fox, Richard. 1971. *Kin, Clan, Raja, and Rule.* Berkeley and Los Angeles: University of California Press.

Frazer, Andrew H. L. 1911. *Among Rajas and Ryots.* London: Seelet & Co.

Frazer, James G. [1890] 1981. *The Golden Bough: The Roots of Religion and Folklore.* New York: Avenel Books: (First published in London by Macmillan in two volumes as *The Golden Bough: A Study on Comparative Religion.*)

Freud, Sigmund. [1913] 1946. *Totem and Taboo: Resemblances Between the Psychic Lives of Savages and Neurotics.* Reprint of edition translated by A. A. Brill in 1918. New York: Random House, Vintage Books.

Fritz, John M., George Michell, and M. S. Nagarajan Rao. 1984. *The Royal Center at Vijayanagar: Preliminary Report.* Melbourne: University of Melbourne, Department of Architecture and Building.

Fuller, C. J. 1984. *Servants of the Goddess: The Priests of a South Indian Temple.* Cambridge: Cambridge University Press.

Gajendragadkar, P. B. 1962. "The Historical Background and Theoretical Basis of Hindu Law." In the *Cultural Heritage of India,* vol. 4. 2d ed. Calcutta: Ramakrishna Mission.

Galey, Jean Claude. 1980. "La créancier, le roi, la mort: Essai sur les relations de dépendance au Tehri-Garhwal (Himalya indien)." *Puruṣārtha* 4:93–163.

Gaster, Theodor H., ed. [1959] 1964. *The New Golden Bough: A New Abridgment of the Classical Work by Sir James Frazer.* New York: New American Library, Mentor Books.

Geertz, Clifford. 1980. *Negara: The Theatre State in Nineteenth-Century Bali.* Princeton: Princeton University Press.

Genct, Jean. [1958] 1966. *The Balcony.* 2d ed. rev. Translated by Bernard Frechtman. New York. Grove Press.

Goldman, Robert P. 1971. *Gods, Priests, and Warriors: The Bhṛgus of the Mahabharata.* New York: Columbia University Press.

Gombrich, Richard. 1978. *On Being Sanskritic: A Plea for Civilized Study and the Study of Civilization.* Oxford: Clarendon Press.

Gonda, Jan. 1939. "The Meaning of the Word *alaṃkāra.*" *New Indian Antiquary* (Bombay), 97–110.

———. 1969. *Ancient Indian Kingship from a Religious Point of View.* Leiden: E. J. Brill.

Gurney, J. D. 1968. "The Debts of the Nawab of Arcot, 1763–1776." Ph.D. dissertation, Oxford University.

Hanchett, Susanne. 1978. "Recent Trends in the Study of Folk Hinduism and India's Folklore." *Journal of Indian Folkloristics* (Mysore) 1:40–54.

Handa, R. L. 1968. *History of Freedom Struggle in Princely States.* New Delhi: Central News Agency.

Hart, George L., III. 1975. *The Poems of Ancient Tamil.* Berkeley and Los Angeles: University of California Press.

———. 1979. "The Nature of Tamil Devotion," in *Aryan and Non-Aryan in India,* edited by Madhav M. Deshpande and Peter Edwin Hook. Michigan Papers on South and Southeast Asia No. 14. Ann Arbor: Center for South and Southeast Asian Studies, University of Michigan.

Haworth-Booth, Mark, ed. 1984. *The Golden Age of British Photography, 1839–1900.* Catalog of an exhibition organized by the Victoria and Albert Museum and the Alfred Stieglitz Center, Philadelphia Museum of Art. New York: Aperture Books.

Heesterman, J. C. 1957. *The Ancient Indian Royal Consecration: The Rājasūya Described According to the Yajus Texts and Annotated.* The Hague: Mouton & Co.

———. 1985. *The Inner Conflict of Tradition: Essays in Indian Ritual, Kingship, and Society.* Chicago: University of Chicago Press.

Hiltebeitel, Alf. 1982. "Sexuality and Sacrifice: Convergent Subcurrents in the Fire-Walking of Draupadi." In *Images of Man: Religion and Historical Process in South Asia,* edited by Fred Clothey. Madras: New Era.

———. 1983. "Toward a Coherent Study of Hinduism," *Religious Studies Review* 9 (July).

———, ed. 1989. *Criminal Gods and Demon Devotees.* Albany: State University of New York Press.

Hobsbawm, Eric, and Terrence Ranger, eds. 1983. *The Invention of Tradition.* Cambridge: Cambridge University Press.

Hocart, A. M. [1936] 1970. *Kings and Councillors: An Essay in the Comparative Anatomy of Human Society.* 2d ed. Edited with an introduction by Rodney Needham. Chicago: University of Chicago Press.

———. 1968. *Caste: A Comparative Study.* New York: Russell & Russell.

Holiday, Henry. 1914. *Reminiscences of My Life.* London: William Heinemann.

Houghton, Walter E. 1957. *The Victorian Frame of Mind, 1830–1870.* New Haven: Yale University Press.

Huntington, Susan L., and John C. Huntington. 1990. *Leaves from the Bodhi Tree: The Art of Pala India (8th–12th Centuries) and Its International Legacy.* Dayton, Ohio: Dayton Art Institute.

Hutchins, Francis G. 1967. *The Illusion of Permanence: British Imperialism in India.* Princeton: Princeton University Press.

Huyler, Stephen P. 1988. "Gifts of Earth: Votive Terracottas of India." *Asian Art* 1 (Summer): 7–37.

Inden, Ronald B. 1977. "Toward an Ethno Sociology of South Asian Caste." In *The New Wind: Changing Identities in South Asia,* edited by Kenneth David. The Hague: Mouton.

———. 1978. "Ritual, Authority, and Cyclic Time in Hindu Kingship." In *Kingship and Authority in South Asia,* edited by John F. Richards. Madison: University of Wisconsin Publication Series.

———. 1986. "Orientalist Reconstruction of India." *Modern Asian Studies* 20:401–46.

————. 1990. *Imagining India*. London: Basil Blackwell.

Inden, Ronald, and McKim Marriott. 1974. "Caste System." *Encyclopedia Britannica*, vol. 15.

Inglis, Stephen. 1985. "Possession and Pottery: Serving the Divine in a South Indian Community." In *Gods of Flesh / Gods of Stone: The Embodiment of Divinity in India*, edited by Joanne Punzo Waghorne and Norman Cutler. Chambersburg, Pa.: Anima Press.

Irving, Robert Grant. 1981. *Indian Summer: Lutyens, Baker, and Imperial Delhi*. New Haven: Yale University Press.

Jackson, William. 1988. "Beyond Within: This World and Transcendence in the Lives of the Early Tamil Saiva Saints." Paper presented at the Conference of Religion in South India on "Exemplary Lives: Hagiography and 'Sainthood' in South Indian Religions" at the National Humanities Center, Research Triangle Park, North Carolina, June 9–12.

Jagadisa Ayyar, P. V. [1920] 1982. *South Indian Shrines*. New Delhi: Asian Educational Services.

————. 1921. *South Indian Festivities*. Madras: Higginbotham.

Janaki, S. S. 1988. "Dhvaja-stambha In *Siva Temple and Temple Rituals*, edited by S. S. Janaki. Madras: Kupuswami Sastri Research Institute.

Kailasapathy, K. 1968. *Tamil Heroic Poetry*. Oxford: Clarendon Press.

Keith, Arthur Berriedale, trans. [1914] 1967. *The Veda of the Black Yajus School Entitled the Taittirīya Saṃhitā*. 2 vols. Reprint. Delhi: Motilal Banarsidass.

————, trans. [1920] 1971. *The Rig Veda Brahmanas: The Aitareya and Kauṣītaki Brāhmaṇas of the Rigveda*. Reprint. Delhi: Motilal Banarsidass.

Kitagawa, Joseph M., and John S. Strong. 1985. "Friedrich Max Müller and the Comparative Study of Religion." In *Nineteenth-Century Religious Thought in the West*, edited by Ninain Smart.

Vol. 3. Cambridge: Cambridge University Press.

Krishnaswami Aiyanger, S. 1931. *Evolution of Hindu Administrative Institutions in South India*. Madras: University of Madras Press.

Lant, Jeffrey L. 1979. *Insubstantial Pageant: Ceremony and Confusion at Victoria's Court*. London: Hamish Hamilton.

Lee-Warner, William. 1894. *The Protected Princes of India*. London: Macmillan & Co.

Leslie, Julia. 1987. *The Perfect Wife: The Status and Role of the Orthodox Hindu Woman as Described in the Strīdharmapaddhati of Tryambakayajvan*. Delhi: Oxford.

Lethbridge, Roper. 1893. *The Golden Book of India: Genealogical and Biographical Dictionary of the Ruling Princes, Chiefs, Nobles, and Personages, Titled or Decorated, of the Indian Empire*. London: Macmillan & Co.

Lincoln, Bruce. 1981. *Priests, Warriors, and Cattle: A Study in the Ecology of Religions*. Berkeley and Los Angeles: University of California Press.

Low, D. A. 1964. "Lion Rampant." *Journal of Commonwealth Political Studies* 2:235–52.

Macdonell, A. A., and A. Berriedale Keith. [1912] 1958. *Vedic Index of Names and Subjects*. 2 vols. Reprint. Delhi: Motilal Banarsidass.

Macnicol, Nicol, ed. 1963. *Hindu Scriptures: Hymns from the Rigveda, Five Upanishads, the Bhagavadgita*. Everyman's Library. London: Dent.

MacQueen, Percy. 1926. *The Pudukotah Portraits*. Pudukkottai: Sri Brihadamba State Press.

Madan, T. N., ed. 1982. *Ways of Life: King, Householder, Renouncer—Essays in Honour of Louis Dumont*. New Delhi: Vikas Publishing House.

Mahalingam, T. V. [1940] 1975. *Administration and Social Life Under Vijayanagar*. 2d ed. rev. 2 vols. Madras: University of Madras.

————. 1967. *South Indian Polity.* Madras: University of Madras.

Majumdar, R. C., ed. 1963. *British Paramountcy and Indian Renaissance.* History and Culture of the Indian People 9 and 10. Bombay: Bharatiya Vidya Bhavan.

Manual of the Administration of the Madras Presidency. 1893. 3 vols. Madras: Government Press.

Marglin, Frederique Apffel. 1977. "Power, Purity and Pollution: Aspects of the Caste System Reconsidered." *Contributions to Indian Sociology,* n.s., 2:245–70.

————. 1982a. "Kings and Wives: The Separation of Status and Royal Power." In *Ways of Life: King, Householder, Renouncer,* edited by T. N. Madan. New Delhi: Vikas Publishing House.

————. 1982b. "Types of Sexual Union and Their Implicit Meanings." In *The Divine Consort: Radha and the Goddesses of India,* edited by Jack Hawley and Donna Wulff. Berkeley and Los Angeles: University of California Press.

————. 1985. *Wives of the God-King: The Rituals of the Devadasis of Puri.* Delhi: Oxford University Press.

Marriott, McKim. 1968. "Caste Ranking and Food Transactions: A Matrix Analysis." In *Structure and Change in Indian Society,* edited by Milton Singer and Bernard S. Cohn. Chicago: Aldine Publishing Co.

————. 1976. "Hindu Transactions: Diversity Without Dualism." In *Transactions and Meaning: Directions in the Anthropology of Exchange and Symbolic Behavior,* edited by Bruce Kapferer. Philadelphia: Institute for the Study of Human Issues.

Mateer, Samuel. 1883. *Native Life in Travancore.* London: W. H. Allen & Co.

Mayer, Andrian C. 1982. "Perceptions of Princely Rule: Perspectives from a Biography." In *Ways of Life: King, Householder, Renouncer,* edited by T. N. Madan. New Delhi: Vikas Publishing House.

Metcalf, Thomas R. 1969. "From Raja to Landlord: The Oudh Taludars, 1850–1870." In *Land Control and Social Structure in Indian History,* edited by Robert E. Frykenberg. Madison: University of Wisconsin Press.

Michell, George. 1992. *Vijayanagar, City of Victory.* New York: Aperture Books.

Miller, David. 1984. "On Literalism: The Letter and the Monkey." *Spring: An Annual of Archetypal Psychology and Jungian Thought.* 1984:151–61.

Mitter, Partha. 1977. *Much Maligned Monsters: History of European Reactions to Indian Art.* Oxford: Clarendon Press.

Mukerji, Chandra. 1983. *From Graven Images: Patterns of Modern Materialism.* New York: Columbia University Press.

Müller, Friedrich Max. [1859] 1968. *A History of Ancient Sanskrit Literature.* Reprint. Varanasi: Chowkhamba Sanskrit Series.

————. [1878] 1964. *Lectures on the Origin and Growth of Religion as Illustrated by the Religions of India.* Reprint. Varanasi: Indological Book House.

————. [1882] 1934. *India: What Can It Teach Us?* Indian edition by K. A. Nilakanta Sastri. Madras: Longman's, Green & Co.

————. [1901] 1976. *My Autobiography.* Reprint. New Delhi: Hind Pocket Books.

Müller, Georgiana Adelaide, ed. 1902. *Life and Letters of the Right Hon. F. Max Müller.* 2. vols. London: Longman, Green & Co.

Mumme, Patricia Y. 1992. "Haunted by Sankara's Ghost: The Śrīvaiṣṇava Interpretation of Bhagavad Gita 18:66." In *Texts in Context: Traditional Hermeneutics in South Asia,* edited by Jeffrey R. Timm. Albany: State University of New York Press.

Narayanan, Vasudha. 1987. *The Way and the Goal.* Washington, D.C.: Institute for Vaishnava Studies; Cambridge, Mass.: Center for the Study of World Religions.

Narayananswamy Pillay, T. C. 1903. *Installation of His Highness Sri Krishnarajen-*

*dra Wadayar Bahadur, Maharaja of My-
sore and the Dassara Festivities* (a poem
in Tamil with an English translation).
Madras: Rippon Press. A copy is available in the Oriental Manuscripts Collection of the British Library.

Neale, Walter C. 1969. "Land Is to Rule." In
*Land Control and Social Structure in In-
dian History,* edited by Robert E. Frykenberg. Madison: University of Wisconsin Press.

Oppert, Gustav. [1893] 1971. *The Original Inhabitants of India.* Reprint. Delhi: Oriental Publishers.

Oster, Akos. 1981. *The Play of the Gods.* Chicago: University of Chicago Press.

Pargiter, F. E. [1922] 1962. *Ancient Indian Historical Tradition.* Reprint. Delhi: Motilal Banarsidass.

Pfaffenberger, Brian. 1982. *Caste in Tamil Culture: The Religious Foundations of Sudra Domination in Tamil Sri Lanka.*
Syracuse: Maxwell School of Syracuse
University.

Preston, James J. 1985. "Creation of the Sacred Image: Apotheosis and Destruction." In *Gods of Flesh / Gods of
Stone: The Embodiment of Divinity in
India,* edited by Joanne Punzo
Waghorne and Norman Cutler. Chambersburg, Pa.: Anima Press.

Price, Pamela G. 1979. "Rāja-dharma in
Nineteenth-Century South India: Land,
Litigation, and Largess in Ramnad Zamindari." *Contributions to Indian Sociology,* n.s., 132:207–39.

———. 1983. "Warrior Caste 'Raja' and Gentleman 'Zamindar': One Person's Experience in the Late Nineteenth Century."
Modern Asian Studies 17:563–90.

———. 1991. "Acting in Public Versus Public
Acting: Conflict Processing and Politi-
cal Mobilization in Nineteenth-Century
South India." *South Asia* 14:91–121.

Radhakrishna Aiyar, S. 1916. *A General History of the Pudukkottai State.* Pudukkottai: Sri Brihadamba State Press.

Raghupathy, M. 1983. *Guide to the Important
Monuments In and Around Pudukkot-
tai.* Madras: Government of Tamilnadu.

Rajayyan, K. 1974. *Rise and Fall of the Poligars of Tamilnadu.* Madras: University
of Madras.

Ramaswamy Poolaver, B. S. 1877. *English
Translation of a Tamil Poem Regarding
the Assumption of the Title of "Empress of India" by Her Most Gracious
Majesty Queen Victoria.* Composed by
S. Ramaswamy Poolaver. 2d ed. Ran-
goon: Albion Press. Filed now as No.
14172 c28(1) of the Tamil Collection,
"Modern Poetry—Panegyric, Satiric,
and Elegiac Poems," Oriental Manuscripts, The British Library.

Ramusack, Barbara N. 1978. *The Princes of
India in the Twilight of the Empire:
Dissolution of the Patron-Client Sys-
tem, 1914–1939.* Columbus: Ohio
State University Press.

Read, Hollis. 1836. *The Christian Brahmun.*
New York: Leavitt, Lord & Co.

Richards, John, ed. 1977. *Authority and Kingship in Ancient India.* Madison: University of Wisconsin Press.

Richards, Thomas. 1990. *The Commodity Culture of Victorian England: Advertising
and Spectacle.* Stanford, Calif.: Stanford
University Press.

Ricoeur, Paul. 1967. *The Symbolism of Evil.*
Boston: Beacon Press.

———. 1971. "The Model of the Text: Mean-
ingful Action Considered as Text." *Social Research* 38:529–62.

Rous, George. 1777. *The Restoration of the
King of Tanjore Considered.* London.
Available in the library of the School of
Oriental and African Studies, University
of London.

Said, Edward W. [1978] 1979. *Orientalism.*
New York: Random House, Vintage
Books.

Saletore, B. A. 1934. *Social and Political Life
in the Vijayanagar Empire.* 2 vols. Madras: B. G. Paul & Co.

Seale, William. 1975. *The Tasteful Interlude:
American Interiors Through the Camera's Eye, 1860–1917.* New York: Prae-
ger Publishers.

Shulman, David Dean. 1980a. "On South Indian Bandits and Kings." *Indian Eco-*

nomic and Social History Review 17:283–306.

———. 1980b. *Tamil Temple Myths: Sacrifice and Divine Marriage in the South Indian Saiva Tradition.* Princeton: Princeton University Press.

———. 1985. *The King and the Clown in South Indian Myth and Poetry.* Princeton: Princeton University Press.

Singer, Milton. 1984. *Man's Glassy Essence: Explorations in Semiotic Anthropology.* Bloomington: Indiana University Press.

Smith, Brian K. 1989. *Reflections on Resemblance, Ritual, and Religion.* New York: Oxford University Press.

Smith, H. Daniel. 1984. "Pratiṣṭhā." In *Agama and Silpi,* edited by K.K.A. Venkatachari. Proceedings of seminar held in December 1981. Bombay: Anathacharya Indological Research Institute.

Smith, Jonathan Z. 1978. *Map Is Not Territory: Studies in the History of Religions.* Leiden: E. J. Brill.

Spear, Percival. 1965. *A History of India.* Vol. 2. Middlesex: Penguin Books.

Standing Order of the Pudukkottai Darbar. 1937. 2 vols. Pudukkottai: Sri Brihadamba State Press.

Stein, Burton. 1969. "Integration of the Agrarian System in South India." In *Land Control and Social Structure in Indian History,* edited by Robert E. Frykenberg. Madison: University of Wisconsin Press.

———. 1975. "The State and the Agrarian Order in Medieval South India: A Historical Critique." In *Essays on South India,* edited by Burton Stein. Honolulu: University Press of Hawaii.

———. 1984. *All the King's Mana: Papers on Medieval South Indian History.* Madras: New Era.

Thiagarajan, Deborah. 1992. "Door and Woodcrafts of Chettinad." In *Living Wood: Sculptural Traditions of Southern India,* edited by George Michell. Produced in connection with an exhibition at the Whitechapel Gallery in London. Bombay: Marg Publications.

Thiagarajan, N. 1932. *A Child's History of Pudukkottai: The Place and Its People.* Pudukkottai: Sri Brihadamba State Press.

Thompson, Edward. 1943. *The Making of the Indian Princes.* London: Oxford University Press.

Thurston, Edgar. [1909] 1975. *Castes and Tribes of Southern India.* Reprint. 7 vols. Delhi: Cosmo Publications.

Tod, James. [1829, 1832] 1972. *Annals and Antiquities of Rajast'han; or, The Central and Western Rajput States of India.* Reprint. 2 vols. London: Routledge & Kegan Paul.

Tondiaman, Radhakrishna. 1897. *History of the Western Palace, Jaghir, Pudukota State.* Trichinopoly: St. Joseph's College Press.

Tottenham, E. L. 1934. *Highnesses of Hindostan.* London: Grayson & Grayson. (Lady Tottenham was in waiting to the Maharani of Baroda.)

Trautmann, Thomas. 1980. Review of *Marriage and Rank in Bengali Culture* by Ronald B. Inden. *Journal of Asian Studies* 39:519–24.

Tupper, Charles L. 1893. *Our Indian Protectorate: An Introduction to the Study of the Relations Between the British Government and Its Indian Feudatories.* London: Longman, Green & Co.

———. 1895. *Indian Political Practice: A Collection of the Decisions of the Government of India in Political Cases.* 3 vols. Calcutta: Office of the Superintendent of Government Printing.

Tylor, Edward B. [1881] 1960. *Anthropology.* Abridged by Leslie A. White. Ann Arbor: University of Michigan Press.

Venkataram Ayyar, K. R. 1938. *A Manual of the Pudukkottai State.* 2d ed. rev. 2 vols. Pudukkottai: Sri Brihadamba State Press.

Venkat Row, 1921. *Manual of the Pudukkottai State.* Published by the authority of the Darbar. Pudukkottai: Sri Brihadamba State Press.

Wadley, Susan. 1975. *Shakti: Power in the Conceptual Structure of Karimpur Religion.* Chicago: University of Chicago, Department of Anthropology.

Waghorne, Joanne Punzo. 1981. "A Body for God: An Interpretation of the Nature of Myth Beyond Structuralism." *History of Religions* 21:20–47.

——. 1984a. *Images of Dharma: The Epic World of C. Rajagopalachari.* New Delhi: Chanyaka Publications.

——. 1984b. "From Geertz's Ethnography to an Ethnotheology?" In *Anthropology and the Study of Religion,* edited by Frank E. Reynolds and Robert L. Moore. Chicago: Center for the Scientific Study of Religion.

——. 1989. "From Robber Baron to Royal Servant of God: Gaining a Divine Body in South India." In *Criminal Gods and Demon Devotees,* edited by Alf Hiltebeitel. Albany: State University of New York Press.

——. 1992a. "Vahanas: Conveyers of the Gods." In *Living Wood: Sculptural Traditions of Southern India,* edited by George Michell. Bombay: Marg Publication.

——. 1992b. "Dressing the Body of God: South Indian Bronze Sculpture in Its Temple Setting." *Asian Art* 5 (Summer): 9–33.

Waghorne, Joanne Punzo, and Norman Cutler, eds. 1985. *Gods of Flesh / Gods of Stone: The Embodiment of Divinity in India.* Chambersburg, Pa.: Anima Press.

Welbon, Guy. 1984. "Mahāsaṃprokṣaṇa 1981." In *Agama and Silpi,* edited by K.K.A. Venkatachari. Proceedings of seminar held in December 1981. Bombay: Anathacharya Indological Research Institute.

Wilks, Mark. 1810–1817. *Historical Sketches of the South of India.* 3 vols. London: Longman, Hurst, Rees & Orme.

Wilson, H. H. [1828] 1882. *The Mackenzie Collection: A Descriptive Catalogue of the Oriental Manuscripts and Other Articles Collected by Lt. Col. Colin Mackenzie.* 2d ed. Madras: Higginbottom & Co.

——, trans. [1840] 1864. *The Vishnu Purana: A System of Hindu Mythology and Tradition.* 2 vols. London: Trubner & Co.

Wilson, John Francis. 1982. *Religion: A Preface.* Englewood Cliffs, N.J.: Prentice-Hall.

Worswick, Clark, ed. 1980. *Princely India: Photographs by Raja Lala Deen Dayal, Court Photographer (1884–1910) to the Premier Prince of India.* With a foreword by John Kenneth Galbraith. New York: Alfred A. Knopf.

Yule, Henry, and A. C. Burnell, [1903] 1984. *Hobson-Jobson: A Glossary of Colloquial Anglo-Indian Words and Phrases, and of Kindred Terms, Etymological, Historical, Geographical, and Discursive.* New edition edited by William Crooke. Reprint. New Delhi: Munshiram Manoharlal.

Index

This index covers basic topics, subjects, names, and places. Technical ritual or royal court terms in Sanskrit, Tamil, or other Indic languages are not indexed here. The reader should refer directly to the Glossary, pages xix to xxvi, for the definitions and derivations of these terms.